Tamakatsuma

Tamakatsuma

A Window into the Scholarship of Motoori Norinaga

John R. Bentley

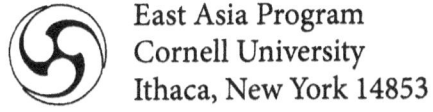

East Asia Program
Cornell University
Ithaca, New York 14853

The Cornell East Asia Series is published by the Cornell University East Asia Program (distinct from Cornell University Press). We publish books on a variety of scholarly topics relating to East Asia as a service to the academic community and the general public. Address submission inquiries to CEAS Editorial Board, East Asia Program, Cornell University, 140 Uris Hall, Ithaca, New York 14853-7601.

Number 169 in the Cornell East Asia Series
Copyright ©2013 John R. Bentley. All rights reserved.
ISSN: 1050-2955
ISBN: 978-1-933947-89-1 hardcover
ISBN: 978-1-933947-69-3 paperback
Library of Congress Control Number: 2013943875

CAUTION: Except for brief quotations in a review, no part of this book may be reproduced or utilized in any form without permission in writing from the author. Please address all inquiries to John R. Bentley in care of the East Asia Program, Cornell University, 140 Uris Hall, Ithaca, NY 14853-7601.

Dedicated to Aoki Shūhei

❧ | CONTENTS

Acknowledgments ix
Introduction 1
Notes on the Translation 9
Abbreviations 11

1 ~ New Fresh Herbs 13
2 ~ Falling Leaves of the Cherry 61
3 ~ The Orange 97
4 ~ Forget-me-nots 113
5 ~ The Eulalia of Kareno 139
6 ~ Cockscomb 161
7 ~ Waves of Wisteria Leaves on the Wind 187
8 ~ The Lower Branches of the Bush Clover 209
9 ~ Snow of Blossoms 237
10 ~ Mountain Sedge 251
11 ~ Kadsura Japonica 277
12 ~ Japanese Yellow Rose 299
13 ~ Broomrape 317
14 ~ Countless Camellias 341

Alphabetical List of Entries 383
Bibliography 393
Index 397

ACKNOWLEDGMENTS

This book began about twenty years ago, when I was translating a variety of works to include in a future anthology of *Kokugaku* scholars. It quickly became clear to me that *Tamakatsuma* dealt with so many varied subjects that it would be more profitable to expand the translation and publish it separately. The original draft included roughly 30 percent of the entries in *Tamakatsuma*, but a reader helpfully pointed out that the work would be of diminished value with such a small amount translated. Taking the challenge, I went back and translated roughly 20 percent more of the entries, and the present work includes half of the entries in *Tamakatsuma*.

I wish to acknowledge my debt to the two readers who went through the manuscript and made a variety of helpful comments and suggestions. I believe this has greatly strengthened the translation. Anyone who has dealt with Norinaga's prose will recognize that some sentences are dense, even as they can be terse, which is the great challenge to the translator. Having said that, I am solely responsible for any errors that remain.

I express my sincere gratitude to the Department of Foreign Languages and Literatures at Northern Illinois University who have been so supportive of my work, especially to Anne Birberick (chair from 2004 to 2010) and Katharina Barbe (chair from 2010 to the present). I am also grateful to Mike Sola who carefully edited the manuscript, and the managing editor at the Cornell University East Asia Program, Mai Shaikhanuar-Cota. As always, I am grateful for the support and love of my wife, Chiemi.

I have dedicated this work to Professor Aoki Shūhei, who taught at Kokugakuin University until his untimely death in late 2008. He will be greatly missed.

INTRODUCTION

When Chikuma Shobō, a medium-sized publisher in Tokyo, decided to publish the complete works of Motoori Norinaga (1730–1801) in twenty plus volumes in the late 1960s, Volume 1, the inaugural volume, included two important works—*Uiyamabumi*,[1] *Tamakatsuma*—and a record of questions and answers to Norinaga's students (unpublished manuscript). When Iwanami Shoten, one of Japan's largest publishers, put together the iconic *Nihon shisō taikei* (*Canon of Japanese Thought*), the only two Norinaga titles they published were *Uiyamabumi* and *Tamakatsuma*. It is significant that *Tamakatsuma* is the work that two separate publishing houses decided to put forth as representative of his "thinking," in spite of its being one of the last major works he published. Regardless of when it came out, *Tamakatsuma* is perhaps the single most important work of Motoori Norinaga for scholars and students alike who wish to have a fuller picture of this multifaceted man in one volume.

Motoori Norinaga was born in Matsuzaka in Ise Province on the seventh day of the fifth month of the fifteenth year of Kyōhō (1730; all dates given are lunar calendar dates). He was born into the Ozu family, believed by his parents to be a blessing child of the Shintō deity Mikumari no kami.[2] As a child, Norinaga was known

---

1. *Uiyamabumi*: Translated by Sey Nishimura (1987). Usually translated as "first steps into the mountains," this small work is an essay for students interested in pursuing scholarship. While admonishing students to avoid Chinese learning, Norinaga notes that the ancient lexicon should be the primary foundation of a student's learning.

2. Mikumari no kami is a Shintō deity originally believed to be connected with running water, and thus worshipped as a deity that enhanced the growing of rice. As Iwai notes, "Due to its domain over the allocation of water, the *kami* was also the object of worship in rites invoking rain (*amagoi*). The gradual change over time in the pronunciation of the

as Tomi no Suke. In his eleventh year, his father, Sadatoshi, passed away, and the family business, cotton wholesale, was taken over by his brother-in-law, Sadaharu. In this same year, he received the name of Yashirō; he was an avid reader and loved literature and poetry; at the age of sixteen, he was sent as an adopted son to the Imaida family in Yamada, a town roughly twelve miles southeast of Matsuzaka. The Imaida family business dealt with papermaking, but Norinaga's talents were not suited for business, and three years later he returned home.

In the first year of Hōreki (1751)—Norinaga's twenty-second year—Sadaharu passed away, and the ownership of the family business passed to Norinaga. As Matsumoto Shigeru explains, Sadaharu had previously liquidated much of the family business in Edo and deposited the sum of four hundred *ryō* so Norinaga, his mother, and siblings could live off the interest: "Although this man (Sadaharu) has so far attracted little attention from Norinaga's biographers, his existence seems to have had a significant effect on Norinaga's life and personality" (1970:12).

Roughly a year after Saraharu's death, Norinaga's mother, Okatsu, sent her son to Kyōto to study. Not long after arriving in Kyōto, he changed his surname back to Motoori, which was the name of his grandfather eight generations removed.[3] We learn that in the third month of the third year of Hōreki (1753) he changed his given name to Norinaga.

In Kyōto Norinaga studied medicine under the tutelage of Hori Genkō (1686–1754) and then later Takekawa Kōjun (1725–1780). He also quickly became a student of Hori Keizan (1689–1757). It was through Keizan that Norinaga became aware of the work of Ogyū Sorai (1666–1728), one of the most influential Con-

---

name Mikumari to Mikomori led to this deity's association with a tutelary of children and childbirth" (Inoue et al., 1999:93).

3. As a samurai, Motoori Takahide (1553–1591) died in battle before his son, Dōin (1592–1648), was born. Dōin took the name of Ozu and established himself in Matsuzaka as a merchant dealing in dyed wool. Dōin's son, Dōkyū (1612–1688), opened a number of cotton wholesale outlets in the Shogun's capital of Edo, thus expanding the family business. After this, three generations of adopted sons results in Sadatoshi, Norinaga's father, inheriting the Ozu line and the family business. Thus Norinaga is a descendant of Takahide in the eighth generation.

fucian philosophers of the Edo period. He also encountered the works of Keichū (1640–1701), a monk who had written a number of books on earlier Japanese texts, the most prominent being *Man'yō daishōki*, an important work on Japan's oldest extant poetic anthology, *Man'yōshū*.

Norinaga's love of poetry seemed to dovetail well with scholars and students who had a love for the ancient learning of Japan. He purchased a large number of works in Kyōto and read what he could about classical Japanese literature and poetry. It is fair to say that at this point in Norinaga's life he was more interested in poetry and literature than in anything more multifaceted. He would later write about how reading Keichū's work opened his eyes, "It is Keichū who discovered the true significance of the way of *waka* poetry" (Matsumoto 1970:32).

After roughly five years in Kyōto, Norinaga returned to Matsuzaka where he opened a humble pediatric clinic. In his spare time, he participated in poetic circles, and in the summer of the eighth year of Hōreki (1758), he began lectures on *Genji monogatari*. He later included lectures on *Ise monogatari*, *Tosa nikki*, and *Makura no sōshi* (Matsumoto 1970:33). Several years later, he penned *Shibun yōryō* [The essence of Murasaki's text (*Genji monogatari*)] and *Isonokami sasamegoto* (Personal Views on Poetry).[4]

Having said that, it is clear that from a rather young age Norinaga possessed a philological knack that would serve him greatly later in his career. At the age of nineteen there is evidence that Norinaga was already reading *Man'yōshū* through the lens of Kitamura Kigin's *Man'yō shūsuishō* (1686), a collection of various commentaries on the poems in *Man'yōshū*. In one of his earliest manuscripts, *Waka no ura*,[5] there is a page titled "Kanatukafi"

---

4. Norinaga completed *Shibun yōryō* on the seventh day, sixth month, of 1763. It is a loose record based on the extensive lectures Norinaga gave on *Genji monogatari*, outlining details about the author, the origin of the work, and a variety of issues surrounding the tale. The majority of the work deals with the meaning and intent of the work. Later in that same year Norinaga completed another manuscript, *Isonokami sasamegoto*, which outlines the basics of good poetic composition, arranged in a question and answer format. He also quotes songs from *Kojiki* and *Nihon shoki* and stitches traditional poetry into a Shintō ideology.

5. *Waka no ura*: Begun around 1747 when Norinaga was eighteen years of age; he completed the fifth volume in 1761.

(character usage). As Ōno notes, this is copied from Fujiwara no Teika's work on proper character usage.[6] During this time when Norinaga appears to have been aware of Teika's attempt to regulate aberrant character usage, he made a list of 246 *man'yōgana* (both phonograms and rebus characters). In a section titled "Differences in *man'yōgana*," Norinaga lists sixty-six words where confusion in the *kana* spelling has occurred. Here he has noticed confusion with *o / wo, e / we, e / fe, i / fi, fa / wa,* and *o / fo*. Ōno concludes, "This matter [regarding this phonological distinction] cannot be recognized without a fair amount of scholarship conducted into the classical language .... It is apparent that while Norinaga was still young, he was not reading *Man'yōshū* simply as a hobby. He was plunging into the study of ancient Japanese literature with a thorough mind of research" (Ōno 1976.5:17–18).

The definitive point in Norinaga's intellectual journey appears to have occurred in the summer of 1763. According to Norinaga's own account, not long after he had returned to Matsuzaka, he obtained a copy of *Kanjikō*, a study on poetic epithets in *Man'yōshū*, written by Kamo no Mabuchi (1697–1769). Norinaga relates,

> Now, after this time, I returned to my hometown [of Matsuzaka], and a person visiting from Edo let me see a recently published book called *Kanjikō*. And this is how I came to know the name of Great Master Agatai [Kamo no Mabuchi]. When I first read *Kanjikō*, it was full of ideas I could not comprehend; it was so different from the other theories that I had read that I felt they were too strange to believe. Nevertheless, because I felt there was some truth involved, I read the work one more time, and found places where I began to agree with the author. Therefore, I read *Kanjikō* a third time, finding many areas where I agreed wholeheartedly with the author. The more I read the work, the greater a strong conviction began to fill my breast, and in the end, I came to the realization that the ancient spirit

---

6. For this section I am greatly indebted to the work of Ōno Susumu (in Ōno and Ōkubo, 1976, vol. 5:16–18). Teika's work on reforming character usage appears in *Gekanshū* (date unclear, though perhaps after 1210, according to Asada 2000).

of Japan and the ancient words were just as Master Agatai had stated.

One day in the fifth month of the thirteenth year of Hōreki (1763), Norinaga got word that Mabuchi would be lodging for the night in Matsuzaka on his journey home from the Shogun's capital. We have nothing but Norinaga's account of the visit, as Mabuchi apparently treated it as a simple visit from another admirer, so caution needs to be exercised when reading this one-sided account. According to Norinaga's account, Mabuchi advised the younger student,

> It appears that you wish to make a commentary upon the ancient record of the deities (*Kojiki*), but first you must rid yourself of the Chinese Heart before you try to study about the true spirit of the ancients. In order to study about the ancient spirit, however, you must have the ability to understand the ancient lexicon. Being able to understand the ancient lexicon means that you must thoroughly study the *Man'yōshū* text. Therefore, I have first tried to elucidate *Man'yōshū*, but in the process have grown old, and my remaining years are few, so I could not attempt to put together a commentary on *Kojiki*. You, however, are in the prime of life, and have a long future ahead of you. If you study without indolence, you will be able to reach your goal of producing a commentary upon the *Kojiki* text.
> Nevertheless, I see some scholars in the present who do not engage in basic research, but immediately strive to do highly specialized work, notwithstanding they do not even comprehend the basics. These scholars can in no way do highly specialized research because they have no foundational knowledge. It seems to me that they are wasting their time producing incorrect works. So you must not forget what I have said, and keep these words alive in your memory. First, get the basics down pat, and then you must strive to do higher, more specialized research. That is why I have not been able to produce a commentary on *Kojiki*

yet. You must not try to do highly specialized research while you are still young and immature in your studies.

This single visit apparently left such a deep impression on the young student that in the twelfth month of that year Norinaga became a student of Mabuchi's, and the two began a lively correspondence, where Norinaga mined the genius of his master regarding *Man'yōshū* and other topics. In spite of Mabuchi's counsel to be patient and master the basics of *Man'yōshū* before attempting to elucidate *Kojiki*, Norinaga began his *magnum opus*, *Kojiki-den*, the very next year. His exegetical work on *Kojiki* would become a thirty-five-year journey that would ultimately make the work accessible to a variety of people, from the common folk to the samurai to the nobility. On the thirteenth day of the ninth month of the tenth year of Kansei (1798), a congratulatory banquet was held, where Norinaga and his students celebrated the conclusion of *Kojiki-den*.

During the many years of work on *Kojiki-den*, it appears that Norinaga felt he should jot down answers to questions that his students might ask in the future, or should have asked in the past. He also kept a record of actual "Question and Answer" sessions he held with his students. Sometimes he felt that a particular problem needed to be addressed with an essay. There were also times that he desired to go back and emend or correct something that he had written earlier. This slowly growing collection of information needed a place to be tethered.

Ōno Susumu imagines that after a quarter of a century of going line by line through *Kojiki*'s text, a text created from a classical Chinese matrix with an inverted order to reflect Japanese syntax, and punctuated with phonograms to help the reader of ancient Japanese process the meaning—the mechanism for deciphering the matrix lost to most in society then—Norinaga would have become weary with his time-consuming annotational work. While that work would have been tedious, it also produced nearly countless opportunities to answer a variety of questions. Norinaga also entertained questions from his students who came from far and near. No doubt, he gained insight into the dialects of Japan that still preserved a number of archaic forms that he found in *Kojiki*. With this large amount of information as a by-product of his work on *Kojiki*, he may have envisioned himself throwing these tidbits into a bamboo basket for later when he could write these thoughts down in Japanese, graceful Japanese sentences created by imitating the elegant language of classical Japanese: "Having assembled (this knowledge), let us try making one bamboo basket for letters. We can imagine that Norinaga's heart moved in that direction. The *katsuma* of *Tamakatsuma* is known in the ancient language as *katama*. It is a basket woven of bamboo one throws in miscellaneous stuff" (Ōno-Ōkubo 1976, vol. 1:18).

Thus, *Tamakatsuma* appears to have been compiled for a variety of needs. As Ōno has hinted at, there was the need to write in free-flowing, elegant Japanese to express his ideas, a natural outcome, as he believed that anyone who had rid themselves of *karagokoro* (the Chinese Heart) and understood *mono no aware* (the profundity of things) would realize. Writing in classical Japanese—as opposed to the learned medium of classical Chinese—may have been something he learned from his master, Mabuchi, who also wrote in classical Japanese, but in a more stilted and artificial fashion, using enigmatic epithets as some use salt and pepper. On the other hand, perhaps using classical Japanese reflects the literary and poetic side of Norinaga, imitating the world he loved in *Genji monogatari*.

The other need was to record the information that he had gleaned from years of work on *Kojiki* and other projects. The reason that *Kojiki-den* comprises four volumes of *Motoori Norinaga zenshū*, even though the actual text of *Kojiki* totals only about 155 leaves, is because Norinaga comments on almost every word or particle in the work. Such painstaking analytical and philological work clearly generated extra material.

As Norinaga's own introduction to *Tamakatsuma* records, he began the compilation of ideas and short essays on the eighteenth day of the first month of the fifth year of Kansei (1793), when he was sixty-three years of age. However, because several handwritten fragments of earlier drafts survive, scholars know that the foundation for this work actually was laid five years earlier, in the first year of Kansei (1789).

These fragments also make it clear that some editing was done, perhaps for pragmatic reasons.[7] This may demonstrate, in a minor way at least, that Norinaga was cognizant that what he advocated would be taken seriously. What is interesting is that if we accept the fact that the subject matter of entry 125 was changed from "An argument about excessive veneration for Confucius by Confucian scholars and their lack of veneration for Shūkō (Zhou Gong)" to "The burial tumulus of Emperor Jinmu," because of a fear of how the authorities, trained on Confucian models, would react, how do we then explain that *Tamakatsuma* includes four other entries that deal rather harshly with Confucian scholars or Confucianism? Could we not also conclude that perhaps Norinaga swapped the former for the latter because he felt it was underdeveloped? On the other hand, perhaps it was too harsh, not politically, but morally. We may never know, but what we do know is that these early fragments illustrate that Norinaga began this new project with the intention of illustrating to his current and prospective students what his thoughts were on *kogaku* (the study of the ancient things,) what later scholars interpret to mean *kokugaku* (national studies).[8] As time went on, this project grew and spread to encompass his thinking on a wide variety of subjects.

The majority of topics covered in *Tamakatsuma* can be placed under one of the following five categorical headings: (i) advice to students, (ii) Japanese history, (iii) linguistics, (iv) native versus foreign ideas (including Shintō and Japanese customs), and (v) philology (including literature and poetry).[9] The following chart illustrates the distribution of these five categories among the entries translated in this work:

Category	Advice	History	Linguistics	Native/Foreign	Philology
Percentage	11	17	24	31	17

---

7. Sugito (1984:477) wonders if the reason one quite caustic entry about Confucianism (originally entry 125) was later deleted was due to the fear of offending the authorities, who were often Confucianists.

8. Tahara (1973:56) writes, "*Kogaku* 古學 = *kokugaku*." I have translated *kogaku* as "the study of ancient things."

9. It needs to be noted that a fair number of entries are a mixture of philology, linguistics, and nationalistic work. This makes it somewhat difficult to categorize some of the entries in *Tamakatsuma*.

It is quite interesting that the distribution is roughly equal between the five categories, though almost a third falls under Norinaga's passion of trying to separate Japanese culture/religion from Chinese influence. What this distribution likely demonstrates is that Norinaga was conscious of these several topics throughout the decade that he compiled, added, and edited the manuscript. One could also claim that he had nearly equal interest in history, linguistics, philology, and eradicating foreign ideas, as well as imparting wisdom to his students. Whatever the conclusion, it seems quite apparent that Norinaga's research was broad and balanced. This helps explain why *Tamakatsuma* is such an important work: it provides a fairly comprehensive overview of Norinaga's thought and scholarship.

This important work came out in installments. The first three books of *Tamakatsuma* were published in 1795. The next three were published at the end of 1797, then three more in 1799, and three more a year after his death. The final two volumes with a volume listing the contents came out in 1812.

One characteristic of Norinaga's thinking that readers generally notice quickly is his almost fanatical loyalty to the ancient traditions of Japan. The Sun Goddess, Amaterasu Ōmikami, *is* the sun in the sky; China's history is violent and chaotic precisely because China is *not* the divine land. Students and scholars could spend much time denigrating his "otherwise academically formidable study" (Nishimura 1991:21), but this scholar thinks we would be missing the more weighty matters.

There is much that is worthy and profound within Norinaga's scholarship: his literary insights, his linguistic sensitivity, and his wisdom in relation to how students should pursue their studies. It is hoped that this translation will open a larger window into the diverse and complex scholarship of Motoori Norinaga.

NOTES ON THE TRANSLATION

Tamakatsuma consists of 1,005 entries, a fair portion of which are little more than quotes from (at the time) rare manuscripts that Norinaga wanted to make a note of and preserve. There are also other entries where a substantial quote from some work is then given a brief evaluation by Norinaga. In the majority of cases, these are of little value for this translation. Overall, I have translated 504 entries (50 percent) from *Tamakatsuma*, and have tried to select entries from a broad range of topics reflecting the thinking and genius of Norinaga.

The text for my translation is Volume 1 of Chikuma Shobō's *Motoori Norinaga zenshū*, which attaches a number to each entry, running consecutively throughout. Volume 40 of *Nihon shisō taikei* also attaches an entry number, but these only run consecutively through each *maki*, returning to "one" at the beginning of the next *maki*. My translation has kept the entry numbers from Chikuma Shobō's text, as it better preserves the "encyclopedic" feeling of the original.

Norinaga was very sensitive to the proper "spelling" of ancient words, though he did not fully understand the underlying phonology of the earlier *man'yōgana* usages. As a matter of point, the minute details of that phonology are still debated in the present. With such a large amount of poetry or literature quoted from a variety of historical periods in *Tamakatsuma*, I have relied on a transparent transcription scheme so the reader can easily decipher it but also have an idea of the dating of the material. In all cases, aside from names of people, I have relied on the *kunrei* system for the spelling. My Romanization scheme is as follows: (i) when written in *man'yōgana* or *kundoku* from the Asuka or Nara eras I have used **bold**; (ii) when written in *kana* or *kanji* from the Heian era or later I have used italics.[10] The following chart demonstrates this:

Text	Old Japanese	Text	Heian-era Japanese
阿米都知	**ametuti**	天地	*ametuti*
國造	**kuni no miyatuko**	はじめ	*fazime*

---

10. The only time I have bent this chronological rule is when Norinaga quotes from *Shinsen jikyō* (ca. 898) or *Wamyōshō* (ca. 935), both dictionaries from the early Heian era, because they continue to use the *man'yōgana* system.

Regarding the vowels of Old Japanese, I have ignored these differences, as Norinaga was not adequately aware of these vocalic values, and my representing these in a Roman transcription was thought to cause confusion. In the endnotes, there has been an occasion to refer to Old Japanese in a Romanization scheme that takes vowels also into account. In these instances, I have rendered *kō-rui* (or type A) with a subscript 1, and *otsu-rui* (or type B) with a subscript 2. When giving a reliable transcription in the notes, I leave the transcription of phonograms in lowercase, and rebus script (or logograms) in capitals. Thus 玉賀都萬 *TAMAgatuma*. When transcribing Chinese words, I have relied on *pinyin* except in cases where the word is better known in its Wade-Giles transcription, such as Confucius.

ABBREVIATIONS

KKS	*Kokinshū*
MYS	*Man'yōshū*
NKBT	*Nihon koten bungaku taikei (Iwanami Shoten)*
SKKS	*Shin Kokinshū*
SNKBT	*Shin Nihon Koten bungaku taikei (Iwanami Shoten)*
SS	*Shūishū*

1 | NEW FRESH HERBS

kotogusa no	My various thoughts
suzuro ni tamaru	unknowingly pile up
tamagatuma	in this jeweled box.[11]
tumite kokoro wo	How refreshing to dwell upon
nobe no susabi ni	these in the field of life.

These various thoughts of mine have piled up profusely, and while I have toyed with discarding them, it seems such a waste, so on this, the eighteenth day of the first month, a day of the rat, I decided to put these together in one book. That is why I have titled the first chapter "New Fresh Herbs." The titles of the following chapters are taken from the season when I put each together.

katami to fa	Here these thoughts remain,
nokore yazawa no	like a marsh in the fields
mizuguki no	with fresh plants growing,
asaku mizikaki	their stems weak and short—
wakana nari tomo	much like the thoughts I leave.

---

11. The present book takes its title from this poem, which also functions as the preface to the book. There is a tradition to read the title as *tama<u>ka</u>tsuma*, but Norinaga's own handwritten copy of this poem has 玉がつま. An earlier fragment has 玉賀都萬 *TAMAgatuma*, written in *man'yōgana*. For the time being I have elected to continue to use *tamakatsuma*.

[1] THE LITURGY OF THE NAKATOMI

The Nakatomi family's liturgy[12] recited during the First Fruits Festival is included in the diary [*Taiki*] of Minister of the Left Uji Yorinaga.[13] The text is:

> We stand before the Great Ruler Yamato Neko who rules over the land of Ofoyasima as a visible deity and pronounce the celebration liturgy of the heavenly deities.
>
> According to the words of the male and female procreative deities who are honorable and intimate, residing in the High Plain of Heaven, the myriad deities have gathered together and according to the words: "The imperial grandson of the honorable deity has first taken the standard of the government of the High Plain of Heaven, and then with it has pacified and subjugated the land of Toyo Akifara Mizufo. He now resides in the heavenly high throne, a mark of the heavenly inheritance, having brought peace and tranquillity to the precious rice stalks of the ever-lasting autumn season, which constitutes the imperial food that insures longevity. You will partake [of this food] in a purified place."
>
> Having heard this pronouncement, the heavenly grandchild descended from heaven, and the distant ancestor of the Nakatomi family, the deity Koyane no Mikoto, went before the imperial grandson and declared: "Ame no Osikumone no Mikoto ascended to the two peaks of heaven, and the imperial grandson received heavenly permission from the male and female procreative

---

12. Of the oldest thirty liturgies, twenty-nine are found in the eighth book of *Engi shiki*, a record of procedures from the Engi era (901–923). We know from his own record that Norinaga copied Kamo no Mabuchi's work on the liturgies in 1772, which only dealt with the liturgies in *Engi shiki*. Roughly seven years later Norinaga found this Nakatomi liturgy in *Taiki bekki*. Norinaga is the first to recognize that this liturgy preserved words that were of ancient date.

13. *Taiki* (diary of Minister of the Left Uji Yorinaga): This is the diary of Fujiwara Yorinaga (1120–1156), known as *Taiki bekki* (台記別記). It is quoted a total of twenty-six times in *Tamakatsuma*. Norinaga often abbreviates the title to just *Taiki*.

deities, and the water used in preparing the meals partaken of by the imperial grandson [and his family] will add water from heaven presented by the water officials of this land in the visible world." When the imperial grandson was instructed thus, Ame no Osikumone no Mikoto rode on the heavenly floating cloud, traveled to the two peaks, and told all these things to the male and female deities. The male and female procreative deities then presented heavenly skewers with the command, "Stick these skewers in the ground from dusk till dawn, and speak the heavenly solemn liturgy. If you speak these words, then wonderful leeks with many leaves and holy bamboo will sprout up in great numbers from that spot. Below these herbs, a sacred fountain will spring forth. You will declare that this is sacred water from heaven."

According to this tradition, in order to prepare the wonderful rice ears to be used in the festival the diviner groups from the four provinces have served the great ruler by performing great divination. Divination has determined that the rice to be used in the first fruits should come from Yasu in Afumi Province, and Hikami in Tanba. The people of the Mononobe, the brewers, assistant brewers, bakers, ash-mixers, lumberjacks, kettle helpers, and rice pullers all will come to the purified ceremonial place, maintaining their own purity, bringing their items on this, the day of the hare, in the middle of the eleventh month of this year.

In a strictly purified state, the ceremonial rice is presented with awe and trembling. Having selected and determined a specific day within the month, the two predetermined provinces [Afumi and Tanifa] will present black *sake* and white *sake* for the great ruler of Ofoyasima to partake of with both broth and fruit, eaten with a sincere countenance, reigning in his luminous glory. May the imperial deities who are worshipped with the liturgy of the heavenly deities in the shrines of heaven and earth prosper. We offer these words of praise together during this everlasting autumn, praying for immovable and everlasting purity. May his reign continue in a straight course, served by the head priest who bears the broad-ax. I, Kiyochika Ason, a member of the Nakatomi who holds the upper fourth rank and title of Vice Administrator in the Office of the Native Cult, do pronounce and establish this liturgy."

He continued, "High princes, low princes, various ministers, the many officials who serve the great ruler at court, and all the common folk of the four quarters, gather together. Revere together, rejoice together, and hearken together. I pronounce these words with awe and trembling, praying that the great ruler's reign will flourish like dense trees."

This is the text. It contains many old and praiseworthy items. Since there are few people in society who know about this text, I have copied it here. There are many orthographic errors in the text, so I have compared three or four manuscripts and have selected what I think are the proper readings. However, that does not mean that I have corrected all the mistakes. Someone should conduct textual criticism to gain a good critical text.

Now, pondering upon the ancient lexicon, and by adding readings to these characters, we can illuminate the meaning to some extent. In the sixth line dealing with the imperial food resulting in longevity, there is the character **wo** (written 遠), and this definitely should be corrected to the linking particle 乃 **no**. It may sound as if the particle **wo** is correct, but it creates a double object with the next clause "rice ears," which also has **wo**. The graph 知 (**ti**) in the sentence "partake [of this food] in a purified place" means "partake of."[14]

If you look at the flow of the words in the tenth line dealing with Ame no Osikumone standing before the male and female deities and telling them about the use of water, you will find that they sound very good. The graph 丁 in the sentence "water from heaven presented by the water officials of this land in the visible world" is found in one manuscript as 尸 and another as 加, but all

---

14. The sentence actually has 知食, glossed as *sirosimese* (please partake), with the graph 知 used as a rebus character and not as a phonogram.

these readings are wrong. This definitely should be the graph 仁 (**ni**). In addition, the graph 立 in the sentence "will add water from heaven" is a copyist's error for 弖 (**te**). I do not know what the verb **mawosu wori** means. This definitely should be read **mawose to**.[15]

The meaning of **mati fa wakafiru ni** is hard to discern, but *Jinmyōchō*[16] says there are two deities enshrined on Second Avenue of the Left Sector of the Capital, those two being the deities Futo Norito and Kuzimati. This seems a proper interpretation.[17] Scholars should consider that Kuzimati is enshrined along with Futo Norito and we later see that they both accept ceremonial food together. The graph read *mira* (韮, leek) might be a mistake for *firu* (蒜, garlic); perhaps the scribe used the graph 昼 (**firu**, afternoon) as a rebus character. Thus, **wakafiru** would mean the period of time just before noon, showing the time after the phrase "from dusk till dawn."

Why would the word **yutu ifo** have a double meaning? **Yutu** is just the same as the next word, many-layered. Yawi is the name of Emperor Jinmu's son, as he was called Hiko Yawi or Kamu Yawi Mimi, so the meaning of this word should parallel this.[18] The graph 依 should appear just before the word "declare" in the sentence "You will declare that this is sacred ... ." The phrase "the diviner groups from the four provinces" is also seen at the end of the Great Purification liturgy as "Also, the diviners from the four provinces," but the corpus mentions that the diviners came from three provinces, Izu, Iki, and Tusima. It does not mean that they came from the four quarters of the land, so the character "also" was added to the text by a later hand. The text here should refer to "four distinct provinces." Thus, that would mean they came from the three provinces mentioned before, and one other province that I am not aware of.[19]

---

15. This is likely a product of Norinaga's texts lacking a clear reading. He appears to have interpreted this as *mawosu wori*, but the reading of *mawosisi wori* makes sense.
16. Jinmyōchō is a directory of the shrines and actually refers to volumes 9 and 10 of *Engi shiki*.
17. In reality, the word *mati* refers to a form of divination, or the result of such divination (Omodaka et al., 1967:680–81).
18. The name is spelled 八井, and actually means "eight (heavenly) wells."
19. Keishi Kurano believes the third and fourth provinces come from Tsushima being divided into upper and lower districts (1976:461).

The particle 仁 in **futomani ni** is a mistake for 乃 (**no**). The phonogram 留 (**ru**) in **tukafe maturu** should be 弖 (**te**).[20] One manuscript also has the character for district after the place name Hikami. If we follow this manuscript, then the same character should appear right after the place name Yasu. The verb 相侯 (serve together) appears in the *Gishiki* as 相仕 (serve together), but in the procedure of the First Fruits Ceremony, it says 共作 (make together). Considering this evidence together, the two graph both read (serve) (侯・仕) are mistakes, and the proper reading should be (make together) (or assistant brewers).

Now, concerning the sentence **yusiri itusiri**, **yu** is ceremonial purity, and **itu** is strict or solemn, and taken together they mean "strict purity." **Siri** is a form of declension like **mafari** in **yumafari** or **kiyomafari**.[21] "Having selected and determined a specific day" refers to something always determined for ceremonies. Maybe the reason it is called **fitoki** is that the ancients were always selecting a proper time to do things. Do we speak these ancient words in the same way in a later era?

The word "both" in "both broth and fruit" is a corruption from a later hand. A later scribe did not know the meaning here and copied the text down carelessly according to the habitual particle cluster *nimo*. The phonogram 弖 (**te**) in "reigning in his luminous glory" definitely should have been 止 (**to**).[22] "Partake together" should be read **afinife**. The reading of **nife** as *mube* is a later phonetic change. The First Fruits Ceremony is read *ofonife*, also called *ofomube*. This partaking of food together means that the Emperor partakes with those in attendance, insinuating that the attendants present the food to him for tasting; this word has the same meaning as "participation" in the vernacular. Therefore, there are many shrines that do not participate in this festival, regardless of the status of the shrine, regardless that some shrines have enshrined deities who must participate in the festival. Places like this that should

---

20. There are no witnesses that support this emendation. It also does not really gain anything grammatically.

21. Kurano says he does not know what *siri* means, but he does quote Norinaga (1976:463, note 1). Philippi ignores the particle altogether (1959:77-78).

22. No witnesses support this emendation.

participate should come forward and take part in the festivities. There are seventy-one shrines seen in the four seasons festival, and like the one I mentioned before, the two deities enshrined on Second Avenue of the Left Sector of the Capital are not included in the list of important shrines, but participate in the festival because of the status of the two deities enshrined there.

The word **akarasi** is a changed form of **akari** and means "light." **Koto ni** is an attending particle attached to the verb "to serve." **Tabe** should always be read this way, and means "to present something." Now, the reader should understand that there should be a **te** after **kikitabe**. "The great ruler's luminous court" in the text should read "The great ruler's court," as the graph "luminous" is a mistake for "morning," which also means "court." The sentence "I pronounce these words" is written "I finish pronouncing my words" in another manuscript, and this rendering is not bad. The words of Ame Osikumone are seen in the records of the Outer Shrine of Ise as being said by Ame Murakumo, so perhaps they are the same deity.

This liturgy was pronounced on the day of the dragon in the Hōraku Chamber of the Palace [of Emperor Konoe], the events recorded in *Yukichō*.[23] The Head Officiator, a member of the Nakatomi, took a branch from a tree and used it as a scepter, and came into the chamber from the south gate and knelt before the ceremonial throne. He then recited the liturgy. This is seen in the codes of the Festival of the First Fruits. I forgot to add that the "e" of "Dajōe no saijō" is a mistake for "palace."

[2] THE COUNCIL HALL OF THE IMPERIAL PALACE

The Council Hall of the imperial palace first appears in the Tenmu record in *Nihon shoki*, where it says, "The emperor was in the Council Hall." It appears here and there in the records, and there are many examples of it in *Shoku Nihongi*. Council Hall is read **ofoyasumidono**, and this refers to the Daigyokuden, or

---

23. *Yukichō*: This is a record of rice paddies located east of the capital that were allowed to present rice for the Festival of the First Fruits.

Council Hall. In the Tenchi record of *Nihon shoki* there is mention of the Western Council Hall, and in the Tenmu record, we see the Interior Council Hall, Inner Council Hall, Outer Council Hall, and the Council Hall of the Abolished Palace.[24] The Eastern Council Hall appears in the Monmu record of *Shoku Nihongi*. These are all read *yasumidono*. **Yasumi** appears in old poetry, like **yasumisisi wa ga ofokimi** and this means "the sovereign who rules over the tranquil country." **Misisi** means "to rule over." That is why they call this the palace of the emperor.

This next example appears much later chronologically, but Saigyō in *Senjūshō*[25] made a progression to the imperial burial tumulus of Emperor Sutoku. In that section is a sentence that says, "And the emperor rested between the Hall for State Ceremonies and the Refreshing Hall, places taken care of by the various ministers." Sometimes ancient usages [like "to rest"] appear in such passages.

Now, in the Kōgyoku and Tenmu records in *Nihon shoki*, the Daigyokuden is sometimes glossed *ofoamudono*, and in the Tenchi record the Western Small Hall is glossed *nisi no koadono*, while the Inner Council Hall mentioned above in the Tenmu record is glossed *uti no amudono*. All of these could have been read *yasumidono*, and that is why some records have this reading written in the margins. Later scribes misread the character 安 with its Chinese reading as *amu*, creating a mistaken reading. There are also manuscripts with the graph 晏 (late into the evening), and the student should remember that this is also a mistake originating from the graph *yasumi* (安), being read *amu*. Since the Council Hall was the most important part of the palace, it was called *ofoyasumidono*, and later the graphs "large-rest-palace" were affixed. In *Shoku Nihongi*, it appears that the Council Hall [Daigyokuden] and Daianden are different structures, but this is not so. They are the same.

24. Norinaga notes four examples of palaces that include 安殿, but only three are actually in the *Nihon shoki* text. Norinaga has the first as 向安殿 (Interior Council Hall), but the text of *Nihon shoki* actually has 向小殿, glossed as **mukafi koandono**.

25. *Senjūshō*: Believed to have been compiled by Saigyō (1118–1190), later research has shown that an unknown author compiled this work, assuming the persona of Saigyō. It is a compilation of tales and stories centered on mystic events connected with Shintō and Buddhist events.

[3] THE TATUTA RIVER

In the second book of autumn poetry in *Kokinshū* is a poem composed when the poet passed Mount Kaminabi and spotted autumn leaves floating downstream as he crossed over the Tatuta River. That poem is

kamunabi no	The spirit of autumn
yama wo sugiyuku	is the one traveling
aki nareba	past Mount Kamunabi,
tatutagafa ni zo	so this is his offering
nusa fa tamukuru	in the Tatuta River. (KKS 300)

This Mount Kaminabi is located in Yamasiro Province, Otokuni District. It is the same place mentioned in a different part of the same poetic anthology where the words, "When the people went from Yamazaki to the grove of Kaminabi to see him off ... " appear (KKS 388). In the poetic collection of Minamoto Shigeyuki, he calls the Yamazaki River the Tatuta River when he is off to Tukusi:

siranami no	It is the only thing
tatuta no kafa wo	left in the wake of the boat
idesi yori	churning up white waves
ato kuyasiki fa	in the Tatuta River:
funazi narikeri	my remaining regrets.

Though this poem says Tatuta River, it is a place beyond Yamazaki, close to Mount Kaminabi in Tu Province, Simagami District, and this is on the road heading down to Tukusi. This river is different from the Tatuta River found in Yamato Province. Thus, since both Mount Kaminabi and Tatuta are revered names in Yamato, people only thought [it referred to] places in Yamato from ancient times, as we saw in the *Kokinshū* poem.

Keichū also understood it this way, and said with skepticism, "Mount Kaminabi is in Taketi District and Tatuta River in Feguri District, and because there is a wide gap in distance between the two, there is no possibility that the autumn leaves of the mountain could have floated down the Tatuta River."[26] Regardless, the introduction says the poet passed the mountain and composed his poem upon crossing the river, making it difficult to declare there is a mistake here.

Thus, to argue as my master[27] did and declare that from the beginning this poem is wrong, even believing that the introduction to this poem is the creation of the compilers [of *Kokinshū*] is extreme. Even if we allow that a poem can be composed under mistaken pretenses, I doubt that this can be said about the introduction of the poem. We see that the fourteen or fifteen poems in *Man'yōshū* dealing with Tatuta in Yamato all refer only to the mountain, and there is not a single poem composed about the river. In other old records, Tatuta always has reference only to the mountain, and never to a river. All references to Tatuta River originated after the capital was moved to its current location [Kyōto], and these poems thus refer to the area beyond Yamazaki as I noted above.

If the poem "autumn leaves in commotion / floating down the river" truly was composed by the "Nara emperor," then it should be Emperor Heizei. The version which reads "the autumn leaves floating in the river / from Mount Kaminabi" with Asuka River instead of Tatuta, is the correct version, and should refer to Yamato. People referred to Yamazaki being across from Kaminabi, but that should not be taken as Mount Mimuro. In spite of this, there is the poem in *Shūishū* in "the name of things" section:

kaminabi no	Has the river bank at
mimuro no kisi ya	Mimuro of Kaminabi
kuzururamu	crumbled to pieces?
tatuta no kafa no	The water of Tatuta River
mizu no nigoreru	has become very muddied. (SS 389)

---

26. Found in Book 4 of *Kokin yozaishō*, a treatise on *Kokinshū*. Keichū argues that Mount Kaminabi is Ikazuchi Hill located in Asuka in Takechi District, which reference he connects to *Man'yōshū*.

27. Norinaga is referring to Book 5 of Kamo no Mabuchi's *Kokinshū uchigiki* (1789). This was not actually written by Mabuchi but is a record of lectures he had given, based on notes taken by some of his students. After Mabuchi's death, these notes were gathered together and Ueda Akinari edited them for publication.

Early in *Kokinshū*, this place name was confused with that in Yamato and these poems were used as reference material. All poems after this show the same influence.

[4] MASTER AGATAI IS THE FATHER OF THE STUDY OF ANCIENT THINGS

The movement to purify oneself of the Chinese Heart and to search into the ancient spirit and ancient words had its origin with our teacher, Master Agatai [Mabuchi]. Before this great man's unprecedented scholarship, people studied poetry from the point of view of *Kokinshū* and later anthologies. They believed *Man'yōshū* to be obscure and hard to understand, and they never thought about the superiority or inferiority of its poetry, nor distinguished older poetry from the newer, nor tried incorporating word usages from *Man'yōshū* as if they were their own.

Thanks to our great master, people now use these old words as their own, composing poetry in the *Man'yō* tradition, even being able to write prose in the ancient tradition. It appears that people in the present believe they received this knowledge on their own, but it is all due to this great man.

Furthermore, when scholars in the present research into ancient records like *Kojiki* and *Nihon shoki*, we have this great master to thank for his well-known studies on *Man'yōshū*. It is because of his work that we are able first to clarify the ancient lexicon and follow the ancient meaning, avoiding the danger of being led astray by Chinese-inspired theories. Our master's devoted work in opening this exalted Way of Japan was truly unparalleled.

[5] CONCERNING *YUKI/SUKI*

Concerning the *suki* of the First Fruits Ceremony, the following appears in *Shiki* of *Nihon shoki*,[28] "The professor believes that

---

28. *Shiki* 私記 (private records) are accounts of a number of lectures held at court over several centuries, centered on the text of *Nihon shoki*. Many of these records have been

suki meant 'next.'" From this period to the present people have only understood this single interpretation and it is mistaken. This commentary comes from the line in the record of Tenmu, "'A purified area' is *yuki*. And *suki* means 'next,'" but the meaning of "purified area" is clear from the graphs. The graph 次 (next) is a rebus character and should not be used lexically.[29] Though there were many synonyms in the ancient lexicon, the Chinese graphs were often borrowed to represent Japanese irrespective of their Chinese meaning. *Suki* had the same phonological value as "next" and the graph "next" was used to represent the word. Both *yuki* and *suki* are really the same thing, making it clear that the meaning of "next" is not intended. Since there is no division between inferior and superior in a continuum, there is no justification for the meaning of "next." It is understood that the character used in the Tenmu record is simply a rebus character.

Suki is the same word as **misoki** [to purify by washing] and means to wash away. Washing also refers to ritual bathing and the words *sosoku* and *susuku* are the same. Putting them together, you get the same words, *soki* and *suki*. Thus, this is the same thing as *yuki* [ritual purification] and means to purify by washing.

[6] CONCERNING MIZUKUKI NO WOKA

The **mizukuki no** in the phrase **mizukuki no woka** is always a pillow word[30] that attaches to **woka** (hill) and is not a place name. Regardless, most people in the old days did not know this and erroneously interpreted this to be a place name in Tikuzen or Afumi.

---

preserved only in fragments. From what remains, it appears that many of the questions asked focused on the meanings of various vocabulary found in *Nihon shoki*.

29. The quote from *Nihon shoki* is often misinterpreted, but it is clear that *yuki* refers to rice paddies east of the capital that were auspicious, so that the crop which is harvested is worthy to be brought to the festival. That $yuki_2$ contains the same ki_2 as $mi_i ki_2$ "sacred wine" should not be overlooked. *Suki* refers to the next place that had the privilege of providing rice or millet for the festival, which by extension pointed to land west of the capital. Thus the graph 次 (next) is appropriate.

30. "Pillow word" is a literal translation of 枕詞. The *Princeton Companion to Classical Japanese Literature* defines this as, "A word or phrase conventionally fixed by meaning, association, or sound to one or more words" (Miner 1985:288). In many instances the word is a place name, and that is why Norinaga comments that the example here is *not* a place name.

Mizukuki means "a fresh stem," and this points to the stem [stalk] of plants. *Kuki* can refer to the stem of a plant or the trunk of a tree. You may know this by remembering that the deity of the trees is named Kukunoti. When this pillow word attaches to **woka** (hill), it means young, and there are many examples of the sounds **wa** and **wo** being used interchangeably, like **wakaduru wokoduru** (to deceive someone), **tawayame tawoyame** (a frail woman). Among many examples are those in Kagura where it says, "the frail (**yowoka**) princess who resides in heaven," but in *Genji monogatari* it says, "the frail (*yowaka*) princess who resides in heaven." These are examples of "hill" and "young" being used interchangeably.

Therefore, this pillow word means "youth, like the young plants," and that is why it modifies the word hill. Now, in Book 6 of *Man'yōshū* this pillow word also attaches to **miduki** (moat) because of a pun on young tree (**miduki**). A poem in Book 7 has "the port of the young hill," and this points to Woka District in Tikuzen Province. The name is also seen in *Fudoki* as the port of Woka [a pun on "young hill"]. This is simply the place name Woka.

Other than these poems, there are no other examples in the ancient corpus of a *mizukuki no woka* found in Tikuzen. In addition, it is a mistake to take the example in the Chūai record of *Nihon shoki*, where it has **kuki no umi**, and interpret that to have the same meaning as **mizukuki**. "Kuki no umi" is a different place than "Woka no mi." Though there is a Mizukuki no Woka in Afumi, there is no evidence to connect the two.

In Book 10, there are poems with just "young hill" with no mentioning of a port, so these examples point to Yamato and not to Tikuzen. The hills of Asuka in Taketi District [of Yamato] are still called Woka to this day and since there is a temple called Woka-dera, would not this be the place? Moreover, is not the example seen in Book 12 simply pointing to a hill somewhere and not a specific place? Furthermore, in *Kokinshū*, in the Popular Music Department Section, is a poem composed in the Mizukuki style, starting with "the temporary hut / built on the tender hill" (KKS 1072). This refers to the place name Woka Yagata seen in *Wamyōshō*[31] as "Wokanoya in the district of Udi in the province of

---

31. *Wamyōshō*: The full title is *Wamyō ruijushō* [An abridged collection of Wa (Japanese) names], compiled by Minamoto Shitagau between the years 931 and 938. It exists in

Yamasiro." The later name of Regent Wokanoya came from this place. "Kata" being read as "gata" is done according to precedence as in Yamagata or Katagata.

In spite of this, all the interpretations of Mizukuki Woka as a place name and *yagata* as "temporary roof" are incorrect. Temporary roofs were things put up on ships, and I believe such usage of the term "temporary roof" to refer to a hut did not exist in the ancient vocabulary.[32]

Now, the Mizukuki style of song is a tradition in the Department of Music and was so named because these songs began with the stanza *mizukuki no* and the term does not refer to just a place. I have given a detailed explanation about all these styles of such-and-such places in *Kojiki-den*, under the heading of "Hinaburi."

Now, the naming of such a record as Mizuguki is the same as Tamazusa (a messenger with a letter), and this again points back to a young tree. In the ancient past when a person sent a messenger to someone, he took a piece of wood from a catalpa (**azusa**) tree and attached a jewel (**tama**) to it as a symbol of authority for the messenger. That is why these messengers are called Tamazusa messengers.

Moving from this usage, we see that such messages were also called Tamazusa, and when someone wished to talk about the piece of wood with the jewel attached, they would say Mizuguki, which referred to the fresh tree. From this, the message itself might be called Mizuguki, also. Taking this one step further, it seems clear that a piece of calligraphy or handwriting could also be called Mizuguki even if it is not necessarily correspondence sent to a person.

---

two variant manuscripts, one in ten volumes and one in twenty volumes. Based on a Chinese dictionary model, it lists Chinese words by category, with a Chinese definition, and then a Japanese reading in *man'yōgana*. It also includes a list of the provinces at the time, with their district and village names often preserved in *man'yōgana*.

32. There are two examples of 屋形 in *Harima fudoki* that can be interpreted as "hut" or "temporary dwelling." In the opening lines of the Sikama District it says, "The reason this is called Sikama is because when Prince Ōmimatsu Hiko built a hut here there was a large deer that cried out. At that time the prince declared, "How the buck cries" (*sika mo naku koto yo*). Thus this district was named *sikama*."

[7] CONCERNING PRIVATELY COMPILED HISTORICAL WORKS

There are many historical works throughout history not compiled by imperial decree, but put together privately. Because all ancient Japanese people revered Buddhism, there is often useless Buddhist thinking included even in these historical works. When we read these works now, many of the statements are bothersome, even insipid. The authors wrote from a pompous point of view, treating events in the "Age of the Gods" as strange, hating whatever was not Chinese. Many of these privately compiled historical works delete the "Age of the Gods," starting their record from the reign of Emperor Jinmu.[33] They believed that it was good for Japan to have records much like China, so they naturally put together works resembling Chinese annals.

In most foreign countries, they did not have an established ruling family, and rulers changed from generation to generation, so the authors of historical works could start their work from any reign they wished; on the other hand, the lineage of our ruling family is completely different from foreign countries. Our ruling family descends from Amaterasu Ōmikami, its reign continuing in unbroken succession, eternal like heaven and earth. Thus, is it proper to delete the beginning, or the "Age of the Gods," and start the record in the middle? Even when one imitates all manner of things from China, depending on the matter at hand, one must be careful.

[8] THE WORDS OF MINISTER IETAKA

Ietaka[34] who held the Second Rank, once said, "How wondrous is poetry. Certainly when I look at what I have just written, I

---

33. In other words, they leave out the "Age of the Gods," a part of the record that explains Jinmu's divine lineage, and the creation of Japan, and why he has the right to rule.
34. Fujiwara Ietaka (1158–1237) was a celebrated poet and helped compile *Shin Kokinshū*. There are over 280 poems composed by him found in a variety of imperially ordered poetic anthologies.

think it is pleasing and not poorly done, but when I read it the next day, the verse is dreadful and trifling. Perhaps that is why I think that poetry is mysterious, because what I originally thought was a good poem, later I think not when I look at it again ... ." These words are certainly true.

[9] CONCERNING CONFUCIAN SCHOLARS WHO FEIGN IGNORANCE WHEN ASKED ABOUT JAPAN

When I ask Confucian scholars concerning things about Japan, they say, "I do not know," not even thinking it shameless to know nothing about their own country. Nevertheless, if you asked them something about China, they would feel humiliated if they did not know everything, so they make up an answer, trying to bluff their way out of the situation when they actually know nothing. This attitude originates from trying to make everything Chinese-like, even themselves. These scholars treat their native land as if it were a foreign country.

Nevertheless, even if they pretend to be Chinese, they are not Chinese by birth. In spite of being Japanese, is it proper if a decent Confucian scholar knows nothing about his own country? Indeed, regarding people from our own country, it may be fine for someone who puts on Chinese airs to take that kind of attitude, but it is difficult to imagine a situation where an actual Chinese person asks another person something, and they answer, "I know a great deal about your country, but hardly know anything about my own."

If they answered thus, the Chinese would no doubt reply, "How can a Confucian scholar know so much about a foreign country when he knows nothing about his own?" The Chinese would clap his hands and roll with laughter.

[10] SIX POINTS ON ANCIENT RECORDS

It is extremely regrettable that some ancient records were not transmitted to posterity, but were lost. From what can be seen in

Shaku Nihongi[35] and Senkaku's *Man'yō no shō*,[36] we know that the court kept most of the provinces' *Fudoki* together up until that time, having them copied and transmitted. Though the fragment of *Jōgūki*[37] quoted in *Shaku Nihongi* may be small, it does appear much older than *Kojiki*, meaning that the Crown Prince [Shōtoku Taishi] actually wrote it. Though the various *Fudoki* were highly respected works, only *Izumo fudoki* has been preserved intact; people often voice their regret that the other geographical annals have disappeared. However, from the time of Ōnin,[38] there was an ongoing upheaval in the capital, and the ancient records were all burnt, scattered, or lost.

If, as in the present, there were many colleagues who wished to study in the various provinces, and required many of these records in their research, then few of these works would have vanished. Nonetheless, in ancient times, there were few people studying in the provinces, because if one was not in the capital, there were few records at one's disposal. That is the reason that we still find ancient Chinese records here and there in the provinces, because people followed the tradition of enjoying learning about China. Thus, the reason that we also find bits and pieces of *Fudoki* here and there is because these works were not originals from the Nara era, but were later rewritings differing widely from the ancient originals; overall, these extant records are not trustworthy.[39]

Among these, *Bungo fudoki* is from the Nara era, but only a

---

35. *Shaku Nihongi*: Compiled by Urabe Kanekata (fl. 1287–1301) sometime between the years 1275 and 1300. It includes a variety of information related to *Nihon shoki*, including quotes from many of the *Shiki* lecture records. It is also one of the most valuable sources for quotes from lost *Fudoki*.
36. *Man'yō no shō*: Compiled by Sengaku (b. 1203) in 1269. The full title is *Man'yōshū shō* (Abridgement of *Man'yōshū*). Sengaku adds annotational notes to many poems, and quotes many of the now-lost *Fudoki* in his commentary.
37. *Jōgūki*: A biography of Shōtoku Taishi that is known only through the quote in *Shaku Nihongi*. The orthography preserved in the quote attests to the age of the source material, but little else is known about its origins or author.
38. During the ten-year carnage and destruction known as the Ōnin War, much of the capital was destroyed by fire and the incessant battles that filled the streets of Kyōto.
39. The general scholarly consensus is that many of the *Fudoki* fragments are originals, or rewritings that incorporated fragments of the lost originals. There is still some debate on the authenticity of some of the fragments, trying to decide which record is genuinely from the Nara era, and which was recompiled due to the loss of the original.

small part remains of the whole. When we ponder upon why the precious originals of these records have vanished, leaving us only bad reproductions, I believe the answer lies in people's disposition for valuing Chinese works above Japanese. People do not like ancient native records, but delight in records that are close to those that are Chinese. This belief of mine is supported by gleaning evidence from a comparison of *Kojiki* with *Nihon shoki*. Later ages revered the "Age of the Gods" section of *Nihon shoki*, but not that found in *Kojiki*.[40] Now, it is very fortunate that within a disastrous event such as the loss of almost all *Fudoki* we find that *Izumo fudoki* has survived. In addition, it is natural that ancient scholars took special care of the *Nihon shoki* text. It is very fortunate for later generations that *Kojiki* and *Man'yōshū* were not lost. Generally, all that we know about the ancient state of Japan has come from these two latter works.

[11] PART TWO

There are mistakes in character usage here and there in the current text of *Nihon shoki*; also, many of the readings—while they are ancient—are in imitation of Japanese spoken in the Heian capital.[41] Furthermore, there are many euphonic usages, some being old, rare, and valuable, but many of the usages are not complete. The whole text is not beautifully done, some areas lacking while others use mistaken characters. The texts are sloppy and this is very regrettable. One printed version is missing in society, while some handwritten manuscripts are very rare, but when we compare the various texts, there is no way to repair the damage. It is

---

40. In other words, the Chinese-based *Nihon shoki* was treasured, but *Kojiki* was ignored, because its text was a mixture of archaic Japanese and Chinese.

41. *Nihon shoki* contains two kinds of readings. There are a variety of words in Chinese that have glosses next to them in *man'yōgana*. An example from Book 1 of *Nihon shoki* is: 至貴曰尊。自餘曰命。並訓美舉等也。下皆效此。"We employ the graph 尊 for deities of eminent reverence. All others are designated 命. Together these are read **mikoto**. All examples hereafter follow this rule." The other type of reading is interlinear readings, many that likely were attached to the manuscript after the earliest lectures held at court. Thus many of these were added in the early Heian period.

nearly impossible to take the manuscripts now and create a handsome and beautiful text. The learned men in present society have the overly optimistic attitude that they can clarify the ancient meaning and lexicon, but their work is full of mistakes. To correct their work requires a great amount of knowledge, but if we desire to carve away mistakes and make corrective emendations to these works, it is best to only correct errors in the characters, and leave the readings of words as they are for the time being.

[12] PART THREE

None of the texts of the historical works after *Shoku Nihongi* is satisfactory. There are many incorrect characters, and some lacunae. Now, because the reading within the *Nihon shoki* text is important, it is not easy to make corrections. Other than the imperial edicts within the historical records after *Shoku Nihongi*, none of the readings is variant between manuscripts, because the scribe simply needed to be able to write acceptable classical Chinese. What must be done now is to go through all the old, good manuscripts of the records up to *Sandai jitsuroku*,[42] and by comparing the various groups, select a critical text so a satisfactory edition will be available for research.

[13] PART FOUR

Let me say a few words about all written works, regarding the pros and cons of woodblock prints and handwritten manuscripts. Needless to say, woodblock prints are easy to find and convenient to use. However, when woodblock prints are first made, the printer makes a copy of the text without thinking about which manuscript should be used. Even when a knowledgeable scholar has selected the critical text to be printed, there are still many er-

---

42. "The venerable records of the three reigns" is the final work of *Rikkokushi*, or the six histories of Japan. The work of compilation was completed in 901. It contains the record of the three reigns of Emperors Seiwa (r. 858–876), Yōzei (r. 876–884), and Kōkō (r. 884–887).

rors in the printed text. After a manuscript has been transferred to a printed form, even if a better handwritten manuscript comes to light, these manuscripts are not widely used in society, and fewer and fewer people look through them. Therefore, only one form of the work is read by society. Some take the mistakes in the printed form and emend them according to the other manuscripts, but it is often difficult to gather enough of the manuscripts to do this work. This is the weakness related to woodblock printed works.

Most of Japan's old manuscripts were converted to woodblock print during the Genwa (1615–1624) and Kan'ei (1624–1644) eras. Almost all of these relied on poor manuscripts and the prints are filled with errors. If we do not obtain better handwritten manuscripts and correct the errors, it is regrettable to say that most of these printed texts will be of little use to us.

On the other hand, there are many varieties of handwritten manuscripts, and though there are mistakes in these manuscripts, by comparing these [manuscripts], we can obtain a near-perfect text. This is one of the strengths of handwritten texts.

Having said that, it is difficult to get one's hands on a handwritten manuscript, as these texts are not widely available in society. These texts are easily lost, and with each consecutive copying, more and more mistakes creep into the text. When some greedy merchant gets his hands on a manuscript, his only desire is to make a profit, so he makes changes in the text, lessening the existence of near-perfect texts.

Therefore, even if there are weaknesses, it is best to have all the various texts converted to woodblock print for preservation. Works like *Jōkan gishiki*, *Saigūki*, and *Hokuzanshō*[43] as well as others from the ancient past are still only available in handwritten

---

43. *Jōkan gishiki* is a record of a variety of rites and ceremonies put together in the Jōkan era (859–876). *Saigūki* (西宮記, also known as *Saikyūki* or *Seikyūki*) is a record of rites and regulations, compiled by Minamoto no Takakira (914–983). The work was completed in various stages, as several different manuscripts with varying degrees of information are in existence. There were many such records through the Heian era, but many have been lost or survive only as fragments. *Saigūki* is the most extensive, which makes it an important record. *Hokuzan shō* was compiled by Fujiwara Kintō (966–1041). It is another record of rites and regulations compiled for the court. It is unclear when this work was completed.

form. It is my plea that these be converted to printed form and spread throughout society.

Moreover, the many personal family histories should be converted to block print. Many of the feudal lords in the land have bought and collected numerous old manuscripts, but they are placed in private libraries where no one can look at them. This prevents the spread of these works and they have no value in and of themselves, unless someone reads them.

If these feudal lords truly prize these manuscripts, then they would command various scholars in many fields to have the various texts compared and collated so that an authorial text can be obtained, and then have it converted to a printed version as a symbol of the wonderful age that they live in. It would be fine if the work were then made available for the people in society. This would be a meritorious service remaining long after the feudal lord has passed on.

For those with authority and money, engaging in this kind of work is no problem, and from this meritorious service, the commoner under heaven is inculcated with a deep sense of gratitude, and this is a [scholarly achievement] that lasts beyond the grave. I wish that someone with this desire would appear on the scene.

[14] PART FIVE

When attempting to obtain a rare manuscript, whether the person is a close acquaintance or not, if the person has the same intentions as you, then it should be easy to lend and borrow manuscripts for exhibition and copying. This is an important task I hope everyone in society becomes engaged in. The person with a defiled heart refuses to show his manuscripts to others, greedily gazing at them by himself; a person who wants to be engaged in scholarship should never do this. On the other hand, it is deeply frustrating if you have a manuscript that was hard to come by, lent it to some person in a far-off, hard to get to province, and it gets lost on the way. It is also vexing when the person to whom you lent the manuscript suddenly passes away, making it impossible to retrieve the document. Thus, if you borrow a manuscript from a far-off place, you should make sure that the manuscript is well taken care of in transit when you return it. Also, because it is very difficult to judge sudden changes in human life, and you might pass away yourself, it is wise to make sure that the manuscript is safe regardless. Therefore, one should establish rules regarding the treatment of such manuscripts to those who carry them back to their owners. Whenever one wishes to borrow a person's manuscript, he should look at it quickly, and return the document as soon as possible, because it is unfeeling to borrow a manuscript and keep it for a long time. This does not apply just to manuscripts, but these rules should be observed whenever you borrow *anything* from a person. I do not quite understand why, but it is especially true of manuscripts that many people when they are finished reading borrowed works leave them strewn around the house for a long time without returning them to their owners.[44]

[15] PART SIX

When you borrow a manuscript from a person, it is very thoughtless to crease a page to show how far you have read. A crease put in a manuscript by someone cannot be remedied.

[17] CONCERNING MINISTER YOSHIDA KANETOMO'S LECTURE ON *NIHON SHOKI*[45]

The same record (*Naka Mikado Gondainagon Nobutane nikki*)[46] goes on to say,

---

[44] Likely Norinaga was vexed by his own experiences. He once petitioned Mabuchi several times to allow him to peruse a manuscript of *Kojiki* his master owned. Mabuchi ignored the request for several years before finally agreeing to show Norinaga the text.

[45] This entry calls *Nihon shoki* by the shortened name of *Nihongi*. I have rendered all cases of *Nihongi* as *Nihon shoki* for consistency.

[46] *Naka Mikado Gondainagon Nobutane nikkii*: Nakamikado Nobutane (1442–1525) was an aristocrat in a time of war. His diary, written in Chinese as was the tradition, covers the years from 1480 to the beginning of 1522. The diary is generally known as *Nobutane kyōki*.

1 ~ NEW FRESH HERBS

The twenty-first day of the tenth month of the twelfth year of Bunmei (1480). Today a lecture on *Nihon shoki* was held in the forbidden quarters, and Minister Kanetomo was to speak ... . After some time, Minister Kanetomo arrived and the first thing performed was the lecture. Next, the lecture was held in the Kurodo, a room in the Cool Hall. On the west side was a lecture stand and the emperor mainly sat there. I sat a distance about halfway from the lectern, serving the minister. The text of *Nihon shoki* [a handwritten manuscript] was placed on a small table, from where the minister read and spoke. First, after Minister Kanetomo had arrived, the audience gathered, and came forward [the names of the ministers have been omitted]. The audience was divided into two equal groups and placed on the left and right. The courtiers [their names are omitted] occupied a place just below the lectern. No one could see in front of them. The masses that overflowed listened to the lecture from the small garden on the west side ... .

Where Minister Kanetomo sat there was supposed to be a bamboo mat in the place that had been determined, and while a line of people were speaking in place I spied a chance to change my location. Today the topic of the lecture was to be on four or five lines on the edge, and we got to talk about the reading of some graphs, but unexpectedly time passed, and we were only able to ask about ten graphs in Book 1, the "Age of the Gods" of *Nihon shoki*.

Again, the twenty-sixth day of the eleventh month of the same year. Today we had another lecture on Nihon shoki. We learned about the sword. First, we heard about the secret tradition of the Nakatomi liturgy, and others were not able to hear. Again, on the fourteenth day of the twelfth month; today the lecture on *Nihon shok*i came full term ... . Regarding the tradition of the mysterious stories today there was praise and admiration.

The diary goes on to record, "The seventeenth day of the first month of the second year of Bunki (1502) I went to Priest Chidō.

There was a lecture on *Nihon shoki* [on the second book of the 'Age of the Gods']. Minister Kanetomo of the Lower Second Rank spoke on this. On the twentieth day of the same month, I went to the First Avenue Palace. The lecture on *Nihon shoki* ended with awards being given, and the lectures covered many things pertaining to Shintō." Reading about the *Nihon shoki* lectures recorded by Minister Kanetomo caused me to imagine how it must have been.

[18] CONCERNING THE DIVINE WILL OF THE THREE SHRINES

In the same record (of Nobutane's) it says, "Tenth day of the second month of the second year of Bunki (1502), the servant of the Lower Second Rank [Minister Kanetomo] witnessed the outpouring of the divine will of the three shrines, together with the names of the heavenly deities … . I write those here now to hand down to posterity." On the seventeenth day of the same month, the record says, "I wrote the divine words of the three shrines for Kanetomo Ason on a one half-meter piece of paper."

[19] CONCERNING *SHINPAI KUDEN*[47]

In the same record, it says,

On the second day of the twelfth month of the twelfth year of Bunmei (1480), I went to worship at Yosida Shrine. I stayed for a short time at the place of Minister Kanetomo and had the pleasure of participating in his discussion on the text of *Nihon shoki*. When we spoke to one another, he said, "Concerning *Shinpai kuden*, various families argue over this and visit each other; however, after sixty or seventy years, nothing has been gained from all this. These

---

47. 神拝口伝 (The oral tradition of divine worship) is an unknown text that apparently had reference to an orally transmitted secret tradition or secret teachings related to worshipping the deities.

families pay no respect to the deities ... I have no other desire but to revere the deities. Since you have come here, I wish you to remember this oral tradition." On the third day, I was sent with a message to the head priest of Yosida Shrine. This was the chance of a lifetime, for the oral tradition regarding worshipping the deities [*shinpai kuden*] stuck deeply in my soul. Such gratitude filled me that my hands and feet could do nothing but dance about. Filled with such ecstasy, I did not know what to say, and gradually presented a shorter version of the message. We should look upon the various teachings of Shintō. We ought to revere these words with awe. Nobutane. Third day of the twelfth month. At Yosida.

[21] ON THE EMPEROR GIVING A NAME TO THE KAMAKURA MINISTER OF THE RIGHT

Gukanshō[48] says, "He performed the coming of age ceremony before the masses and received the name of Sanetomo from the palace.[49] On the eighth day of the twelfth month of the third year of Kennin (1203), he gave the order as Shogun. ... "

[22] YOU SHOULD READ CHINESE WORKS ALSO

It is very good to read Chinese works, also, when you have free time. If you do not read Chinese records, you will not know about the evil customs of other foreign countries. In addition, since all ancient Japanese records are written in classical Chinese, if you do not know how to read Chinese, it is difficult to pursue a course of learning. When one comes to the realization that there is evil in all

---

48. *Gukanshō* was written by a Buddhist monk named Jien (1155–1225). The author attempts to provide a political analysis of the past that illustrates how society can avoid disaster in the future. He starts with the first ruler, Jinmu, and outlines the history of Japanese rulers with the intent of illustrating the decline of fortunes at the court.

49. Minamoto Sanetomo (1192–1219) is famous for receiving a name from the crown.

foreign customs, it strengthens his own native Japanese spirit, making it unmovable. Then even if you read Chinese works day and night, your heart will not flinch. However, as the Chinese custom is to put on airs of knowledge by using logic and reason in relation to everything, Chinese works debate things in minute detail, and advocate things to their own advantage. Thus, when reading Chinese works, do not forget that even a shrewd person may find that his own mind is spontaneously following the argument, and he easily falls into confusion.

[23] FINDING THE WAY THROUGH STUDY

If you desire to find the Way through studying, first you must purify your heart by removing [the influence of] the Chinese Heart. If you do not rid yourself of the Chinese Heart, then even if you read and ponder the ancient records, you cannot grasp the ancient meaning. Without knowledge of the ancient meaning, you cannot know about the Way. [Knowledge of] the Way was originally something unobtainable through studying. It is the true heart a person is born with. "True heart" means the disposition a person was born with, whether good or bad. Nevertheless, people of later eras followed Chinese learning in case after case, and because they lost this true heart, a person in the present cannot restore himself to the ancient Way without studying it.

[24] SCHOLARSHIP

Scholarship in the world today refers to the study of Chinese texts, and there is a distinction between this and the study of ancient things in our country. It appears that others believe that the study of Japan consists of theology, Japanese studies, and *Kokugaku*.[50] This definition of scholarship is built around the study of China,

---

50. At this point in time, Norinaga did not mean what we later call the National Learning Movement (*Kokugaku*). When he refers to that, he usually uses *kogaku* (古学, "the study of ancient things").

with Japanese studies relegated to a secondary status. This current state of scholarship is unpardonable, but ancient learning originally centered only on Chinese studies. Since there was no one who tried to specialize in the study of our august land, society naturally defined scholarship in this [Chinese-centered] way. In the present era, however, many people have decided to specialize in studies on our imperial land, so scholars now divide Chinese learning into two fields: Chinese and Confucian learning. People should openly refer to national studies simply as "scholarship." Even in respect to Buddhist studies, which has split off from other fields, priests openly call their study just "scholarship," and not Buddhist studies. This is how it should be. When hearing the term *kokugaku*, people may think it is extolling our country, but the usage is restrained by the use of the character *kuni* [country, national].

In general, regarding how people in society label things, people do not comprehend the distinction between native and foreign, but use foreign words treating foreign things as if they were native. This is the problematic result of these people having become accustomed to Chinese things, as that is all they have read.

[25] THE CHINESE HEART

The "Chinese Heart" does not only point to an attitude that prefers Chinese customs and highly values China. Most people in society today debate about the good or evil of everything, and when they have to judge the rationale of something, they make statements taken right out of Chinese works. This tendency is not only seen with people who read Chinese works. Even people who have never even opened a Chinese volume react in the same fashion. Most people who are ignorant of Chinese works should not feel as if they are responding to a foreign stimulus, but people believe that everything Chinese is superior to Japanese things, and this trend of learning things from China has continued for over a thousand years; thus, this foreign influence has naturally pervaded into the very fabric of society. It is inculcated in the hearts of the people, forming the foundation for everyday life. Thus, people think, "I do not have a Chinese Heart"; "This is not related to

Chinese thinking. This is logical; this is how things should be." Even this form of thinking is a custom difficult to rid from people with Chinese Hearts.

The idea that the hearts of people, Japanese or foreign, are not different, and there should not be two standards for judging good and evil, so there cannot be something like "Chinese thinking," is reasonable on the surface, but even this way of reasoning is Chinese in origin. This very attitude is extremely difficult to erase from people's minds.

The human mind is the same from country to country, and this points to the original state of the heart of a person, but the ideas and philosophies in Chinese works were written upon the foundation of the Chinese habit of bothersome sophism, where most of the feelings of a person are decorated with falsehoods, and this is not the pure heart of man. There are many examples where things the Chinese label "good" are not really good, and what they label as "evil" are not really bad. Thus, we should not proclaim that there are not two versions of good and evil. In addition, this philosophy of "required norms" comes from the required norms of the Chinese Heart, but there are many aspects where things are not actually following a required norm.

Concerning these points, if people were well versed in the ancient Japanese records and came to a clear understanding of the Chinese Heart, they would realize the truth of what I say. It is extremely difficult to distance oneself from this foreign philosophy, as everyone in society has the Chinese Heart as his or her foundation.

[26] CONCERNING THE DIFFERENCE BETWEEN *OKASI* AND *WOKASI*

Tanaka Michimaro[51] theorizes that we say *okasi* when a person praises something, and this word is a shortened form of *omukasi*

---

51. Tanaka Michimaro (1724–1784) was born in Mino Province. He became a student of Kamo no Mabuchi's around 1758 and was interested in *Man'yōshū*. In 1780 he became a student of Norinaga's.

and it starts with the phoneme /o/. The word *wokasi*, which signifies something that makes us laugh, comes from the root *woko*, thus the word starts with the phoneme /wo/. Therefore, these two words originally were separate and distinct, and when phonological confusion came about, these two were confused, written, and understood to be the same word, and it is a mistake to think they are the same.

This is certainly a correct and well thought out theory. The meanings of "to praise" and "to be funny" are fundamentally opposite, so how could both meanings come from the same word? **Omukasi** is an ancient word, for *Nihon shoki* reads the graphs "virtue" and "joy" as **omukasimi**. The imperial edict in *Shoku Nihongi* has the word **umukasi**, while some poems in *Man'yōshū* take the o/wo off and write just **mukasi**.[52]

This Michimaro was a person from the village of Harinoki in Tagi District in Mino Province and he later lived in Ofari, Nagoya. He was very fond of ancient things and taught them to others. He indeed researched deeply into *Man'yōshū*. He was somewhat older than I am, but became my student and has come to see me two or three times, and we have exchanged letters several times. He has since passed away. I have had students who study ancient things come from Nagoya all because of the guidance of this elderly man.

[27] ON TRYING TO GIVE THE POSITION OF CROWN PRINCE TO EACH OTHER

In this same village is another of Norinaga's students, named Suga Naomi. He was a poet and one of Norinaga's students who has enjoyed reading Chinese and Japanese works ever since he was a youth and is well versed in them. He also produced poetry and his understanding of things is very sound, but he passed away be-

---

52. First, the older of the two words is *omukasi*, which means joy or ecstasy. A related form is *umukasi* and the truncated form is *mukasi*. Scholars are split over the etymology of *wokasi*, but it does seem related to the word *woko*₁ (stupid or foolish). Interestingly, the ancient lexicon does not show any traces of *wokasi*, *Shinsen jikyō* (890) being one of the first. Norinaga is right, however, in saying these two words do not share the same etymology.

fore he even reached his fortieth year. What a pity that we should lose such a man!

Suga once said, "Anciently, we find in one of the marginal comments in the preface to *Kokinshū* the scene where Ōsazaki and his brother [Uji Waka Iratsuko] try to give each other *the eastern palace* [*tōgū wo*]. It is a phrase that does not make sense to anyone.[53] I suggest that *tōgū wo* should be *tōgū to*, and because the graphs を (*wo*) and と (*to*) are easily mistaken, a scribe mistakenly copied the wrong particle.[54] This usage of 'eastern palace' points to Uji Waka Iratsuko." This theory makes a lot of sense.

[29] CONCERNING HOW THE POSTHUMOUS NAME OF EMPEROR SHIJŌ WAS SELECTED

Heikoki[55] says, "On the nineteenth day of the first month of the third year of Ninji (1242), the various ministers gathered together to discuss the posthumous name of the deceased emperor. Some said to call him Shijōin, others said Gorokujōin, others Gojōin, still another group suggested they call him Gotobain .... The body of deceased Shijō was moved from the place of mourning and placed in the villa of the Right Major, land measuring four *chō*. Perhaps that is what they used to decide on his posthumous name [*shi-chō* > *shijō*].

[30] CONCERNING HOW THE POSTHUMOUS NAME OF EMPEROR GOTOBA WAS SELECTED

Heikoki says, "On the twenty-sixth day of the sixth month of the same year (1242) ... the emperor told a story today, saying that

---

53. Here Naomi is calling attention to the fact that the particle *wo* does not make sense.

54. Norinaga means that in cursive script the graphs 度 (*to*) and 遠 (*wo*) are easily confused.

55. *Heikoki* is the diary of Taira no Tsunetaka (1180–1255) who was an aristocrat of the Kamakura Shogunate. The title of the diary apparently originates from his surname 平 (*hei*) and the fact that he was Minister of Civil Affairs, which in the Tang Codes was called 戸 (*ko*). While the diary has not been preserved in a complete manuscript, what remains is important for a look into the legal affairs of the day.

the posthumous name of Kentokuin should be changed to Gotoba. Perhaps this is something requested by the previous internal minister. Having pondered on this, I think such an action is unprecedented in our court. At the Chinese court, they often switched names. The Great Minister said as much. It was very difficult to know the reason for the ceremony of altering a name. The reason announced was that the first name did not suit the divine will of the deities and Buddha. What should be done?"

[34] THE FESTIVAL AT SIRAYAMA SHRINE IN KAGA

Heikoki says, "On the sixth day of the fourth month of the same year (1242) ... today was the festival of the Sirayama Shrine in Kaga Province. Thus, the provincial governor and I went by ship early this morning to attend ritual purification and the divine ceremonies. The person in charge of the moon and water appeared. Lower people with heavy and light clothing did not enter beyond the gate. When it came to eating fish, no one acted reserved. And like the eleventh month of the previous year, the eating of everything from birds to rabbits was strictly forbidden, for this was the tradition of the shrine." Until the Middle Ages, when a shrine held a festival, even the provincial governor attended. Nonetheless, in this present era of confusion, the divine ceremonies are neglected in the various provinces.

[35] TWO POINTS ABOUT THE CHINESE HEART

In China, everything that happens to people, happiness or sorrow, peace or war, is viewed as the workings of heavenly forces. They call these things "the Way of heaven," "the will of heaven," "the logic of heaven," and so on; thus these are called "the natural Way of heaven and earth," "things decreed by heaven," and "the logic of heaven and earth." These things are prized above all else, revered with awe. This came about because in China there is no true "Way," and the Chinese cannot comprehend that everything that goes on in the world is the doing of the deities and their will.

Thus, the Chinese recklessly created the philosophy of "the Way of heaven," "the will of heaven," and "the logic of heaven."

"Heaven" is merely the place where the heavenly deities dwell and this spatial entity has no mind of its own, and it is impossible that an entity with no existential power can "send down heavenly decrees." The Chinese do not respect, awe, or revere the deities, but only respect the place known as heaven. It is much like recklessly revering and feeling awe for the imperial palace and knowing nothing about respect and reverence for the ruler who resides inside.

Since those in foreign countries cannot comprehend that everything is the doings of the deities, they easily believe in "the Way of heaven" or "the logic of heaven." This is not hard to understand. Nonetheless, Japan to this day has transmitted the correct and true "Way," but Japanese Confucian scholars do not search or ponder this, believing the empty sophistry of foreign countries, calling this "heaven" and offering their respect to it. How can they have come to this point, believing that everything works according to heaven, singing the praises of ideas from China?

Also, in China the exaggerated and bothersome ideas of "the great limit," "the great nothingness," "*yin* and *yang*," "heaven and earth," "the eight seals," and "the five natural elements" are all theories created by the Chinese. None of these has any truth to them. When people discuss the texts of *Kojiki* or *Nihon shoki*, they generally employ these Chinese ideas to expound upon the texts, and this is very foolish.

In the recent past, there have been people who have tried to get away from Confucian thought, but even these people have not come to realize that the ideas of "the logic of heaven" and "*yin* and *yang*" are flawed theories. These people cannot escape this frame of mind because they have not rid themselves of all Chinese thinking, and these dreamlike ideas are leading them around in the dark, but the people have not yet awakened. The idea that Ama-terasu Ōmikami is not the heavenly globe in the sky shows these people are still fettered by the petty reasoning of the Chinese Heart, and they have yet to comprehend that the logic of the true "Way" is sublime and profound. Amaterasu Ōmikami is the heavenly globe in the sky and her descendants came down to this earth and rule over our country. One cannot fully comprehend these truths by using the limited knowledge of humans. Is it not another example of this Chinese Heart and its adherence to petty rationalizing that causes these people to use the excuse that since they cannot comprehend these things according to their own wisdom, there can be no such thing as this "Way"?

[36] PART TWO

This is not to say that the Chinese are completely ignorant of the deities. There is proof that fragments of our orthodox traditions have been transmitted to China, because some people worship the deities and have festivals in their honor. Regardless, the Chinese have no way to come to a perfect understanding about the creation of heaven and earth, the formation of the countries and the myriad objects, the way of man, the beginning of all creation, the deities' ruling over all events in life, as well as the behavior of all deities. With regard to these great affairs, they only speak of "heaven," and then only speak of the deities in connection with unimportant and petty affairs. They belittle the great Sun Goddess, who illuminates this world, treating her as if she were nothing important. It is sheer stupidity that they do not know the true form of this goddess, or how much she deserves our respect.

[37] CONCERNING THE PEOPLE OF THE YIN DYNASTY REVERING DEMONS AND DEITIES

It seems that the people of the Yin dynasty honored ghosts and deities.[56] The saying that this was a mistake came from the people

---

56. Norinaga appears to have reference to *Li ji* where it says, "Confucius said, 'The people of the Yin dynasty honored spirits and led the common people to serve these spirits. They put service to the ghosts of the dead first and ceremonies last.'" It is interesting that this argument revolves around a misunderstanding of the graph 神, which in Japan was used to represent *kami*, the deities of the Japanese pantheon, while in Confucius's day it referred to spirits or spiritual things. *The Analects* states, "The Master (Confucius) did not talk about extraordinary things, strength, chaos, and spirits" (子不語怪力亂神).

of the later dynasty of Zhou. This was not a mistake discovered in the Yin dynasty. The idea that the people of Zhou felt that worshipping the deities was barbaric, when viewed from the perspective of the true Way, shows that the people in the Yin dynasty were even more barbaric, but this whole subject is built on the sophistry of the sages who treat the deities lightly.

[38] READING THE CHINESE GRAPH 言 AS *MOZI*

Recent scholars of the study of ancient things avoid using the graph 字 (character, graph) when they talk about the thirty-one characters of song [*uta no misodifito mozi*], calling it thirty-one syllables.[57] In addition, they call each stanza five or seven syllables, instead of five or seven graphs, but even in the preface to *Kokinshū*, it records that song is composed of "thirty plus one graphs." This is how they described song from long ago. When *mozi* is spoken of, this is a pronunciation of the graphs 文字, and though this is not originally Japanese, we do not say *monzi* [reading 文字 according to the Chinese]. The Japanese word for character does not sound like it would in Chinese, but the pronunciation is a form created so it sounds native.[58] Words like *fousi* (bonze, monk), *zeni* (money), or *fumi* (record) are words where the Chinese pronunciation has been altered, and there are many examples where an originally Chinese word has become part of the native lexicon. Therefore, there are many places in the ancient tales where it was improper to call a morpheme *kotoba*, so they called it *mozi*. These all belong to the category of X *no mozi* or X *wo mozi*. Recent scholars of antiquity believe that these examples of "*-no* word," "*-wo* word" sound like Chinese phrases. In stories like *Genji monogatari*, it says, "the graphs for parting," and in the "Aoi" chapter, it talks about using such a character like that now, and this means "word." In spite of it

---

57. Early in his work Norinaga did the same thing, however. See *Isonokami sasamegoto* (Ōno and Ōkubo 1976, vol. 2:89).

58. Norinaga's work on the proper spelling of Chinese words (*Kanji san'onkō*) makes the following remark, "Now, the ancients were not fond of the pronunciation of Chinese graphs, so though they read Chinese works, they read them in Japanese as far as possible" (Ōno and Ōkubo 1976, vol. 5:423).

being proper to use *kotoba* for "word," there were times when people used the word *mozi* in its place; thus, it is even more proper to say five or seven *mozi*, or "the word ... ."

[39] PUTTING FORTH A NEW THEORY

Recently, the way of scholarship has made good progress and because scholars have sharpened their methodology in a variety of fields of study, there are many people putting forth various new theories. When those theories are good, they are praised. Therefore, anyone who considers himself a scholar rushes to announce new and rare theories concerning research he has yet to finish. They do this to surprise society. This practice springs from the desire of scholars to avoid losing the scholastic race. Among these new theories, there are some good ideas, but overall, scholars with shallow experience become anxious and announce theories with the intention of trying to better their peers. They take announcing a theory lightly, cutting corners on thorough research without making sure there are no contradictions in the theory.

Because of this, many of these theories are full of mistakes. In all cases, bringing forth a new theory is an important act. The scholar must spend time thinking deeply about the issue, obtaining concrete evidence, making sure that there are no problems in his logic, and ensuring that his theory is free of contradictions. If a scholar does not believe that his theory can withstand other scholars' scrutiny, then the theory should not be announced lightly. There are many times that one is full of confidence about his theory at the time of announcement, but after reconsideration and scrutiny, the scholar himself comes to find that his theory is erroneous.

[40] A WORD ABOUT READING CHINESE WORKS

When reading Chinese works, the reader will notice that many of the words therein differ from the current usages in society. This is due to the works having been read traditionally from ancient times, and the older words have been preserved as they are, but the pronunciation has deteriorated through syncope. The current pronunciation of *notaumaku* (to say) is a syncopated form of *notamawaku*, and there is even a form *notabaku*. In the ancient lexicon, the word *tamau* was also pronounced as *tabu*, and that is why one poem in *Man'yōshū* reads the verb *notamawaku* as **notabaku**.[59] The phrase stating a certain reason, *kakaru ga yuwe ni* can be read as *karu ga yuwe ni*, with one syllable [*ka*] removed. This is not an example of syncope.

The pronunciation of "nevertheless" as *sikausite*, with *u* added to *sikasite* is much like saying "eighth day" (*yoka*) as *yauka*, or "wife" (*nyobō*) as *nyoubau*. "With this" is not pronounced *kore wo mote*, but *koko wo mote*, an example of the ancient lexicon preserved as is in the present. There were many examples in the ancient lexicon where "this," which is *kore* in the present, was pronounced *koko*. Pronouncing the particle *yi mote* [instead of *motte*] is an example of low-class syncope. Pronouncing "pondering" as *omonfakaru* and "thinking" as *omonmiru* are examples with *n* attached in place of *i* (*omoifakaru / omoimiru*).

"A little bit more" being pronounced *nannan to su* is just *narinamu to su*, but pronouncing "in spite of" as *nannantari tomo* is wrong. The pronunciation of *fotusu* (desire) is a form of *forisu*. *Kudan* (paragraph) is just a form of *kudari*. Certain examples like "friendly" pronounced as *sitasinzu*, "to value" as *omonzu*, "base" as *iyasinzu* are left in the ancient form [the modern form being *sitasimisu*, *omomisu*, and *iyasimisu*]. Also, the pronunciations of *yominzu* (like) *nikuminzu* (hate) are also examples of ancient forms with *n* attached. Pronouncing "when" as *tokinba* is an example of *zuwa* added to a word, and the suffix changes to *zunba*. "Tears" becomes *nanda*, "has become" is *nannu*, "to end" becomes *wowannu*, while "accomplish" is *togenzi* and "becomes" is *narinzi*. These are all examples of syncopated forms with *n* attached, and there are many more examples of this phenomenon.

---

59. Norinaga has reference to MYS 4408 (奈氣伎乃多婆久 *nage₁ki₁ no₂tabaku*, said lamenting). This is a nominalized form: *no₂tamapaku*, where the loss of the vowel causes prenasalization: *notamapaku > notampaku > notabaku*.

[41] CONCERNING SYNCOPE

It is extremely rare to find syncope in the ancient lexicon, and this phenomenon is completely different from later eras. Syncope as found in later eras originated at the end of the Nara era, and at any rate, it slowly appears on the scene with each successive reign. As I noted at the end of *Kanji san'onkō* [ca. 1771], syncope is something that came about naturally and systematically, and there are not more than five kinds of this change. Not all examples of syncope are correct, because some are examples of phonetic confusion, where the change in one phoneme causes a change in a neighboring phoneme, so when later learned scholars read the ancient works, and they have failed to understand the original word, they read it with the current pronunciation—though one should not mix ancient and new—which is careless.

In all later eras, there are many examples of words that have undergone a phonological change, so it is very easy to become confused. It is best to search the origins of the word and pronounce these properly. Among these examples of syncope, many have *n* added, but this is not the original phonetic structure. The reader should remember that such are all later examples of syncope. Now after the syncopated *n*, the original morpheme had a voiceless phoneme that has been voiced, so all examples of this kind are labeled "voiced." For example, the ancient word **nemokoro** (generous) later became *nengoro*. After the *n*, the phoneme /ko/, which was a voiceless syllable in the ancient language, has become voiced because of the /mo/ in the upper position.[60] All examples of voiced phonemes in syncope follow this pattern. In spite of this, the palates of modern people have become accustomed to syncope, so even when they try to read the ancient texts correctly, they still say *nemogoro*, leaving the third syllable voiced, and this is a mistake. There are many examples like this, and the student should beware.

---

60. Norinaga is very astute to see this phonological change. What actually appears to have happened is that the second vowel of $nemo_1ko_2ro_2$ was raised to *nemukoro*, and then when the vowel later devoiced, the *m-* underwent syllabification to *n*, and prenasalized the following velar: *nemokoro > nemukoro > nengoro*.

[42] CONCERNING THE TITLES OF OFFICIALS

Among the various titles of officials, there are some actual titles from the ancient past, while others were provided with Chinese graphs at a later date [which then influenced the reading of the title]. The title is indeed old, though some posts were established much later. There are also some titles that were recreated by using Chinese titles, and there are people who want to know how to distinguish between the various kinds.

First, minister [*daijin*] was anciently called **ofo-omi**, a title [Omi] with the word "large" attached in order to elevate the post. Therefore, this post was originally limited to those with the title of Omi. The post of Ofo-murazi was treated the same, given to those with the title of Murazi. In spite of this, in the ancient era Ofo-omi and Ofo-murazi should not be seen as governmental posts. The period when "Ofo-omi" became the name of a ministerial post is during the reign of Emperor Kōtoku, when the ministers of the left and right were established. Before this time, any group, not just those with the title of Omi, could rule in the government.

Now, during the reign of Emperor Tenchi the posts of internal minister and prime minister were established. These originally were related to the ancient title of Ofo-omi, and later were used as distinct posts in the government, with the addition of left and right. These posts along with that of prime minister are based on the Chinese system of government, and are not typical of the ancient Japanese system. *Wamyōshō* says that the true reading of the post of prime minister is **ofo maturigoto no ofo matugimi**, and this is a reading of the attending graphs. Even in works from the Middle Ages, we find the reading of *ofoki ofo imautigimi* or *ofoki otodo*. These other readings came about because the one in *Wamyōshō* was so long that people in the Middle Ages removed the second graph [read *maturigoto*].

Ministers of the left and right were called **ofo imautigimi**, and this is nothing but a reading attached to the Chinese characters. However, the reading of **matugimi** and **mautigimi** are ancient posts and the title means "the ruler in the front"; the current word is a syncopated form of this ancient word [*mafetugimi*].

The post of **mafetugimi** appears in one poem contained in the

1 ~ NEW FRESH HERBS 51

record of Emperor Keikō in *Nihon shoki*.[61] *Wamyōshō* has the reading of **mautigimi**, but later commentaries like *Hokuzanshō* and *Ejidai*[62] have the reading of *mafutigimi mafutikimudati*, and the syllable *fu* is incorrect. These syllables became *u* through syncope and should be understood to underlie the phoneme /u/.

The posts of *dainagon* (great councilor), *chūnagon* (middle councilor), and *shōnagon* (lesser councilor) are based on Chinese government systems and these readings are based on the reading of the graphs.[63] *Ben* (controller) was read **ofotomofi**, a reading that sounds ancient, but I have my own doubts about the meaning. I have not been able to reach a decision.[64] It is also unclear what meaning the character itself has or why it was affixed to the post. The example seen in *Saigūki*, *Hokuzanshō*, and *Shōyūki*[65] has the title written 大鞆火之官 (the official of the large arm pad fire), but these are merely rebus characters.

All the posts of *geki* (head inspector), *naiki* (document official), *daishi* (major recorders), *shōshi* (minor recorders), and *shishō* (scribes) are imitations of Chinese posts. Calling all head officials **kami** is something from the ancient past. The vice official is called **suke**, something that is perhaps also archaic. Judges were called **maturigotobito**, a name created later. I have not found a reading for the post of *sa* [viz. *sakan* (assistant)]. The reading of *saukan* comes from syncope on the first syllable.

Among the eight ministries, the treasury is ancient. Perhaps the Imperial Household Ministry is also old. I am not sure about

---

61. NS 24 contains the following: 魔幤菟耆彌・伊和哆羅秀暮 *mape₁tuki₁mi₁ iwatarasu mo* [Courtiers cross over (the little tree bridge)].
62. *Ejidai*: Written by Ōe no Masafusa (1041–1111), an aristocrat at court and a poet. This work deals with regulations and rites at the court.
63. According to the readings preserved in *Nihon shoki*, Dainagon (Great Councilor) is read **ofoki mono mausu tukasa** (the great director who humbly says things). The title Chūnagon (Middle Councilor) is read **suke no mono mausu tukasa** (the vice director who humbly says things). There is no example of Shōnagon in *Nihon shoki*.
64. The reading for controller as **ofotomofi** is first seen in *Wamyōshō* (Yosano and Masamune, book 5:2v.). The post itself is first seen in *Shoku Nihongi*, second year of Taihō (702); see Aoki et al. (2000, vol. 1:53). The word itself is likely composed of *ofo* (big) plus *adomofi* (to lead) and monophthongization resulted in *ofotomofi* (Nakada 1982:289).
65. *Shōyūki*: The personal diary of Fujiwara Sanesuke (957–1046). It covers the period from 982 to 1032. Unfortunately, this large diary has many gaps, mostly due to faulty textual transmission.

the Civil Affairs Ministry. The Central Affairs, Ceremony, War, and Punishment ministries are all imitations of Chinese organs. The Inspectors Bureau is also based on a Chinese example. Among the various posts, the post of chamberlain is indeed ancient. Among the various bureaus, retainers (*toneri*), the cleaners of the internal storehouse, and the cooks of the palace are all ancient. The internal storehouse was always known as just **kura** because these people officiated in the forbidden precincts. The cleaners were originally called **kanimori**, a syncopated form of **kamumori**. The present form of *kamon* is a terrible corruption of the original.

Among the various administrative agencies, the chamberlains, sake brewers, and water overseers are ancient. The water overseer is **mofitori**, written as such in *Wamyōshō*. The present form of *mondo* is an awful corruption of the original.

The *konoe* (bodyguards), *hyōe* (military guards), and *emon* (palace gate guards) are all based on Chinese models. The title of archers preserves an ancient reading. The original reading was **yugefi**, and the modern reading of *yugie* is a corruption of this. Viceroy is an ancient name. Attendants were called **omotobitomeutigimi**, but I am not sure about the reading of /me/. The attendants in the Central Affairs Ministry were called **omotobitomatigimi**. *Hokuzanshō* says these are *omotomafutigimi*. Posts other than those mentioned above are from later eras, but many have preserved ancient readings, and are not necessarily modeled after China. One may know the meaning of those posts that originated with Chinese titles by the characters.

[43] ABOUT THE UPPER AND LOWER DESIGNATIONS IN THE RANKS OF COURTIERS

Concerning the reading of upper and lower designations [in ranks], upper was **opoi**, while lower was **firoi**.[66] This is seen in the fourteenth year of Emperor Tenmu (685), where the record says,

---

66. This explanation is somewhat garbled. The text in *Nihon shoki* actually has 毎階有大広 with the last two characters read in the texts as *opoki firoki*. Norinaga appears to have taken the bound forms, *ofo* and *firo*, and attached *i* (rank) to this, but the etymological spelling is *wi*, which he knows. It is unclear where his spellings of 於保伊 (**ofoi**) and 比呂伊

"The court revised the 'cap and rank' system ... and each level shall have an upper [large] and a lower [broad] division." This distinction of large and broad was incorporated into the later system. Originally, these were pronounced as *opoki* and *piroki*, but syncope changed the final /ki/ to /i/. While I do not understand the sentence in the preface to *Kokinshū* where it says "Kakinomoto no Hitomaro, *ofoki mitu no kurai*" (upper third rank), writing it as *ofoki* instead of *ofoi*, at least fits the ancient precedent.[67]

[44] SONGS THAT HAVE NO VOICED SYLLABLES

There is a song in *Kokinshū* that does not repeat a single syllable,[68] and this variety of poetry shows that some poems did not use even one voiced phoneme. A few other examples are:

otofa yama	Like Mount Wings of Sound,
oto ni kikitutu	I have heard rumors of her.
afisaka no	But I grow old
seki no konata ni	waiting on this side of
tosi wo furu kana	Meeting Hill Barrier. (KKS 473)

komu yo nimo	How I wish the next life
faya narina namu	would hurry along and come.
me no mafe ni	I want the memory
turenaki fito wo	of that cruel person here
mukasi to omofamu	to be a thing of a former life.
	(KKS 520)

There are still other examples like this.

(firoi) are from, unless he is simply imitating *man'yōgana*. He is correct when he later notes that lenition of the medial -k- results in -i (*ofoki* > *ofoi*).

67. It is interesting that Norinaga mentions no surprise that Kakinomoto no Hitomaro is recorded as having the third rank in the preface to *Kokinshū*, when *Man'yōshū* makes it clear Hitomaro died a very low-ranking courtier.

68. KKS 955. The poem is:

yo no ukime	I wish to enter
mienu yamadi fe	that mountain path
iramu nifa	of easiness,
omofu fito koso	but the woman of my heart
fodasi narikere	is a shackle around my ankle.

[45] HOW TO READ CHINESE POETRY

In *Dōmōshō*,[69] a certain person went to Kitano [Tenmangū] and composed a Chinese poem:

Going east and going south, the clouds appear so small.
The days of the second and third months passed lazily.

This person dozed off and in his dream, the divine Sugawara no Michizane said, "Read this poem in Japanese: 'I went hither and thither and the clouds all cleared up. The days of the second and third month passed peacefully.'" ...

Anciently poetry had to be a thing of beauty and that is why they composed such poetry. Even when Japanese people composed Chinese prose in the ancient era, they read these in Japanese because reading these according to the Chinese pronunciation of the graphs sounded awful. Regardless of this, such things in the present are exactly opposite. All the words used in verse are believed to sound beautiful if they are read aloud using Sino-Japanese readings. Moreover, regardless of whether the text is written or orally reproduced, people believe it is good to use Chinese readings, because these people are learned in Chinese texts.[70]

[46] CONCERNING LONG VERSE IN *KOKINSHŪ*

The first long poem [*chōka*] included in *Kokinshū* is dreadful. That poem (KKS 1001) contains the following: "and why should I / be bitter toward you, my love?" This phrase is inadequate in connecting the upper portion of this poem with the lower. The poet should have composed this poem without these two stanzas. And while having the verb "think of" nine times in a single poem

---

69. The full title is *Waka dōmōshō* (An abridgement of ignorance of *Waka*). A poetic treatise written by Fujiwara Norikane (1107–1165), which was completed around 1145. It categorizes poetic vocabulary, starting with *Man'yōshū* and other anthologies.

70. It should be mentioned that much of the beautiful Japanese prose written in the nineteenth and twentieth centuries owes a great deal to Norinaga's own elegant Japanese prose.

grates on the ears, the poet goes on to add "and if I should die / I think I would be happy to die." I have my doubts about repeating the same thought [to die] in two places. The phrase "I think ... but" is one example, and then there is the clause "my thoughts so deep," while the closing two stanzas wallow limply.

Next is Tsurayuki's poem (KKS 1002) attached with an index of old poetry, but the flow of the poem is horrid and lacks coherence. Tadamine's poem (KKS 1003) sounds like it has only one rhythm, while Mitsune's poem (KKS 1005) has no rhythm at all. There are some good points in Ise's poem (KKS 1006), and I have argued this way because her stance in the poem does not fit her status, and this should not be.

[47] CONCERNING THE THEORY ABOUT THE THATCH ON ISE SHRINE

Concerning the thatch used on the roof of the main shrine at Ise, it is said there was an order to use simple materials for thatch, but this idea is a mistake coming from scholars of Shintō in the recent era who curry favor based on that bothersome Chinese Heart. The idea of placing a high value on simpler materials comes from this same source. In all ceremonies connected with the deities, it is not true that everything should be simple. Not only the main shrine, but also all the commodities presented for the deities should be unparalleled in their beauty, dignity, and splendor, and this is how people should revere the deities. It is a show of disrespect and shallow intent to make the shrine building or the articles of presentation unadorned.

The method and material of the thatch of the great shrine of Ise follows and preserves the ancient precedent without deviation. In addition, the unparalleled beauty and splendor of the thatch of the shrine is a symbol of the emperor's generous reverence to the great deity. Therefore, one may know that the movement toward the idea that simplicity equals beauty for the emperor's palace as well as those items presented to the shrine originated in the recent past from scholars of Shintō who have gone against the ancient tradition and follow the Chinese Heart.

[48] ON THE CHINESE OFFICIALS WHO HAD BOTH AUTHORITY TO WORSHIP THE IMPERIAL DEITIES AND PERFORM FUNERALS TOGETHER

If you look through the work *Zhou li*, you will notice that it says it is proper for the head priest and subordinates to take charge over all festivals related to the deities even as they had authority to conduct funerals. There was no distinction between living and dead, clean or defiled. Viewed from our [Japanese] perspective, this is a very abominable practice.

[49] THE POEM COMPOSED BY THE GO KYŌGOKU REGENT

In the fifteen-hundredth poetic composition match, Go Kyōgoku wrote,

kumo faruru	The clouds disperse
yuki no fikari ya	and the snow sparkles.
sirotafe no	On heavenly Mount Kagu
koromo fosu tefu	is where the robes are hung—
ame no kaguyama	those white ceremonial robes.

He has simply changed the first two stanzas of a song by Empress Jitō,[71] but because the song he created was novel, it is not jarring with its happy sound. That is why the judges could not criticize it.

[54] CONCERNING THE LIMITED AMOUNT OF MONEY IN THE PAST

In the same record [*Azuma kagami*][72] there appear the words "four rolls of excellent quality silk measuring 75 feet in length worth 120 *mon* [divided into 20 *mon* each]," "two *tan* of indigo

---

71. A slightly revised form of MYS 28.
72. *Azuma kagami*: An important military chronicle of the Kamakura Bakufu. It out-

1 ~ NEW FRESH HERBS 57

cloth [with no pattern] worth four *mon*." You realize from this record that anciently money was very rare. The same record also notes, "The Villa Proprietor, Kudō Hiromitsu, wore a hemp robe and *suikan*." The modern word *saime*, meaning "tightly woven cloth," is a corruption of *sayomi* (hemp robe).

[55] THINKING IT RUDE TO CALL A PERSON
BY HIS GIVEN NAME

In the same record [*Azuma kagami*], we see the following in the words of Taira Masako when she reproved Yoriie, "The Minamoto family has been one family of Shoguns. The Hōjō are our relatives. Thus, those before us often benefited from their kindness. You are always summoned to be in their presence, but now you get nothing like a warm commendation. Moreover I have heard that everyone is summoned by their given name, and this is why people harbor vengeance." This excerpt makes it clear that it is rude to call a person by his given name.

[56] CALLING A NEW YEAR ILLNESS "PLEASURE"

In the same record [*Azuma kagami*] it says, "On the eleventh day of the first month of the second year of Shōgen (1208) ... since pleasure visited the house of the Shōgun, he put affairs off until today." This survives even today. During the New Year people have a taboo on the word "illness," and instead call it "pleasure."

[57] ON THE POEM OF PRIEST KEIGETSU
AT KIYOMIZU TEMPLE

During the upheaval of the Jōkyū era (1219-1222), there was a priest named Keigetsu at the Kiyomizu Temple who gave his al-

---

lines the first six Shoguns, from Yoritomo in 1180 to Munetaka Shinnō's return to Kyōto in 1266. It is thus believed to have been completed sometime after 1266.

legiance to the capital. He joined the emperor's army and the enemy captured Keigetsu when the army headed to Udi. When the enemy was about to put him to death, he composed a poem and showed it to them.

choku nareba	It being a command,
mi wo ba suteteki	I have forfeited my life.
mononofu no	Surrounded by warriors—
yaso udigafa no	I am not one of them—
se ni fa tatanedo	in the rapids of the Uji River.

The enemy admired this poem and spared the priest's life, banishing him to some faraway place. This is seen in the same record [*Azuma kagami*].

[58] THE NUMBER OF *SAKE* JARS DURING THE KAMAKURA ERA

It says in the same record [*Azuma kagami*], "On the thirtieth day of the ninth month of the fourth year of Kenchō (1252), the government said there should be prohibitive measures on the regulation of selling alcohol in the various places in Kamakura. A command was given to the Hoho magistrate and his officials and through this an investigation into the *sake* jars of the various families in Kamakura revealed that there were 37,274 jars. ... "

[59] CONCERNING THE LAST WORDS OF HŌJŌ TOKIYORI

In the same record [*Azuma kagami*] it says, "On the twenty-second day of the eleventh month of the third year of Kōchō (1263), the monk Hōjō Tokiyori left the world at Saimei Temple and left these words of praise: 'The mirror of leaves hangs high. For thirty-seven years I have swung one hammer and spread the great Way. On the twenty-second day of the eleventh month of the third year of Kōchō, I have revered and loved the Way.'" Like the era of the Hōjō and Ashikaga, everyone, whether high or low, had become lost in Zen, and when they faced death, they thought that these kinds of fabrications about having found enlightenment are wonderful. This is bothersome and stupid.

[60] CONCERNING PRINCE MUNETAKA'S PRINCIPAL WIFE BEING LABELED "MIYASUDOKORO"

In the same record [*Azuma kagami*], every time there is mention made of Prince Munetaka's principal wife she is referred to as "Miyasudokoro." The paragraph before this appears to mention why. Generally, "Miyasudokoro" refers to women of the *kōi* rank who give birth to princes or princesses. In addition, it is very easy for such a title to be used for the principal wife of Prince Munetaka. People in later eras misunderstood this and called the consort in the palace of the Crown Prince "Miyasudokoro."

2 | FALLING LEAVES of the CHERRY

On the tenth day of the ninth month [in 1793], the leaves of the cherry I planted in the front garden were dark red and as evening arrived, the color of the leaves left me with a deep sense of sorrow. I composed a poem when the evening breeze scattered the leaves.

fana tirisi　　　　As the autumn leaves
onazi kozue wo　　scatter from the treetops,
momidi nimo　　　it is this cherry
mata mono omofu　standing in my garden
nifa zakura kana　that brings back sad memories.

I decided to include this here, and title the second chapter accordingly.

[61] CONCERNING THE PRESENTATION OF THE CEREMONIAL ARTICLES AND THE RECITATION OF THE LITURGY AFTER AN IMPERIAL ASCENSION

Shōyūki says the following in the fifth year of Chōwa (1016), "After the imperial ascension, the liturgy that accompanied the presentation of the divine offerings said: 'The Emperor proclaims with great words of praise the divine will before the many imperial deities. Accepting the command of the male and female procreative deities who reside in the High Plain of Heaven, the Emperor has ascended the high throne of the heavenly globe in this, the land of Luxurious Reed-Plain of Precious Rice Ears. He took control of the machinery of the successive government on the twenty-eighth of the fourth month, and I, Nakatomi no Takakuni of the Senior Sixth Rank Upper, have been sent to proclaim the state of this event. With this, we hold up and present divine offerings. I proclaim these words as the Emperor has commanded me.'" I believe these words are a liturgy and are not an imperial decree.

The clause "proclaims with great words of praise" contains an error because it should not have "words," but should have "finished proclaiming." The graph for "words" (言) is an addition, because the word "finish" is insufficient to complete the meaning. The verb "proclaim" is an addition. I think the original had "humbly proclaim," but there is no ancient precedent for this reading. I have never heard of any clause using "successive," also. There is an example of "following precedent," so maybe a graph has been dropped from the text. The date of twenty-eighth of the fourth month is a mistake for twenty-ninth of the first month. A critical text of this diary should have these corrections.

Texts for liturgies and imperial edicts became more and more corrupt into the Middle Ages, most of the words lacking any cohesion, with many places that do not make any sense. No one has spent time doing thorough research into these liturgies, because people have no interest in the ancient meanings and know nothing about the ancient lexicon. These texts all have a literary quality in their vocabulary; everything about antiquity is praiseworthy. It is mortifying when people treat these events as if they were nothing of any importance. I have brought this up to arouse greater caution in people.

The same diary goes on to say,

> Fifteenth day of the fourth month of the ninth year of Tengyō (946). The Emperor ascended the throne and caused that divine offerings be presented to the heavenly deities and earthly deities in the five provinces of the interior and the various provinces in the seven circuits. [The offerings from the interior provinces were assigned to the various provincial governors. The offerings from the other various provinces were assigned to be provided from taxes.]

2 ~ FALLING LEAVES OF THE CHERRY 63

A messenger from the Nakatomi and Imibe families was sent to each of the circuits [each received one relay bell as proof, but the messengers in the interior received no such bell].

The diary further says,

On the day that the offerings were presented from the five interior provinces and the various provinces of the seven circuits, a check was made to see if everyone had fulfilled their duties. On the twentieth day of the third month of the first year of Tenryoku (970),[73] it rained and the ministers of the government did not appear at the ceremony, so the ceremony was cancelled. Today, messengers were dispatched to present the divine offerings to the various deities of the five interior provinces, and the various provinces of the seven circuits, following precedent after the ascension of an emperor. The head of the bureau of the native cult spoke to the various messengers several days before and put someone from the Ōnakatomi and Imibe families in charge of the messengers. He gave each a token showing authority to be given to each province. However, each messenger was assigned according to the decision of the head of the native cult.

The diary also notes, "There were eight checks for the interior provinces and the provinces of the seven circuits. There were five tokens stating that the divine offerings from the seven circuits shall come from the taxes. Altogether, there were fifteen tokens of authority." This record appears in the diary of Minister of the Right Ono Miya Sanesuke.

---

73. Context makes it seem that this is the first year of Tenryaku (947), the following year of the imperial ascension. Scribal error here, having mistaken the second character, has thrown this date twenty-three years into the future.

[64] ON THE DAMAGE DONE TO THE DIVINE MIRROR WHEN THE PALACE CAUGHT FIRE

The same record [*Shōyūki*] notes,

At the first hour of the fifteenth day of the eleventh month of the second year of Kankō (1005) ... the inner chambers of the palace caught fire ... . The fire started in the Unmei Chamber, and the divine mirror [the so-called place of awe], the great sword, and other divine articles could not be taken out [and rescued] ... . On the seventeenth day ... the damage to the divine mirror was investigated and reported ... . A mirror, the great sword, and some documents were lost in the fire. The divine mirror was slightly damaged. Other than this, no damage was found. The frame for the mirror was lost. ... In the Murakami record it says, "On the twenty-fourth day of the ninth month of the fourth year of Tentoku (960), everything was lost in a fire ... . On the twenty-fourth day, Sugemitsu Ason reported, 'We reached the Unmei Chamber and I searched the tops of the roof tiles and found one mirror. (The mirror was eight *sun* in diameter, and while it had one nick there was no other visible damage.) ... ' On the twenty-fifth day Kiyotowo Korenobu and others together reported that they had again searched and found one charred mirror ... Thus in the palace daily record it says, 'How awe-inspiring that even though it was in the coals and ashes of the fire it was not completely destroyed by the fire ... . (Among the three mirrors was the great deity of Ise of the Hinomafe District of Kii Province ...).' Similar to this theory regarding this incident are the three mirrors we have ... . On the ninth day of the twelfth month the Middle Captain of the Office of the Left came and while standing said, 'Today at the tenth hour we transferred the divine mirror from the office of the Prime Minister to the Palace of the Eastern Third Avenue. As I served in this transfer [I report] ... .' On the tenth day the Middle Captain of the office provided proof and reported,

2 ~ FALLING LEAVES OF THE CHERRY 65

'We transferred the divine mirror yesterday. However, upon opening the old august peninsular box and holding the lid, from between the new *kara* box that was provided there suddenly appeared a ray of light like that of the sun, and the female attendants from the inner palace all saw it together. The divine sign was renewed and all were again filled with awe.'"

[66] THE IMPERIAL EDICT WHEN THE IMPERIAL PROCESSION WENT TO KAMO

In the same record [*Shōyūki*] on the twenty-fifth day of the eleventh month of the first year of Kannin (1017), an imperial edict was issued for an imperial procession to Kamo:

The Emperor declares this decree before the awe-inspiring great imperial deity of Kamo with fear and trepidation. During this year we have had prayers and offerings presented, and furthermore with the power of the light and the assistance of the unseen deities together we find that now the bright symbol is apparent. We have pondered the awe-inspiring reason for this repayment. Thus we selected an auspicious day, a day of fortune, and with gold and silver offerings decorated with silk brocade streamers, with flat swords, and belts for Chinese swords, with august bows, august arrows, an august halberd and the august mirror, together with these various divine treasures, we sent a runner on a horse to the eastern quarter accompanied by music. With song, we advance and come forth to make our offering.

In the previous year there was one district, the Atago District, which brought forth a petition and we put forth that petition in prayer. However, in certain places in this district, there is land that is not controlled by any one man, some saying it is the capital of a certain king, others saying it is the territory of a deity of light, a land that has been handed down from ten thousand generations. Thus, the south extends as far as the great highway of the north of the imperial castle. The east extends to the boundary of this district. The west extends as far as the great highway east of the palace. The north extends to the border of this district, and they have made a petition. Within this area, there is a village of the Ryō Ice house. Because this place has the responsibility for the hundred princes, it is difficult to reach for a temporary change. Supposing that we were in the district of the deities and were able to set aside this one village, and then we could equally divide the district in question according to the superiority or inferiority of the various shrines. However, it would be difficult suddenly to determine the number of cultivated fields, and towns and villages. Thus, on a future day, we will set the boundaries of the various areas involved and will make a report to the great imperial deity, one of pacification and calm, and eventually receive the divine response, and there will be no movement of the court of the emperor. On the eternal bedrock watch over us night and day, providing protection for us, purifying and pacifying the four seas, and the myriad people will be at peace, and while we ask for the removal of the omens of flood, drought, famine, and pestilence, we also pray for the constant blessing of the work of the farmer and silk producer, and provide us with the same virtue as Yao of China. Compare our name with that in Chinese literature, and without going against the superior thoughts of the imperial feelings, we declare that we will provide protection and blessings. This we pronounce with fear and trembling.

In a separate petition, we declare that the Queen Dowager has also come here, and with the assistance of the unseen deities, she has not vacated her duty, but the feelings of the imperial body reach into the darkness. The small gate to the Empress's palace has been bright for a long time, and the ways of the duty of a mother at last bear fruit, and for myriad years and a thousand autumns, watch over her night and day, providing protection for her, we

2 ~ FALLING LEAVES OF THE CHERRY 67

ask with fear and trepidation. The eleventh month of the first year of Kannin.

[70] TATUTA RIVER, PART TWO

As I stated in the previous chapter about Tatuta River, it refers to the Yamazaki River, but in the present most do not know which river it refers to or what area it is. I have said this for several years, and in the third month of this year, the fifth year of Kansei (1793), on my way down from the capital [Kyōto] to Ofosaka, I took a boat by the Yamazaki River and went downstream. As I looked around the area, I asked about the river I was on, and was told that generally from Yamazaki in the opposite direction after the Minase River there are no more rivers. As I carefully thought on this, I realized that Minase is the name given later and this river is actually the ancient river called Tatuta. It is on the border between the Yamazaki and Minase, as the boundary of Yamasiro and Tu provinces were just a ways from the river. That river is located in the Upper Sima District of Tu Province. Presently it is narrow as the dikes here and there are high, and as I think about how the flow of the river is good, I believe that anciently the river flowed in a wide area, but later with the construction of high dikes, the river is narrower as it is at present.

Now the names of Mount Kaminabi and the Kaminabi Shrine as found in the Tatuta poems appear in *Jinmyōchō*: "Located in the Otokuni District of Yamasiro Province. People come from Tamate to worship at the Sakatoke Shrine" [important deity, major shrine, receives offerings from court for the biannual "Monthly Festival" and the "Rite of Tasting the First Fruits"]. As this is also known as the Yamazaki Deity as found in *Shoku Kōki* and *Rinji saishiki*,[74] the name Kaminabi originated from this shrine, so Mount Yamazaki

---

74. The first title is *Shoku Nihon kōki*, the fourth history in *Rikkokushi*, compiled in 869. It covers the years 833–850, or the reign of Emperor Ninmyō. The second title, *Rinji saishiki*, is a section in volume 3 of *Engi shiki*. It outlines details for provisional (or extraordinary) festivals.

must be Mount Kaminabi. This shrine is presently also known as the Heavenly King Yamazaki.

Now when I passed through the village of Minase in the far distance there was the village of Kaunai, and on the edge of the village there is a small forest, which is known as the Kaminabi Forest, but it does not match the scene about which the ancients wrote poems. There are no rivers nearby. Pondering this, I believe that the name of Kaunai migrated here at a later date from somewhere else, but it preserves the ancient name. The boundaries of the forest must also be from a later era. The introduction to this poem in *Kokinshū* says, "From Yamazaki as far as the forest of Kaminabi." This sounds as if the poet is heading away from Yamazaki, meaning that while it is confined to the Yamazaki area he must have headed from the village toward the forest.

[71] MINASE RIVER

Anciently the name Minase River was not used as a specific name for a river. It originally referred to a river with very little water, or a river where the water flowed under the sandbars, so there was no water above in the riverbed. In Book 4 of *Man'yōshū* we find:

kofi ni mo so	People also will die
fito fa sinisuru	from yearning.
minasegafa	Like the river with no water
sita yu ware yasu	I waste away, chasing
tuki ni fi ni ke ni	the moon after the sun. (MYS 598)

And:

kotitaku fa	If their talk is annoying,
naka fa yodomase	then please rest in the middle.
minasigafa	Like the river with no water
tayu to ifu koto wo	never allow yourself
arikosu na yume	to cease to exist. (MYS 2712)

2 ~ FALLING LEAVES OF THE CHERRY 69

And:

uraburete	Cast down with regret
mono fa omofazi	I do not let my heart be troubled.
minasegafa	Like the river with no water
arite mo midu fa	my water shall flow
yuku to ifu mono wo	though no one sees it. (MYS 2817)

These all have the same meaning ... .
Thus, it is a mistake to understand these poems above as referring to the Minase River in Yamazaki. The river in the area around Yamazaki anciently was called both Yamazaki River and Tatuta River, as I have argued above. The label Minase River only becomes the name of a river after the era of *Kokinshū* and other works. *Ruijū kokushi*[75] notes that during the years of Enryaku (782–805) and Kōnin (810–823) the emperor often went hunting on Minasi Moor, and a number of times it mentions the village of Minasi. This is Minase in the present. Thus, the name of the river originated from this place name. Now the two graphs 水成 should be read *minasi*. In *Man'yōshū* the three graphs 水無川 should also be read the same way. The graphs 成 and 無 became difficult to read [as *na*]. Nevertheless, from ancient times both the place name and the name of the river were *minasi* and *minase*, which pronunciation must have been similar enough to make the connection.

[72] CONCERNING *RYŌBU* AND *YUIITSU*

Among the various shrines in society today, the ones where a Shintō priest serves are called *yuiitsu* (singular), while the ones where a Buddhist priest serves are called *ryōbu* (dual). There is also one sect within Shintō called Ryōbu. What they call *ryōbu* is a form of secret teachings within Buddhism, dealing with the two

---

75. *Ruijū kokushi*: A historical work that categorizes events found in *Rikkokushi*. It was compiled by Sugawara no Michizane, and completed in 892. It is important because it helps augment lost parts of *Nihon kōki* and other records.

circles, the Garbhadhātu and the Vajradhātu, and splicing these two in with the Way of the Gods is called *ryōbu shūgō*. Thus, these two circles [*ryōbu*] are merged together with the Way of the Gods. You can see this from the graph 部 (form together). It *does not* mean "both *kami* and Buddha." Now the term *yuiitsu* (singular) came about in relation to *ryōbu* Shintō, with the intention of avoiding confusion with this *ryōbu*. Therefore, while from the very start there was the "singular" Way of the Gods, this name itself only came about after the existence of *ryōbu* Shintō. However, it is a pernicious mistake to interpret *ryōbu* as not referring to the two circles, but insisting that it refers to the union of heaven and humanity. What reason is there for insisting that heaven and humanity are one? This idea is simply based on the Chinese philosophy that heaven is supernal and wonderful, which goes starkly against the ancient spirit of Japan.

Heaven refers to the domain where the heavenly deities reside, so what is the reasoning behind saying that humans are one with this sphere? Scholars in our society cannot remember the spirit of the ancients, and because they are blinded by Chinese philosophy, they try to debate in all cases the profundity of things, and end up reaching forced conclusions like this one.

[73] THINGS IN THE WORLD THAT DO NOT SUIT THE WAY

It is bad suddenly to try to get rid of customs that have existed in society for a long period simply because they do not suit the Way. Some ought to get rid of just the problematic points and continue in their search for the true Way. If we were to force everything in the world to conform to the Way, then we would create something that does not suit the spirit of the Way. Since everything in this world, creation and obliteration, prosperity and decline, are controlled by the will of the deities, man and his limited power cannot change anything. People who have an understanding of the true Way should elucidate these principles and understand them.

[74] PRINCIPLES TO ADHERE TO WHEN FOLLOWING THE WAY

It is the obligation of a ruler to apply himself to the Way. It is not something reserved just for scholars. It is the calling of scholars to consider and search into the parameters of the existence of the Way. Since this is my philosophy, I do not try to apply myself to the Way. I spend my time trying to ponder and elucidate what exactly constitutes the Way.

Originally, the ancient rulers followed the Way, and these are the attributes of ruling over everything under the heavens, so that present-day government is not in agreement with the principles of the Way. It is not the spirit of the Way for those below the rulers to rebel against the system, and individually apply themselves to the Way. The people below the rulers should be obedient, whether the rulers' actions are good or bad. The ancient Way is not to come to an understanding of the spirit and then apply it privately.

[75] THE PLACE WHERE PRIEST SŌGI WAS BORN

It is recorded in a certain record[76] that Tuno Village in the lower quarter of the Fudinami Villa in Arita District in Kii Province, on a strip of land between 40 and 50 *ken* in length [236 to 295 feet] is the site of the house where Priest Sōgi[77] was born.

[76] THE AUSPICIOUS SIGNS OF THE SAGES OF CHINA

Anciently in China during the time of the sages, the records state that in honor of the virtue shown by these sages various auspicious signs appeared, such as unicorns, phoenixes, or a variety of birds and beasts. However, in spite of the fact that these kinds of rare animals appear from time to time without any warning, the

---

76. The record in question is *Nanki meishō ryakushi*, a gazetteer-like work of unknown authorship.
77. Priest Sōgi (1421–1502) was a famous *renga* master.

Chinese caused the people of the time to believe that these things had appeared because of the presence of the sages, a demonstration that heaven had bestowed these symbols because of the virtue of the ruler.[78] It is the behavior of the Chinese to act like this related to a myriad things.

[77] TWO POINTS CONCERNING *UDI* TITLES

In our present society, many people do not comprehend [the term] *udi*.[79] No matter how lowly in station a farmer or woodcutter may be, they are all the posterity of someone in the ancient past, so there is not a single person who does not have an *udi*. However, from the time of the Middle Ages, the custom developed of people only having surnames, but the lower classes were not obligated to put both their surnames and *udi* together in one name, so naturally the *udi* became completely supplanted by the name. After a long period had passed, these people no longer knew what the *udi* of their own family was.

Now, regarding people who were originally of a lower social status, but through their own efforts obtained a higher rank, they felt that they were missing something because they had no *udi*,

---

78. In *The Works of Mencius* we find where people praise their Master and mention that this kind of sage is also found in the animal kingdom, where the unicorn is of the highest order among quadrupeds, and the phoenix is of the highest order among fowl ("Gong-sun Chou-i" chapter). *Li ji* records, "Therefore the sagacious kings demonstrated this obedience thus: mountain dwellers were not forced to live by the river. Islanders were not forced to dwell on the plains .... Thus heaven sent down fat-dew, and earth sent forth spring water of wine. The mountains sent forth implements and chariots, and rivers sent forth the map-horse. Phoenixes and unicorns were all in the distant forests" ("Li yun" chapter).

79. *Udi*: A label that anciently designated a group of households recognized by the crown. It is sometimes translated as "clan," but this usage is somewhat misleading. There were two different ways to represent *udi* in early Japanese: 氏 (clan) and 姓 (surname). In general, different Japanese readings were applied, with 氏 read *udi* and 姓 *kabane*. Norinaga here has 姓 glossed as *udi*. Aoki (2005:170) explains that 氏 refers to a group of households that are directly or indirectly related by blood and are recognized as a legitimate unit by the crown in Yamato. On the other hand, 姓 refers to a political status conferred on an individual (and thus his descendants) by the crown. These generally were of two types: a postal status, and a geographical status. Many *kabane* were granted in honor of the post the person held, while others originated from the locale of the family.

and there were many cases where these people would recklessly select an *udi* like Fujiwara, Minamoto, or Taira. These all appear during the times of upheaval in the Ashikaga era [Muromachi era], when all the *udi* in the realm were erroneous, and everything was in a terrible state of confusion. Among these, in the present we find that of ten people with an *udi*, nine of them will have Minamoto, Fujiwara, or Taira. So one may wonder that if so many of the ancient *udi* have disappeared, then most of the people of these three families must have survived down to the present, but such is not the case. In the Middle Ages, most of the high-ranking positions were filled with people who had one of these three *udi*, and people with other *udi* all occupied lower positions, so naturally their *udi* began to disappear, and most people did not know what their *udi* was, and these naturally were lost.

Another reason is that people in the present know nothing about the various *udi* from the ancient days, but believe that *udi* only include names like Minamoto, Taira, Fujiwara, Tachibana, and others. When people choose an *udi* according to their own preference, they always choose from among these, so the various ancient *udi* are unknown, and this has resulted in names like Minamoto, Taira, and Fujiwara increasing in number. And because people yearn [to be like] an ancient, talented individual, they will pretend they are of this person's lineage, so some scholars then become Sugawara or Ōe, just like most warriors are of the Minamoto family. Generally, because even people of high social standing in the recent past have only relied on the surname, we now have the practice where the *udi* does not appear in public. That is why everyone attaches an *udi* as he or she wishes.

Now in the present we have people learning to compose poetry in the *Man'yō* style, and studying about the ancient past, and they think that the ancient *udi* are interesting. Among these are many who like to start using unfamiliar but ancient *udi* within their own names, but this is very annoying, just like the person who pretends to be Chinese and chops his own surname down to using only one graph. It shows how extremely childish and intemperate the person is. If a person longs for the ancient past, he should follow the ancient rules, though one should not recklessly play with these titles; can a person claim to enjoy things from the ancient past if he is not afraid of the judgment of scalding water[80] conducted before the deity Magatsubi?

Generally speaking, an *udi* is something handed down by our ancestors, and because it was not bestowed by the ruler above, it should not be attached to one's name recklessly. And when one has an *udi* that was not actually from the family, but one's ancestor in the Middle Ages, or from the days of one's grandfather, or father, started using it, then it is probably not an issue to continue using it. However, one should not attach an *udi* to one's name. This is something you should not do. If one does not know about *udi* but only uses a surname, there likely is nothing wrong with that. Because people enjoy things from the ancient past, it goes against the ancient spirit to change everything in the present into something neoclassical.

[78] POINT TWO

In society, people generally call the names Minamoto, Taira, Fujiwara, and Tachibana "the four *udi*" (四姓). Of these, the Minamoto, Taira, and Fujiwara have been widely used since the Middle Ages, so that is probably why they were included in this designation. Tachibana, on the other hand, has been used in only a very few family lines, compared to the other three, so the reason it was included with the others is not clear. I think it is probably because during the reign of Emperor Saga, his empress was of the Tachibana lineage, and the custom of revering that title probably started from that time. You even see something about these "four *udi*" in Chinese works. The Chinese apparently heard from a Japanese visitor that the Japanese lined up four of their titles, so they recorded this, and because this news reached all the way to China, people in Japan think that this appellation is very famous.[81]

---

80. *Nihon shoki* describes a method used to determine if a person was innocent or guilty, by thrusting the person's arm into a vat of boiling water. If the person was innocent, they would not be scalded, but if they were guilty, they would be harmed.

81. Found in *Ishō Nihon-den*, a compilation of quotes from China and Korean put together by Matsushita Kenrin (1637-1704) in 1688. The second volume contains the following, "In Japan, those who are labeled 'king' come from the Genji, Tachibana, and Taira down to the Hada. These are the Fujiwara family."

It is truly silly for people to think it a big deal when anything Japanese appears in Chinese works. It is all so ridiculous for people to think that anything Japanese appearing in Chinese works is important. Because all foreign events and items appearing in Chinese works were simply recorded by scribes as explained by foreigners, there is nothing great or rare about these entries.

[79] CONCERNING SURNAMES

There are numerous people in society with the same lineage name (姓) like Fujiwara, Minamoto, and others, and so many of these that we cannot number them, and if we did not divide these names into surnames (苗字) it would become extremely confusing; thus, people are always using only the surname, resulting in this becoming the main name. This became the natural, evident course of events, so that today the surname has become like the lineage name of old. People who do not know the lineage name act as if it is right to protect the correct surname. Now, the character 苗 of 苗字 (surname) has no reasonable etymology. The original word was 名字 (name-graph, surname). However, when writing the character 名 (name) it is possible to confuse this with *azana* (alias), so people altered the graphs [from 名 to 苗]. Thus if someone decides they will write 名字 instead, this does not fix the problem, though, as in the Middle Ages 名 also became connected to the lineage name, and in general people used 名字 in a very broad sense. Thus, people have said that 名字 is a small division within the lineage name system. In the present people say that the child and the father have the same name (同苗). Originally, this was written 同名, which has its origins from the usage 同姓 (same lineage name).

[80] ON ALIASES

The word *azana* (alias) refers to more than just names like Bun-Rin [Funaya no Yasuhide, also known as Rin], Sugasan [Sugawara no Michizane, also known as San, "the third"], Heichū [Taira no Sadafumi, also known as Chū], or Naka. From ancient times, there were many instances where a name used in place of the correct name was called *azana*. In the Middle Ages, what we presently call a secular name was also called an *azana*, and other than these instances, there were cases when an alias came from the name of a field or place, or came from some *thing*. None of these examples shows the correct way to establish a name, but was established simply by the custom of usage, and all of these originate from the customs of naming people in China. Among some of these, the custom of secular names has the same function as names of Chinese people.

[81] WHY COMMENTARIES ON POETIC WORKS ARE CALLED *SHŌ*

From ancient times commentaries on poetic works have been called *shō* (抄, excerpts, abridgments), and there are many titles like "such and such-*shō*." And while the character 抄 does not mean "a commentary," this blurred usage came from China, and we find in Buddhist texts, regardless of the content of the work, designations such as "records," "anthologies," or "excerpts." This custom of calling commentaries on poetic works "excerpts" also was originally done in imitation of the names of Buddhist texts.

[85] INTERPRETING SHINTŌ WORKS

From the Heian era on, people have interpreted Shintō works without thinking deeply enough about the ancient meaning of the words. They have blindly clung to foreign Confucian and Buddhist interpretations, committing themselves based on Chinese reasoning without looking into *Man'yōshū*. Because they have no knowledge of the ancient meaning of these words, other than that from Chinese-induced logic, they do not see the special, ancient substance nor can they figure out the clear meaning of the words. Therefore, the ancient contents of the work remain submerged, without illumination, and the records of the deities themselves, too, are interpreted based on Chinese thinking. As a result, scholars have failed to elucidate the Way.

Thus, the methodology I employ to expound the records of the deities is very different from the prevailing theories found in society. In addition, since I advance theories that have never been propounded throughout history, scholars often chastise me. Nevertheless, this is due to said scholars' affinity to Chinese learning through time, where they have listened to theories deliberated in the same manner. Because they have yet to purify themselves from this Chinese Heart, they cannot yet understand the incorrectness of their theories. What I expound is simply the ancient legends as recorded in *Kojiki* and *Nihon shoki*. The refutations from these people in society are nothing but private opinions twisted through the confusing influence of the Chinese Heart. The opinions voiced by these scholars are vastly different from the ideas in the ancient legends and ideas of Japan. How clearly one would naturally come to see the difference if he would read *Kojiki* and *Nihon shoki* closely! Before one tries to denigrate my theories, he should first criticize *Kojiki* and *Nihon shoki*. As long as one believes in these records, he cannot chastise my theories.

[86] THE POEM OF THE JINGI

In the "Section of the Divinities" (神祇部) in *Fūgashū*[82] we find the poem:

moto yori mo	Even from the beginning
tiri ni mazifaru	there was a deity
kami nareba	who mixed with the dust.
tuki no safari mo	What is so painful about
nani ka kurusiki	the monthly sickness?[83]

This was written when Izumi Shikibu went to the shrine in Kumano and was blocked from entering, so she was not able to

---

82. *Fūgashū*: This is the seventeenth imperially ordered poetic anthology, completed sometime before 1348. It was compiled by Emperor Hanazono.

83. *Tuki no safari* "obstruction of the moon" refers to monthly menstruation, which prevents women from doing various things because of the perceived defilement. Here she could not approach the shrine.

present her offerings to the deities. She then composed the following poem,

>   *fareyaranu*   The floating clouds that
>   *mi no ukikumo no*   trail, like this body of mine
>   *tanabikite*   that finds no appeasement—
>   *tuki no safari to*   how distressing
>   *naru zo kanasiki*   this monthly sickness.

In a dream that very night as she slept, she was told that her petition had been communicated to the deities. This event does not agree with the Way [of the Japanese deities] at all but is a Buddhist interpretation. From the Middle Ages on this has been the general custom; people are used to hearing only what Buddhists have to say about people like this Izumi Shikibu, and thus think that she had such a dream after being imbued with the feelings of a Buddhist Heart. Why should the deities have a mind to possess her? Even the phrase "mixed with the dust" is carelessly based on the words of the Chinese writer Laozi, who said, "Lessen the light and mix with the dust,"[84] and she used it in this poem. Furthermore, there is nothing above the deities. One should not let their hearts be troubled by such mistakes as in this dream, and a person should not defile the deities.

In the same section of the same anthology is a poem by a person called Watarai no Asamune,

>   *katasogi no*   The mitered extension poles
>   *tigi fa uti soto ni*   of the roof are different according
>   *kafaredomo*   to the angle they are cut,
>   *tikafi fa onazi*   but the vow is the same—
>   *ise no kamukaze*   to that divine wind at Ise.

Not only in this poem, but all usages in poetry where they make vows to the deities, or mention "coming down among men

---

84. This phrase evolved in Buddhist thought, and it came to mean that in order for Buddha to save humanity, he hid his light, and came down and mixed with the dust of the earth (humanity).

in the form of a deity," are incorrect. From the Middle Ages down to the present people have industriously clothed themselves in the philosophy of Buddhism and composed poetry about things related to the [Shintō] deities, being deceived by the belief in "original substance and manifested traces",[85] where they identify with the concept that even the Shintō deities in the original land are all Buddhist entities, and using this terminology, even officials who serve the deities at the Ise Shrine commit this kind of blunder. In addition, there is no reason for entities like Buddhist Bodhisattvas, vows, or ideas like "coming down among men in the form of a deity" to be imposed over everything dealing with Shintō deities. Things like "this is a poem about such and such a deity" or "this is a poem from such and such a shrine" are deceptions created by many Buddhist priests in unison to entice people in society into their own branch of Buddhism. These types of poems are not suitable to the intention of the Way of the deities, and are all based on Buddhist theology. All of these things are based on the custom of "a teaching of expedient means"[86] which from ancient times these Buddhist priests have taken after that person, Shaka, to entice people, using falsehoods without any reservations.

[87] CONCERNING POETRY IN *KOKINSHŪ* THAT DEALS WITH THE MOON

The appearance of the moon in poetry should be listed under the topic of "autumn," but in *Kokinshū* poems on the moon are found in the "Miscellaneous" section, and there are only five poems about the moon included in the "Autumn" section if they were connected with autumn or wild geese.

---

85. This is the concept that Buddhist spiritual entities came to Japan in the guise of Shintō deities in order to save people in Japan. Such sentiment first appears in the early Heian era.
86. "A teaching of expedient means": This term is from Charles Muller's "Digital Dictionary of Buddhism" (2012).

[88] POETRY IN *FŪGASHŪ*

In *Fūgashū* there is a poem composed by Emperor Go-Uda where we find the words:

amatu kami	To worship and serve
kunitu yasiro wo	the shrines of the heavenly deities
ifafite zo	and the earthly deities—
waga asifara no	this indeed is how our wonderful land
kuni fa wosamaru	of the reeds is so well governed.

This grand, august poem properly suits the spirit of the Way. Unlike other countries, our country has not engaged in bothersome practices, but we have simply worshipped the deities, and the reason that our land under the heavens has been governed so well is because our native, divine land is so exceptional, and it was definitely true in the ancient past. In the same anthology, in the "Celebratory poems" section, we find the following poem from the former Interior Minister of Kazan-in [Fujiwara Morotsugu]:

waga kimi no	Surely the sun
yamato simane wo	that rises from the roots
iduru fi fa	of the islands of Yamato
morokosi made mo	ruled by our lord
afugazarame ya	shines even upon the land of Cathay.

This song also suits the spirit of the Way.

[89] AN EXAMPLE FOR READING WORKS

Among the sayings of Suga Naomi is one where he said, "Reading a fulfilling work—fulfilling in content and volume—is like taking a long trip. There are many boring places along the way, but after having passed through them, one comes to the eye-opening interesting places like the coast or the mountains. In reading, too, those who make fast progress are like those with strong legs who move quickly, and those who make slow progress are like those with weak legs who move slowly." This example is very interesting.

[90] SCHOLARS DO NOT ACCEPT NEW THEORIES READILY

Generally, when a scholar advances a new theory that differs from the accepted theory of the time, the scholars of society tend to despise and criticize the theory, regardless of whether the idea is acceptable or unacceptable. When some of these scholars hear that the new theory is dramatically different from the theory that they have adhered to, some refuse to accept the new theory without even examining whether it is good or bad. Other scholars think in their hearts that there are many reasonable points about the new theory, but because they are jealous, they refuse to follow the new theory from a person of the same generation. They do not state whether the supposition is good or bad, but adopt the attitude that they cannot accept such a theory.

A more serious example is of a person who is very envious of the new theory though he feels in his heart that the theory is good, and searches for the slightest defect so he can reject the entire hypothesis. Concerning an old theory, in general when seven or eight points are unacceptable out of a total of ten, scholars often do their utmost to try to hide the defects of the theory, emphasizing the two or three satisfactory points in an attempt to support the older belief. On the other hand, when there are eight or nine good points to a new theory, these same scholars emphasize the one or two bad points to repudiate it, so they and their colleagues will not have to follow the new idea. This is the general trend of scholars today.

In some rare cases, however, a few scholars will hear of a new theory, notice the defects in the old way of thinking, and change their attitude to follow the new idea. There are also some scholars who harbor doubts about the points of the old theory, but because they have no power to change things, they continue as before, until they hear about a new theory. Upon getting wind of the new theory, they are overjoyed with the new doctrine, and immediately follow it.

In general, no matter how satisfactory the points of a new theory are, it is rare that scholars accept the theory right away; however, most scholars in society gradually accept new theories, even if it takes years. When a certain theory is widely accepted, even when those scholars who originally were envious and did not join the group following the theory feel regret, they feel a greater sense of vexation because now they are latecomers, and their hesitation has damaged their reputation. There are many examples of scholars who though they feel these unpleasant thoughts, continue to hold onto old theories. When society widely accepts a new theory, those who from the start quickly abandoned their old ways of thinking and followed the new theory are considered wise and intelligent, while those who stuck with the old theory, refuting this or that, are considered foolish.

[91] PART TWO

Lately, we have seen an increase in the number of people who understand the importance of studying the ancient eras. Among many of these people are those who revere Keichū. If a person understands the importance of Keichū's perceptive scholarship, then he naturally will come to an understanding of the greater importance of my teacher, Master Agatai. Why is it that many of these scholars fixate on Keichū and cannot take the next step? And those who do discern Master Agatai's importance adopt the attitude that they cannot accept theories advanced by people after him, so we have the same problem. This attitude is much like "not wanting to admit defeat," a very debilitating way of thinking. This is an accurate appraisal of most of this society's scholars.

[92] WHY PROVINCES ARE CALLED "STATES"

It is not clear in which imperial reign the names of the provinces were determined, which [in the "Age of the Gods"] are known as "such and such a region" (某州). Anciently even in private records within Chinese works one very seldom sees this usage. In official documents all place names were called "such and such a province" (某國), and one does not find any usages of "region" (州). So why is it that in spite of this, people in the recent past who did not understand the principle I have mentioned above enjoyed recklessly putting on Chinese airs, and determined that using "such and such a region" in their speech and writing sounded more beautiful than "such and such a province"? They write things like Upper No Region or Lower No Region, or Etizen Region or Tikugo Region for provinces that anciently were divided into east and west, or north and south. Now, while both graphs 國 and 州 are read *kuni*, from the Nara era onward, the standard for writing all these toponyms has been established and one cannot just write the name any way he pleases. The position put forth by a certain Confucian scholar states that *kuni* is based on the feudal system, and in the era when the imperial court was in power and the system of districts and counties was in force we should speak of these provinces as "regions" (州), insinuating that the usage of "province" (國) was already established. This theory is a deplorable error biased toward Chinese precedent up to the present, and our system does not fit with the system of that country. First, regarding precedent in that country, in the so-called feudal eras there were areas known as the Country of Qi and Country of Lu,[87] but after the establishment of districts and counties we no longer find examples where regions were labeled "provinces." However, the reason people are biased toward this is due to the half-baked way of thinking that it is not in the hearts of the people of China, and in spite of everything in that country being determined in the way mentioned in the previous examples, from era to era things were settled based on the mind of the king, and even if the idea was poorly thought out, there was no way they could avoid implementing it. Thus, the situation of dividing land varied in later eras, and there were various things without precedent in former eras, but at any rate, one should not follow China's precedent.

---

87. Norinaga has taken his example from Book 4 of *Shiji*, where King Wu enfeoffs Shang-fu with Qi and his brother Dan with Lu.

[93] CONFUSION IN CONFUCIAN NAMES

Confucius considered it a laudable thing to correct the names of things.[88] Recent scholars here [in Japan] appear to be engaged in throwing names into confusion. It is probably a misdemeanor when they take place names and change them as they wish, making them longer, or shorter, in imitation of Chinese practices, but is it not something to be honestly feared when they recklessly change appellations related to the royal court?

Recently, a certain Confucian scholar said something like, "In the present the name of many things is not correct. 'A' is presently called such and such, which is without reason. It is proper to call it this or that." Is it not terribly shortsighted and questionable when they change everything to a more modern-sounding word in an egoistic manner? Generally, Confucius took no thought for the reckless behavior of the feudal lords of his day, but preserved the things originally established by the Zhou kings. Now the behavior of recent Confucian scholars who follow the current practice of ignoring the present labels, and willfully change those that had existed since the ancient times, trying to create new things privately, is in direct violation of the spirit of Confucius's teachings in *Chunqiu*.[89] This is a terrible way of throwing things into chaos.

Now in our country, though the circumstances of things may change over time from the ancient past, the label of things does not change according to these circumstances, and it is truly something to be grateful that we have preserved the old names of all kinds of things; as Confucius would say, it is very good that the names of things be correct. To stand this on its head and claim that this is improper springs from a heart that desires to badmouth our country from all angles, and the person often does not notice that he is wrong.

---

88. *The Analects* says, "Zi Lu said, 'The Lord of Wei is waiting for you, so you can arrange the government. What are you going to do first?' The Master said, 'Definitely we should correct names'" ("Zi Lu" chapter).

89. What is often known as the *Annals of Spring and Autumn*. It is the earliest surviving history of China. Tradition states that Mencius claimed that the text was compiled by Confucius, but most scholars now doubt this tradition.

2 ~ FALLING LEAVES OF THE CHERRY 85

[96] *SHUNKI*

The work called *Shunki* (Spring Record) is a diary of [Fujiwara] Sukefusa who resided in the Spring Palace.[90] It is said that only one volume of the diary survives in the present. The manuscript I looked at was one volume with eighty-five leaves.

[97] CONCERNING *MATSUSHIMA NO NIKKI*

This refers to a diary kept by Sei Shōnagon when she traveled to Matusima in her old age, and it was later titled *Matsushima no nikki* (Matsushima Diary). People viewed it as a rare find, but it was quickly determined to be a terrible forgery, and there are fewer things worse than this work in the whole world. I believe that it was put together in recent years by a student of the ancient past, and it contains sentences made up by the perpetrator. There are truly many people like this in recent years who create forgeries. What kind of crazed person would spend so much time and sweat putting together a pointless and trivial work to deceive society? If a person who has some skill in discernment were to look at the work, he would easily see the deception and make a very clear judgment, but people with such skill are quite rare, and our society is filled with people who have no sense of discernment—they are deceived by these forgeries; it is such a terrible pity and so lamentable that people play with things of importance.

Lately there are many people who seek after compositions, which are rare in the world, but there are so few people who can tell the truth from the fraudulent. One should remember that when we talk about rare works most of these are fakes, and one should be careful in his selection.

There are works like the one called *Suma no ki*[91] supposedly

---

90. Fujiwara no Sukefusa (1007–1057) was a courtier who kept a very detailed journal of events at court, but as Norinaga mentions, much of this journal has been lost. What does survive sheds great light on the court of Emperor Go-Suzaku (r. 1036–1045).

91. At present this is known as *Kanke suma no ki*. While most people in the present agree with the assessment of Norinaga that this is not the work of Michizane, some scholars believe the work to have been written around the Kyōhō era (1716–1735). Seno (2010) ar-

written by Sugawara no Michizane, minister of the right, which are gradually spreading throughout society, and almost everyone believes these to be authentic, but in the case of this work, it is an atrocious forgery. These types of forgeries are numberless. One should be careful.

[99] WHY *MORI* IS WRITTEN 杜

In the San section of the "Zhou benji" of *Shiji* we find, "It is said, 'The Duke of Zhou was buried in Bi.' Bi is in Tu (杜) located southeast of Hao." There is an annotational note, "杜 is written 社 in one manuscript." Also in the "Qin benji" there is the line "(He dispatched troops to smite) Dangtu," and there is an annotational note that says, "杜 is written 社 in one manuscript." This discrepancy arises because of the graphic similarity of 杜 and 社, so perhaps the mistakes arise from that. Or perhaps it originates from the two being interchangeable. If the character 杜 is understood as an interchangeable usage of 社, then perhaps it is because there is always a forest where there is a shrine.[92] Or within the confines of the shrine, one understands that there is a forest there.

[102] WHY IT HAS BECOME EASIER TO LOCATE VARIOUS WORKS

Until the last twenty or thirty years, people studying poetry concentrated only on recent anthologies and no one studied [the poetry in] *Man'yōshū*. Even people known as scholars of Shintō studied Chinese learning and did not try to understand anything about the true heart. Since no one researched into *Man'yōshū*, no one realized that in order to understand poetry and the Way, they must start with this work. Thus, Priest Keichū spent most of his

---

gues that the author is actually Maeda Tsunanori (1643–1724), the text discovered after his death and taken to a Kyōto scholar, Tsuboi Yoshichika (1657–1735), who revised the manuscript and then disseminated it.

92. The reasoning is that *mori* means forest or grove, and 杜 (shrine) is also read *mori*.

energy on this work, while he began to elucidate the ancient spirit. While his work is fragmentary, there was not a poet or Shintō scholar who realized that they should rely on this man's suggestions.

When I was still in my youth and residing in the capital, few people knew that *Daishōki* existed. Copied manuscripts of this work were rare at the time and it was difficult to get one's hands on it. Even Keichū's commentary on the "One Hundred Poets, One Hundred Poems," titled *Kaikanshū*, was difficult to locate. While I was in the capital, I was finally able to borrow these works from someone and read them. I wished to buy the manuscripts and searched for a bookstore, but could not locate one that had these manuscripts. I asked one bookstore proprietor why it was hard to find a printed version, let alone a handwritten copy. He told me that no one has any need for this work, so they do not print it. After trying this and that, at last I got my hands on a manuscript.

This was how difficult it was several years ago, but now handwritten copies of *Daishōki* are widely available and it is not challenging to find one, all because there have been advances in the Way of ancient learning, and there are so many people searching after it.

This is not only true of *Daishōki*. Originally, all handwritten copies of works and household records were difficult to locate, but now it is easy to get one's hands on almost any work, because of this prosperous era.

[103] THE WAY I CAME TO SCHOLARSHIP

When I was very young, I thought that reading books was more interesting than anything else was. However, my reading was not done under the tutelage of a teacher, and was not any special kind of study. I did not intend to study anything in particular, and I did not study toward the direction of scholarship. I simply read Chinese and Japanese works, anything that was available, and when I was able to get a hold of some work, I started reading ancient works and modern works without making a distinction between the two. While reading in this manner, I turned seventeen or eighteen, and had a desire to write poetry. I had a desire to try my hand at poetry, but again, it was not done under the guidance of a teacher, and I did not show people my poems; I merely produced poetry in private. I read ancient and modern poetic anthologies to learn from them, and I composed poetry in the average, modern style.

Thus, when I was more than twenty, I went to Kyōto to study. It was in my eleventh year that as soon as my father died, our family business in Edo failed, and later under the advice of my mother, I went to Kyōto to study medicine. In addition, in order to learn this trade [of medicine] I studied the general trend of Confucianism taught in society. While I was in Kyōto, I borrowed *Hyakunin Isshū Kaikanshū* to read, and this was the first time that I came across the theories of Keichū. I realized the excellence of Keichū's learning, and while I was searching for other works by Keichū, like *Yozaishō* and *Seigo okudan*,[93] I gradually came to see the distinction between poems of good quality and those of poor quality.

Studying in this manner, I found that I did not like most of what the modern poets were thinking, and though I thought that their form of [modern] poetry was uninteresting, since I had no other friends who shared my opinions, I went to various poetry gatherings just like other people and composed poetry. In spite of my aversion to the modern style of poetry, I composed in that style and no one criticized me. This is as things should be, but I will discuss this topic another time.

Now, after this time, I returned to my hometown (of Matuzaka), and a person visiting from Edo let me see a recently published book called *Kanjikō*. And this is how I came to know the name of the great Master Agatai. When I first read *Kanjikō*, it was full of ideas I could not comprehend; it was so different from the other theories that I had read that I felt they were too strange to believe. Nevertheless, because I felt there was some truth involved,

---

93. *Kokin yozaishō* is a commentary on *Kokinshū* that Keichū completed in 1691. The title word *yozai* means "extra material," and apparently refers to material he had left over after completing *Man'yō daishōki*, a commentary on *Man'yōshū*. *Okudan* is a thorough commentary on *Ise monogatari*. It was completed in 1692, the product of a number of years of research. Keichū originally interpreted *Ise monogatari* to be biographical in nature but later changed his mind and came to the conclusion that it was fiction.

2 ~ FALLING LEAVES OF THE CHERRY 89

I read the work one more time, and found places where I began to agree with the author. Therefore, I read *Kanjikō* a third time, finding many areas where I agreed wholeheartedly with the author. The more I read the work, the greater a strong conviction began to fill my breast, and in the end, I came to the realization that the ancient spirit of Japan and the ancient words were just as Master Agatai had stated. Now that I think back on it, there are many shallow points within Keichū's theories about *Man'yōshū*. This is the sum of the progress of my poetic research up to the present.

Now in my study of the Way, first from the beginning I read this and that from old and new varieties of records about the deities, and from about the time I was twenty years of age I had a desire to study this area in particular, but I did not put forth any special effort to study. However, from the time I went to Kyōto the desire to study the Way increased, and though I followed the theories in the poetic research of Keichū and thought about the ancient spirit of the imperial land, I quickly discovered that the opinions put forth by the scholars of Shintō of the day were all incorrect, so there was no one I could rely on to be my teacher. Thus, I had a strong desire somehow to figure out the true, ancient spirit of our land.

Right about that time, I obtained a copy of *Kanjikō* and as I diligently read and reread it my desire to research the ancient spirit of our land grew stronger, and my desire to follow the great master increased day by day. Then one year my master received an order from his Lordship Tayasu[94] and when he was touring from this province of Ise to Yamato, Yamasiro, and others, going here and there, he was able even to come to where I live in Matuzaka and spend two or three days. I knew nothing of these events, but later learned of his visit and was terribly disappointed (that I had missed him), but on his return he spent one night here and I was able to wait and receive instruction from him, and was greatly pleased. I

---

94. At the time Mabuchi was in the service of Tokugawa Tayasu Munetake (1716-1771). He was the second son of Shōgun Tokugawa Yoshimune (1684-1751). As his father passed over him as heir, Munetake turned his attention to scholarship. He had an interest in Japanese things, and hired Kada no Arimaro (1706-1751) and then later Mabuchi to be his teacher. Munetake had a great interest in *Man'yōshū*.

quickly hurried to the inn where he stayed and met him for the first time. I added my name to his list of students and received instruction from him.

[104] THE WISE ADMONITION OF MY MASTER

When I, Norinaga, was around thirty years of age, I first heard the teachings of Great Master Agatai. From that time forth, I desired to put together a commentary on *Kojiki* and I announced such to my master. At that time, he said to me,

> It appears that you wish to make a commentary upon the ancient record of the deities (*Kojiki*), but first you must rid yourself of the Chinese Heart[95] before you try to study about the true spirit of the ancients. In order to study about the ancient spirit, however, you must have the ability to understand the ancient lexicon. Being able to understand the ancient lexicon means that you must thoroughly study the *Man'yōshū* text. Therefore, I have first tried to elucidate *Man'yōshū*, but in the process have grown old, and my remaining years are few, so I could not attempt to put together a commentary on *Kojiki*.[96] You, however, are in the prime of life, and have a long future ahead of you. If you study without indolence, you will be

---

95. *Karagokoro* (Chinese Heart): This usage to show influence from Chinese thinking was created by Norinaga in contrast with *magokoro* (true heart), showing that his account of this visit is not completely accurate (Nosco 1990:175). Matsumoto's comment (1970:70), "It is not very important here how accurately Norinaga remembered Mabuchi's words," assumes that Norinaga highly valued Mabuchi's encouragement, so the actual account is of less value than the fact that Norinaga recorded it. Nosco (1990:175) sees a tension between the two that is never resolved, likely because Norinaga had certain literary values he was unwilling to compromise.

96. The other point that makes the accuracy of this account suspect is the way that Norinaga frames Mabuchi's words. The retelling of the account assumes that a study of *Kojiki* was a higher, perhaps more important goal, a goal that could only be attained if the student starts with *Man'yōshū*. As Nosco (1990:175) points out, Mabuchi never viewed *Man'yōshū* as second to any other work. It is probable that the actual account between the two was one where Mabuchi was pleased to see "so promising a student," but felt the young man did not have sufficient training in *Man'yōshū* to even begin work on a text as difficult as *Kojiki*.

able to reach your goal of producing a commentary upon the *Kojiki* text. Nevertheless, I see some scholars in the present who do not engage in basic research, but immediately strive to do highly specialized work, notwithstanding they do not even comprehend the basics. These scholars can in no way do highly specialized research because they have no foundational knowledge. It seems to me that they are wasting their time producing incorrect works. So you must not forget what I have said, and keep these words alive in your memory. First, get the basics down pat, and then you must strive to do higher, more specialized research. That is why I have not been able to produce a commentary on *Kojiki* yet. You must not try to do highly specialized research while you are still young and immature in your studies.

These were his extremely generous words of admonition.
I thought that these words of admonition were very astute, so I buried myself in the study of the *Man'yōshū* text, deeply searching, going back time after time. When I came to comprehend the spirit of the ancients and their language, I came to find that the scholars of the day who had produced commentaries upon *Kojiki* were all incorrect, their ideas grounded in the Chinese Heart; they had not even been able to comprehend the true spirit of the ancients in this work.

[105] ON MY LEARNING FROM MASTER AGATAI

My, Norinaga, meeting with Master Agatai took place one night when he was lodged in this town [Matuzaka]. I met Master Agatai only this once. After this meeting, I often asked questions [via mail] to my master concerning my work.[97] The answers I received from him piled up in great numbers, and I took care to keep each, but since people have come here, begging to see them, I gave

---

97. At the time Norinaga was engaged in work on *Man'yōshū* and the Imperial edicts in *Shoku Nihongi*.

them out one or two at a time until I now have very few left. Now, I told my master about my ardent desire to put together a commentary on *Kojiki*, and he lent me the first section of *Kojiki* in which interlinear readings had been attached to certain ancient words. I also borrowed the middle and last sections of the manuscript that contained actual alterations in the reading done by the hand of my master.[98] Many of the quotations in my *Kojiki-den* noted as "my master's theory" have reference to this manuscript. Now, needless to say this scholarly giant was the one who opened the way of the study of ancient things, and as his words of counsel toward me show, he spent the majority of his energies expounding *Man'yōshū*. Therefore, when it came to *Kojiki* and *Nihon shoki*, his theories were shallow. Many of his ideas were not well thought out. Thus, when it came to his exposition on the Way, his theories lacked precision, and the bulk of his ideas were plagued with inaccuracies. In the end, these theories were merely blind gropings along the periphery of the issue. In addition to this, my master did not break completely away from the impurity of the Chinese Heart, and occasionally his theories fall into that trap.

[106] DO NOT STICK TO YOUR MASTER'S THEORIES

When I expound upon ancient records, I often take sides against my master [Mabuchi]; there are many times when I give my own opinion distinct from my master's theory when his is not satisfactory. It appears there are many people who think this is improper, but this follows precisely the teachings of my master, for he said, "After one has established a theory, if a better line of thought comes along, do not hesitate to abandon the original theory, even though it came from your master."[99]

---

98. This is the manuscript of *Kojiki* mentioned before. Norinaga appealed to his master several times before Mabuchi finally obliged.

99. In a letter to Norinaga dated the ninth day of the fifth month of the sixth year of Meiwa (1769), Mabuchi responded to a letter he received from Norinaga in which the latter had written some ideas about the edicts found in *Shoku Nihongi*. Mabuchi writes, "These [archaic words] survive in the vocabulary in old poems of our courtly tradition, and while

2 ~ FALLING LEAVES OF THE CHERRY   93

This is a respectable principle taught to me by my master, showing what an excellent scholar he was. Generally, research into the things of the ancient past is not something easily accomplished by one or two people. Are there not also mistakes in theories that good scholars have established? Surely, they cannot escape having something incorrect creep into their theories. Even scholars who believe in their own hearts, "With this theory the ancient past is now clarified. There should not be any theory superior to this!" There are often other excellent theories, which later appear. Because one's theory passes through more scrutiny after it has been published, it becomes refined in detail, so clearly one cannot be trammeled by his master's theory. It is damaging to the way of scholarship to protect old theories entirely without regard for whether they are good or bad.

Though it is terrifying to declare in public that something in one's master's theory is incorrect, if you do not do it, then other scholars cannot come to an understanding of the truth, being blinded by that old theory. Knowing your master's theory to be incorrect but continuing on in your studies without saying anything, and not correcting it toward the truth is the act of only worshipping your master and not giving any heed to the Way. Because I, Norinaga, revere the Way and ponder ancient things, searching for ways to elucidate that Way, I make it my priority to clarify the spirit of the ancients. If a person cannot help but reflect upon something, and believes that something I have theorized is incorrect, then that person should criticize me. There is no way around criticism, regardless of how much people examine my theories. I would like to become a scholar not censured by people, a person labeled good by others, incapable of perverting the way of scholarship, unable to remain content with myself if I have twisted the thoughts of the ancient Japanese. Since this is what my master

---

Kojiki writes in this style [like that of the edicts], the songs are limited by [the number of syllables in] stanzas and so it abbreviates some auxiliaries. If *Kojiki* had also been written in Chinese we would not know about these auxiliaries. But the fact that these auxiliaries are found in the liturgies and edicts and I have not yet realized this leaves me completely struck with admiration [for your research]" (Ōno 1993:391).

taught me, does not this attitude in return show respect for him? Regardless, that point is meaningless.[100]

[107] INSTRUCTIONS I LEAVE TO MY STUDENTS

Students following me in learning should not stick to my theories when other good ideas surface after I have gone. Discuss the faults of my theories, and spread those good ideas throughout society. Since everything I teach my students seeks to illuminate the Way, in the end, the first thing my teachings will do is to help elucidate that Way. It is not my wish for you revere me above thinking about the Way.

[108] EXPLAINING THE FIFTY LINKING SOUNDS TO THE DUTCH

One of my students is a man named Ozasa Daiki Minu,[101] a Confucian scholar who serves the feudal lord in Hamada, Ifami. It seems that around autumn time in the eighth year of Tenmei (1788), he took a trip to Nagasaki in the province of Hizen, and he met some Dutchmen who had come ashore there. They had a discussion on phonology with some Japanese, when Minu told them of the fifty sounds of our imperial language. When the discussion centered on the *wa* section of Japanese sounds, Minu said that in his speech the *wa* line of sounds all started with *u*. He said that he pronounces /wi/ like /ui/ and /we/ is really like /ue/, while /wo/ is much like /uo/, meaning that he makes a distinction.[102]

---

100. In the end, what Norinaga wants people to understand is that respect for one's master should not take priority above correcting mistakes, even if the mistakes come from one's own master. Norinaga's main goal was to elucidate the Way by bringing ancient truth to light, and ridding the world of the mistaken ideas imported from foreign cultures.

101. Ozasa Daiki Minu (1722–1801) became a student of Norinaga's some time before 1784, which appears to be the first time that he visited Matsuzaka. A rather large stele marks his grave but the inscription has deteriorated to such an extent that it is now difficult to decipher. The inscription is preserved by Shimane Prefecture historian, Yatomi Kumaichirō, in his work *Ozasa Minu*.

102. To most Japanese the sounds *i u e o* are indistinguishable from the earlier sounds

When he asked why that was, they told him it was because it was done in imitation of *wa* /ua/. In other words, the Dutch language makes this same distinction. This matches perfectly with what I have argued in my work, *Jion kanazukai*.[103] Minu was so happy that he wrote a letter to me telling me all about this. Within the story, he related to me in his letter there are other interesting things, but I have left them out here.

---

wi we wo (*wa* being the only exception). Minu has thus noticed that his dialect of Japanese preserves an older distinction, which tries to keep the *a*-line of Japanese distinct from the *wa*-line.
 103. Building on the work of Keichū who tried to recover the historical spelling of Japanese words, Norinaga looked into the spelling of native and Chinese words, based on his knowledge of *man'yōgana*. Completed in 1776 Norinaga was the first to realize that the centuries-old idea of grouping *a-i-u-e-wo* and *wa-wi-u-we-o* was actually backwards. For the theory that Fujitani Nariakira noticed this *after* Norinaga, see Ōno (in Ōno and Ōkubo 1976, vol. 5:18–25).

❦ 3 | THE ORANGE

tati yoreba　　　Drawn by its very aroma—
mukasi no tare to　whose scent was it anciently
ware nagara　　　that made me doubt
wa ga sode ayasi　the scent from my own sleeves,
tatibana no kage　here in the shade of the orange?

This is a shallow poem written on the topic of "orange," and it seems affected to place it here at the beginning of this chapter, something I should think better of doing; however, I leave it according to my system of naming each new chapter with a poem.

[110] THE PILLOW WORD *ARAKANE* THAT MODIFIES THE WORD "EARTH"

The pillow word *arakane* that modifies *tuti* "earth" is written 殿舎根. Anciently it was the tradition to read 殿舎 (ceremonial building) as **miaraka**. It is also clear that the word was used without the prefix *mi-*, as found in *Kogo shūi*, "who constructed the palace now reside in Araka." And in a note, "The ancient reading for 'ceremonial palace' is **araka**." Now anciently these ceremonial palaces were like the building of the Great Deity at Ise, and as these were built with the pillars buried into the earth, that gives the etymology of *araka* (ceremonial palace) and *ne* (root).

[111] A POEM ABOUT *KOTATU*

Around the twelfth month we had a gathering of this and that person, and we were to compose poetry on the topic of "buried fire," when someone said, "Compose a poem on *kotatu*." So I composed,

musibusuma	Into the buried fire
nagoyaka sita no	below where I am in soft
udumibi ni	ramie pajamas,
asi sasinobete	I stick my feet—
nurakusi yosi mo	and how nice and warm it is.

No one there could stop laughing.[104]

[112] WHY THE CHINESE AVOID THE GIVEN NAME OF CONFUCIUS

In China, in the present Qing dynasty the current ruler desires to avoid the given name of Confucius, Qiu, written 丘, so they have started writing the graph minus one stroke [thus 㐀], and they claim, "From the ancient eras of the Qin and Han down to the Ming, no one has realized how noble Confucius was." They boast of this thing of themselves, but it is very silly. If one really says he respects Confucius, then he would put his heart into following the Way of Confucius. However, they do not follow his Way completely, but recklessly worship the man, so what is so great about that? If people have been following the Way of Confucius to the best of their ability, then there would have been no need to alter the graph for his name, because of a desire from long ago to avoid it. In reality, all they are doing is feigning allegiance to the Way, intending to have people think that they are great. In general, the actions of

---

104. This appears to have been interesting to those gathered because Norinaga referenced a poem from *Man'yōshū* (MYS 524): **musibusuma / nagoyaka sita ni / fuseredomo / imo to si neneba / fada si samusi mo** (I sleep in soft ramie pajamas, but because I am not sleeping with you, my skin is cold).

the Chinese have been like this since ancient times, and when we hear that they say it is good to respect sages and wise men, it is simply an act to gain a false name, not an idea where they revere something truly good.

[114] CONCERNING THE PASSING OF SHŌHAKU

In the same record [*Nisuiki*],[105] it says, "In the fourth year of the same regnal period (Daiei, 1524),[106] fourth month, fourth day, Muan [the recent cognomen of Priest Shōhaku, who was also known as Botange] passed away."

[115] CONCERNING THE RAISING OF THE BOW

In the same record, we see, "At the hour of the ox on the third day of the second month of the third year of Kyōroku (1530) we went inside the palace, and [the ceremony] of the raising of the bow occurred." How interesting that they did such things even inside the forbidden precincts.

[118] CONCERNING THE FESTIVALS OF THE FOUR BORDERS AND FOUR CORNERS

In *Saigūki* it says, "The festival of the 'four borders' is an exorcism where an official of the Bureau of Divination faces each of the four borders [of Kyōto].[107] An official of the Office of the Chamberlain was used as a messenger." The festival of the "four corners" was a rite in the Bureau of Divination that exorcized the

---

105. *Nisuiki*: A diary kept by Washinoo Takayasu (d. 1533). The diary covers twenty-nine years, from 1504 till his death in 1533. It is of value because of its eye-witness account of the destruction of the capital during the Ōnin War.

106. Shōhaku actually passed away three years later in 1527, or the seventh year of Daiei.

107. Usually called "the festival of the four corners and the four borders," this is a rite of the Bureau of Divination performed by officials of that bureau on Kyōto's four bordering roads to exorcize epidemic spirits, deities, and evil spirits (Inoue et al., 1999:28, 29).

four corners of the palace buildings. The officiator was a person from an office that had a person available. These two festivals were used when epidemics appeared throughout the realm, and the Bureau of Divination would come forth with the preparations [an edict to the officer of raw materials]."

[121] ON THE *WAZA UTA* IN THE SAIMEI RECORD OF *NIHON SHOKI*

I have thought about the *waza uta* found in the sixth year of the Saimei chapter of *Nihon shoki*, being persuaded by the theories of a certain person.[108] Perhaps the stanzas should be laid out thus: **towa toyomi** / **wono feda wo** / **kari gari no kurafu** / **towa toyomi** / **wono feda wo** / **kari gari no kurafu** / **firakuduma no** / **tukurisi** / **osafeda wo** / **kari gari no kurafu**.[109] Now, it appears that because this song portends a deplorable outcome [regarding the battle at Paekchong Bay], people were afraid of this song and deliberately scrambled not only the stanzas, but also the syllables, so that it would be difficult to figure out the meaning of the song. Near the end of the song are the characters 甲子, and the song should be read starting here.[110] This also vaguely marks the spot where the individual syllables should be rearranged and read. Therefore, I start reading this song from this spot onward. The first stanza, 騰和與騰美 (**towa toyomi**), originally was **yoto** and was rearranged as **toyo**. Now, **towa** should be **tawa**, and this refers to the ridge of a mountain, as seen in *Kojiki*. Since the allophonic variation of **tawa**

---

108. It is generally believed that Norinaga is quoting from Keichū's theory, but the theory he discusses is not the same as that put forth by Keichū; thus, we do not know for sure who influenced Norinaga here.

109. The difficulty with this song is that it uses what appear to be cryptic words, making it challenging to know where to parse words. This difficulty resulted in the idea very early on that the song was actually an anagram, and to solve the puzzle, one needed to unravel the syllables. Thus, many have tried to rearrange the syllables to make an intelligible song. Needless to say, no other song in *Kojiki* or *Nihon shoki* is constructed in such a way, so it is better to deal with the song on its own terms. See Bentley (2006a:136–40) for a modern explanation and translation.

110. The graphs 甲子 are not phonetic, and are a striking disparity in a song that is composed almost entirely of phonograms. Norinaga's novel idea is that this date, which is the first one in the Chinese calendar, shows where the unraveling should start.

3 ~ THE ORANGE

and **towa** is a known phenomenon, where we have examples like **tawamu** and **towomu**, or **tawawa** and **towowo** and so on as found in *Man'yōshū*, this **tawa** points to the ridge of a mountain. **Toyomi** means "be in commotion." The second stanza, 烏能陛陀烏 (**wono feda wo**),[111] means "tail-above-paddy" and refers to a rice paddy on the edge of the mountain. The third stanza, 歌理鵝美能俱邏賦 (**kari gari no kurafu**), means the "wild geese eat." There are many examples [in the literature] where "wild geese" are used allegorically in relation to mountains, rivers, provinces, and people.[112] Reading up to this point it means there is a group that is in commotion, and someone rises up noisily to eat the rice of the paddy. The fourth stanza, 騰和與騰美 (**towa toyomi**), is the same as that above. This stanza originally was recorded in *Nihon shoki* as 美和陀騰能理歌美 (**miwata yo nori kami**), and the graphs 美・陀・能・理・歌 were all reordered, and then the two graphs 騰・與 were dropped. The fifth and sixth stanzas are the same as explained above.

The seventh stanza, 比邏矩豆摩能 (**firakuduma no**), according to the certain individual means "flat-squat down-hunchback." That is based on the name of a hunchbacked person in this chapter of *Nihon shoki*, where the graphs for "squat down-hunchback" are glossed as **kuduma**. **Fira** (flat) is also said to mean terribly bent over. It is the same kind of label as a bent-over pine tree being called *fira matu*.

The eighth stanza, 都俱利伺 (**tukurisi**), means to cultivate land. The original has 俱例豆例 (**kureture**). We should take 豆 and put in 都 at the beginning of these four graphs. In addition, the first 例 is perhaps a mistake for 利, and the second 例 a mistake for 伺. Thus, this would be rearranged as **tukurere**, which perhaps means to be cultivated. Either way, this is what it should be.[113]

---

111. Interesting that Norinaga has not realized—or perhaps forgotten—that 陀 in *Nihon shoki* represents *ta* and not *da*, as much of *Nihon shoki*'s orthography is based on Late Middle Chinese.
112. As Norinaga points out, *kari* "wild geese" are very prominent in *Man'yōshū*. I have counted the following number of cases of poems with wild geese paired with other objects: "hill" 2, "mountain" 14, "river" 1, "rice paddy" 10, "foliage" 7, and "people" 15.
113. Here Norinaga unwittingly brings to light the major problem with deciphering this song in this manner. Difficult-to-defend emendations and fudging of the text must be done to make the puzzle theory work.

The ninth stanza, 於社幣陀乎 (**osafeda wo**), means "the paddy that has been checked and fortified." The word **osafe** appears in Book 20 of *Man'yōshū* in the song:

tukusi no kuni fa   The land of Tukusi
ata mamoru   is a fort of check,
osafe no ki zo to   where we protect against our enemies ...
                                    (MYS 4331) ...

It is the same *osafe*, and is a check and protection from the enemy. Because this *waza uta* symbolizes the defeat of the imperial armada that was sent to save Paekche, it points to the rescue mission, known as *osafe*, and as the rice paddy is on the mountain, this song weaves in fact with allegory. There are many examples where the actual object and a metaphor are woven together in *Man'yōshū*, as we seen in this one stanza here. The tenth stanza is the same as the one above. According to the certain individual, the meaning of the entire song is that the imperial armada would be defeated, and all the glory and meritorious service would be good for nothing; their bodies would become like the deplorable hunchback, laid low, as if they were enduring suffering and anxiety by plowing a mountain rice paddy, where many geese appear and consume their crop of rice, and everything has been laid to waste.

However, there are errors here and there in this individual's theory. First, it is bad to make **firakuduma no** the first stanza, because there are six syllables here, and ancient song in Japan always, without exception, started with five syllables.[114] Above that, from this stanza down to the third should be used as the ending, because it sounds like it is winding down. Also, he states that **wonefeda** is a mistake for **osafeda**, but in all the songs contained in *Nihon shoki*, there is a stanza that is repeated two or three times, but the same kind of graphs are used in other songs, and the

---

114. Here is another difficulty with this song because if we ignore 甲子 in the latter part of this song, we are left with sixty-two phonograms. Theoretically that should work out to a rotation of five- and seven-mora stanzas with two seven-morae at the end. However, to do so results in sixty morae, which leaves us two morae over. In other words, this *chōka* is clearly not following the strict convention of alternating five and seven morae.

stanza with "paddy on the edge of the mountain" replaces 烏能陛陀 **wono feda**, which appears twice in this song; thus, wanting to write the graphs 弘 and 幣 goes starkly against precedent.[115] Next, the two ideas that the stanza 美和陀騰能理歌美 should be 美歌理能陀和美騰 (**mikari no tawami to**) and mean "while he tried to stop the imperial hunt, the geese came," or having this stanza mean "the waves of the water are in commotion" are both bad. Canceling an imperial hunt is not known as **tawami** or as **miwada**.

In addition, making the stanza 騰和與騰美 that appears after the two graphs 甲子 read as **wa to yodomi** or even as **wa totoyomi**, and interpreting this as "I am in commotion" or "I plus the verb *totoyomi*" makes absolutely no sense. Now, Master Azumamaro said that it was a mistake to rearrange the graphs to make sense of this song, but should be read as it is written and understood thus; this theory is nonsense, because none of the words is well constructed, and the import of their theories is difficult to comprehend. This theory of Azumamaro's is a secret tradition, so it is difficult to elucidate it any further here.

Now, no matter how old the ancient songs, there are times when a song will contain words we cannot understand, but any of these songs can be understood well, and there is not one song that does not sound good; only in the case of this one song do we find that we cannot understand what it says right from the very beginning. Thus, we should conclude that the order of the stanzas or placement of the syllables has been altered; it is like the Yabatai poem,[116] so how is it that no one has been able to pay attention and

---

115. Norinaga has made another valuable suggestion in solving this riddle. He has noticed that certain stanzas in the song are repeated throughout the song. The most important stanza is **kunori kari ga**, which is six morae in length. If there are repeating stanzas, then the song *cannot* be an anagram. It is unfortunate, however, that he does not make that suggestion.

116. "Yabatai": A Chinese poem originally believed to have been produced by Bao Zhi (418–514), a prophetic Buddhist monk of the Southern dynasty. Many now believe the poem to have been the work of someone else. There is even a theory that the poem was composed in Japan. It first appears quoted in *Enryakuji gokoku engi* (ca. 790). The title 野馬台 is clearly a cleaned-up version of the name of Yamato found in *Wei zhi* (邪馬台), replacing "wicked" (邪) with "field" (野). The poem is written in vague stanzas, meaning that anyone can interpret the work as s/he sees fit.

figure this out? However, I myself have not found a suitable solution to this puzzle, but I believe it is a good idea to have *towatoyomi* as the beginning line of the song.

[122] ABOUT THE CHINESE ASCETIC PRACTICE OF MOURNING THE DEATH OF A PARENT

The practice in China handed down from generation to generation in relation to mourning the death of a parent is that the person shows deep filial piety by becoming skinny and weakened while mourning.[117] The scholars of China have written much about this practice. Among some of these writings are sayings like, "When true sadness does not reach a proper depth, then drop the amount of food given to the mourner, emaciating him and making him visibly weakened." And this is the custom of the Chinese, to make things *appear* as something when they are actually not. This is terrible, and it is quite foolish for others to think it a superior practice and praise it.

If the pain a person feels at the loss of a father or mother is indeed deep, then it is dangerous to treat one's body in such a manner. To do so makes the person weak, exhausted, and prone to sickness, and if that person should pass away from this experience, how could you call that deed filial? If a person must experience sorrow, which will bring him close to death, then surely the deceased is feeling deep sorrow, too. Why should something like this be pleasing? There is nothing good in ignoring the wishes of the parent, making the children put on airs because society deems it such, labeling it "filial piety." This is not pious in the end. It is one of the habits of the Chinese in acts of filial piety and everything else, to make these actions obvious for others to see, labeling this escapade something worthy of the praise of the world.

---

117. *The Analects* record, "Regarding mourning, it is better to have sincere grief than an organized ritual" ("Ba Yi" chapter). In the "Shu Er" chapter of the same work it says, "When the Master ate next to someone who was in mourning, he never ate till he was filled."

[123] CONCERNING THE DEBATE ABOUT IT BEING GOOD NOT TO SEEK RICHES AND FAME

Confucian scholars through the ages have not felt sorrow for their state of poverty, nor have they had any joy for wealth and prosperity. They have thought this indifference is good, but this is not an expression of true human emotion. What it is, however, is one of the falsehoods these scholars engage in so they may obtain prestige. Even if there were a rare example of such a person actually feelings that riches are not desirable, then he would be an example of the perverse sort. What kind of good comes from this kind of thinking? I think it is mistaken. Certainly, it is wrong to go against logic and force oneself to seek after riches, but if a person works hard in his station, advancing in life until he obtains riches and fame, then this is an act of filial piety to his parents and ancestors. Unfilial action knows nothing worse than a person who falls on hard times, placing his own family in dire straits. It is the trend of the Chinese to covet excessively a lofty reputation, while forgetting true filial piety.

[127] ON THE KOSIZUKA TOMB

A person from the province of Yamato told me that in Tobi Village in Upper Siki District there is a burial mound called Kosizuka. The top part is circular with a boulder partly visible inside at the front. People do not climb to the top of the burial mound. Now to the south there is a gentle slope so that the mound appears to be an imperial burial mound. Personally, I wonder if this is not the burial tomb of Nigi Hayahi. On the other hand, there are many burial mounds in Yamato Province that are of the same shape, so what do people think? It is unclear. The place known as Tobi anciently was called Tomi.

[128] THE VARIOUS PALACES IN ASUKA

The sites of the ancient palaces in the Asuka area are as follows: the Okamoto Palace is at the base of the Oka Temple. The Kiyomigafara Palace is a slight distance south of the Oka Temple. The Kafafara Palace is near the knoll by the Kafafara Temple. The Itabuki Palace is in the field east of the Asuka River.[118] These are the theories of the Asuka family, who are in charge of the Asuka Temple.

[129] ABOUT A PERSON CALLED UEMURA NOBUKOTO

In the area of Nara in a place called Fikita Village there was a man called Uemura Nobukoto.[119] He wrote a book called *Kōdai wana shōshi*[120] in thirty volumes. This individual enjoyed pondering the events of all the provinces and areas, and among the many entities on this and that, he has thought about various things and recorded very detailed information about ancient places in Yamato Province. On the seventh day of the second month of the second year of Tenmei (1782), I received the news that he had passed away. He once had come to see me and I met him here. He talked in great detail about ancient things he had pondered deeply.

---

118. The Okamoto Palace was used by Jomei, Saimei, and Tenmu. The Kiyomigahara Palace was used by Tenmu and Jitō. The Kawahara Palace was used by Saimei. The Itabuki Palace was used by Kōgyoku and Saimei.

119. Uemora Nobukoto died apparently early in 1782, though we only know that because of Norinaga's record of the date when he heard the man had passed away. Nobukoto enjoyed traveling, and thus became interested in the etymologies and histories of toponyms in central Japan. Very little is known about him, other than what is found in the several works that he produced.

120. A topographical encyclopedia of Yamato Province, arranged by district. Information about each toponym is gleaned from a variety of works, including *Kojiki*, *Nihon shoki*, *Sendai kuji hongi*, *Engi shiki*, and *Shaku Nihongi*.

[133] THE STATE OF COMMENTARIES ON SHINTŌ WORKS

Anciently, it was the occupation of Confucian students at the Imperial University engaged in historiography to publish commentaries on the "Age of the Gods" sections of the ancient works. The compilation of these commentaries came about after the Kōnin era (810–824), and these constitute what is known as *Nihongi shiki*.[121] These commentaries were put together relying solely on Chinese thinking, and this does not mean these scholars studied the works from a Shintō point of view. Therefore, these people had no understanding of the ancient spirit or the lexicon, and their commentaries are generally infantile and shallow; of course, they say nothing about the ancient Japanese Way. They only give superficial comments dealing with word usage.

That being the case, the ancient Confucian scholars of Japan entirely took after Chinese ways, and did not have any particular ideas of their own. Therefore, even when they discuss works about the deities, one hardly finds any arbitrary arguments distorted by the Chinese Heart. There were no forced theories based on Confucian ideas, and things were at peace. As time went on, one group called *shingaku* (divine study) appeared, and specialists on the Shintō works engaged in minute analytical study. Nonetheless, the trait of scholars at that time was one of thoughtless sophistry, so they did not analyze the texts in any faithful manner. Some merely twisted the sentences and reached forced conclusions, while some used Buddhist philosophy, and others relied on Confucian ideas.

These scholars increased in vain cleverness, and now they have finally awakened to the mistake of mixing Buddhist philosophy with Shintō and have eradicated that mistake. Regardless, they did not come to this conclusion through an understanding of the ancient state of the Japanese Heart; they merely discarded Buddhism because Confucian learning surpassed Buddhism in popularity. Due to these things, scholars in the present who proclaim

---

121. This is not exactly true. *Shaku Nihongi*, a work from the Kamakura era that quotes many of the *Shiki*, says that the commentaries started in the fifth year of Yōrō (721). The next one was in the third year of Kōnin (812).

that they follow the Way of the gods [Shintō] really follow Confucianism. This does not agree with the true spirit of Shintō.

While these scholars understand the problem of having become trapped in Buddhist philosophical interpretations, they do not realize that they are still trapped in Confucian philosophical interpretations, a state I find hard to comprehend. In the recent past, some people have come to the realization that Confucian ideas are out of place, and they have attempted to rid themselves of Confucian thinking, but they still have trouble eradicating every trace of the Chinese Heart from their minds. These people still believe in the truth of the logic of heaven, or *yin* and *yang*, and this sophism causes them to interpret the High Plain of Heaven as the capital of the emperor. They deny that Amaterasu Ōmikami is the heavenly globe in the sky and make the palace of the sea deity some island. They cannot rid themselves of these warped theories because they are still sullied by the Chinese Heart, nor have they come to a level of cognizance where they become aware of this foreign thinking, all because they are stained by Chinese philosophy. This is proof of how deeply the Chinese Heart has pervaded the very minds of the people in society.

[136] DISMANTLING AND REBUILDING THE VARIOUS SHRINES

In the same work [*Saigūki*] regarding the dismantling and rebuilding of the various shrines, [it notes that] "the Grand Shrine of Ise is rebuilt every twenty years ... . Usa Shrine is rebuilt every thirty years [which is overseen by the Dazaifu], Sumiyosi Shrine is rebuilt every twenty years ... and Kasima Katori Shrine is rebuilt every twenty years."

[137] ON THE COLOR OF THE DOCUMENT PAPER FOR EDICTS

In the same work, it says that the document paper for edicts to the Grand Shrine of Ise was to be green, the color for Kamo Shrine was to be crimson, and the rest were to be yellow.

[143] WHY WE CALL CHINA *KARA*

A certain person said that it was a mistake to label China *Kara*, because originally *kara* was used in reference to the Three Han [Koguryŏ, Paekche, and Silla].[122] There are errors in his reasoning, however. In Book 19 of *Man'yōshū*, in a poem composed by Yakamochi on the third day of the third month we find:

karabito mo	Even today when it is
ikada kabete	said that the people of China
asobu to ifu	enjoy themselves floating on rafts—
kefu so wa ga sekwo	Let us all put flowers
fana kadurase yo	in our hair. (MYS 4153)

This poem is also found in *Shin Kokinshū*, and though the graph 漢 (Han China) is generally read *aya*, in the case of this poem 漢人 should not be read *ayabito*, but definitely should be read *kara*. In the same chapter of the same anthology, we find a *chōka* (long poem)[123] given to Fujiwara Asomi Kiyokawa, the ambassador being sent to Tang China, written by Fujiwara Taikō. In this poem we find the words **kono ago wo karakuni fe yaru** (I send off this, my son, to China; MYS 4240). And even in a poem composed by Ōtomo Komaro Sukune, the vice ambassador, there are the words **karakuni** (韓国) **ni yukitarafasite** (Going to China and fulfilling my duty; MYS 4262), where we find that Tang China is actually written 韓国 (the land of the Han). Does this not make it clear that the two usages were interchangeable, because both were read *kara*? Also anciently, it was common to use the graph 唐 (Tang) to represent *kara*.

---

122. As Yoshikawa et al. (1978:94, headnote) point out, this "certain person" Norinaga has reference to is Amenomori Hōshū (1668–1755), a well-known Confucian scholar. He was closely connected with events related to the Korean Peninsula, and was stationed in Pusan for several years as an assistant in charge of Korea (from 1703 to 1705). While there he learned some Korean. He wrote a work, *Tafaregusa* (published in 1789), which notes that anciently the three kingdoms on the peninsula were labeled *kara*, and at a later date the name *kara* became confused and was then used on China, which he criticizes as a mistake.

123. It is interesting that Norinaga calls MYS 4240 a *chōka*, when it is a *tanka*. But the headnote matches, so it may merely be a slip of the brush.

[144] CONCERNING THE GRAPHS 朝臣

The status title of 朝臣 (court-vassal) is read **asomi**, and means "my older brother the vassal" (吾兄臣). In spite of this, in the reign of Emperor Tenmu, from the time that the eight titles were established, the court began writing this title as "court-vassal."[124] They borrowed the reading of *asa-omi*, and while the title is a contracted form, the characters helped people remember the meaning of the title. Even in Chinese works, there is an example where Cai Yong wrote, "The dukes, ministers, and Palace Gate overseers in *Shangshu* appeared at court dressed in silk cloth and this is called 'morning officials' (朝臣)." The various captains of the schools of the various agencies and councilors on down are called "morning officials" in *Duduan*, but this title only appears very rarely in works from that country.

[145] CONCERNING THE DEMON OF THE MIND

In tales and stories when someone has unknowingly committed a blunder, a terrifying thing comes out of that person's mind, which is called *kokoro no oni* (demon of the mind). In an annotational note in the Chinese work *Liezi*, there is the line, "Doubting the heart which produces a ghost in the dark." The intentions of this thing are very similar to that here.

---

124. There are generally two competing etymologies for this title. One is that advanced by Norinaga. His theory of contraction: *ase* (my older brother) + *omi* (minister) > *asomi* is plausible. The weakness in this theory is the disparity between that meaning and the characters in the title. The other theory works backward from the title: 朝臣 (morning-vassal) < *asa* (morning) + *omi* (minister). Martin (1987:506) believes that *omi* is itself a contraction of *opo* (large) *imi* (taboo), and points to a person who ministered in place of the lord or a deity. This may explain how the graph 臣 (vassal, steward, minister) came to be applied to this Japanese word.

[148] CONCERNING THE GRAPH 妹

Among the august words spoken by Izanami as recorded in the liturgy "Chinkasai" are the words "my beloved sister" related to Izanagi, written 吾奈妹乃命 or 吾名妹乃命, and in a section before this we find "the two sister deities." Regarding the graph 背 (back; a rebus graph for *se*) works like *Shaku Nihongi, Gengenshū*,[125] and others, write this as 妹, which shows what the ancient archetype was. Now in the Kaya District of Bitchū Province section of *Wamyōshō* there is a village called 庭妹, which has the reading note of **nifise**, and is the place currently known as Nifise (庭瀬). This character 妹 (younger sister) is a mistake for 妹. In the same province, there is a village name **kurese** (呉妹) in the Simomiti District, and Firose (広妹) and Tofose (遠妹) in the Fusaga District of Simotukeno Province. None of these has reading notes attached, so we do not know how they were to be pronounced, but as all three employ the character 妹 and all have the gloss *se* attached, truly they sound like toponyms that have *se* in their names. Regarding this, when we also consider that there is a place name written 弟翳 in the Simomiti District of Bitchū province with the reading note of *se* it makes you think that this could also be written 妹, but anciently there are examples where older and younger brothers of men and women were called *se* among themselves regardless of whether the female was addressing an older or a younger brother. Thus, the graph 弟 (younger brother) had that kind of origin. As we are labeled such, and people call us that, there was no reason why they could not write 妹 and read it as *se*; all these examples prove that 妹 (younger sister) is actually a copyist's error for 妹.

---

125. *Gengenshū*: Written by Kitabatake Chikafusa (1293–1354) and completed sometime around 1378, apparently as preparation for his later work, *Jinnō shōtōki* (1339). The work expounds on Ise Shintō, demonstrating to the reader that to understand Shintō one must begin at the beginning (*gengen*).

❧ 4 | FORGET-ME-NOTS

I unexpectedly had to look through some Chinese records and doing this caused me to reflect on several things. I vaguely remembered which record I wished to look at, but could not remember which volume I needed. I guessed here and there but could not locate what I wanted. I could have searched successive volumes, but this would have taken a great amount of time, so I gave up searching, having gained nothing for the effort. I composed the following poem with this feeling of dissatisfaction still in my breast:

fumi mituru	I have been there before,
ato mo natu no no	but left no trace the last time.
wasuregusa	Forget-me-not!
ofite fa itodo	The longer my life becomes
sigerisofi tutu	the shorter my memory is.

I was originally born with a poor memory, but lately it has become so bad that I cannot even seem to recall what happened just moments before. This is a very disheartening chain of events.

[155] ONE'S NATIVE AREA

At present when people are on a trip, they call where they live *furusato* (old village), but originally this word pointed to where a person had lived before they had moved to a different province. It is not proper to use this word about where one was before one goes and returns from a trip. Thus, we do not see any songs in *Man'yōshū* or *Kokinshū* where this word is used that way. In

Man'yōshū when the poet has gone on a trip and he refers to where he left, he will use the word **kuni** (province) or **ife** (house). In later generations we have all become so accustomed to using the word *furusato* that this usage has become commonplace, so there is no sense in trying to change it now. However, if one wants to produce *Man'yō*-like poetry then he must be careful; and yet some people still use the word *furusato*, and I do not think that is proper.

[156] UKIYO

The word *ukiyo*[126] refers to a world of regret, and the phrase is used in reference to a world that is full of anxiety. If one looks at the usage in old song, it will become clear. However, in some Chinese works the graphs 浮世 (floating world) are used, causing confusion, and people have become accustomed to writing "floating world" instead, and it is a mistake to use this in a vague reference to things in the world. One should carefully look through old songs, and if you do, you will find that the usage has reference to anxiety.

[157] THE HUT WHERE THE PRIEST KEICHŪ LIVED

The hut called Enju where the priest Keichū lived is located in the area of Kōzu in Ofosaka, in the town of Wesasi, and even now, there is a small temple there. He passed away there, and a burial plot is located in that town. There is also an epitaph written by a Confucian scholar named Goi Toshisata[127] from around the

---

126. Because it is often written with the graphs 浮世, most Westerners interpret it as "the floating world," but as Norinaga points out, the original meaning appears to have been one of regret.

127. Goi Toshisata, better known as Goi Ranshū (1694–1762). When Nakai Shuan (d. 1758) opened Kaitoku Shoin (later known as the Kaitokudō Academy) in 1726 Ranshū became a lecturer there. He later left and went to Edo to serve the Lord of Tugaru. He retired from this position in 1739 and returned to Ofosaka to teach at the academy. His lectures centered on Zhu Xi philosophy. He wrote *Hi betsu hen*, where he criticized Sorai's philoso-

time of Kanpō (1741–1743). Now this hut originally was located at a place called Nusagaki Garden within the homestead land of a certain Fuseya family in the village of Manchō of Ikeda Township in Izumi District of Izumi However, there are still poems at the house of the Fuseya familu that were composed by Keichū a long time ago, which someone had written down, that exist to this day.

[158] CONCERNING 者 AS "ACCORDINGLY"

In all kinds of documents there are many examples of "such and such, (者) accordingly, such and such." Writers in the Middle Ages attached this graph 者 to the beginning of words in the last part of sentences, and read this as *tefereba* (accordingly), which is a mistake. This graph should be attached to words at the beginning of the sentence, and read as *teferi*, which is a form of *to iferi* [(thus) it is said].

[163] INNER ATTENDANT

There is a post at the Ise Shrine, divided into major inner attendant (大内人) and minor inner attendant (小内人). A certain person asked me about the meaning of "inner attendant," and I responded that in *Nihon shoki* we see where the throne bestows on Nakatomi Kamatari the post of inner minister (内臣). In the first year of Tenpyō Shōhō (749) in *Shoku Nihongi* as well as in an imperial edict in the first year of Tenpyō Hōji (757), we see that the Ōtomo family is referred to as "inner military" (内兵). In that same record, we also see the name Inner Mononobe. All examples of "inner" originate from the meaning of "being especially intimate." Therefore, these inner attendants are labeled thus because they are especially intimate in their service at the Great Shrine.

---

phy as leading to absolutism in government. He also studied *kokugaku*, which appears to be why he wrote the epitaph.

[164] THE WORDS OF THE CHILD SEEN IN THE SUJIN RECORD, WHO WAS DIVINELY POSSESSED

A certain individual asked about the meaning of the words spoken when a child of Hika Tobe of Fikami in Tanba Province was divinely possessed, as seen in the sixtieth year of Sujin in *Nihon shoki*. This is my response to the query: the words in question should be read thus:

> There is a rock like a jewel sunken beneath the water plants. It is the perfectly beautiful mirror that is worshipped by the people of Idumo. It is the mirror of the wonderful deity who exudes power. The treasure at the bottom of the pond, the actual shape of the treasure. The spirit of the cleansing water of the mountain river. The sunken mirror of the splendid deity. The treasure at the bottom of the pond, the actual shape of the treasure.

If you read this according to the present text, it sounds forced. The word **sidukasi** (sunken stone) is the same form as **yukasi** from **yuki** (going), or **fakasi** from **faki** (girded), and is a word based on **siduki** (sunken), so it continues as "gem weed sunken beneath the pure water plants." It is a preface[128] for the word Idumo. **Idu** means pure, and originates from the gem weed that is sunken to the bottom of the river being pure. I have not been able to figure out the meaning of **matane**. The word **osifabure** means to hold out and shake the mirror, lifting it as a presentation to the deities. **Sokodakara** (bottom treasure) means the ultimate treasure. All things that are of such an extreme quality are labeled **soko**. **Umasi** (sweet and beautiful) modifies **sokodakara**, and does not modify **mikami** (august deity). **Mitakaranusi** is a shortened form of **mitakara no usi** (director of the august treasure), and refers to the person in charge of this ceremony. These are all words that praise the mirror. **Mitama** points to the august jewel, and it is known as the jewel at the bottom of the

---

128. "Preface" translates 序. The *Princeton Companion to Classical Japanese Literature* states that a preface is "the use of some lines in a *waka* to prepare for a later idea or word" (Miner 1985:279).

mountain river. The words **sidumekakeyo** mean to pacify, hang, and present [the mirror]. The words **umasi mikami no** ... are the same thing as the mirror, and are words that praise the jewels. The entire meaning is that the vassal of Idumo should worship the deities with the utmost divine treasures, the mirror, and jewels.

[165] AN EXAMPLE OF PEOPLE IN SOCIETY BEING DECEIVED BY FALSE APPEARANCES

If we were to give an example about the state of our imperial land and foreign countries, then we could say that anciently the people of our imperial land were beautiful in a natural way, avoiding decoration and ornamentation, leaving themselves in a genuine, untouched state. Foreign countries, on the other hand, had ugly women who applied cosmetics to their hair and face, adorning themselves with beautiful clothing. Viewed from afar, it is difficult to judge the good or bad traits and the person with makeup and attractive apparel *seems* more beautiful. When people today approach such a woman, they do not know how to distinguish whether she is beautiful or ugly. Why should people think these women are beautiful when viewed from afar? Since everything from China lacks sincerity, these scholars must wrap their ideas up in beautiful apparel and peddle them thus.

[167] DEBATING FROM ONE POINT OF VIEW

Scholars in society who do not criticize the mistakes in a person's thinking, who do not follow one point of view, but argue from the attitude that this way of thinking is as good as that way, are the ones who say things contradictory to what they truly believe. They try to look favorable to a wide audience, being insincere and corrupt. It is not proper to alter what you believe to be true, and follow someone else's theory, no matter how much criticism you may receive from others. A scholar must not be flattered or intimidated by what others say.

It is the widely accepted view of people in the present that it is unacceptable and narrow-minded to stick to just one point of view, criticizing other theories as bad, while is it open-minded and generous to freely switch from theory to theory, avoiding criticism from other people, but this opportunistic attitude is not as acceptable as people believe. If a theory you deeply believe and follow has been confirmed, then you should adhere to it, avoiding other theories that differ from your point of view. All theories differing from the point of view you esteem to be good is unacceptable. The logic is that if your way of thinking is good, then that other way of thinking is surely bad. This attitude that a certain theory is good, while another theory is not bad demonstrates that the person does not have an established point of view, and that he does not believe any one theory very deeply. If one has a deep belief in an established theory, then that person will feel obligated to criticize the bad points of a theory differing from his own. This is the sincere attitude of a scholar who believes his own point of view to be true. I do not necessarily believe it to be bad to stick to my point of view and criticize beliefs that differ from my own as unacceptable, no matter what other people may think of me.

[168] ON A PERSON'S THEORY CHANGING FROM TIME TO TIME

When a person's theory has contradictory points, or lacks any unity, it is confusing to someone who does not know which facts to believe. Thus, the average person may feel that this scholar's entire theory is unfounded. This situation is true to some extent, but it is not always the case. In other words, it is difficult to admire a scholar whose theory remains unchanged from the beginning when he proposes the theory and holds to it until he dies. We often see where a scholar's theory changes over the course of time, as he accepts good ideas along the way that differ from what he originally proposed. Thus, the theory is now better than it was when he first proposed it.

As time passes, scholarship makes progress, and so a theory must surely change. In addition, it is very admirable when a scholar

4 ~ FORGET-ME-NOTS 119

makes a clean break and changes some aspect of his theory that he has noticed was originally mistaken without hiding it. This is especially true of our recently established Way of the study of ancient things. People cannot expect us to research everything, as our field is newly established. We will elucidate the Way only after the research of many scholars has been completed, and sufficient time has passed. It is only natural that points within a person's later theory differ when compared with the original theory. This is something that will become clear throughout the life of the scholar. That is why it is logical to accept the later ideas of a person as his established theory. Nevertheless, because it is impossible to claim that it is unlikely that a person's original ideas will be better than the ideas later altered, the final choice of which idea to follow is thus left up to the reader.

[175] ONE POINT ABOUT THE USE OF THE HONORIFIC PREFIX *MI*

In *Genji monogatari* there are usages such as "Buddha's august *kalavinka* voice," "single august belly," "august crossing before his presence," "the daughter of Jijū, Her Highness's august nurse," "the curtain stand before the same august presence of the Buddha," and "the august person of the second avenue of the palace." These examples of the honorific prefix [*mi* = august] as interpreted in the present are pronounced differently than they should. One should be careful. Even in the example of "crossing before his presence," the prefix should be attached to "crossing" and not to "before."

[176] CONCERNING THE WORD *FABERU*

The word *faberu* appears only twice in *Ise monogatari*; those two examples both appear in the context of letters.

[177] THE READING OF THE TEN TRUNKS[129]

The graphs 甲乙 are read *kinoe* and *kinoto* because of the underlying meaning of "older brother of the tree" (*ki no e*) and "younger brother of the tree" (*ki no oto*).[130] The rest can be discovered by thinking in this way. The reading of *kanoe* for 庚 and *kanoto* for 辛 is due to contraction of an older *kane no e* and *kane no oto*, where **no** of **neno** elides.

[178] ON THE GRAPH 乙

The reason the graph 乙 is read *oto* is because of the pronunciation *otu*. However, some may consider that in the usage of these graphs (of the calendar readings) 甲乙 these are read *kinoe* and *kinoto*, then perhaps it also has the meaning of **oto** (younger brother), or that we also write **wotome** (maiden) as 乙女, but both of these ideas are mistaken. The word **wotome** is written 処女 and 未通女 and so on in *Man'yōshū*, but the phonogram **wo** (乎) is used. Whether we see 乙 as having the pronunciation of *otu* or the meaning of **oto** "younger brother," both have **o** as the initial vowel, so there is no reason to write **wotome** with this graph.

[186] CALLING PEOPLE "MIYA"

Attaching the word *miya* to [the name of] offspring of the lineage of the emperor anciently was limited to royal princes and princesses. A child of a royal prince did not have the word *miya*

---

129. "Ten trunks" (十干) refers to the first half of a system known as *kanzhi* 干支 in Japanese (and *ganzhi* in Chinese), which was made up of ten trunks and twelve branches. The ancient Chinese divided a lunar month into three time periods of ten days each. Each of these ten days was given a designation, which forms the ten trunks. This designation of "ten trunks" comes from the Latter Han era. According to *Nihon shoki*, the Japanese first instituted a Chinese calendar in the eleventh month of 690, though some believe a calendar was already in use before this time. The naming of these trunks is based on the five elements, each divided into a greater [elder brother] and lesser [younger brother].

130. Norinaga is very astute to notice that these forms are contractions of earlier, longer forms, and *ki* here is likely "wood," from "tree," one of the five Chinese elements.

added to his name. However, after the time around the Middle Ages children born of royal princes also began to have this added to their names, and recently the successive offspring of the brothers of emperors all have *miya* attached to their names.

[188] EVENTS AFTER A PERSON HAS DIED

What events occurred in the ancient past after people had died? When Ama no Waka Hiko passed away in the "Age of the Gods," the record says "there was singing and dancing for eight days and eight nights." What appears [in the record] is that people enjoyed themselves with music, and it is difficult to know any more details about this. However, it is the tradition that they sang and danced. I have already explained these things in *Kojiki-den*.

The fact that there is defilement from death was set forth from the "Age of the Gods," but establishing the number of days to deal with the defilement likely was decided later. In addition, the practices of taboo [avoidance] and mourning robes are done in imitation of Chinese practices in later eras. In the record of Emperor Nintoku in *Nihon shoki*, the text uses the graphs 素服 (white hemp mourning clothes), but this is a typical usage based on Chinese texts.[131] Our land did not have mourning robes in the ancient past. When Emperor Chūai passed away they had nothing of the sort, and it is clear from Empress Jingū's preparation [to invade Silla] that she also did not have any mourning clothing.

It seems to be a charitable act when China established the detailed rules governing mourning robes, but in the end, it is an emotionally shallow and superficial practice. The grief from losing a parent to death cannot be rigidly delimited to a specific time up to a certain month or day, but it is the bad habit of China to draw a strict time limit and force these rules on people. In the end, spreading this kind of practice simply teaches people to how to deceive each other.

---

131. *Li ji* notes, "When something distressful happened to the army, the commanding officer wailed outside of the Ku Gate [of the palace], dressed in white hemp mourning clothes" ("Tan Gong," Part Two).

A son who has only shallow feelings for a parent will be over his grief before even three years has passed, but will still wear robes and pretend to be grieving. On the other hand, a son who has deep feelings for his parent will still be grieving for the parent even after three years have passed, but at that point even though his grief continues he will put away the mourning robes and erase any traces of his feelings. Are not both of these superficial and deceptive? That our imperial land originally did not have this practice shows that our ancient people could grieve without a set time limit, be it long or short, and this is how one should truly mourn. Even if one does not wear mourning robes, the person can still grieve, while even if one wears the robes, he can still feel no grief. Therefore, this formality of wearing robes is worthless.

Thus, even in China, during the reign of Emperor Wen, the emperor tried to shorten the length of the mourning period,[132] but Confucian scholars at his court thought this was a very bad idea and disagreed with him; however, the actions of this emperor were logical. Even though our country took this practice from China, we have shortened the period, determining that in the case of the death of a parent, the period of mourning should not exceed one year. Nevertheless, this is still an exceedingly long period of time, and since there is no need to forsake one's business for such a long time, what would it hurt if one were to go to work even though they were still mourning?

Now the reason I have said this basically is to argue about the existence of mourning robes. If these things had already been established in our country, then I would say that they should be strictly complied with and people should not go against them. It is very frightening that people who revere the past in all aspects will go against customs from the past if they feel that these do not suit themselves. It is very selfish.

---

132. *Shiji* records, "Let Us issue an order to the officers and commoners of the world: after the order arrives [that the sovereign has died], people should hold a memorial service for three days, then all should take off their mourning apparel … . For those who should arrange mourning affairs, wear mourning apparel, and hold memorial services, none of them need to wear unhemmed mourning apparel" (Nienhauser 1994.2:181).

[190] CONCERNING CALLING CHERRY BLOSSOMS JUST "BLOSSOMS"

We do not see any examples until the era of *Kokinshū* where cherry blossoms are called simply "blossoms." This is explained in detail in Priest Keichū's *Kokin Yosaishō*. In Part One of the "Wakana" chapter of *Genji monogatari* there is a line dealing with plum blossoms where he says, "I want to compare this [plum] blossom to cherry blossoms when they are at their peak." This is a proper way to make a distinction between cherry blossoms and other blossoms.

[192] CONCERNING POETS AND PRIVATE POETIC COLLECTIONS

Regarding the labeling of people who compose poems (poets, 歌人), in the seventeenth volume of *Shūishū* there is the line where "poets" are gathered together at the house of Prime Minister Sanjō. He has them compose poetry on a variety of topics. Also, regarding private poetic collections (家集), these are seen in the "Mana" preface to *Kokinshū*, and in the same volume of *Shūishū* it notes, "During the Tenryaku period (947–957) Ise collected poetry for a private collection." Also in the twentieth volume of *Shūishū* we see where it mentions that poetry was written down in private collections, and in the collection of Minamoto Shitagau it mentions that Taira no Kanemori had a private collection as well as others. *Ruijū kokushi* also notes under the entry of Minister Sugawara no Koreyoshi that he had a private literary collection in ten volumes.

[196] CONCERNING THE READING OF *FASE* FOR *FATUSE*

The ruler Yūryaku in *Nihon shoki* is named 長谷雄朝臣, which is traditionally read **fasewo**,[133] but in *Kokin waka rokujō*,[134] it records his name as *fatusewo*, written in *kana*. However, in Minister Kensuke's anthology, and Tsurayuki's anthology, in the head notes it has the reading of *fase*. In the Saneakira collection there is a poem written on the topic of "banana tree," which has a stanza where it has the words *fasewoba kaku ya*.[135]

[197] CONCERNING WRITING "CUCKOO" AS 時鳥

In the "How Lamentable" poem in *Wenxuan* is the stanza: "birds who waited for spring chirp wonderfully."[136] This refers to things in spring, when all kinds of birds who chirp in spring are called "birds of the time" (時鳥). Now people also write the name of the cuckoo as 時鳥 because it certainly is one of the birds that chirps in the springtime, and in the end, it really became like its name.

[199] *RIHŌŌKI*

The use of the graph 李 in the title of *Rihōōki*[137] is difficult to comprehend. In the quotations of this work found in *Saigūki*,

---

133. The manuscripts of *Nihon shoki* generally agree that the older reading was *Fatuse*.

134. *Kokin waka rokujō*: A privately compiled poetic collection in six volumes, compiled between 976 and 987. The extant manuscripts contain over 4,300 poems, though the original appears to have contained closer to 4,700 poems. One of its most striking characteristics is the 1,000 or so poems quoted from *Man'yōshū*.

135. *Bashō* (banana tree) is mentioned in *Wamyōshō* with the vernacular reading of **fasewoba**. Saneakira has written this as 長谷をば (Yosano and Masamune, 1978, book 20:5r).

136. "How Lamentable." This is a poem by Lu Shiheng (261–303), contained in volume 28 of *Wenxuan*.

137. This is the diary of Prince Shigeakira (906–954), the fourth son of Emperor Daigo (r. 897–930).

Hokuzanshō, and other works, the title is recorded using only the graph 吏. Even in the work Taiki, the title is written with 吏. The graph 李 is an error someone made later.

[208] ON THE SHRINE OF SAHO HIME

Was there not a Saho Hime Shrine in Nara? In *Takano sankei no ki*, a record by Sanjōnishi Kin'eda,[138] it says that he visited the shrine of Saho Hime, located near Nara.

[209] CONCERNING THE POETRY COMPOSED BY MINISTER TAMEKANE

In the preface to the work *Nomori no kagami*, written by the Rokujō no Uchi Minister Arifusa,[139] it says, "Lately there is a person called Minister Tamekane whose poetic style goes against that of his ancestors [starting with Teika], and he breaks the principles that have been upheld by successive generations of poets in his family. Many of the poems he has composed are not proper *waka*." I had been thinking, "Regarding that minister [Tamekane], his poetic style within the way of *waka* likely followed the set poetic style, because it was handed down by his family in unbroken succession." However, I did not follow up on this thought because I did not have a more detailed inquiry for anyone. However, now that Tamekane has come under criticism again, I realized that there actually was a problem with his poetic style. When we remember that having said that, the priest [to whom I was talking] laughed and scorned me, and he said, "The son of Emperors Yao and Shun, and the younger brother of Liu Gehui were all fools, and just because one is born into a family of prestige does not guarantee

---

138. Sanjōnishi Kin'eda (1487–1563) was a courtier and poet of the Warring States period. The record Norinaga mentions is a record of temples and shrines he visited with Satomura Jōha, a renga master.
139. Rokujō Arifusa (1251–1319). *Nomori no kagami* is said to have been written by Arifusa, but some scholars in the present doubt this association.

that the person obtains the associated wisdom. Even the great Buddha once said that his disciples would lose his teachings. He used the example of a parasite on a lion eating the lion. In the same vein, because people who have transmitted the way of Buddhism or Confucianism have made mistakes these ways become worn and discarded. Therefore, it is unavoidable that the proper way of poetry would eventually disappear even from a house of great prestige. That minister was a person of such stature that he was greatly esteemed by Emperor Fushimi, but even though he was bad-mouthed and lost his position, which act was accomplished on rather weak pretenses, it is difficult to talk about his weaknesses. I simply want him to be remembered with words of praise."

In general, *waka* has the heart as its center, but it cannot be composed only with the heart. The heart is honest but it should not be overly honest. The poet should stay away from using flowery language, but should use poetic language in a skillful manner. In order to have an affected air in the poetry the poet should stay away from pretense. In order to imitate ancient poetry, the poet should not imitate the form. By copying the ancient style, one should not reproduce the ancient style. I was told other things, too.[140]

[211] ON THE DIVERSITY OF COMMENTARIES ON THE CONFUCIAN CLASSICS

When one compares the ancient commentaries on the Confucian classics of China from the Han era with Confucian commentaries from the Song era, you find many discrepancies between the thrust of each text's argument. Some commentaries from periods after this even deny the veracity of Song Confucian commentaries.

These Confucian classics essentially lay out the principles for the Way and are important works of unparalleled value, so these commentaries must agree on a set principle from which the com-

---

140. Interesting that in *Uiyamabumi* Norinaga is critical of the poetry of Tamekane. He wrote, "Lord Tamekane's ... style of poetry is eccentric, base, and inferior, and it was considered unorthodox even in his own time" (Translation by Nishimura 1987:487).

mentary begins. Since there are so many disparate theories from the ancient days, how can the reader know which is worthy or faulty? Most things in our imperial land were already established and there was no sense in spending much time arguing about minute points, and this proves that the Japanese ideas were superior to those of China. And the Confucian school from the Song era known as Zhu Xi teaches the student to "investigate things, extend your knowledge, and seek the principle," but this is the epitome of foolishness. These scholars could not even make a thorough search into these important classics, their theories exploding into ever-growing numbers, proving that no one can understand the logic of all creation without erring.

[212] ON CHINESE THEORIES BEING PROFUSE AND VERBOSE

Chinese propose verbose and profuse theories, many of which are dry and boring. There are many Confucian scholars who criticize Chinese works from the Song era as excessive, but even the arguments of these Confucian scholars, while not as numerous as those from the Song era, are still profuse.

[213] *RYŌBU SHINTŌ*

In general, of all the Shintō shrines in the land, from the Middle Ages, the majority has been headed by Buddhist monks, and those that have not were called *yuiitsu* (singular) while the shrines administered by monks are called *ryōbu* (dual). Aside from this, there is also a group with the name *ryōbu Shintō* [both (parts) are Shintō], and they have a tradition that states, "Shōtoku Taishi and Prince Toneri are both *ryōbu Shintō*. Kūkai was well versed in a variety of philosophies and comprehended the mysteries of Shintō, so he revitalized *ryōbu Shintō*. Emperor Saga praised this and granted the label of *ryōbu Shintō*." This is all a fabrication.

These teachings state that these groups have taken the best of the three teachings from Shintō, Confucianism, and Buddhism, and discarded what is inferior, relying on the logic of the myriad things in the natural world that appear before our eyes, and they are able to comprehend the beginning and end of heaven and earth. I now provide my judgment by saying that these are all terrible mistakes. First, while they claim to have taken the best from these three teachings, if you examine what they teach you find that they have only taken philosophies from Confucianism and Buddhism, and they have taken nothing from Shintō. Everything is based on the Way of Buddhism with Confucian ideas intermingled, and they talk much about astrology.

Thus, they have only selected ideas from Shintō in relation to the creation story recorded in the "Age of the Gods" section of *Nihon shoki*, with its Chinese-infused text with deity names like Kunitokotachi (forever-standing-land).[141] You cannot even see a hint of the focal point of Shintō, so how can one label this as Shintō? Furthermore, astrology does not fit into these teachings, either. It is also very strange when they say that they take the best and discard the inferior. What criteria are they using to judge which is superior and which is inferior? They are simply labeling "superior" things that suit their own feelings, and "inferior" things that do not suit their own feelings; it is all based on personal criteria. What kind of proof do they provide regarding their standard? As true logic is something hard to discern, if someone thinks that this is superior, and naturally fits the logic of things, he will find that many times he misses the target. Based on the feelings of a simple man, how can one determine the myriad creations of heaven and earth by relying on the logic of some small thing you see before your eyes?

Teachings such as "to gain a perfect knowledge of natural laws" found in Song Confucian philosophy are terribly erroneous. Beyond that this label "Ryōbu Shintō" is something where you do as you please, making the heart of the person the "master," and the deities and sages "slaves," nothing but a temporary vessel, where

---

141. Norinaga is saying that since these scholars quote from the "Age of the Gods" section of *Nihon shoki*, instead of *Kojiki*, they end up with a few Shintō tidbits, like the names of the deities, but everything is dressed up in Chinese.

the difficult to expound portions of the sacred words of the deities, the teachings of Buddha, the words of Confucianism—difficult to expound according to one's feelings—are all explained away as "a teaching of expedient means," "theory," or "allegory." Recklessly expounding things as one pleases is not the way of Buddhism or of Confucianism, and it goes without saying that it does not follow the Way of the deities! It is a new Way, pioneered by people's feelings, so why would anyone label it Shintō? The answer is that Confucianism and Buddhism came here from foreign countries, and the Way of the deities itself is a system that existed from the beginning in the imperial land, and while we are talking about events in a later era, people in society should revere the Way of our country and not that of some foreign place. Fortunately, many people feel thus, so in order to attract people who adhere to this thinking, some individuals have borrowed the name of our Way and attached it to this philosophy. The ancestors of the people who have done this were monks from long ago. The people of the land back then generally revered the deities, so these people first took Shintō deities and oriented these within their foreign philosophy, and very cleverly expounded doctrine like the knaves in Buddhism, and led their hearts to this Way. You should use this as a touchstone to discern Shintō as it has existed in the recent past, which is now labeled "Ryōbu Shintō."

[214] PART TWO

In the Way of Confucianism, everything is expounded based on the reasoning of *yin* and *yang*, as well as expounding upon the "great limit and the limitless." However, if you ask these people what kind of reasoning this "great limit and limitless" is, or about its origins, they have no way to answer, simply stating that it is the "great limit and limitless." Thus in "Ryōbu Shintō" they expound one upper level of things according to the doctrine of secret teachings of Buddhism, and claim that these are the doings of *aji* of Tantric meditation, the unchanging nature, a sea change, or self-existence. Though these people boast that this ideology is superior to any other philosophy, when pressed about the origin of the logic of the Tantric meditation and the unchanging nature, they say it is a sea change and self-existence. No matter how they try to answer, no matter how they try to explain the reasoning of all things, when they explain the origins of one thing after another, even dealing with how these things came to be, or the logic behind them, the listener is never able to come to an understanding. In the end, everyone falls into this (trap) of mysteriousness ... .

[215] PART THREE

Someone belonging to "Ryōbu Shintō" said, "According to the fluctuations of the unchanging nature, this gives birth to the immeasurable mastery of all things, and while there is nothing left of the physical object, it is so profound that it cannot be explained by words, nor can it be seen by the human eye. And though you hear it you do not comprehend." While saying this, why does the speaker then always claim that there is no such thing in the world as a mystery? Does not the phrase "so profound that it cannot be explained by words" refer to something mysterious?

[217] THE THEORY THAT BEGINNING STUDENTS SHOULD COMPOSE POETRY

Recently I read a book written by a Confucian scholar.[142] Within his teachings to beginning students about writing Chinese poetry, he said, "In the end, do not show your first two or three hundred poems to people outside the circle of people you study with. Moreover, since these poems should not be included in later poetic collections, the student should copy certain stanzas of poetry from the ancient poets without reservation to master poetic composition. While your poems still lack substance, feel free to lift words and phrases from the poetic commentaries *Tangshi chu*,

---

142. As Yoshikawa et al. (1978:127, headnote) point out, Norinaga is referring to Emura Hokkai (1713–1788).

Mingshi chu, and *Shiyu suijin* in order to fill out your poems." This is truly good advice on how to learn.

It is the same when composing Japanese *waka*, also. In poetic composition, too, a person generally wants to produce new poetry, as he likes, so mistakes not typical of poetry appear, and then the poet forms bad habits that are hard to erase. If the student is a beginner, then it is important for him to rely on ancient precedent for the linking of words and the contents of emotion.

[218] YOU COMPOSE POETRY BY CAREFULLY SELECTING THE WORDS

In *Dōmyōshō* it says, "In the poem

mizu no omo ni	On the surface of the water
teru tuki nami wo	is the shape of the shining moon.
kazofureba	When we count them
koyofi zo aki no	it is tonight that
monaka narikeru	is the very middle of autumn.

we find the word *monaka*. People at that time did not think that *monaka* was a proper word for poetry, and so they criticized it, but it was still included in an imperial anthology because the poem itself had such wonderful style."

[230] ON THE WORK *A TREATISE ON VOICELESS AND VOICED WORDS IN THE ANCIENT LEXICON*

When considering voiceless and voiced words in the ancient lexicon, there are many words that differ from those in the modern tongue. So, in answering the question: "How can one tell the difference?" we know the standard because *Kojiki*, *Nihon shoki*, and *Man'yōshū* are very accurate in their *kana* usage, making a distinction between voiceless and voiced phonemes; thus, the student may know the difference through these records. Among these three records, *Kojiki* is especially accurate, next comes

132	Tamakatsuma

Man'yōshū, and then *Nihon shoki* in that order. *Nihon shoki* has many examples of confusion in voiceless and voiced phonemes, but overall the distinction is clear.[143] There are few examples of confusion in *Man'yōshū*. There are almost no mistakes in *kana* usage within *Kojiki*. Because the scarcity of mistakes testifies to the acute accuracy of these records, then most mistakes [one finds] are a product of later scribal error.

Now concerning voiceless and voiced phonemes, there are many instances where the pronunciation is different from the present. Most people think [voiceless and voiced sounds] were not distinguished in writing, or they believe there to be confusion in the usages, or that in this certain instance they can use a voiceless character with a word that requires a voiced one; this kind of thinking shows these people are ignorant in this area of linguistics.

Nevertheless, that is not really the problem, for voiceless and voiced words in the ancient lexicon have changed from those in the modern. With this, we see that like the case of the pillow word for mountain, **asifiki no**, the sound **fi** is generally voiced to **bi**, but this word also appears in *Kojiki* and *Nihon shoki*, and is especially conspicuous in *Man'yōshū*. Each of these examples is written with a voiceless phonogram, and not a voiced one. There are one or two examples that scholars believe to be confused, but from the many examples recorded exhibiting unity we know that this specific sound anciently was voiceless. With other words, the case is the same. One should read the ancient records and compare the *kana* usage in order to know whether a syllable is voiced or not. People get tripped up by the present custom of reading aloud old records without following the *kana* usage, voicing syllables when they are not, and making a sound voiceless when it is voiced—the so-called method of interpreting these according to personal inclination— this is very disturbing. When one reads from old works, the reader

---

143. This statement needs to be clarified. Regarding the phonogram usage of the songs, *Nihon shoki* is quite consistent, but the overall confusion in usage surely is because *Nihon shoki* is a compilation of a large corpus of material, while *Kojiki* is really a reworking, a rewriting, of earlier material, and hence the phonogrammatic usages were standardized. In other instances, *Nihon shoki* contains a wide array of materials, both from kingdoms on the peninsula, as well as older material from within Japan. Norinaga is correct, however, that beginning students would do well to start with *Kojiki*, which is very consistent, and has a smaller pool of phonograms than either *Man'yōshū* or *Nihon shoki*.

should strictly follow the *kana* usages, whether they are voiced or not.
Now the change from ancient times to the present of voiceless and voiced sounds has interested me, and I would like to follow the ancient phonology in writing, without feeling compelled to follow modern precedent. What I thought early on is written in the first volume of *Kojiki-den*, but because I did not have sufficient time, I could not consider various words in relation to voiceless or voiced sounds. Feeling regret for this, I often tell my friends how I feel. One of my students, Ishizuka Tatsumaro[144] who is from Tofotafumi Province, Futi District, Fosota Village, took an interest in this phenomenon, and looked through the ancient records, thinking deeply about *kana* usage. Not long ago, he published a work called *Kogon seidokkō* (*A Treatise on Voiceless and Voiced Words in the Ancient Lexicon*).[145] Looking at this treatise, I find ideas that I had not even thought of, even in such previously published works of mine, such as *Kamiyo no masakoto*. Colleagues who wish to study the ancient lexicon must read *Kogon seidokkō*.

[231] THE ARGUMENT OF PRIEST KENKŌ

What are we to make of the words of Priest Kenkō who wrote in *Tsurezure gusa*,[146] "Should we look at the blossoms only in full bloom, or the moon upon when it is unobscured by clouds?"[147] There are many more examples of ancient poems composed under the beautiful blossoms, regretting that the wind would scatter the

---

144. Ishizuka Tatsumaro (1764–1823) is well-known as a linguist. He became a student of Norinaga's in the eighth month of 1789.

145. *Kogon seidokkō* (A Treatise on Voiceless and Voiced Words in the Ancient Lexicon), finally published in 1801. Tatsumaro is also famous for another work, *Kanazukai oku no yamadi* (ca. 1798), where he posited fifteen different phonemes showing the type A and type B distinction (the *kō-otsu-rui* distinction), something later made famous by Hashimoto Shinkichi.

146. *Tsurezure gusa*: Translated as "Essays in Idleness." Yoshida Kenkō (d. 1352) came from a branch of the Urabe family who were in charge of the Yoshida Shrine. He later took Buddhist vows and changed his name to Kenkō. His essays are primarily focused on Buddhist themes, especially the impermanence of life.

147. This is from section 137. I have used the translation by Steven D. Carter (in McCullough 1990:410).

blossoms, or lamenting that the clouds would hide the moon. At other times, people composed many poems with a feeling of helplessness, waiting for the blossoms to scatter or for the clouds to conceal the moon. These types of poems outnumber those written when the blossoms were at their height, or when the moon lit up a cloudless sky. Moreover, the reason that many of these examples are seen in poems with deep sentiment is because the poet lamented their passing, though he would like to have seen the blossoms at their best, or be able to gaze up at the shining moon in a cloudless sky, it was almost impossible to catch that moment. Is there a poem where the poet is viewing the blossoms at their height and is waiting for the wind to scatter them, or is viewing the moon in a cloudless sky and waits for the clouds to come out and hide it? Regardless that there are no such poems, what Kenkō is stating goes against the emotions of people. It demonstrates a false sense of refinement coming from the pretentious feelings of people in the Middle Ages, concealing the true state of refined sentiment. There are many examples of this false refinement in the words of this priest. No matter how Kenkō portrays them, they are the same.

In all matters, there is great deception involved when one takes feelings that go against what the average person in society hopes for and makes this something elegant. Even in love poems where the poet is happy to meet his (or her) lover, there is no deep sentiment; however, there are many poems written about the anxiety of not being able to meet one's lover, and this is because everyone wishes to have close personal relationships with someone else. People's feelings are such that there is little deep sentiment in experiences of joy. Because our thoughts sink deep into our hearts when things do not go as planned, many poems exist to move our hearts, written when things have not gone as desired, and the poet feels pathos and grief. Poems written on joyous occasions tend to lack emotion. Though this may be true—that painful, sorrowful poems are refined—we cannot say that the hearts of people are actively seeking for bitter experiences.

Also, this priest argues, "The best thing a man can do is to die before he reaches forty."[148] These words have been used in poetry

---

148. This is from section seven (ibid.:395).

and prose by people from the Middle Ages onward. These people believed that the desire to live long showed that one's heart was unsightly, so they feigned that dying young was attractive; all these ideas about the purity of abandoning the world come from the flattery of Buddhism, and many of these ideas are false. These people may say things like this, but who would really wish in their hearts to die young? For example, even in the rare event there is someone who thinks this way [about dying young], that person certainly was not born with this attitude; he has become lost and confused within the teachings of Buddhism. The true heart of humanity is such that even if they experience great hardships, they do not desire to die early; everyone treats life carefully. Because of this, poems written during the *Man'yōshū* era expressed the desire to live long, but the significance of poems composed after the Middle Ages are the opposite. In all respects, the movement making worthy strange things that go against the true hearts of the common man is inspired by foreign practices; thus, one may know that this is an extreme adornment of one's heart.

[232] ON THE PRACTICE IN SOCIETY OF BUILDING FACADES

The desire to eat good food, wear fine clothing, live in a nice house, find one's fortune, be respected by people, and live a long life are the true feelings of everyone's heart. Yet, people label these as evil desires, saying that it is splendid not to desire this form of life. The practice of many people today who put on a facade of not wanting anything is a bothersome misrepresentation. In addition, scholars of learning and training or respected priests of honor put on countenances of "Oh, what profound beauty" when they gaze at the moon or cherry blossoms, but when they see a beautiful woman, they pass by as if her image had never met their eyes. Is this how life should be? If one feels profound emotion when gazing at the moon or cherry blossoms, then why do not their eyes notice the beauty of a woman? If one is to say that the moon or cherry blossoms are profound, and that the beauty of a woman is not worthy of notice, then that is not the heart of a living person, but is a terrible lie. As this is the case and the general disposition of society is to adorn one's heart with superficial feelings, should we not censure these people?

[233] CONCERNING ADOPTED SONS

The practice in present society of adopting the son of another family so one can have an heir is not an ancient custom in either the imperial land or China. Thus Confucian scholars teach that this is something that should not be done, saying that in general not having a son is the will of heaven deciding a certain person should not have an heir; and as there is nothing a person can do about it, that is the way it is. Taking a person's son who is not related to them by blood and making him an heir goes against the way of reason and is a worthless act and in the end is a transgression of going against heaven. Confucian scholars say things like this, but it is very one-sided.

If one must adopt a child from a family with no blood relation, then this should be done so that the family lineage will not die out, the graves of your ancestors will not be forsaken, and festivals will not cease, rather than have everything simply end. In ancient times, this custom did not exist in the world. If things became like they are in the world today, would the Duke of Zhou and Confucius have labeled these as evil? In spite of that, another certain Confucian scholar has said that even if the adopted son of a different lineage holds a festival for those ancestors, the deities do not accept it. The reason that the deities of the ancestors accept a festival from an actual birth-son is because he is of the same bloodline. When someone of a different bloodline conducts the festival, the spirit (of the deceased ancestors) has no reason to come and receive the worship. The reasoning of these words is very difficult to comprehend.

In this world, does not the spirit of a person who dies, leaving a deep grudge, come, possess another person, and even cause calamities? Regardless that this person has no blood relation to the dead spirit, if there is just one point to the relationship there can be a connection. Is a relationship not more secure if one were intently to ask the person to join the family, have him become the heir, and hold a festival for that family—would the deities and spirits not accept this?

[234] ON STUDENTS ASKING DIFFICULT QUESTIONS FIRST

When a student in the field of scholarship meets someone learned and addresses a question to him, the first thing these students often do is ask questions on difficult topics gleaned from among the ancient corpus, questions nobody can answer. For example, they ask about the cryptic *waza uta* in the Saimei chapter of *Nihon shoki*,[149] or the ninth poem in the first volume of *Man'yōshū* (which starts 莫囂圓隣之大相七兄爪謁氣).[150] The general desire of every scholar is to first clarify such difficult points, but if this is the case, when you ask a simple question that everyone should be able to answer, you will find that they cannot even expound upon easy subjects. It is completely meaningless for people like this to skip over the basics and try to elucidate difficult points first. Because there are many things that are unexpectedly different from what one had imagined understanding—and thus failed to pay attention to—one should first think repeatedly about simple questions, searching to clarify them. After one has obtained these easy answers, then he may ponder upon questions that are more difficult.

[237] ON THE DEITY HOMUSUBI

From the beginning when the two deities Izanagi and Izanami give birth to the land of our country and the myriad deities until

---

149. A very difficult song from the seventh year of Emperor Saimei (NS 122). Many have attempted interpretations, but the scholarly world has yet to decide on a set meaning. Norinaga attempts to clarify it in [121].
150. A poem written in difficult script, making the reading unclear. The interpretation in Omodaka's *Man'yōshū chūshaku* is, "The waves that were calm in the bay are now violent. Did my Lord once stand here at the base of the oak tree?" (1977, vol. 1:112-20) For Norinaga's own interpretation, see [354].

they give birth to the fire deity, Homusubi, these are auspicious events of the formation of things. There is nothing evil here. Through the birth of the deity Homusubi, the great deity Izanami hid in the rocks and this is the beginning of evil in the world. Regardless, Homusubi is the final deity born from a process of auspicious events, and was born on the margin of the beginning of evil events, and is thus a deity who is a combination of good and evil. Fire in society has many good attributes as it warms up objects, but also has the evil power to burn and destroy all creation— it has no parallel. It originates from the spirit of this deity, which was formed on the edge of good and evil, and thus is a mixture of good and evil.

Regarding this a person once said, "Being a female deity, Izanami spoke the auspicious words first, and because of this she gave birth to Hiruko Awashima, who was a good-for-nothing child. Thus, this should be called the origin of evil in the world. So why do you consider Izanami hiding in the rocks as the beginning of evil?" I responded, "Having the female deity utter her words first went against logic, but her words of praise, *ana ni ya*, are good words. Also, it was rare to give birth to an evil child, and because this is a good event, it is difficult to label it a truly evil occurrence. Thus we are forced to say that in all things in the world it is natural that you cannot have something without some evil being involved."

❧ 5 | THE EULALIA OF KARENO

Autumn has passed and all the grass has completely withered. On the lonely plain, there is only the miscanthus, clinging to life, flourishing heavily on the field, so I composed the following poem as I saw this scene and felt profound emotion:

karenu beki	It should have withered
kareno no obana	the miscanthus of Withered Moor.
karezu aru wo	I will keep watching
karezu koso mime	unwithered as it is—
karenu kagiri fa	as long as it does not wither away.

People will think that the person who saw this scene is a fool, because he used such trivial words in the poem, but I thought it does not really matter what they think, so there it is.

[239] ON THE DISCUSSION BY MR. KUMAZAWA ON SHINTŌ TEXTS

Mr. Kumazawa[151] argued in *Miwa monogatari*[152] that the works of Shintō were not written based on ancient oral traditions, but

---

151. Norinaga is referring to Kumazawa Banzan (1619–1691). He was an early neo-Confucianist of the Yang-Ming school. He worked at reforms but soon incurred the wrath of scholars in the Zhu Xi school of neo-Confucianism.
152. *Miwa monogatari*: A text in eight volumes written by Banzan, although the date of completion is unclear. It is an exposition on Shintō from the point of view of a Confucianist. He wrote it in the form of a dialogue between a variety of "factions," including priestly families connected to the shrines, priests, Buddhist thinkers, nobility, and elderly thinkers. The work rejects Buddhism and calls for a union of Confucian thought and Shintō.

were allegories written much later. As these records contain no moral teaching, it suits the idea of a metaphor, but even as metaphors, if they had elucidated logic like Zhuang Zhou[153] it would have been better. As the things in the works of Shintō are written from an allegorical stance that exceeds the average person's intelligence, they are generally hard to comprehend.

I, Norinaga, will argue against this point. First, it is not unusual for people to view Shintō texts and say that these are so-called allegories. This is an example of the hearts of magicians. All Confucian scholars argue that there is nothing supernatural in the world, and as this can be taken as a kind of crestfallen attitude, they interpret everything in the "Age of the Gods" as allegorical. This is true not only of Confucian scholars; it is also true of most recent Shintō scholars, who have failed to rid their minds of the Confucian heart. It seems wise on the surface not to believe all these things in spite of truth or error, but it is half-baked sophistry, because they cannot comprehend that the intelligence of man is limited, and there are many things we cannot fathom. They think they can appreciate the myriad things in the world according to their own understanding, and this is a fallacy taught by the Chinese Heart. The all-inclusive reasoning in the world is boundless, and as man cannot comprehend all these things with his limited knowledge, how can they say that the average person can comprehend the supernatural things of the "Age of the Gods"? The author of the above words said that the works of Shintō are metaphorical to the point of being silly, because there is no moral teaching in these texts. The events in these works have no profound reason, but are nothing more than very shallow stories.

These are just vague ramblings. Even in a poem from *Kokinshū*:

sokofi naki   In a bottomless pool
futi ya fa sawagu   does the water churn?

In the same vein as this poem, when something has a profound depth, the result is that the surface hides any sense of the depth of its truth, but still has the truth ... .

---

153. Zhuang Zhou (Zhuangzi) was a Chinese thinker, born 369 BCE, but his death date is unclear. He lived around the time of Mencius and belonged to the Laozi school of thought.

[240] THE THEORY ABOUT STRANGE PHENOMENA, PART ONE

Let's say that in the present world there are no humans, but in the "Age of the Gods" there was a record that mentioned humans, and then it states,

> Regarding humans, they have a place called the neck on the upper part of the body, with things on either side called ears, which can pick up the sound of voices very well. On the front there are two things called eyes that can well discern the color and shape of any object. Below this is a thing called a nose that can discern smell. Below this is something called a mouth that can emit a sound from deep within, and by moving the lips and tongue is able to generate a voice that changes and produces sound that creates words that describe all kinds of things. Below the neck on either side are things called hands, which are divided at the ends into things called fingers. By moving the fingers, they can do all kinds of things, being enabled to make all kinds of objects. Below this there is something called feet, and there are two of these. The body is carried about by moving these, and by moving these repeatedly, the human is able to climb a high mountain, and can walk to any place. Now hidden inside the breast is a thing called the heart [mind].[154] This is the most extraordinary organ among all things, because while it [the mind] has no color or shape, it regulates all things, including the ears, that hear things, mentioned above, as well as the things the eyes see, what the mouth says, and how the hands and feet move. Now related to this human, at one time he became very ill, and the disease grew severe and at last nothing worked and he could not even move, and everything stopped.

Now if Confucian scholars should read this they would typically not believe it, and say that because this is recorded from the

---

154. Here Norinaga is using the word *kokoro* (heart, mind) to refer not only to the heart, but also to the mind, the organ of reason.

"Age of the Gods" where in the world would one find such a strange story? They would claim that this is a meaningless, worthless story, and that would be the end of it.

[241] PART TWO

Continuing in the same vein as above:

In the "Age of the Gods" it is recorded that there were things called humans, created in the beginning. This human who was called a "person" originally came from such and such a place. They lived together, man and woman, and because they slept together at night and did this and that together the woman became pregnant and gradually became large. After about ten months, her belly grew painful, and suddenly from her front, something appeared. She had created something that moves and cries. When the person lifts it up and looks at it, he calls it such and such. Now this thing was created inside the woman's womb in the beginning, and now a white liquid comes out of her breasts, and continues without stopping, so the woman puts the breast up to the hole in the thing's face which she has created and from which a cry issues forth, and it takes the breast in its mouth and drinks very peacefully. The woman feeds the thing both night and day. With the passing of days and months it gradually grows bigger, and it begins to do things it could not do in the beginning.

If this was recorded in a record, as I mentioned above, and if these Confucian scholars were to read this what would they say? They would say it was a typical allegory. Thus, they label anything that existed in the "Age of the Gods" but no longer exists in the present as "strange." Why should things that do not exist now be looked upon as suspicious? Because things in the world still exist now, no one thinks they are strange. If one really thinks about it, there is not a single thing in the present world that is not really strange; if you follow everything along, you will find that everything is strange.[155]

[242] THE DIFFERENCE BETWEEN CHINESE WORKS AND SHINTŌ WORKS

Concerning the three entries above [239-241], I thought of an interesting lesson. Compared to Chinese works that sound wise and full of logic regarding all things, stories from the "Age of the Gods" come off sounding tedious and ignorant. This common distinction is used as a method for teaching. For example, let us say someone wanted to create this thing we call a human. No matter how wise he is, or how skilled, no matter how much he studied about *yin* and *yang*, and their union, though he slaved over this idea for months and years, even if he were able to create something, he would not be able to make a human being who acts and moves like we do. But as noted above the man and the woman spend one night together in a bedroom doing something secret, without even applying their minds, without even using so much as a little knife, and they are able to create life without hardly any trouble. Nevertheless, if one were to inspect the actual act in the bedroom, where is the wisdom and the profound logic? One cannot speak openly about the situation. It is very embarrassing and unmanly. It is not even as good as a child's trick. Moreover, while it is an incoherent, silly act, almost all humans come into life in this way, a way that man himself with all his skill cannot reproduce. The acts of the deities are incomprehensible and mysterious.

The stories in Chinese works generally sound wise, but because there is a limit to human intellect, there are areas that it does not reach. It is much like the example I just gave, where a person cannot create another living being, no matter how much skill he has, but it is the same as that scene in the "Age of the Gods" where those two deities perform what on the outside is an

---

155. The purpose of this is to attempt to convince people who believe that the mythological stories are nothing more than make-believe that just because those things do not exist in the present does not mean they did not exist in the past.

embarrassing, stupid act, but end up producing a living being in a brilliant manner.

If you consider these two allegories together you see that on the surface the things in the "Age of the Gods" do not appear to have any logic, sounding incoherent and stupid, but I want the reader to understand that in reality these things extend beyond human comprehension and are difficult to fathom, having a profound logic to them.

[244] *KARAZAE*

In *Gukanshō* it says, "Although Minister of the Center Korechika was deficient in personality and in ability to handle administrative affairs, he was accomplished in Chinese learning and very good at composing Chinese poems."[156] It is rare to see this usage of *karazae*. It refers to someone who has Chinese learning. All examples of *karazae* found in tales and stories have reference to scholarship.

[245] WRITING THE WORD *TOMI NI* WITH THE GRAPH 早

In the imperial edict in the thirteenth volume of *Sandai jitsuroku*, we find **tomi ni tumi nafe tamafazu** (hurriedly punish him and do not bestow [anything on him]). This graph 早 should be read *tomi ni* (quickly, in haste). This word fits very well in this context. Texts that have it glossed as *tuto ni* (early in the morning) have it wrong.

[250] ON KANDE KŌJI

"Through the street of 勘解小路" is glossed as *kande kōji* in *Ōkagami*.[157]

---

156. My translation is taken from Brown and Ishida (1979:56).

157. This presents a slight problem. As the editors of *Motoori Norinaga* note, the various manuscripts of *Ōkagami* have 勘解小路 glossed as *kade no kōdi*. They do not know of any

[257] ON REARING A CHILD SAFELY

In *Eiga monogatari*, in the "Separation of the Brothers" chapter it says, "If you can manage to rear him safely, he will be ruler for all under heaven."[158] To put this into the vernacular of the present, we say "celebrate the oldest being secure," which is the same meaning.

[259] SABURŌ

In *Genhō ryōiki*,[159] there is a section where a man of the Fumi Imiki family is said to have been given the nickname of Ueda Saburō (上田三郎). This event occurred in the reign of Emperor Shōmu,[160] so the name can be dated back to that period, and *azana* is the same as what is known today as a nickname.

[260] ON THE WORDS *FOKASU* AND *FIKI*

In the vernacular, people say *fokasu* to mean discarding something, a word that also appears in *Ochikubo monogatari*,[161] as *fofokasitamafu*. In the same tale, we see where, "Shōnagon ... came because she had a connection with the Lady Ben."[162] This usage of *fiki* is what we called *fiiki* (be partial to) the present.

---

manuscripts that have *kande* (Yoshikawa et al., 1978:146, headnote). Interestingly, Yamagiwa translates both instances of this name as "Kande Kōji" (1967:64, 170), but he does not mention which text he is using.

158. I have slightly modified the translation of the McCulloughs (1980, vol. 1:210), as they translated 一天下の君にこそおはしますめれ as "he will sit on the throne." Norinaga's text only has 一天の君, lacking 下.

159. The full title is *Nihonkoku genhō zen'aku ryōiki*, believed to have been compiled sometime around the beginning of the Heian era, perhaps as early as 822. It was compiled by a Buddhist Bonze named Keikai, who served at Yakushiji. It contains many stories and tales, most belonging to the Nara era.

160. Emperor Shōmu (701–756) reigned from 724 till 749. He was born the eldest son of Emperor Monmu.

161. *Ochikubo monogatari*: A tale of unknown authorship, though some believe it to be the work of Minamoto Shitagau. Written some time at the end of the tenth century, it is one of the oldest examples of a Cinderella-type story, in which a maiden is harassed by her stepmother.

162. Slightly altered version of Yanagisawa and Whitehouse (1965:142). They translated *fiki* as "on the recommendation of," but *fiki* here means to "have a connection to" someone.

[261] THE WAY OF POETRY AND CHERRY BLOSSOMS

The label "the Way of Shikishima" or "the Way of poetry" is commonly used in the present, but if you read the preface to *Kokinshū*, it says, "In that (Nara) era everyone understood the spirit of *waka* ... " or "Here people understood things of ancient times or the spirit of *waka* ... ," or "Though Hitomaro has passed on, *waka* will remain with us." If these things were in a record from a later era then it would have certainly included the words "the Way of poetry" (*waka*), but here it refers to the *spirit* of *waka* or things related to *waka*. It does not mention a "Way." In the "Mana" [Chinese] preface of the same anthology, it does mention "this Way" or "our Way," but in the "Kana" preface, there is no reference at all to a "Way."

Now when we speak of cherry blossoms it is customary to run it together as one word, *sakurabana*, but in *Kokinshū* whenever it appears in a head note, it is always *sakura no fana*, with the connecting *no*. Examples of *sakurabana* always occur in the poems, and never in the prose. Therefore, when one composes poetry or writes prose in imitation of the ancient past, he should take care to recognize this kind of distinction. One should remember that there is a distinction between Chinese and Japanese writing, as well as being sensitive to the changes that have taken place in poetry and in prose. Regarding this, every time I read *Kokinshū* this causes me to be a little more careful in my own work.

[265] *KYŌKA*

Kyōka [mad poetry] is mentioned in the first chapter of *Honchō monzui*,[163] in the small preface attached to a poem by Minamoto Shitagau. However, this is a Chinese poem and is not the same as what we call *kyōka* in the present.

---

163. *Honchō monzui*: Originally compiled in imitation of *Wenxuan*, this work of Chinese poetry arranged by category was compiled by Fujiwara no Akihira (989–1066) sometime between 1058 and 1064.

5 ~ THE EULALIA OF KARENO 147

[266] SHŌYA

In the provinces in present-day society, the village headman is called *shōya*. In an official order dated the thirteenth day of the third month of the second year of Engi (902) as found in volume two of *Honchō monzui* it says, "Estate houses were newly established, with many subject to the strict provisions of the law." This also appears in *Ruijū sandaikaku*,[164] and these are chiefs of the territory. The government set up organizations called estate houses, and these were caused to govern that specific area.

[267] CONCERNING THE OBJECT CALLED *FATA NO KAZARI*

At present the object called *fata no kazari* (decoration of a loom) is seen under the entry of "loom" in *Wamyōshō*. There is the line "the place where one skillfully pulls the strings" and this is glossed as **wakaduri**. This name mentioned above is a corruption of this **wakaduri**. In the present edition of *Wamyōshō*, it has 和加豆和 **wakaduwa**, but this last 和 is a mistake for 利. Older manuscripts have 利.

[268] VARIOUS PLACE NAMES IN EDO

Priest Sōgi recorded the following in *Kaikoku zakki*,[165]

On the following day I left Asakusa and headed toward Nippa, and while on the way as I was visiting various

---

164. *Ruijū sandaikaku*: A compilation of legal regulations, compiler unknown. The work appears to have been completed sometime in the eleventh century. It originally was compiled in thirty volumes, but over time parts of the manuscript have been lost, and now it is only preserved in two witnesses, one in twenty volumes and another in twelve volumes. It is a catalog of previous regulations, organized by subject. It includes regulations from the three reigns of Kōnin (810-823), Jōkan (859-876), and Engi (901-922).

165. Interestingly, *Kaikoku zakki* was not written by Sōgi, but by Dōkō (1430-1527). It is a geographical work, recording various place names in Japan.

famous places I stopped on a hill called Bi Hill, and rested in the shade of a tree in a pine grove.

simo no noti	After the frost
arafarenikeri	had appeared
sigure woba	then there was the drizzle.
sinobi no oka no	The pines on "wait it out" hill
matu mo kafi nasi	were of no use to me.

After passing here we arrived at Koisi River .... When we arrived at Torikoe Village ... we arrived at the Bay of Siba.

Pondering the places along the path, the place he called Sinobi Hill sounds like a locale on present-day Mount Tōei. Thinking about it, perhaps the place Sinobazu Pond came from Sinobi Hill.

[270] *TIKUSIYAU*

Presently people say in jest, "You are a bastard" (*tikusiyau* > *chikushō*) to parents or children, or to any other relative. Even in China, during the reign of Emperor Wen of Sui, Crown Prince Guang tried to woo Lady Chen [wife of Wen], and when Emperor Wen heard of this he was greatly angered and said, "That bastard! Why did I ever entrust such an important task to him [to be the heir]?"

[271] *FUTON*

In the present people call the thing that you spread out on the floor and sleep in *futon*. Anciently people would use a simple cloth, written 布単 *futan* (a measure of cloth), or sometimes written 布毯 *futan* (cloth blanket). The word *futon* is a corruption of this.

5 ~ THE EULALIA OF KARENO   149

[273] THE POEM IN *ISE MONOGATARI*

There is the poem:

ifama yori	From between the boulders
ofuru mirume si	the sea pine continually grows—
turenaku fa	Unchanging as the tide of the sea
sifo fi sifo miti	if we continue to see each other
kafi mo arinamu	perhaps there will be some value.[166]

The meaning of this poem is, "If there is no change in our seeing each other, at any rate in the end there will have been some value to it." It is speaking of meeting the man again. The fourth stanza means "at any rate." The connection of *mirume* is "seeing eyes" but also "sea pine," a reference to seaweed in the ocean. No one has been able to understand the fourth stanza because people are tripped up by the words.

[274] THE *MANA* EDITION OF *ISE MONOGATARI*, PART ONE

Among the editions of *Ise monogatari* is one called the *Manabon*,[167] a text written in imitation of the writing style of *Man'yōshū*, so it is written in *mana* [Chinese characters]. It has been said from the beginning that this is the work of Prince Rokujō,[168] but if you examine the text, wondering if this is actually the work of the prince, you realize it is not his work, but a later fabrication. Foremost, the use of the graphs to represent each sound is very crude and haphazard. There are many places where it is hard to

---

166. This poem appears in *dan* 75 of *Ise monogatari*, and is generally believed to have been corrupted over time, because the meaning is not readily apparent currently.
167. The text is actually written in *man'yōgana*, a phonetic script. Tradition assigns authorship of the text to Prince Tomohira (964–1009), a son of Emperor Murakami. He is also called Prince Rokujō. His authorship of this text, however, is far from certain.
168. Perhaps this points to Prince Masanari (1200–1255), the younger brother of Emperor Juntoku. He was actually raised by Princess Kinshi in a palace called Rokujō Palace. He was called by that name.

understand the meaning. For example, *kurau* (darkness) is transcribed as 苦労 (hardship), or *oyobi no ti* (blood of the fingers) is transcribed as 及後 (and then later) and so forth. These kinds of usages are word association puzzles and there are examples like this in *Man'yōshū*. "East" (*aduma*) is transcribed as 熱間 (*atuma*) and "so on and so forth" (*ni keri*) is transcribed as 逃利 (*nigeri*), so the author has confused voiced and voiceless syllables. These kinds of errors are permissible, but when the text has *nan* (particle) and the writer uses 何 *nan* (what), or when the text has *zo* (*kakari musubi* particle), the author uses 社 *zo* (society) or 諾 (agree) for the particle *to*—these choices are very difficult to fathom. But this is not all.

Words like *omoferu* (thinking) are spelled 思恵流 (*omoeru*), or *tamafe* (give) as 給江 (*tamae*). Also when a word has the particle *fe* as in *koko fe* (this way) or *kasiko fe* (to way over there), the author writes all of these with 江 (*e*), and when double particles are used, like in *mi wo mo* (also to me) or *kore wo ya* (this), where the direct object marker *wo* is used with the inclusive *mo*, or the direct object marker *wo* is used with *ya*, the author writes these as 面 (*omo*, face) or 親 (*oya*, parent), or when *wasure* (forget) is transcribed as 者摺 (*fasure*).[169] These kinds of spelling errors are rarely made by well-versed poets even in the present, so errors of this kind demonstrate that the author was horrible at understanding how to write. I view this as the work of a forger, so it is difficult to accept any of the graphs in this edition.

While this is the case, looking at the [spelling of] words in this edition, compared with the known editions in the present, we find that there are strengths and weaknesses with each. It does appear that *kana* was later converted to a Chinese [rebus] script. Therefore, even now this is one edition that should be available [for research]. Regardless, there is one thing that is very difficult to comprehend. When my teacher, Master Agatai, expounded on *Ise monogatari* he

---

169. The issue of spelling errors, and when the change had occurred in the vernacular of society, is difficult to date precisely, but Martin (1987:79) provides a rough-and-ready chart, based on a number of texts. According to these data, the phonological changes and mergers that result in the kinds of spelling errors that Norinaga brings up had all occurred by the eleventh century, which still matches the dating of the author, Prince Rokujō.

5 ~ THE EULALIA OF KARENO   151

called all the *kana* manuscripts modern works, and labeled them all bad, but he called this *mana* edition an "old work" and lathered praise on it. He used it, saying it was wholly worthy, so what are we to make of his quoting from this edition as a testimony of correct usages when it is such a worthless text? In addition, while he talked so much of ancient *kana* usages, the usages in this edition rarely match those of the ancient era. How could he not notice that the *kana* spellings in this edition are horribly confused and very clumsy with what is in the world?[170] There are sections here and there that cannot be understood.

Now lately there is a certain person who has published a variant *mana* edition that is labeled "an old text." The basis of this text quite surpasses that of the others, being full of graphs that are difficult for people since the establishment of the present capital to understand. Regardless, this is not an authentically old manuscript. In the final analysis, this is the publisher's own work. I can declare this because first, manuscripts presently in the capital employ graphs without any distinction between voiced and voiceless syllables. However, this manuscript attempts to distinguish between voiced and voiceless syllables without any confusion, which suggests it must be someone who appeared after the recent emergence of the study of ancient things or they could not create this. Also the creator writes about the five "syllables" (五言) *ka-ki-tu-ba-ta* at the beginning of a stanza. If the author had been someone from the ancient past, he would have called these the five *mozi* (characters). An allusion in poetry is called *waka* glossed as *kafesi*, while "waterfall" is written *tagi*, and the eleventh day of the month is written *towo marito fi*. These types of [mis-] spellings are only created by those of today who study the ancient words, and while the forms are fine, they do not represent the form of the story as it should be if it was from the ancient past. It is the product of someone who has not thought about the flavor or character of the specific era. "Eleventh day" and other words would have been

---

170. The *Mana-bon* text appears to be an amalgamation. Structurally it is close to the *Teika-bon* manuscripts, but an examination of the actual sentences makes it fairly clear that it was transcribed, likely from a manuscript belonging to the newer branch of manuscripts called 広本系 (Kōhonkei) (Katagiri 1968:391–95).

written 十一日 and not spelled out in a story from the past, and even if the author had written in a more elegant style he would have certainly written *towoka amari fi to fi*. Letting the *a-* of *amari* elide here is the work of students of the ancient past. Also ignoring the *ka* (day) in *towoka* demonstrates that, as we might expect, this student of the ancient past does not understand the ancient language well enough.

In addition, in the section "*utu no yama*"[171] in the orthodox manuscripts where it has "they met a monk" (with *afitari* in *kana*) this manuscript has 仁逢有 (*ni afitari*); adding the particle *ni* shows the creator does not know the elegant speech of the old language. This text is the sophistry of someone in the present with a crude mind. These kinds of errors are mixed in here and there, and the text is filled with fabrications.

[275] THE *MANA* EDITION OF *ISE MONOGATARI*, PART TWO

The reason that the historical spellings in the *Manabon* version of *Ise monogatari* are so confused is not simply due to mistakes. There are even people who argue that the work contains mischievous writings, and we should not trust the historical spellings, because these inform us that we also should not be obsessed with those spellings, because the spellings were purposely muddled up. This is not necessarily the case. However, if such were the case it would be strange and very uninteresting. Some people in later eras have examined all the historical spellings and tried to correct these after the spellings have become confused. In addition, those who do not trust the spellings and argue that we should not be obsessed with these means that we already know what should be corrected and have done so, and this again is something that people do in later times.[172]

---

171. In *dan* nine.
172. Norinaga is arguing that in the early Heian era when *Ise monogatari* was written, the spellings were correct. So the confusion in spellings came about later, as people tried to

[280] THINGS I WANT TO SAY ABOUT READING *ISE MONOGATARI*, PART ONE

The line in the opening section of *Ise monogatari*, "The hunting robes worn by a man ... " has a *no* right after the subject "man," which is incorrect.[173] The *mana* edition lacks *no*, which is correct. As for referring to a man, when composed in poetry regarding this or that, it will refer to the woman's actions.

In the section where there is the poem "Isn't the moon the same moon as in the past," we have the line *foi nifa arade*, a string of words that do not make sense.[174] The *mana* edition has this written as 穂には, which is not satisfactory. It says *fo nifa idezu* "It did not appear on his countenance." Words such as *fo nifa arade* do not sound right.

Regarding mistakes in characters, the line *utu no yama*[175] has the clause "*wa ga iramu to suru miti fa ito kurau fosoki ni, tuta kafede fa sigerite ...* " (The path that they were about to embark on was very dark and narrow, plus it is overgrown with vines and maple trees). The *fa* after *kafede* should be regarded as a particle [and not as leaf]. This *fa* is used in combination with *fa* after *miti* mentioned above, and in this way functions as a contrastive. A poem in *Kokinshū* has three of these [case marker] *fa*:

aki fa kinu	Autumn has come.
momidi fa yado ni	The crimson leaves cover
furisikinu	the ground around my dwelling.
miti fumi wakete	There are no visitors
tofu fito fa naki	to tread through and open the path.
	(KKS 287)

---

correct what they *perceived* were spelling errors, because their vernacular had changed and it no longer matched the earlier spellings.

173. Norinaga is correct, as most witnesses of *Ise monogatari* simply have "*wotoko kitarikeru ...* " without *no*, but the complete manuscript (which is generally used as the critical text) has a *no* here, which should be interpreted as a nominative case marker, but then it is difficult to understand what the meaning of the sentence is.

174. This appears in *dan* four. Modern scholars still struggle with this line, but interpret it to mean, "He did not intend to have feelings for her ... ," based on the assumption that *foi* is 本意 (intention), where *fon'i* elides to *foi*.

175. In *dan* nine.

There are many examples like these. The *mana* edition transcribes this *fa* as "leaf," and if you interpret the line that way, it renders it into a ridiculous sentence.[176]

There is the poem *kimi ga tame / taworeru eda fa* (The branch I broke for you ...).[177] The meaning of this poem is "Reflecting the depth of my feelings for you, while it is still spring, the leaves on this branch are deeply colored as if it were autumn." In the various commentaries, the commentators have been tripped up by the word *aki* (autumn), and I wonder about the appropriateness of interpreting this to reflect the change in the feelings of the woman. There is nothing unusual about the poem the woman sends back in reply. There is also nothing in the story to suggest that we should be suspicious about the intentions of the woman.

Then there is the poem *idete inaba / kokoro karosi to* (If I were to leave here [people would] say I was a woman of shallowness ...).[178] The reference to "leave" here is usually interpreted as being from the woman, but the context makes it difficult to determine whether it was the man or the woman. The text has "then something trivial happened," which should refer to the woman. After this poem, it then says "this woman," which does not make sense. It does not make any sense to have the woman appear again here. This should be the man and not the woman. Now because of the vagueness of the text, one person has suggested that the woman did not leave; the man did. However, the description here for the reason of the breakup does not make any sense if we make it the man. And if the subject is the man, it matches well with the words "this woman," but it does not work, because right after the poem "Is that person thinking of me?" it says, "It had been a long time and this woman ... ." The words "this woman" fits here, because it is not the man who is the referent.

In the poem *tutu widutu ... imo mizaruma ni* (The round well ... I want to see you as a grown up) should be *imo ga mizaruma*

---

176. Mabuchi, in his *Ise monogatari koi*, falls into this trap. He takes the graph at face value, and says that the sentence should be interpreted to mean that the path is overgrown with maple leaves.
177. This appears in *dan* 20.
178. This appears in *dan* 21.

ni.[179] There is no need for *ni* if the direct object marker comes after *imo*. Because the previous stanza mentions the man's own height, we know that he is talking about the woman having grown up. Now later in this section we have the words, "That woman looked in the direction of Yamato" and the man from Yamato came back to enjoy the well, so we know that these events are placed in Yamato. Therefore, in the beginning it should say something like, "A long time ago in Yamato Province," instead of just, "A long time ago a man living in a rural area," which certainly makes me think this is a person originally from the capital. The words "The woman gladly waited for him, but each time it came to nothing" are lacking something. Because the clause *matu ni* (waits for) refers to a one-time event, having the words *tabi tabi sugi* (with the passing of each time) leaves the sentence unbalanced. Thus, it should say, "The woman gladly waited for him but he did not come. And each time she waited ... ."

The line "A long time ago a man lived in a slightly rural area"[180] is correct in the *mana* edition, where it says, "A long time ago a man *and a woman* ... ." It makes no sense as the next line mentions the man and how he longs for the woman, if there is no woman mentioned in the beginning. I wonder what the first two stanzas of the poem *adusa yumi / mayumi tuki yumi* (a catalpa bow, a sandalwood bow, a zelkova bow) mean, because it does not make sense to me.[181] Furthermore, the *mana* edition transcribes this as 神言忠令見 *ga goto urufasi mise yo* (show me your intimate feelings ...), but because these are simply rebus graphs, it is a very crude way to transcribe this part of the poem. The end

---

179. This appears in *dan* 23. There are some texts that only have *tutu wi tu*, which makes little sense here. Norinaga has relied upon a variant tradition, but the poem and its interpretation are still problematic. Katagiri et al. (1994:136, n. 2) wonder if the *no* in the critical text is the product of scribal error.
180. This starts *dan* 24.
181. In *Seigo okudan*, Keichū interprets this as, "A man takes a bow in his hand, so there are many examples in ancient poetry where this is used as a metaphor for a woman." Mabuchi comments in *Ise monogatari koi*, "Here the bow is made to sound in preparation for the situation of coming before the gods and making a vow. The man says, 'Show me the beautiful token of my beloved's divine words.' These are words he used to pray to the deities at that time."

of the poem means: "As I have shown you my intimate feelings in the past, now show this present fellow your intimate feelings."

I have discussed the circumstances surrounding the poem *miru me naki / wa ga mi wo* (I who have no good qualities ... "[182] in *Kokinshū no tookagami*, but it does not go well with the end of the last stanza when placed here ... .

[281] THINGS I WANT TO SAY ABOUT READING *ISE MONOGATARI*, PART TWO

Among the various tales, *Ise monogatari* is interesting, with wonderful diction, a tale loved by many in society, but there are a number of places where it is difficult to comprehend the meaning here and there, perhaps because of scribal error in transmission by a later person. If you try to interpret these sections, then you end up with ridiculous readings. In addition, we should not criticize those places where the story deviates from the truth, because it is all a work of fiction anyway. Rather we should appreciate the work on its own merits, because of its skillful telling of the tale, and its ability to assist people in composing poetry and writing sentences in the vernacular.[183] In a few instances, the poetry in the tale is dreadful beyond expression, so one should read the tale with that in mind. Among the many commentaries on the tale, those worthy of note include Keichū's *Okudan* and my master's *Ise monogatari koi*, but both have their strengths and weaknesses. There are also a great number of places where you will likely wonder if the argument is correct. I also noticed a number of things when I read the tale, and have wanted to write these down in detail, but I have been busy and have not been able to find the time, and now I find that I cannot achieve that goal [of writing a commentary], which is a pity. Therefore, I decided to select a number of points and comment on them, which I have already done.

---

182. This appears in *dan* 25.
183. As opposed to writing in classical Chinese, which is what educated males knew.

[282] THE LAST WORDS OF NARIHIRA ASON

In *Kokinshū* it says, "A poem composed by Narihira no Ason[184] when he had fallen ill and was frail:

tufi ni yuku	I have heard people
miti to fa kanete	say that men must proceed down
kikisikado	this path after all.
kinofu kefu to fa	And yet I never dreamed that my turn
omofazarisi wo	would be yesterday or today."

(KKS 861)

Keichū says the following about this, "This is the true state of the human heart, and this poem is a model example for instruction. In later ages, when people were on their deathbeds, they composed poems of exaggerated sorrow, or poems about having obtained enlightenment regarding death; however, there is no truth to these poems, and they are all displeasing. In regular circumstances, it is fine for a person to put nonsense or unduly ornate words into his poetry, but when the person meets his end, it would be nice if the poet would for once be sincere. The sum of the sincerity in the life of Narihira is seen in this last poem, but later poets all depart from this world showing us that their lives have been one continual round of deception."

These words are not the words of a priest, but are truly precious gems. Even a Buddhist priest, if endowed with the pure Japanese spirit, can become worthy like Keichū. A person following in the path of Shintō or poetics who is adorned with the Chinese Heart could never say something like this. The priest Keichū taught the world about truth, but those who follow the [current] path of Shintō and poetics teach the world lies.

---

184. Ariwara no Narihira (825–880) was a famous poet, and some believe him to be the basis for the hero in *Ise monogatari*.

[283] MITI NO KUNI MUTU

The province of Mutu, as recorded in poetry, is read *mitinoku*, and in *Wamyōshō* it is spelled **mitinooku** and means the place in the deep interiors of the path, so when we add the graph "province," it should be called *mitinoku no kuni*. However, in tales and stories from the Middle Ages they only call it "Miti no kuni," shortening the name, because of the bothersome repetition of *noku*. Later the province was called Mutu, which is a corruption of *miti no kuni*. Because the graph 陸 (dry land) was a substitute for 六 (six),[185] and as people used these two interchangeably for *mutu*, this is how the alternative name came to be. However, anciently they did not call the place Miti no kuni or just Miti. Calling the province just Mutu in the present is a terrible custom that has lost the original form.

[284] ON THE GRAPH 和 IN THE NAME IZUMI (和泉)

In response to the question of why the graph 和 is used in the provincial name 和泉 (Izumi), what the reasons were for adding it,[186] this has bothered me for years, and as I have pondered this, it seems to me that first *izumi* appears as the name of a district 和泉郡, and there is an Upper Izumi Village and a Lower Izumi Village, so there is no argument that the name came from here. Thus in the territory of this village is a hamlet called Fuchū (府中), which has a place called the "well of Izumi," and it has splendidly pure water. In that place there is Izumi no Wi no Ufe (Upper Izumi Well Shrine), Izumi Shrine and others. These also appear in the list of shrines in *Engi shiki*.

---

185. As most numbers in Japan and China are composed of only a few strokes, in order to prevent changes when money is involved, other homophonous graphs have been used. In the case of six 六, the graph 陸 was substituted. This was well-known to the Japanese, so Norinaga is arguing that the confusion in the name originated from a graphic and homophonic usage.

186. *Izumi* means "spring," which is what the graph 泉 represents. So the question is why add another graph, which contributes nothing to the name?

5 ~ THE EULALIA OF KARENO

In spite of this, *Izumi-shi,* which is written by Mr. Namikawa,[187] mentions the well of Izumi, and considering that it describes the water of the well as pure and delicious, this water has been pure and delicious since the ancient period, so it was called *nigi izumi* (soft fountain) and written 和泉 (soft fountain), but the people of the locale only called it Izumi, which spread, and as the water is renowned, even people in the capital learned to call it Izumi, so that the district name also became the provincial name, and as the tradition was to write all toponyms with two graphs, the graphs always referred to the original name, so they wrote it as 和泉. The province of Yamato also is always pronounced in speech as *yamato,* but when written in graphs, the graph "large" 大 is always attached, so when we write 大和 this is analogous to the two graphs used for Izumi. I believe, however, that the character 和 was included because originally people called it *nigi izumi.*

---

187. Namikawa Seisho (1668–1738) was a student of Itō Jinsai. He was not only a Confucian scholar but also studied geography. He is known for compiling a geographical work on the Kinai area, titled *Go Kinai-shi,* in sixty-one volumes. He finished it in 1734 and published it in Ōsaka in 1735.

6 | COCKSCOMB

In one of my poems I had composed "plucking the crimson blossom / of the cockscomb." A certain individual said, "Anciently this was composed using *kurenawi no*,[188] and not as *karaawi no*. Why not compose it thus?" I responded that in *Man'yōshū* we find poems with both examples of *kurenawi no* and *karaawi no*. Now there is a theory that *kurenawi* refers to something that came over from China, and this word is a contracted form of *kure no awi*, while *karaawi* is something that was brought over from Kara [on the peninsula], and is sometimes spelled 韓藍 (Han, indigo). However, *kara* is a general name for foreign countries to the west of us; if it points to China, then the word is the same thing as *kurenawi*.

In spite of that, in Book 11 of *Man'yōshū* we find 鶏冠草 (cockscomb grass) glossed as **karaawi**, and some interpret this to be *tukikusa* (spiderwort), or *keitouge* (cockscomb flower). There are many confusing theories, but it is incorrect to interpret these as "spiderwort" or "cockscomb flower." There is no doubt that these refer to *kurenawi*, so I am told that *karaawi* means "a crimson flower," and that is why I included it in the poem. Let me add that in Book 7 of *Man'yōshū* there is the following poem:

aki saraba	When autumn comes
utusi mo semu to	I will use you even as dye
wa ga makisi	that cockscomb that I planted.
karaawi no fana wo	Has someone gone and
tare ka tumikemu	plucked the blossoms? (MYS 1362)

188. *Kurenawi* means crimson, perhaps based on something loaned from Koguryŏ (*kure*), as the word is likely composed of *kure no awi* (indigo from Koguryŏ), while *karaawi* is likely "Kara indigo."

Here **utusi** is a dye, and the graph 移 (to transfer) is miscopied as 影 (shadow) in the original text, at which point the person nodded in agreement with my argument and did not ask any further questions. The poem I composed was:

karaawi no	Like the crimson flower
sufe tumu fana no	of the safflower
sufe tufi ni	I try to hide my deepest feelings
iro ni ya iden	but I cannot endure it—
sinobikaneteba	it has likely appeared on my face.

I composed this on the topic "Showing one's feelings through herbs." Perhaps there will be people who will criticize me because this poem closely resembles the one in *Kokinshū*:

wa ga kofi wo	As I cannot endure
sinobikaneteba	this longing for you
asibiki no	I will display the color
yama tatibana no	of the orange on the mountains
iro ni inu besi	that cause one's legs to cramp.

(KKS 668)

[287] WHEN ONE COPIES DOWN A MANUSCRIPT

When one is copying a manuscript, it often happens that when there is the same word twice in the same line, or in neighboring lines, the copyist makes a mistake and leaves out the words in between.[189] Also, there is the mistake of accidentally turning two leaves together, when you thought it was just one leaf; this means that your copy ends up skipping one page of the original. One must be careful of such mistakes.

Also, one must be careful to copy the characters correctly and not mistake two characters that look alike. This does not only apply to copying manuscripts, but one must be careful anytime he undertakes to write something. Since we write to convey meaning

---

189. This is called haplography.

to someone else, the writer should strive to write clearly. There are many instances where writers show off their calligraphy skills, making the passage almost unreadable. This is meaningless.

Even in letters and memos in daily life, if you do not write legibly, then your message hits a dead end, and the reader must expend great energy to figure out what you wrote. He tilts his head and reads it repeatedly. When a passage is unclear, then he must come back to you: "I can't read this." You may think it is indeed rude to ask, but forcing the reader to guess at the meaning will only lead to more mistakes.

[288] ON PENMANSHIP

Above all else, it is nice to be able to write beautifully. When people who compose poems or do research have terrible handwriting, it makes their work look bad. The attitude that it makes no difference if one's handwriting is poor is reasonable on the surface, but it leaves much to be desired, and is not a fitting attitude for such a person.

My own handwriting is atrocious and I feel great regret every time I pick up a brush, and when people ask me to write anything, I become impudent and write one sheet of *tanzaku*. Having written something, I stare at my work and think how terrible my handwriting is. If I feel this way, how do others view my poor writing? This brings me shame and sorrow. I often wonder why I did not spend more time on my handwriting when I was younger.

[289] CONCERNING THE *TUKI YA ARANU* POEM BY NARIHIRA ASON

The poem

tuki ya aranu	Is it not the same moon?
faru ya mukasi no	Is it not the same spring as anciently?
faru naranu	But it is not the same spring.
wa ga mi fitotu fa	My body is one and the same,
moto no mi ni site	but things are not the same. (KKS 747)

has been interpreted in a variety of ways by many people, but their interpretations are bothersome, and they have not captured the significance of the poem. If I were to give my own impressions of this poem that I have gleaned from my own study, [I would say that] the two particles *ya* [after *tuki* "moon" and *faru* "spring"] are to be interpreted as *ya fa*, meaning that both the moon and spring have not changed from the previous year. Thus, the meaning of this one poem is, "The moon is not the same moon as before, and yet it is the same moon. Spring is not the same spring as before and yet it is the same spring. In spite of this, my body is still one and the same, but it is not the same as before."

"Anciently" refers to having seen his lover in the past. The words *moto no mi* refer to his body when he was seeing the woman. Now the words *mi ni site* mean "while it is still my body" and are an abbreviated segment, but include the significance that his body is not the same as it was last year. The *ni site* reflects an emphasis on the upper stanzas, in contrast to where it said that the moon and spring are still the same, and you can naturally understand that it contains that inference. Perhaps the poem of Narihira was one source for Tsurayuki's criticism as seen in the preface to *Kokinshū*, where he said, "There is an abundance of meaning but a dearth of words." In *Ise monogatari* before the poem the text notes, "He went to [Fifth Avenue] and stood there looking, sat there looking, but the scene did not feel the same as last year." This illustrates that this inference is included in the poem. The idea that things are not the same as last year does not mean that the moon and spring have changed, but that the feelings inside him as he gazes at the scene have changed.

In the miscellaneous poems of *Shin Kokinshū*, there is a poem composed by Kiyowara Fukayabu:

mukasi misi	While the spring
faru fa mukasi no	that I beheld a long time ago
faru nagara	is still the same spring
wa ga mi fitotu no	my body is not one and the same
arazu mo aru kana	though they are. (SKKS 1450)

It is as if this poem has commented on the meaning of Narihira's poem. This poem has well understood the import of his poem.

[298] CONCERNING SOGA NO UMAKO

Gukanshō records,[190]

Why was it that when Emperor Sushun was assassinated by Great Minister Soga no Umako, the great minister was not censured in the least, but this act was treated as a good deed? Even people in ancient times thought [this kind of treatment] was odd. People in the present also should understand this. In the land of Japan anciently there generally are no examples of the king of the country being put to death. And the country was founded on the principle that this [type of behavior] should not occur. But on the contrary this king and Emperor Ankō were assassinated.

The assassination of Ankō by Prince Mayuwa who was seven years old is allowable as he, the prince, was soon put to death afterward .... The assassination of Sushun ... without Umako receiving the least punishment and [he was] allowed to go free. Among those in power was Crown Prince Shōtoku, so why did the crown prince not do anything, but in the end united his intentions with Umako? It is something society could not comprehend ...

Thinking deeply about this event the important point is that Buddhist law exists to protect imperial law. And these events took place to demonstrate the principle that when Buddhist law permeates society imperial law cannot exist without Buddhist law. In the logic of things, when there is something of significance and something of insignificance, people should adhere to the significant thing and discard the insignificant .... This Great Minister Umako clearly was a model official who converted to Buddhism. When Sushun, who had not even the slightest virtue, but had ascended the throne as king only because he was the princely son of Kinmei, was about to put this great minister to death, Great Minister Umako who had

---

190. The editor of the *Tamakatsuma* notes that the version of *Gukanshō* that Norinaga relied on was not very good, being full of errors (Yoshikawa et al., 1978:177, headnote).

power because of his belief in Buddhism, realized he was about to be killed so he [acted defensively and] killed the king .... It is also possible that [the assassination] adhered to principle in that it also followed the inclination of Suiko.

To this Norinaga responds: this theory irrationally sets up Buddhist law as something superior, and demonstrates the extreme errors in the world from among things in this way. It is exceedingly trivial and wrong.

[302] THE SPOKEN TITLE OF GOKYŌGOKU

The [title of] Regent Gokyōgoku is usually pronounced with the character 後 pronounced *go*, but in *Gukanshō* quoted above, it is written with *no* between the graph and the rest as Go [*Noti?*] *no Kyōgoku*.[191]

[303] A BIOGRAPHY OF MASTER AGATAI

Master Agatai was a descendant of the Kamo Agatai Nushi family, and his distant ancestor is Kamo Taketsunomi, a descendant of the deity Kami-musubi. The story that he turned into the Yata crow and guided Emperor Jinmu appears in *Shinsen shōjiroku*.[192] The posterity of this deity resided at the Kamo Shrine in Sagara District of Yamasiro Province. One of these descendants, a person named [Kataoka] Morotomo, received an edict in the eleventh year of Bun'ei (1274) to serve in the newly built Kamo Shrine in Okabe Village of the Famamatu territory in Sikiti District of Tofotafumi Province. He was granted possession of this village

---

191. Suggesting that perhaps the *Gukanshō* record intended the title to be pronounced as *Noti no Kyōgoku* instead of *Gokyōgoku*.

192. *Shinsen shōjiroku*: This is a register of families within the capital and the five capital provinces, arranging the various lineages into one of three categories: imperial lineage, divine lineage, and foreign families. It was compiled by a committee headed by Prince Manda, son of Emperor Kanmu. It was completed in 814, but all that survives is an abbreviated version.

6 ~ COCKSCOMB 167

and became the head priest at the new shrine. These events are recorded in a work called *Hikima gusa*,[193] and it contains a copy of the document containing the edict. Furthermore, in the first year of Kengen (1302), the family received another edict and they were granted the land of Okabe. There is an official copy of the edict in possession of the family.

Thus, they have served as priests at the Kamo Shrine in long succession. Masasada, a grandfather to the great master in the fifth generation, achieved military valor in the battle of Fikimafara, and he received from Lord Tokugawa Yasukuni a sword fashioned by Rai Kuniyuki and a dragon suit of armor. These events appear in *Mikawaki*.[194]

Now Master Agatai was born in this village of Okabe in the tenth year of Genroku (1697). From the time when he was young, he had interest in studying ancient things, and in the eighteenth year of Kyōhō (1733), he went to the capital and became a student of Kada Ushi no Sukune Azumamaro of Inari. In the third year of Kan'en (1750), he moved to Edo and later served Lord Tayasu. When Lord Tayasu gave him a robe inscribed with a hollyhock design, he wrote a poem:

afufi tefu	The robe with the
aya no onzo wo mo	beautiful hollyhock design—
udibito no	were the servants of the deities
kadukamu mono to	to try and rend it
kami ya siriken	the deities would surely approve.

On the thirteenth day of the tenth month of the sixth year of Meiwa (1769), he passed away at the age of seventy-three. He is buried on a mountain within the precincts of Korin-in, which is within the larger land of Tōkaiji, a temple in Sinagawa of Ebara District of Musasi Province. These events were recorded by one of his students, so I have taken that report and recorded it here. I

---

193. *Fikima gusa*: It is unclear what work this is. Yoshikawa et al. (1978:180) wonder if this was not a private family history written by Mabuchi.
194. *Mikawaki* is a record outlining the events and achievements of members of the Tokugawa family up to Ieyasu.

should also record things about his parents, and since I have left that out of my record, I will ask someone who knows the family well to provide that information, and I intend to write that down also.[195]

[304] CONCERNING THE CRITICISM OF FLOWERS

Of the blossoms, the cherry is wonderful.[196] Within the species of cherry, the mountain cherry has thin, illustrious leaves scattered here and there. When the blossoms are in full bloom, there is nothing with which to compare its beauty, and you believe that its beauty is out of this world. Cherry trees that have green leaves mixed with the blossoms are very exquisite. There are many varieties of cherry trees among the general name of "mountain cherry," and if you look carefully, you will discover subtle changes between the varieties. No two are exactly alike. Presently, there are various beautiful mountain cherries, like Kirigayatu, double-flowered cherry, and the single-flowered cherry.

If you look from the base of the tree up into it on a cloudy day, the color of the blossoms becomes obscured. It is the same with fir trees or any other tree growing luxuriantly, for the white blossoms of the cherry stand out brightly against the green background. On sunny days, looking at the blossoms with the sun behind you, the color stands out in peerless fashion, and it makes you wonder if they are the same blossoms. Of course, the dawn is splendid [for viewing the blossoms].

Evening is beautiful, too; at dusk when the plum is blooming, the beautiful one is the red plum. As the plum blossoms reach their peak of beauty, the petals begin to turn white and it is a shame that at this point they are worthless to look at. Even when the cherry is in bloom, the plum does not realize it is time to scatter, the petals hanging on listlessly, wilting away. Gazing at this sight,

---

195. Norinaga either forgot about this, or never got around to collecting the information, as it does not appear in *Tamakatsuma*.

196. Norinaga is clearly imitating the style of Sei Shōnagon in *Makura no sōshi*. Her work starts off with *faru fa akebono* "As for spring, it is the dawn [that is most beautiful]." Norinaga starts this section off with *fana fa sakura*.

one gets the feeling that this represents the state of aging in the world and that hanging on so late in life is pitiful. I feel this every spring when I see the blossoms. The white blossoms are all very fragrant, but the visible ones are inferior. Plum blossoms bloom from tiny branches, and they are better than viewing them while you are in the treetops.

It is better to gaze at peach blossoms from far away, because they bloom in such numbers. If you observe the peach close up, it looks rustic. Other various varieties of blossoms, like the Japanese yellow rose, rabbit-ear iris, wild pink, Japanese bush clover, eulalia, and Valerianaceae, all have their splendid points. Even a chrysanthemum, if picked at the appropriate time, is nice. If one selects a bold, large flower, it is not elegant, and difficult to enjoy. Azaleas blooming in their splendor in fields or mountains make one doubt one's eyes. The aronia is exotic with minute detail in its beauty.

What I have said above is mainly my own opinion, and others may feel differently about these blossoms, so we should not set down strict guidelines. Also, there are many flowers that people in society enjoy now, and it may seem pretentious not to bring all of them up, but I have little appreciation for those flowers, since they do not appear in poetry or in the ancient records. Perhaps this is one example of a twisted mentality.

[307] A KEY BEING DRAWN IN *TAKARADUKUSI*

In society, we have a type of picture called *takaradukusi*, where people gather as many valuables as they can and draw them. I pondered the reason that some of these portray a key within them, and realized that there is an account in the third year of the reign of Emperor Tenchi. The wife of Ihaki Suguri Oho of the Kurumoto District in Afumi Province went out into the yard when two keys fell from heaven. She took these and gave them to Oho, and for the first time he became wealthy. From this time, keys have been prized in society, and people have even painted them in their pictures.[197]

---

197. Kitamura Nobuyo (1783-1856), a scholar of the Kokugaku movement, criticized this description by Norinaga, saying, "This phenomenon does not go back as far as *Nihon shoki*. Because in all examples, the seven gods of fortune depicted in these pictures are

[308] CONCERNING AN INNER BUDDHA HALL

An imperial edict issued on the twenty-seventh day of the third month of the fourteenth year of Emperor Tenmu (685) says, "In every house in every province let them make a Buddhist temple, and place a statue of the Buddha and a copy of a sutra, and worship and make offerings to these." This is found in *Nihon shoki*. It seems that having an inner Buddha hall[198] to worship the Buddha in the dwelling of every person started at this time.

[309] APPEALING DIRECTLY TO THE FACE OF THE EMPEROR

Shunki records,

On the twenty-second day of the tenth month in the fourth year of Chōryaku (1040), today [the Emperor] moved to the residence of the Interior Minister on Second Avenue … . This evening while on an imperial excursion near the intersection of the Great Eastern Road of Tōin and the Small Road of Kamude, one subordinate of the Usa Shrine [it was a monthly complaint; we had accepted the complaint, but had not yet ruled on its merits], wearing a robe and a cap approached the royal palanquin from the right side. He raised his voice and made an appeal directly to the emperor. It was a rare event. The guards of the right and others were supposed to prevent anyone from following, but they had let their guard down. I was charged with sending the man away. He would have to be stopped.

---

holding these keys in their hands, these are actually depictions of the Sarasvatī holding something, which makes these vital objects within which the power of treasures resides. In *Shiojiri* by Amano [Sadakage] it says, 'The Sarasvatī holds a key in her right hand [which is not a key to a Japanese treasury!], and in her left hand she grasps the seal of knowledge [it is incorrect to say that she is making a treasured pearl]'" ("Intei zatsuroku," Nihon Zuihitsutaisei Henshūbu, 1974:143).

198. I have followed Charles Muller's (2012) "Digital Dictionary of Buddhism" in translating 持仏堂 as "inner Buddha hall."

However, as this was an excursion to move the Emperor to his new residence the guards of the right and left were hesitant to do anything. Thus, they were unable to catch the man. This kind of event is abnormal.

Again,

On the twenty-fifth day of the twelfth month of the same year, there was an imperial excursion to Firano .... This evening while we were returning to the palace, at about a place near Figasi Dōin and Second Avenue, farmers from Izumi Province presented a written paper [of complaint] and raised their voices to utter their complaint ... I wonder why the attendants did not chase them off? This kind of thing has happened from time to time. There is no need to announce the ban again.[199]

It is very rare for someone to go before the awe-inspiring ruler and just voice a petition. The era of Chōryaku was the era of Emperor Go-Suzaku. *Shunki* is the diary of Great Chancellor and Minister Sukefusa.[200]

[311] CONCERNING THOSE WHO CALL SHRINES THE ANCESTRAL TEMPLE AND THE ALTARS OF SOIL AND GRAIN

It is an informal matter of Chinese imitation when people of later ages say with airs of importance that shrines are "ancestral temples" or "altars of soil and grain." Anciently shrines were labeled neither of these. Here and there in *Nihon shoki* and other records the graphs 宗廟社稷 (ancestral temples and altars of soil

---

199. My translation of this entry has been aided, in part, by the French translation of *Shunki* by Hérail (2004:180, 343–45).
200. As Norinaga mentions, *Shunki* is the diary of Fujiwara Sukefusa (1007–1057). The diary is important, not only because of its portrayal of things at court, but also because Sukefusa gives his opinions and criticisms about things in general. The surviving manuscript of this diary includes entries from 1038 to 1054, but there are still some gaps.

and grain) appear, but this is simply embellishment from Chinese records,[201] and originally shrines were not called that. However, the early compilers took these characters and glossed them as *kuni ife*, and this is a gloss from Chinese texts that refers to the state. Now the reason that shrines should not be labeled "temples," is because there is only one example in the province of Tikuzen, the Kasifi Temple, which appears in older documents, separated from other designations. This temple is not included in the list of shrines in *Jinmyōchō*. Now aside from this, there is the temple-shrine of Ofo-obifime in Buzen Province and its origins are explained in Book 30 of *Kojiki-den*. One should read that and think about it.

People called shrines "ancestral temples" or "altars of soil and grain" without tracing the origins of these because they have abandoned the ancient regulations and recklessly follow Chinese tradition. People who expound upon Shintō simply repeat sayings from China. What kind of a mind do they have when they cannot comprehend that this is the same thing as the Buddhist priests who try to entice people by saying that the Shintō deities are actually Buddhist entities?

[312] ON CALLING PEOPLE *JIN*

It may appear to people that calling a person *jin* (仁) is a colloquial usage of recent years, but in a document quoted in *Monzui* from Ōe no Masahira we find, "I apologized and treated that person (其仁) well, and then finally recorded the auspicious event."

[313] EASTERN QUARTER AND WESTERN QUARTER OF THE CAPITAL

The city of Heian was arranged in (two halves), an eastern and western quarter, but from the beginning only the eastern quarter

---

201. 宗廟社稷 (ancestral temples and altars of soil and grain): This designation is quite old, first appearing in *Li ji*. It also appears in *Shiji*, *Hanshu*, and *Hou hanshu*, to which the compilers of *Nihon shoki* clearly had reference.

has prospered, analogous to the present, and the western quarter has not. In Yoshishige no Yasutane's work, *Chiteiki*,[202] it says, "During the last twenty years I have watched both sides of the capital, the east and west. In the western side of the capital, the dwellings of people have gradually become sparse and it is almost like a ghost town. People are leaving the area and none comes to stay. Roofs are falling down and none are being built up."

[315] *YAGI*

The designation of rice as *yagi* (八木, eight trees) is old. In *Shōyūki*, we find examples like "*yagi* ten *koku*" or "*yagi* forty *koku*."[203]

[319] *DAIMYŌ*

In *Shirakawa Akihiro Ōki*,[204] we find during the fourth month of the third year of An'gen (1177) that "the various *daimyō* [feudal lords] did not respond to the request for laborers." It would appear that the title *daimyō* existed during that time.

[321] CONCERNING *KUNI NO MIYATUKO*

What is known as *kuni no miyatuko* were not as large as in the present, but in all aspects they generally were like the *daimyō* [feudal lords], and there were many in the various provinces. Among these there were *kuni no miyatuko* (provincial chieftains), as well as *kimi* (lords), *wake* (provincial officials), *atafe* (peninsular chiefs), *inaki* (rice tax collectors), and *agatanusi* (district chiefs).

---

202. *Chiteiki*: A *zuihitsu* written in Chinese by Yasutane (ca. 1002). It was critical of society, and thus contains a number of descriptions of the capital and how the nobility lived.
203. Yagi (八木): This is a verbal description of the graph 米 (rice), describing it as constructed from the graph 木 (tree) and 八 (eight) inverted.
204. *Shirakawa Akihiro Ōki*: This is the diary of Prince Shirakawa Akihiro (1095–1180). He became the head of the native religion in the government, and this post later became hereditary in the Shirakawa family.

There were a variety of these titles, and while there was a distinction between higher and lower in authority, records that document the criteria for each distinction do not survive. It is difficult to discern which were superior and which were inferior, but in general, these were all like the *kuni no miyatuko*, and so these various provincial officials were all grouped under the title of *kuni no miyatuko*. Now this system closely resembles the system of various titles of nobility found anciently in China during their feudal periods. Those lords were divided into five ranks of honor: duke, marquis, count, viscount, and baron. These five ranks resemble that of the division of the various titles in the *kuni no miyatuko* system. The Chinese took one of these ranks (marquis) and labeled the whole system after it, which is much the same as taking the provincial officials and labeling the whole system *kuni no miyatuko*. Regarding things in China, anyone who studies the culture of that country will know about the five titles of the nobility, but when it comes to the ancient things of our imperial land, there are few who really understand these, and in relation to the *kuni no miyatuko* they do not even know that there were a variety of titles. How can they not know what kind of titles there were among these?

[322] CONCERNING EVENTS OF IFAWI, TUKUSI NO KIMI

Anciently in the land of Tukusi there was a *kuni no miyatuko* called Ifawi,[205] Tukusi no Kimi. This title "kimi" is one of the divisions in the group of *kuni no miyatuko* discussed in the section above. In *Nihon shoki* he is recorded as a *kuni no miyatuko*. However, his son, known as Kuzuko, is recorded as Tukusi no Kimi, so he is truly a *kimi*. During the reign of Emperor Keitai, Ifawi rebelled against the imperial court and lacked any rules of propriety, so the court dispatched a messenger of chastisement who destroyed him. While this Ifawi was alive he had a tomb constructed beforehand. The plans for it to be an unusually

---

205. Ifawi: This name is usually rendered in English as Iwai (石井), but Norinaga includes the gloss イハヰ, so I have spelled the name as Ifawi.

large and dignified tomb are seen in the *Fudoki* of Tikugo Province, which notes, "Upper Tuma District. Two *li* south of the district seat is the tomb of Ifawi, Tukusi no Kimi. It is seven *jō* in height [seventy feet], and six *jō* in diameter [sixty feet]. The area surrounding the tomb is sixty *jō* to the north and south, and forty *jō* to the east and west. It is surrounded on all four sides by sixty stone figures of men and sixty stone shields placed in alternating positions. In the northeast corner there is a separate enclosure, called *gatō*. Inside this is one stone figure standing in a composed manner on the ground. He is called *tokibe*. There is another figure in front of him who is naked, laying face down on the ground, and is called *nusubito*. To the side are four stone boars that are called *zōmoti*. In that area there are also three stone horses, three stone dwellings, and two stone storehouses. An elderly person relates that in the reign of Emperor Ofodo [Keitai], Ifawi, Tukusi no Kimi, was fierce and ruthless and would not become educated in the ways of the imperial throne. While he was alive he had this tomb constructed. The imperial army was suddenly dispatched and tried to attack him, and he realized that there was no way for him to be victorious, so he fled alone to the Upper Mike District in Buzen Province. His life ended between steep peaks in the mountains to the south. The imperial army chased after him there but they had lost his trail. The soldiers were infuriated, so they broke off the hands of the stone figure people, and broke off the heads of the stone horses. The elderly people here relate the tale that the reason so many people become sick in Upper Tuma District is because of this event." …

[325] CONCERNING *MAN'YŌSHŪ* USING THE GRAPHS 義之 TO TRANSCRIBE *TESI*, AND THE WRITING OF 大王 FOR THE SAME

In *Man'yōshū* we have examples where 義之 transcribes **tesi**, as in Book 3 with 我定義之 (**wa ga sadametesi**, that I made my own) (MYS 394), and Book 4 言義之鬼尾 (**ifitesi mono wo,** I have made a promise) (MYS 664), and in Book 7 and Book 12 we find the same phrase 結義之 (**musubitesi,** that has been tied) (MYS 1324, 3028), and in Book 10 we find 織義之 (**oritesi,** that was woven) (MYS 2064) and 逢義之 (**afitesi,** and met) (MYS 1066), and in Book 11 we find 触義之鬼尾 (**furetesi mono wo,** we have touched (MYS 2578). There is no debate about the reading of these two graphs; they should be read **tesi**. However, this is not because the graph 義 (upright, read *gi*) can be read **te**. It is always read **tesi** when used in combination with 之, and there are no examples where 義 alone is used to transcribe **te**. In all cases this graph is a corruption of 羲, which is the name of a Chinese king, 羲之 Xi Zhi. He had a high reputation regarding composition, being someone without parallel, and even in our divine country it was considered auspicious if one had a fragment of his actual writing, and so they called this **tesi** "master of the hand." It is an ancient custom of calling writing "hand," and in *Nihon shoki* when professors of literature are mentioned, they are called **te no fakase** (professors of the hand) or even **te kaki** (hand-writing). You will realize this is true because even within this same *Man'yōshū* there are places where the same **tesi** is transcribed with the graphs 手師 (hand-master).

Now in Books 7 and 11, there are places where **tesi** is transcribed as 大王 (great king), such as 結大王 (**musubitesi,** having tied) (MYS 1321, 2602), and in Book 10 where we have 定大王 (**sadametesi,** having decided) (MYS 2092), and Book 11 言大王 物乎 (**ifitesi mono wo,** the thing that I have said) (MYS 2834). These examples of 大王 also clearly should be read **tesi**. Anciently, however, scribes did not realize [the true reading], and greatly erred when recording the wording. These two graphs are also based on King Xi Zhi, and likewise mean "hand-master." Xi Zhi's son, Wang Xianzhi, also was gifted in writing, so when people spoke of writing, they called this father and son "great king, minor king," and that is how the rebus writing of "great king" came about. Therefore by comparing the name of Xi Zhi and the usage of this label "great king," you may know that both should be read **tesi**, and that these have reference to Xi Zhi.

Now Master Agatai's own commentary says that these should

6 ~ COCKSCOMB 177

be read **tesi** because 義 is a mistake for 篆 (ancient style of writing, read *ten*). Also the reasons that the transcription "great king" is to be read **tesi** is because it points to the son of heaven [heaven is *ten*]. In spite of this argument, 篆 is never used to transcribe any Japanese sounds; the graph 義 is never used alone to transcribe **te**, so we realize that the only way to understand this usage is to look at the two graphs together, a graphic set transcribing **tesi**. Also, if "great king" had reference to the son of heaven then the poet should have simply written 天子 (son of heaven) or 天皇 (heavenly ruler). By simply writing "great king," you do not get either meaning. Furthermore, if the intended meaning was "son of heaven," I do not see why the poet could not have just used phonetic script.

[326] *ARIKINU*

In Book 14 of *Man'yōshū* there is **arikinu no / sawe sawe sibumi** (Sinking among the noise, like the rubbing of silk cloth) ... (MYS 3481), and in Book 15 **arikinu no / arite noti nimo** (being here afterward, like the rubbing of silk cloth) ... (MYS 3741), and in Book 16 **arikinu no / takara no kora** (my precious children, like the rubbing of silk cloth) ... " (MYS 3791). The word **arikinu** is fabric that is vivid in color. The first part, **ari**, means "vivid color." It is the same as *ari ari*, which we also find. The usage of *arituki* does not mean that there is a moon in the sky, making the nighttime sky bright. As the daybreak can appear especially dazzling from the light of the moon, we say *ari ari tuki* because the sky is bright and glowing. We also call it *ariake no tuki* (the morning moon).

In *Nihon shoki* in the record of Kinmei, the graphs 㲲毯 (light woolen quilt) are glossed as *ari kamo* (vivid colored woolen quilt), which originates from "vivid."[206] This comes from *Hou Hanshu*, where we find, "In the land of India they have finally woven cloth which is good for woven quilts." Now in some poems in Book 14 of *Man'yōshū* quoted above and Book 4 there are examples of 球衣乃

---

206. Interesting that most manuscripts have *ori kamo* "woven quilt" instead of *ari kamo*.

(pearl-robe-**no**), which my master stated should also be read as *arikinu*, and though he interpreted *arikinu* to be "pearls," the example in Book 4 is "pearl-like robes," which refers to clothing that are jewel-like.[207] Also, in Book 16 when it is used as a pillow word for *takara* (treasure) it has the extended meaning of vividly colored fine robes being precious [like treasure]. Whether it is robes or whatever, things that are extremely rare and precious are called *takara* (treasure). This is obvious.

[329] ON THE COLOR CALLED LIGHT YELLOW

"Light yellow" (*asaki*) in the present refers to a light blue color, but anciently it referred to a light yellow color. It also was used for green. This fact appears in *Kichibu hikunshō*,[208] in the twelfth month of the second year of Kenkyū (1191), also in *Gyokuzui*[209] in the twelfth month of the second year of Kenryaku (1212) when the prince had his coming-of-age ceremony, and it records that there are a variety of opinions about the color of his outer robe, but there are some manuscripts that say it was a light yellow color. The color green comes from the meaning of *azagi* (a light green color, like young leeks), which is different, but as people pronounce it the same (as *asaki*) they have confused the two. The later usage of light blue is a semantic change from the usage of green.

[333] *MEKAKAU*

In *Ōkagami*[210] we find, "Also, the picture he drew of a man frightening some children by wrapping each finger with the peeled

---

207. Norinaga is correct that examples like 珠衣乃 found in MYS 503 should be read *tamaginu no*; it should be stated, however, that this poem in general is very difficult to interpret.
208. *Kichibu hikunshō*: A Heian era record of customs and rites at the court in five volumes. The compiler is unknown.
209. *Gyokuzui*: This is the diary of Kujō Michie (1193–1252), kept between the years 1209 to 1238.
210. *Ōkagami*: "The Great Mirror" is the first of the four *kagami* "mirror" historical

skin of a bamboo shoot and pulling at his eyelids to show only the reds, with the faces [of the children] flushed in the horrible fright they felt."[211] *Mekakau* (make a face) is called *bekakau* in the present.

[334] *AWIKUTI*

In the present a small dagger is called *awikuti*. In *Jōkan gishiki* in the list of items to be used in the Festival of the First Fruits it says, "Forty *awi* daggers." This name (*awikuti*) originated from this [earlier] word.

[338] FROZEN ICE

In a poem in the *Horikawa-in hyakushu*[212] it says: *fuyu samumi / idesi kofori wo / udumi okite* (With winter so cold, we bury the ice that forms for later use) .... In the present when something hardens from the freezing cold we say *itesi*, which is this word.

[339] ROOSTERS ANNOUNCING THE DAWN

People say "announcing the dawn" when roosters crow at daybreak. This appears in a poem from the same *Hyakushu*: *akatuki no / toki wo tukuru nari / nifatori no / kowe utikafasi / fane wo narabete* (It is as if they are announcing the dawn—the roosters mix their voices together and line up their wings). Here *tukuru* makes one think that this is *tugeru* (to announce), but it should be

---

tales. It is unclear who the compiler is or when it was completed. The tale focuses primarily on the court of Fujiwara Michinaga (966–1028).
  211. See Yamagiwa (1967:128). It would seem that Yamagiwa has tried to give a literal translation of *me* (eye) *kakau* (make red), but the word's etymology is unclear.
  212. *Horikawa-in hyakushu*: This work has a complex history. It appears that it was originally compiled by Minamoto no Toshiyori and others who belonged to a circle during the reign of Emperor Horikawa (r. 1087–1107). It was put together in two parts, the original and what Norinaga calls "the later" volume.

taken as the same *tukuru* in the present vernacular. Also the usage of *toki no kowe wo tukuru* (announce the time with one's cry) also appears in the later *Hyakushu*: *karabito fa / sika no wosima ni / funadesite / fakata no oki ni / toki tukuru nari* (The foreigners put out to sea from the small island of Sika, and in the offing of Fakata they seem to be announcing the coming of the dawn).

[340] MOUNTAIN PASSES

In the same *Hyakushu* we see: *asigara no / yama no tauge ni / kefu kite zo / fuzi no takane no / fodo fa siraruru* (I came today to the pass of Mount Asigara, and I now understand the height of the peak of Mount Fuzi). This poem was written on the topic of "mountain passes." The graph 峠 was written by a later person, but the graph is written such because of the meaning of *tauge*. It is the same type of euphony you see in examples like *fimuka* becoming *fiuga* [Hyūga] or Tamu no Mine becoming *tau no mine* [Tamu Peak]. Thus at that time *tamuke* (offerings to the gods for safety on a trip) quickly changed to *tauge* (mountain pass).[213]

[341] AROUND THE FIRE

In the games that children play, there is one called *fimafasi* (around the fire).[214] In the same *Hyakushu* there is the following: *midoriko no / asobu susabi ni / mafasu fi no / munasiki yo woba /*

---

213. Norinaga seems to be making two interrelated arguments. First about the graph: 峠 (mountain pass) is a Japanese native creation, consisting of 山 (mountain), 上 (climb), and 下 (go down). Hence, a place in the mountains where you are at the point of having climbed up and are about to go down. The second point is to explain the etymology of the word *tauge*. He follows earlier scholars, such as Keichū, who see it as contraction of an earlier form of *tamuke* (an offering). Thus *tamuke* > *ta^muke* > *tau^mke* > *tauge*. The earliest known usage is this poem Norinaga quotes.

214. In this game the children would sit in a circle. A kind of paper candle would then be lit and one child would hold it. They would then start playing *shiritori* and pass the candle. The child who could not come up with a word or the child who held the candle when it went out would then lose.

6 ~ COCKSCOMB 181

ari to tanomazi (One cannot rely on this futile world, which is just like the fickle game of *"fimafasi"* that small children play).

[342] *KUDOKU*

Toshiyori Ason[215] composed this poem, which appears in the same *Hyakushu*: *fazime naki / tumi no tumori no / kanasisa wo / nuka no kowegowe / kudokituru nari* (It seems that the voices of those praying who have been petitioning the gods are for the sadness of the piling up of transgressions that have no beginning).[216] The word *kudoku* is not a vulgar usage. To comment further on this poem, the stanza *fazime naki tumi* refers to transgressions that have no beginning, as seen in Buddhist scripture. There it is written 無始 and means that there is no beginning, and thus it is read this way in Japanese as *fazime naki*.

[343] THE SACRED STONE

In the same *Hyakushu* there is a poem by Sakaki Kenshō:[217] *ikoma yama / tamuka fa kore ka / ki no moto ni / ifakura utite / sakaki tatetari* (On Mount Ikoma, is this the offering for safety? At the base of the tree I strike a sacred stone and place a branch of the *sakaki* tree). The final stanza of this poem sounds like *fimorogi ifaki* as found in the record of the "Age of the Gods." The meaning of *ifakura utu* is to take stones and create a throne.

---

215. It is possible that Norinaga is referring to Minamoto no Toshiyori (1055-1129). He was a courtier and a poet. An active poet, he wrote a treatise on poetry called *Toshiyori zuinō*.
216. Norinaga must have liked this poem, as he also quotes it in Book 6 of *Kojiki-den*, regarding the story of the Sun Goddess hiding herself in the cave and casting heaven into darkness. That section also deals with the meaning of *kudoku*.
217. Sakaki Kenshō: It is believed that this points to Minamoto no Kenshō [dates unknown], a middle-ranking courtier during the early twelfth century. He was also a poet with a small number of poems that appeared in several imperially ordered anthologies.

[346] TAMA ARARE

Recently I, Norinaga, wrote a book titled *Tama arare*,[218] and pointed out many mistakes in the writing style used by people in society. I did this for the benefit of the new student. In spite of this effort, many students who come to me and follow my every word still make the exact same mistakes that I pointed out in *Tama arare*, a work at their disposal. How can they misunderstand?

Of course, people who do not wish to take my advice are not on my mind, but even people who pretend not to agree with me find places where my theories make sense, and they quietly correct their own mistakes. Furthermore, there are students under my tutelage who believe my teachings to be correct but do not emend their writing; they read my work, fail to memorize the mistakes, and forget everything they read. This occurs because they do not peruse the book, because they think that they are above correction.

Something pondered and understood will not be forgotten in time, even if they have only heard it once. Are not people who put on airs shameless? What I have said above does not apply just to *Tama arare*, but applies to every work that a student reads.

[347] ON *KANA* USAGE

Kana usage lately has been elucidated, and since students of ancient studies have been careful, mistakes have been kept to a minimum. So why are there so many mistakes in the poetry my students compose and then show me? This is because a beginning student does not have the knowledge to arrange properly the particles *te*, *ni*, *wo*, and *fa*, and we may pardon them for making these mistakes. If one reads about *kana* usage in works like *Shōkanshō*[219]

---

218. *Tama arare* was published in 1792. It points out mistakes that students and others make when trying to write in elegant Japanese. While the work is essentially divided into two sections: poetry and prose, much of what is said in the poetry section is also found in the prose. Norinaga argues that students should imitate the prose and poetry of the Heian era.

219. Written by Keichū and published in 1695, *Shōkanshō* is important in that it points out mistakes in the *kana* system that Teika had tried to correct.

and *Kogontei*,[220] even a child who knows nothing can distinguish the usage very well. Then why do students make mistakes?

These students do not pay close attention, clinging to the opinions of their master, thinking, "If something is incorrect, then my master will correct it." They become sloppy and do not put their heart into the work; thus, the task becomes bothersome. There is no way to come to an understanding of *kana* usage by relying on such a person. Thus, all usages that are even the slightest bit suspicious, like *i / yi, e / ye, o / wo*, or *fa, fi, fu, fe, fo, wa, yi, u, ye, wo*, or sounds that undergo voicing, like *si* and *ti, su* and *tu*, must be checked—though it is somewhat of a bother—in those records elucidating *kana* usage. In all tasks, if one does not put his heart into his work, then it is difficult to complete. Moreover, is it not true that there is absolutely no value in saying this about a child who never leaves his parents' side until he comes of age?

[348] RESEARCHING OLD NAMES

There are many places where old shrines have been abolished, or even shrines that still exist, but nothing is known about which deity the shrine worships, and this very lamentable. We believe that the shrines included in the list of shrines in *Engi shiki* should never be put on the abolished list, or neglected to the extent that no one knows which deity the place worshipped. Nonetheless, during the revolts of the Middle Ages, everything fell into chaos, not only shrines, but old rules and customs, and this reflects the sad aspect of upheaval, for everything ceases to exist as it had before.

The present day is a rare example of tranquil rule, to an extent rare even in the ancient past, so prosperity follows prosperity, allowing us to research the past and reestablish things that had ceased to be. We are also able to rescue those things that are near the point of extinction. Thus, it is the era where shrines should be renewed to their prosperous state, like in ancient times. In order to

---

220. *Kogontei*: Written by Katori Nahiko (1723–1782), a student of Mabuchi. It is arranged like a dictionary and builds on the work of Keichū.

restore shrines that have ceased to exist, someone must search the remains, while others must research the existing shrines that do not know which deity they traditionally worship, and make this clear.

Next, many place names are seen in old poetry that are currently unclear. The present day is a wondrous period of prosperity, so we should spend time researching these things.

Therefore, whether it is shrines, or the burial mounds of emperors and empresses, or place names seen in old poetry or any other name, many things existed in the ancient past, but have been lost in the upheaval of the Middle Ages. It is difficult, but someone must research these things and reestablish them. The reason it is difficult is that, first, the only evidence we have for old place names is their existence in some old record, making it hard to find an exact location. No matter how detailed your investigation into a record, when you actually go to the spot, it often appears different from the record, and the resulting conclusion is often different from the actual place. As for a place about which there are unclear points when viewed from afar, there are cases where there are after all both written and oral transmissions at that locale, leaving no confusion.

When a person does go to a certain province, the first thing he must do is find local records or oral traditions that he can trust. Your work will be insufficient unless you actually visit the place and talk to people there. Also, it is insufficient to visit the place just once. The researcher thus needs to visit the place, look and ask around, then return home and search the records again and compare the two sets of information. Then you must go out again. Without doing this, it is difficult to reach accurate conclusions.

There are various things to keep in mind when you go to the provinces and start asking questions of the people. People who talk in great detail, as if they know a lot, are difficult to trust, because a person who has spent half his life looking into one section of a work tends to talk as if he knows a lot more than he actually does. This ends up hampering your research. It is also the tendency in the world for people to claim that a famous place name existed in their province, even in their own village, and these people stubbornly cling to the frailest evidence, terribly twisting the facts in an attempt to prove that the place was originally here, in their locale. Also, there are many cases where people have fabricated ancient evidence [stone relics and the like]. The researcher must beware so that he is not led astray by these things.

Lower-class people who have never opened a record may talk about things they remember, saying things that are contradictory, so they declare things that sound interesting, and the researcher must beware of such fabricated stories. Sometimes you may hear about a past scholar who visited the place, made a mistaken decision on some evidence, and told the people that their place was once the scene of "such and such" an event. The villagers will thus believe what they were told, and this has been handed down from generation to generation. So things that may sound reasonable cannot be trusted, either.

And when you visit the place and hand down a decision, there are various things you must keep in mind. First, is the place hallowed, befitting a shrine? Are the trees luxuriant? Do they seem of great age? The place may seem like the ancient ruins of some shrine, but you cannot openly trust that feeling. Even in places where nothing remains, there are many old and lush forests and groves. As standing trees over two or three hundred years old appear majestic, it is difficult to determine if they are really old. One must also take care when researching into the old names of villages, mountains, rivers, bays, and beaches. One must also be careful of even the *azana* names of rice fields.

In addition, the researcher must take care and look carefully into the district names of villages in the provinces. Many temples also have preserved very old names. Because of this, it is easy to make a mistake on the larger name. The history of temples often comes from those priests who have a bad habit of making up stories, but sometimes there are kernels of truth imbedded in these stories, so one cannot discard an oral history merely because it comes from a temple. There are cases where priests in the Middle Ages took some old relics and deceived the people by telling them that the relics proved that the area was a hallowed area for Buddha, so the researcher must also look into the truth of those claims.

Old temples often have old records and many of these contain old fragments of history. Places that you might suspect contain nothing but fabrications often contain truth, so you must search through the records carefully and thoroughly.

[350] ON THE GRAPH 俵

The graph 俵 (a bale of rice) appears in *Engi shiki*. Now before that period (that *Engi shiki* records), it also appears in a tally from the Council of State, dated the second day of the eleventh month of the eleventh year of Jōwa (844). This is recorded in *Ruiju sandaikaku*.

[353] REGARDING THE GOVERNING OF THINGS UNDER THE HEAVENS AND PUTTING SHINTŌ AFFAIRS FIRST

In the Taihō Codes in the section on positions, the posts of the Shintō religion [the native cult] appear first, followed by the Dajōkan. In *Engi shiki* the first group listed is the Shintō officials, followed by the Dajōkan. In the later-era work, *Shokugenshō*, by Kitabatake Jungō,[221] he lists the officials following the same order as the Taihō Codes. Considering how much Tang influence had been introduced into our country by these periods, it is truly a testimony of the divine establishment of our country that things should be ordered thus. It is truly noble and something to be celebrated. In all facets of life I wish that such things could be properly ordered.

---

221. Kitabatake Jungō: This refers to Kitabatake Chikafusa. The work *Shokugenshō* is believed to have been written around 1338, around the same time that he was finishing *Jinnō shōtōki*. Chikafusa wrote *Shokugenshō* as a commentary to explain the customs and rituals of the various offices and posts in the imperial government.

7 | WAVES of WISTERIA LEAVES on the WIND

Whenever I see the wisteria blooming very wondrously at certain places, I never fail to recall the poem " To the People About to Leave" (KKS 119), so I composed this poem:

fudi no fana	The blossoms of the wisteria—
wa ga tama no wo mo	twisted in the pine branches
matugaye ni	like my own jeweled life-string
matufarete mimu	firmly attached to me,
tiyo no faru made	until a thousand springs have come.

On the following day I started to compile this chapter, so I named it after this poem.

[354] ON *MAN'YŌSHŪ* POEM 9

In the first volume of *Man'yōshū* it says, "A poem written by Princess Nukata when the imperial procession stopped at a hot springs in the province of Ki."

kama yama no	At Kamayama
simoki ete yuke	the hoar frost was very deep;
wa ga se ko ga	my beloved one
itatasu gane	stood beneath the aged oak
itu kasi ga moto[222]	waiting patiently for the frost.

---

222. My gloss and translation to this poem follows Norinaga's interpretation, regardless of what later scholars have said about this poem.

The graphs 莫囂 are read **kama**. The reason for writing *kama* in this manner comes from the ancient custom of causing a person to be quiet, known as *anakama*, with the *ana* dropped. To put it into modern colloquial language, it is the same as saying, "You are noisy!" This word for noisy (*yakamasi*) is **kamabisusi** with *kama*, meaning, "do not make such noise." Now, Mount Kama is seen in *Jinmyōchō*, located in the province of Kii in the district of Nakusa, Kamayama Shrine. Also, in *Shoryō shiki*,[223] we see the Mount Kama Tomb in the same Nakusa District. This tomb is the resting place of Emperor Jinmu's older brother, Itsuse, and is seen in *Kojiki* and *Nihon shoki*. The shrine and the tomb are both located close to the ancient road to Kumano, and so the characters 國隣 should be read *yama*.[224] *Yama* are the mountains forming the border between the neighboring provinces, and that is why the author used these characters [literally "neighboring province"].

The character 國 (province) is written 圓 (round) in the Kanei edition of *Man'yōshū*, but 國 in another manuscript. The reason for the character 霜 (frost) written 大相 (great–together) in the Kanei edition is because the former was written in cursive script, and appeared to a scribe as the latter two characters. Thus, a scribe made a mistake in copying.[225]

This excursion [to the hot springs] is seen in the record of Emperor Saimei in *Nihon shoki*, fourth year, winter, tenth month, fifteenth day, where it says, "The imperial procession proceeded to the hot springs in Ki." Because we also see that in the eleventh month they stayed there, it was a time when the frost was heavy. Concerning the characters 木兄氐 (tree–older brother–base), in the Kanei edition, the first character is mistakenly written 七 (seven), while in another edition it is written 土 (earth) or 云 (say). Also, the third character is mistakenly written 爪 (claw).[226] In

---

223. That part of the *Engi shiki* that deals with the management of Imperial tombs.

224. Most manuscripts have 圓隣 and not 國隣, so Norinaga's theory of this meaning *yama* will not work. He notes the discrepancy in other manuscripts, but chooses 國 over 圓 based on his perceived meaning of the poem.

225. Again, textual evidence shows that the original was 大相, and Norinaga's emendation is not justified.

226. It is generally agreed that the archetype was 七兄爪 (seven–older brother–claw). As

addition, 湯 (hot water) is mistakenly written 謁 (announce).[227] The reference of **wa ga se ko** (my beloved one) is to Emperor Tenchi, who was crown prince at the time.

The record in *Nihon shoki* shows that the crown prince also went on the imperial excursion. Now, I have already explained in the second chapter (of *Tamakatsuma*) that Princess Nukata was the wife of Emperor Tenchi. That is why this poem by Princess Nukata uses the words **wa ga se ko**. The characters 為兼 should be read **sugane**. This stanza thus reads, "Surely it was he who was standing at the base of this oak tree." Nevertheless, the reading of *seriken* is far off the mark because this stanza is talking about when the crown prince came to this spot.

The stanza **itu kasi ga moto** refers to an old oak tree located at the Kamayama Shrine. Therefore, the princess wrote this poem when the frost was heavy, and she followed the crown prince the morning of the day that he had come to worship at this Kamayama Shrine. The meaning of this one poem is, thus, the frost was heavy at Kamayama, and under the aged oak tree my beloved stood quietly for a short time, waiting for the frost to disappear.

[355] ON WANTING TO KNOW WHICH DEITY IS WORSHIPPED AT WHICH SHRINE

There are many old shrines where we no longer know which deity was worshipped. None of the deities are listed in *Jinmyōchō*, only the shrine name is mentioned. In *Izumo fudoki* there is a list of shrines, but the names of the deities are not listed. Because the name of the deity became the name of the shrine, we should have the shrine name listed, and for the people making the list it was not really necessary at the time to know which deity they worshipped. Later eras believed that people had to know what deity was worshipped. Those who felt they must know researched into the shrine's history and other areas, or tried to find connections

---

this does not make much sense, scribes over time appear to have either been careless in copying, or have tried to make sense of the stanza by altering some graphs.
227. Again, current scholarship views 謁 as the archetype.

with the shrine from records within the "Age of the Gods" as mentioned in *Kojiki* or *Nihon shoki*. If these people found the name of a deity that fit even part of some vague criteria, in many cases, they claimed that this deity was worshipped at a certain shrine. Many of the stories handed down at shrines cannot be taken at face value.

The ancient tradition says there were eight million deities,[228] and numerous other deities inhabit the High Plain of Heaven and the earth, so in most cases we do not know what shrine worshipped what deity. The deities mentioned in the "Age of the Gods" section of *Nihon shoki* represents only one-ten millionth of the posterity of the deities. Is it possible for those researchers to go through these records and say, "Ah, it is this deity," when most names of deities never made it into these records? Why do most scholars fail to realize there are many deities whose names never were recorded? Therefore, it is a reckless mistake for these people to search in the darkness and arbitrarily decide that this shrine worships this deity, when the older traditions say nothing about what deity the place venerated.

If one were truly to determine the deity a shrine actually worshipped, then precedent must be followed. As an example, the great shrine Isuzu Miya at Ise Shrine is labeled thus, because it worships Isuzu Hime, the deity of the bells. The Outer Shrine of Ise is called the Watarai Palace because it worships Watatsumi, the deity of the dragon. In recent times, most scholars engaged in this kind of work have followed this type of precedent in deciding what deity a shrine once worshipped. Nonetheless, most of the conclusions these scholars reach are rash and beyond the realm of certainty.

Rather than arbitrarily deciding which deity a shrine worshipped by a priori deciding when there is no evidence, it is closer to the ancient spirit to just leave the shrine name as the

---

228. Modern scholars do not take this as a concrete number, but one with the meaning much like "myriad," or "numerous." Interestingly, the ancient tradition in Japan appears to have vacillated between eight million (in *Kojiki*) and eight hundred thousand (in *Nihon shoki*) deities. Norinaga later takes offense at this, as if *Nihon shoki* had purposely decreased the number of deities. It seems clear that the tradition fixated on the number *eight* plus some larger digit.

name of the deity. People in the recent past have the insipid idea that nothing can be done with just the name of the shrine. In society today, some names of shrines are so widespread that they have become the names of the deity worshipped there. Is it not true that most people do not look deeper into what deity the Fatiman, Kasuga, or Inari Shrines worship, but just say the place worships Fatiman, Kasuga, or Inari? Many shrines are in the same boat, and the name of the shrine reflects the name of the deity.

[356] WHY YOU WANT TO REVERE THE DEITY YOU WORSHIP

In the Heian era, the Shintō priests and officials in charge of the liturgies revered certain deities among the many they venerated at shrines, secretly hiding their names by taking them out of the ancient oral traditions. They then said things like, "We are worshipping Kunitokotachi, or Amaterasu Ōmikami or Emperor Jinmu," giving the ceremony a mysterious atmosphere. There are many examples of this type of deception in society. It is dreadful for someone who is a fervent servant of the deities to deceive the deity he reveres and worships. Is not this reckless?

[357] THE TITLES OF KŌSON AND TENSON

Nihon shoki calling the successive emperors who have reigned since the advent of Ninigi *kōson* (imperial grandson) or *tenson* (heavenly grandson) instead of calling him the grandson of the imperial deity or the august son of the heavenly deity is not an ancient usage. The label *kōson* refers to being a grandson of the imperial deity, but it is modeled after Chinese usages.

In other ancient records we only see that the emperors are all called the grandson of the imperial deity, and in a song in *Shoku Nihongi* there is an example where the emperor is called the august grandson, with the word "imperial" dropped from the title. However, you never see an example where the character 命 (*mikoto*) is dropped. Furthermore, we never see any examples of *tenson* in the ancient records. *Tenson* refers to the august child of the heavenly deity, and is believed simply to be this older title rewritten. The reason people in society have a custom of generally being attracted to beautiful Chinese prose is, I believe, similar to the popularity of titles like *kōson* and *tenson*, and the truly beautiful titles of the ancient past have become hidden and rarely used. *Kōson* is generally read as *sume mima* (imperial grandson), and *tenson* is read *ame mima* (heavenly grandson), but instead of getting hung up on the graphs, these should be read *sume mima no mikoto* for "*kōson*," and *amatu kami no mikoto* for "*tenson*," and in this way I want to spread the true reading again in the world. The reading of *ame mima* (for *tenson*) is particularly grating on the ears and is a reading without logic.

[367] THE USE OF *SAMA* TO SHOW RESPECT TO PEOPLE

The usage of *sama* to show esteem for people began in these records some 440 or 450 years ago, and one finds examples here and there. One can find examples of *ufe-sama, zenchō-sama, kinri-sama, gosho-sama, kubō-sama, miya no onkata-sama, tokudaiji-sama*, and *jochū-sama*.[229] Even with the names of addresses of letters, there are such as O-tsubone-sama. In addition, we even find examples where *dono* and *sama* have been combined together, as in Rokuonin-dono-sama and Muromachi-dono-sama.

---

229. In order of appearance, these are: 上様 (*ue-sama*, for members of the imperial family or nobility); 前朝様 (*zenchō-sama*, for the previous emperor); 禁裏様 (*kinri-sama*, for the emperor or a person in the forbidden precincts); 御所様 (*gosho-sama*, for the palace or someone powerful in the palace); 公方様 (*kubō-sama*, for the emperor or powerful people in the Kamakura government); 宮御方様 (*miya no onkata-sama*, for those residing in the palace); 徳大寺様 (*tokudaiji-sama*, for a member of the Tokudaiji family); and 女中様 (*jochū-sama*, for servant women serving in the households of nobility or the Shogun).

7 ~ WAVES OF WISTERIA LEAVES ON THE WIND   193

[369] LAMENTING THE DECLINE OF SHINTŌ FESTIVALS

One thing I certainly desire is to see the decline of many shrines arrested, their stations solidified, and the various festivals and ceremonies restored to what they were in the ancient past.

Many shrines and their festivals in the present have fallen into severe decline because of the upheaval in the Middle Ages, some shrines even having been abandoned. People in the present only see the end result and think that it has always been like this. A rare person who reads the ancient records spends most of his time in Chinese records, debating about everything from this foreign point of view, and there are very few people who read our oldest native records. Thus, they do not know that in the ancient era, our native shrines and ceremonies were revered and venerated. Then there is the rare exception where someone knows these things, but he is blinded by popular custom, and I find it lamentable that there is no one who compares the past with the present.

[370] MOST PEOPLE IN SOCIETY ADMIRE SHRINES THAT LOOK DESOLATE

The attitude of people in the present that a place which worships the Shintō pantheon should look lonely and desolate shows they do not know that shrines once were very active and vibrant in their own day. Today, most of the major shrines are in decay and falling into ruin, and people gaze at this condition and believe that this is the way it has always been. This is a mistaken perception.

[371] THE OFOTORI SHRINE IN IZUMI PROVINCE

In a work called *Izumi-shi,* when you read the section that records events related to the Ofotori Shrine in that province, such as "During the Keichō era (1596–1615) it sustained damage from the fire in battle," or " ... during the Genroku era (1688–1703) the monk Kaien erected a temple, Shinhō, within the precincts of the shrine. On the corner of the temple it says 'small shrine'"; reading these events makes one weep. How sad it is that this august shrine, whose name is seen in the list of shrines in *Jinmyōchō* as the Ofotori Shrine of the Ofotori District, with the name of the deity it worships, its status as an important shrine, and its ability to present food for the tasting of the first fruits, has been treated thus. It is a shrine with very high standing, but its precincts have been made into one of Buddhism. The doings of the evil deity Magatsubi cannot be avoided.

Now this shrine only remains in one small corner of its land. I have never been to worship at this shrine, but I present my empathy for it. How is it that there are no other people who grieve with sorrow when they see this shrine? There are likely many other similar cases throughout the various provinces, but I just happened to read about the state of this one in this work, and I could not endure the feeling of lament, and have experienced such shock. How pitiful it must be to those who have a sensitive heart to such matters.

[372] THE CHINESE KNOW NOTHING ABOUT OTHER COUNTRIES

The ancient people of China knew nothing about other countries. They believed the sages of their country were the first to do everything, like govern the state and establish a way to govern the individual. They boasted that theirs was the greatest country under heaven. Nonetheless, not much time later, Buddhism came to China from a country called India, so they must have known that there was at least one other superior country.

In the present, they have come to know something about other countries in the West that rival India in greatness. There are few who truly know nothing about the various countries in the world, but in these far-off Western countries there are many things that have existed there since ancient times that also existed in China. There are also many things in these Western countries that are not in China. Many of these countries did not have relations with

China until the recent past, and there was no such deficiency in the past.

In China's ancient past, the people only knew about the land of the barbarians that was nearby, and they knew very little about countries that were relatively close. They knew of the existence of other countries, but it was a fuzzy sort of knowledge, and when they spoke about other countries, they always said unreasonable things filled with erroneous information.

And even when it came to the neighboring land of the barbarians, the Chinese thought it was a broad area with low-class people, being an evil land, and this perception pervades the Chinese records. Thus, in everything, the Chinese perceived their own country to be superior to all others, an attitude that led to reckless boasting.[230] Anciently to the extent that the Chinese had a shallow knowledge of other countries, it is indeed true that in the recent past when they do know more about countries far away, they cling to their ancient traditions and do not update them.

Even in our own country, most people have some knowledge about the situation of various countries, but they stick to the ancient habit of blindly believing the lies of China, worshipping it and thinking that everything originated in China. What kind of misinformed person believes there are no other countries than China?

[373] THE LEARNING OF HOLLAND

In the recent past, people have begun studying things from Holland. And in the city of Edo there are people who say this and that about the country. Some people—usually those studying about Holland—say that the Dutch travel the world over engaging in trade, so if people study about Holland they will know about

---

230. It is fairly well-known that the ancient Chinese historiographers referred to their neighbors with unflattering renditions of their names. In the third-century chronicle, *Wei zhi*, the Chinese mention neighboring lands such as 挹婁 (ladle out-drag), 濊 (deep water), 倭 (dwarfs), and 黒歯 (black teeth).

various far-off lands. Thus they know about the bad habits of people who only study Chinese texts. There are many separate countries in the world, and a person should not be particular about just one country. They say these things and lead others to study about Holland. This is better than being blindly loyal to Chinese studies, and this sounds reasonable on the surface. So do these people really not know that our country is the best and most respected country in the world? People should naturally come to understand how superior our country is by studying things connected with other countries. The reason even these people do not respect their own country is because they think it bad to persist in one view, but thinking it good to not persist in one view of things means the problem remains—they are still getting hung up on things. There are many people who think this way, even among scholars who do not study Dutch learning.

[374] THINGS NOT FOUND IN CHINA

When scholars engaged in Chinese learning hear someone say there are things in Japan that do not exist in China, they treat them condescendingly, claiming they are ignorant of the facts. Yet, if the same person tells one of these scholars about things in China that also exist in Japan, then these scholars are the first people to agree. What kind of attitude is this? Do they actually believe that everyone in China is learned? People engaged in Chinese learning talk as if they know everything, and I wonder if there is anything that parallels this in stupidity.

[389] THINGS TO KEEP IN MIND WHEN YOU WRITE

There are many things to keep in mind when you compose poetry, but there are other things to be careful of when you write in other styles.

When people write *areba, yukeba, kikeba, sakeba,* or *tireba,* they all write the Chinese character plus *ba* (like 有ば), but this could be read *arufa* or *araba* (as well as *areba*), and it is confusing

7 ~ WAVES OF WISTERIA LEAVES ON THE WIND

to the reader. People who do not know a word make mistakes when they read, and if they are copying a manuscript, they copy it incorrectly. So an original *yukeba* (since he will go) becomes *yuku fa* (going), or *yukaba* (if you go). To avoid such mistakes, the writer must write the parts that conjugate in *hiragana*.

Nouns like "mist" (*kasumi*, 霞) or "promise" (*tigiri*, 契) become declinable morphemes when you add, for example, the past tense ending *keri* to make *kasumikeri* (misted), or the negative ending *nu* to make *tigiranu* (does not promise). You should not write these, though, simply by attaching endings to the graph for the noun, such as by writing 霞 (*kasumi*) + *keri*, or, for *kasumu tuki* (misted moon), 霞 (*kasumu*) + *tuki*. In such declinable forms, you must alert the reader by writing the declinable portion with a combination of the graph and a *hiragana* symbol, like 霞 [(*kasu*)*mi*] + *keri*, 霞 [(*kasu*)*mu*] + *tuki*, 契 [(*tigi*)*ra*] + *nu*, or 契 [(*tigi*)*ru*] + a noun (to describe a thing that is promised).

In order to make a distinction between declinable and indeclinable words, declinable forms should have attending *kana*, because forgetting this will just confuse the reader. It is the last syllable that tends to conjugate, like *kasuman*, *kasumi*, *kasumu*, or *kasume*. And when one writes "autumn leaves," he should not just write the graphs for *momizi*, but should write *momiziba*. This is the proper way to write. You must write it this way, adding the second graph for "leaf," because it is confusing for the reader who might mistake the *kana* for the topic particle *fa*.

In addition, it is a mistake to write the graph for "house" when writing the *ka* for *kakurega* (a place to hide), or *sumika* (a place to live). This *ka* means "place" and not "house."[231] But you should not write the graph for "place"; just leave it in *kana* script. Writing the first half with Chinese and leaving the last *ka* in *kana* looks ridiculous, so all these mannerisms should be treated in the same way. I wonder about using the Chinese graph for "lonely" (淋). What about the graph for *nagame* (to compose poetry, 詠)? *Nagame*

---

231. The problem Norinaga is trying to get his students to avoid concerns homophones. The graph 家 is read *ka*, but etymologically this *ka* and the *ka* in *sumika* "a place to live" are different.

means to lengthen one's voice in singing poetry, and has nothing to do with gazing at something (*nagameru*).

It is improper to use obscure graphs. The kinds of mistakes I have addressed abound in the prose people currently write, and I have only written down a point or two regarding this. The people in the past did not pay attention to such minute detail and wrote freely, using any kind of script their heart desired. So how should people in the present write? There will surely be some who wonder if it is proper to set up so many rules in governing the prose written by modern people.

There will be people who denigrate as vulgar and infantile those who find pleasure in ancient customs and try to resurrect those noble traits, but I find nothing here worthy of such criticism. People in the ancient past knew each other's thoughts and there was no chance of a misreading. Writing as one pleased in the ancient past was fine, but in the present era, what you personally understand is often cryptic to those around you. It is thus easy for the reader to misunderstand, and copy your words incorrectly. Thus, I constantly feel that we should pay special care to what we write and how we write it.

My own habit is to constantly reflect on what I have written, thinking, "Could someone misunderstand what I mean?" or "Will someone copy this sentence down incorrectly?" While I worry about this, I also worry about my penmanship, something I have struggled with since my youth, and I end up not being able to write anything but an abbreviated version of what I set out to compose.

Ancient words are infamous for being misread and miscopied. I have pondered how we could write these words down without the reader misunderstanding, and this led me to create rules that perhaps go beyond necessity, asking people to add *kana* script here and there. I realize the educated person will make fun of me, but habits from one's youth are not easily nullified.

[390] POETRY WRITTEN ABOUT *SAMISEN*

On paintings painted by some depicting a lutelike instrument called a *samisen*, which many people play in the present, it is the

7 ~ WAVES OF WISTERIA LEAVES ON THE WIND   199

custom for someone to compose a poem and then ask that it be inserted into the painting, it being a form of being playful. People who enjoy the ancient past see this as a way to look down on things. I wonder why they do such shameful things, but certainly while it is what offensive people say, what in the world should one do with a poem that was composed and written on a picture?

kikaseba ya	Since you let me hear it—
inisife fito ni	to a person of the ancient past,
san no wo no	the three melodies of
mitu no sirabe wo	the three strings,
kokoro fiku ya to	how it pulls at my heart strings.

It is likely that certain people will laugh at me, but on the other hand while they are being slothful, they also do the following, requesting that the following poem be written to the side of a picture of a monkey who is satisfied, having eaten what he likes:

umakeredo	While it was tasty
kufanu zo kufu ni	I ate while I could not eat.
masaru beki	Because I ate what I liked
konomite kufeba	the desire that should increase
fara fukurekeri	expanded my belly.

[392] THE KOREAN LANGUAGE

The same person[232] also said that the lower-class people of Korea speak a language where the native sounds (in this case Korean) and Chinese sounds are strung together. People belonging to the higher class only use Chinese sounds. For example, a lower-class person calls "a sword" (*handō*), or "fire" (*furuhaa*). *Han* is the native reading for sword, while *tō* is the Sino-Korean reading. Also, *furu* is the native reading for fire, while *haa* is the Sino-

---

232. "The same person" refers to the section just before this where Norinaga mentions a man who entered his school to learn, a Confucianist named Osaza no Minu.

Korean.[233] Higher-class people say *tō* for sword and *haa* for fire. This man said, "All words fit this pattern." This same person often met Koreans in the province of Ifami during the third year of Tenmei (1783) and heard how they spoke to each other. "Native reading" means Korean, and Sino-Korean refers to the Chinese reading in that country.

[393] WHAT A PERSON ONCE SAID

Once when the cherry blossoms were at their best, a few of my poetic-circle friends and I went to view the blossoms. On our way back we talked about the beauty of the blossoms when one friend said, "While I was thinking about how to phrase my poem and how the blossoms appeared, I forgot to look up and view the blossoms." This no doubt sounds foolish, but in reality I think everyone probably has experienced something like this. I found this experience quiet amusing.

[394] *SAFABOKURI*

In Tosa Province they have something that you wear (on your feet) when going into a deep rice paddy called *safabokuri* (沢木履), and it prevents you from falling down. A person from there related this to me.

[395] TOSA PROVINCE DOES NOT CREMATE PEOPLE

The residents of Tosa Province do not cremate their dead. That means that when people in Tosa hear that other provinces cremate their dead, they think that is a strange custom. When a person

---

233. In the Korean vernacular "fire" is *pul*, which likely was transcribed as *furu* in Japanese. The example of "sword" is problematic. "Sword" in the vernacular is *kkal*. It is possible that the word *handō* that Norinaga mentions is a Korean version of 太刀, where *han* is the vernacular word for "large" and *dō* is the Sino-Korean for *to* "sword."

from Tosa told me this I said, "Is this a recent development?" He replied that it is a custom from ancient times.

[397] *FOYA NO IZUSI*

A person from Safeki once told me that in the Safeki Sea of Fizen Province there is something called *foya*. It is purple in color, and shaped like a sea cucumber. Another person once said to me that if this true then *foya no izusi*, which appears in *Tosa nikki*, is what people made *sushi* out of.[234]

[398] *FUGUSI* AND *KUGUTU*

A person from Bungo Province related that they have a thing called *fugusi* (shovel) in their province even now and still use it. They also have *kugutu*, which is called *kugu* (hemp bag). He related to me that it is woven of rope and is something you put small tools in.[235]

[399] CONCERNING A FISH CALLED *ISIBUSI*

A certain person told me that in various tales you find mention of a fish called *isibusi*, which people in the present call *gori* (goby). This fish is found in abundance in rivers like Kamo River or Katura River, and they usually hide themselves under rocks, so he searched for them under the rocks and caught some. So the name fits the nature of the fish (*isibusi* means "hiding under a rock").

---

234. This part of *Tosa nikki* seems to have been misunderstood. *Foya* in classical Japanese was understood to be a "sea squirt." However, perhaps because of the shape of a sea squirt, this word later became a vulgar word for the genitals of a woman.

235. Norinaga seems to have written this down because both words appear in *Man'yōshū*, and he was pleased that these words were still used in the dialect of Bungo. *Fugusi* appears in MYS 1 as 布久思 **fukusi** (scoop). *Kugutu* also appears in MYS 293 久具都 **kugutu** (bag made of woven sedge).

[401] THE BRIDGE OF FAMANA

In *Sarashina nikki*[236] there is a section where it says, "The bridge of Famana—When we went out from the capital [to Upper Fusa Province] we crossed a bridge built of black timber, but when I returned there [four years] later there was nothing there—no bridge, no traces—so we had to cross by boat. This log bridge was built over the inlet. The waves of the sea are very high, and the area around the beach is devoid of any scenery; there is nothing else there. We could see through the thick pine forest where the waves come in and recede out, and we could see the waves wash over the pine branches, and this truly made the pine needles shine like jewels. It was indeed fascinating. Then we headed upward toward the capital to a hill called Winofana, which was forlorn beyond words, and after we climbed to the top of the hill we came to Takasi Beach in Mikafa Province."

[409] I HAVE NOTHING SPECIAL TO TELL PEOPLE

I have come to an understanding about the Way and ancient Japanese poetry only because I have pondered the ancient records according to the teachings of Master Agatai. Regarding the secretly passed poetic traditions handed down within certain families, I have not learned any, and so as far as these things are concerned, I have no knowledge concerning even one tradition. Thus, I have nothing special to pass onto people.[237] I want all good things to spread throughout the world, so I have pondered the ancient records, and as far as I believe I have come to an understanding, I have made these ideas public through my writings and nothing in the least has been held back. If there is a person who naturally wishes to follow and learn something from me, all he needs to do

---

236. *Sarashima nikki*: The diary of the daughter of Sugawara Takasue, finished around 1060. Rather than a diary or journal in a modern sense, this is more of a record of events seen through the lens colored with romance and dreams of a noble woman.

237. There were various secret traditions floating around during the Middle Ages in Japan. Norinaga is demonstrating to people that what he has is public not private.

is peruse my works. I have nothing else to add aside from what is in these works.

[410] THERE ARE SOME POINTS IN THE DOCTRINE OF THE CHINESE THINKER, LAOZI, THAT RESEMBLE PARTS OF OUR WAY

I am presently engaged in illuminating the true Way, but there are some scholars engaged in the study of Chinese texts who claim that my research is based on the doctrine of Laozi. When I expound upon the Way, I do not add one iota of my own limited wisdom, but have learned these things by reading the accounts in the ancient records and comparing these with various commentaries. It is those careless scholars engaged in Chinese learning who believe that my words tend to resemble some points of Laozi's doctrine, and they claim there was no country before China and China is the mother of all learning, but these are chance similarities and not the influence of Laozi.

There are other countries that anciently had no contact with China, and these countries and China did not know of the existence of the other, so each country had its own origins. Among these countries, our own imperial land was the origin of all the others, it being the ancestral country. The orthodox Way was transmitted only in our land, and no other country received the orthodox Way in its fullness, so other countries have no way to know about the true Way.

On the other hand, Laozi was a brilliant and wise person who studied the heart of man deeply. He gradually came to the conclusion that these superficial teachings and sophism were extremely detrimental, in the end damaging the Way. With this realization, he pondered on the true image of the Way, and partially reconstructed it. Some of these thoughts parallel what I have said and these coincidentally agree with the true Way.

The original, orthodox Way never contained human wisdom or sophism and was established in the imperial land, and it is only natural that Laozi should detest the sophism he found in his country, and parts of his new doctrine should parallel our true Way.

Nonetheless, Laozi's doctrine is after all a product of his own limited thinking and experience, and he was not born in the imperial land, nor did he hear about our true Way. Thus, he could not come to a true understanding of the foundation of this philosophy. Between his doctrine and the true Way, there are great rifts and places that have irreconcilable differences. Those Chinese scholars do not know about these differences, but jump to conclusions by seizing upon only the parallels. It is quite ignorant to claim that our true Way comes from the doctrine of Laozi.

In all things, there are always parts and places that resemble other things. Our true Way has parallel ideas with Confucian doctrine and with Buddhism. Therefore, it is natural that some part of Laozi's doctrine should parallel ours, but why should that attract attention?

[411] EXPOUNDING UPON THE WAY, WHETHER OR NOT IT RESEMBLES OTHER WAYS, IS NOT CONDITIONED ON WHETHER PEOPLE ACCEPT IT

When one expounds upon the true Way, it is a meaningless exercise to seize upon the common points between our Way and Confucianism, Taoism, or Buddhism, elucidating things in whatever direction the person prefers, enlightening his students on topics in which he has special interest, while he expounds upon the differences. It is also meaningless for a teacher to draw marked lines between other doctrines while ignoring the similarities, and change certain points in his doctrine to make the difference more pronounced. Whether there are similarities or differences, whether points are identical or dissimilar, at any rate, these have nothing to do with the significance of a different Way.

In addition, a teacher must never change subtle points in his doctrine, trying to control the emotions of people by saying, "This does not work in our society," or "If you say this, people will believe you." This is a barbaric method, and the person should not think about the praise or the criticism of the world. Even if your doctrine does have points related to other philosophies and not a single soul believes what you say, one should expound upon the

Way as it is written in the "Age of the Gods" sections in the ancient records.

[412] THE VULGAR USAGE OF *KŌ WO KIKU*

The phrase *kō wo kiku* (to smell incense) is originally a Chinese phrase, and is not an ancient Japanese one. In all aspects *kō* (incense) is something lit (*takimono*) or smelled (*kagu*), which points to refined ways of speaking, and even in poetry in *Kokinshū* we have the phrase "the blossoms of the orange tree / as I smelled that fragrance ... " (KKS 343). And in *Genji monogatari*, in the "Umegae" chapter we have where the minister of arms (*hyōbushō*) debates the best and worst kinds of incense, and judges these by smelling those which have a deep or shallow scent.

There are no examples of using the verb *kiku* related to incense in the ancient records. People in the present do not realize this, and it is a terrible mistake when they think that using the verb *kagu* is horribly vulgar. The word *kiku* used this way is just slang.

[413] REPUTABLE SCHOLARS IN CHINA
ALSO BELIEVED IN BUDDHISM

Buddhism in China was also venerated by many reputable Confucian scholars through various ages, and it appears there were various people who believed it was difficult to abandon. However, in that country, there were actually few who truly believed and worshipped Buddhism sincerely. That is why it appears that many honorable Confucian scholars believed in the religion, but they mainly did it for recreation.

Buddhist teachings are mysterious and broad, expounding about the former life as well as the afterlife, dealing with enlightenment. There are various rules for governing the heart, and the whole religion is quite strange and interesting, so it appears that poets and nonpoets alike made it a form of amusement or an aid in refinement.

Also, there were eminent priests in the various sects who neither believed in the religion nor followed Buddhism's precepts. These left wondrous, glorified names for themselves in society after they left the world, and there are many people who were touched by these priests' work, so they too search the sutras diligently, suppressing various desires, leading the difficult life of an ascetic, believing deeply in the religion. Since there are people who are not even afraid to lay down their lives for fame and merit, why should there be anything shocking about some priests being hypocritical?

[414] WHY BUDDHISM IS EASY TO BELIEVE

It is not necessarily because Buddhism has such profound teachings that there are priests who seem overly wise and can get people in the present to believe easily in the doctrine. It is simply that from ancient times preaching was done with vigor, and later everyone in society belonged to the religion. One reason is that most people invited others to come and share the experience. When anything is practiced widely in society, it is easy for a person to join in, simply because everyone else is doing it.

[415] ON ANCIENT ELEGANT WORDS THAT STILL EXIST IN THE PROVINCES

There are many instances of ancient elegant words existing to this day in the [languages of the] provinces. Especially, there are interesting words still in use in the customs of people in provinces located far away from the capital. These last few years I have paid special attention to the words that visitors from far-off provinces who have come to see me have used, and I always ask questions about those usages. But if we were to collect the vocabulary from the various provinces on a wide scale, how many interesting things we would come upon.

Recently, a man from the province of Figo came, and for the words we currently use in society like *mieru* (visible) and *kikoeru* (audible), he used the words *miyuru* and *kikoyuru*. Because these are elegant usages no longer heard at all in the present, when I asked, "Is this how you generally speak in your province?" he replied, "People with no education, or those who live in the mountains use words like *miyuru*, *kikoyuru*, *sayuru* (clear sound), and *tayuru* (to cease). But many of the people have changed their speech and now say *mieru* or *kikoeru*." This type of speech is vulgar nowadays, but since the people in the provinces use these types of words, it appears that they believe that it is proper speech.

No matter what province it may be, the language used by those who are uneducated and of low status as well as those who live in the mountains includes many ancient words, though they may be somewhat slurred. When many people are living together in a bustling town, however, people from other provinces are likely to be there, also, and some people have the opportunity to travel back and forth to the capital. With this, these people become accustomed to hearing words from other regions, and a person is able to choose his words, creating a pretentious modern style of language far removed from the ancient, which gradually falls into a vulgar form of Japanese.

Another person from the province of Figo once said, "In my birthplace of Figo we call a toad *tangaku*, which is believed to be a corrupted form of the ancient word *taniguku*." And this really appears to be the case.[238] I have heard many other examples like this from other regions too, but for now I have only given the examples that suddenly came to mind. When I remember others I will make those public.

[416] *SETI* AT THE BEGINNING OF THE YEAR, AND CALLING ONE'S WIFE *UTIKATA*

The so-called banquet served at the beginning of the new year is called *seti*. In the private anthology of Mibu no Tadami[239] (it says) that by some folding screens they were eating *seti* (and he

---

238. The word *taniguku* "toad" appears in *Kojiki* and *Man'yōshū*.
239. (Dates unclear). Mibu no Tadami was a poet who lived in the tenth century.

composed): *faru kasumi / tatu to ifu fi wo / mukafetutu / tosi no aruzi to / ware ya narinamu* (On that day when spring mists arise, is it I who is the master of the new year that is approaching?) In the private anthology of Tsurayuki we see the usage of "the wife (*utikata*) of Middle Counselor Tsunesuke." It turns out that calling one's wife *utikata* is an ancient usage.

8 | THE LOWER BRANCHES OF THE BUSH CLOVER

fito fa kozu　　　　No one comes to visit me—
fagi no simofa mo　　The blossoms on the lower branches
katutirite　　　　　of the bush clover have scattered.
arasi fa samusi　　　The storm feels cold
aki no yamazato　　at my mountain lodging in autumn.

Looking at ancient poems with multiple usages of *fa*, I have enjoyed the rhythm, and I wanted to compose a poem that does the same thing. Will people pick up the meaning of the poem? Or will they not? Even though I understand the meaning, someone else may read it and not get it. I wonder if anyone will get the meaning. I have no idea either way.

[419] ON THE REMNANTS OF ANCIENT PRACTICES SURVIVING IN THE PROVINCES

There are many examples of remote villages that not only preserve the ancient vocabulary, but also preserve various ceremonies with fragments of elegant customs. Moreover, when one of those people infected with learning is among the group that practices one of these customs, he takes a stand against the ancient custom, proclaiming it to be old nonsense. He wants to alter and modernize everything, and it is regrettable that this trend continues all over the country, and various old customs are slowly fading away. There are many interesting examples of funerals and weddings preserving old customs in the provinces. How I would like to travel from shore to mountain and write down all these old customs. What later-era people have done in rearranging funerals and festivals has mostly been influenced by the Chinese Heart, and this is a very unbecoming and bothersome problem.

[422] ANCIENT RECORDS AND THEIR IMPOSTORS

Recently, there are many colleagues who love the things from the ancient past, and when they hear there is something ancient, no matter what it may be, they are quick to excitement;[240] because of this, there are many items that appear to be thousands of years old, items handed down at old shrines and old temples, or artifacts buried for thousands of years excavated from the ground. Now, since these old, rare items have appeared, it goes without saying that a diagram of these items is copied onto paper, and these are in turn copied by those in far-off places, and then shown to friends. It is very regrettable and heart-rending that in the world now there are many people who manufacture suspicious forgeries, and deceive people, saying these things are stored away in "such and such" a shrine located in "such and such" a province. They then hold up a diagram of the object and claim that some person excavated it from some mountain.

The other day, in the Sakaori Shrine located in the province of Kafi, a statue said to be of Hoage no Mikoto, the old man who lit the fire and provided the finishing stanzas for the poem of Yamato Takeru, was said to have been discovered a few years ago located between two rafters in the attic of the building. Someone made a copy and showed it to another person. Because the object appeared to be the work of high antiquity, people believed this to be a rare find. I was suspicious about the copy, and I asked one of my students living close to the shrine[241] to go see what he thought

---

240. It should be remembered that a number of discoveries around the time of Norinaga had fueled this excitement. In the spring of 1784, the famous gold signet was found on Shikanoshima by Hakata Bay.

241. Yoshikawa et al. (1978:240, headnote) identify this individual as Hagihara Motokatsu (1749–1805). He came from the Yamanashi District of Kai Province. In 1783 he wrote *Kai Meishō shi* "A Record of Famous Places in Kai." It seems logical that Norinaga would ask him, as he was an expert in things related to that area.

8 ~ THE LOWER BRANCHES OF THE BUSH CLOVER 211

about the discovered statue. The item was quickly found to be a fraud. I asked the head priest of the shrine, Iida, about the discovery, and he wrote back saying in reality there was not even a diagram of the statue in existence.

Also, during the same period, a person in the province of Figo [somewhere in Figo but I have forgotten where] claimed to have excavated a wooden block said to have been engraved by the woman Hikaki.[242] A rubbing was made and transmitted to places here and there. When I inquired about the origins of this wooden block, it sounded authentic, but there was something I still did not understand, and I still have my doubts. These kinds of unexpected examples are hard to accept. One should be on his guard.

[423] ON WANTING TO KNOW THE ETYMOLOGY OF WORDS

Scholars should naturally want to know the etymology of ancient words, and this should be the first thing they inquire after. Etymology concerns questions such as, "What does 'heaven' mean?" Or "What does 'earth' mean?" This is one facet of scholarship and is all well and good, but it should not be the major concern of your work.

Your concern with the ancient lexicon should be more about researching and elucidating how ancient Japanese used these words, rather than what the origin was. If you can make clear how the word was used, there is little lost even if you do not know the etymology. It goes without saying that one should elucidate the beginning of things, and do the rest later, but you must not become overly concerned with this principle. In some cases, you can research the later stages and work backward.

In most instances, it is difficult to elucidate the etymology, and even when you come to some conclusion about the etymology, it is often difficult to prove you are right. Thus, the study of linguistics should not give etymology priority, but should concentrate on il-

---

242. Hikaki appears in *Yamato monogatari*.

luminating how a certain word was used by the ancient people. For example, even if a scholar discovered the etymology of a word, without knowing how it was used anciently, his work has little value. Without knowing the proper usage, a scholar cannot use it in his own writing.

This is especially true of people engaged in the study of ancient things. When they discover a fairly old word, the first thing they do is look into the etymology. They do not even wonder how the word was used, and when they use the word in their own work, they often commit terrible blunders in usage. On the whole, there are many cases where the etymology of a word and its usage are not the same. For example, *naka naka ni* is usually used to mean "neither there nor here, somewhere in the middle," but the overall significance is "halfway." You can also use it to mean "on the other hand." It is a mistake to use it according to its original meaning [from the etymology] of "in the middle."

Another example is *kokorogurusi*, which in the present vernacular means "how pitiful." It is a mistake to take the word at face value and use it as "my heart is pained." Thus, students should understand this principle by what I have said and make the ancient usage your first priority in study. If you spend all your time on the etymology, then you end up creating a mountain of mistakes.

[424] CONCERNING STANZAS REPEATING 5 AND 7 OR 7 AND 5 IN CHŌKA

When I hear ancient *chōka* composed by people in the present, many of these are composed in 7-5-7-7 meter, but when we examine how the stanzas are composed in the majority of the *chōka* in *Man'yōshū*, we find that they continue in 5-7-5-7 meter. *Chōka* with a 7-5 repeating meter are extremely rare. Because of this people should compose poetry so that the meter is 5-7-5-7. Nevertheless, *chōka* from the *Kokinshū* onward will start with 5-7 meter, but many of the continuing stanzas will flow in 7-5 meter. When one attempts to compose poetry according to this standard, with all stanzas repeating the 7-5 syllable meter, you find that it is sturdy and the rhythm is fine. This originates from the time of

Kokinshū, and because it quickly became the standard, poetry written at that time by a poet was found to flow naturally. *Imayō* [or popular songs] of the Middle Ages, as well as later types of songs, such as more common songs of the present, all start with a standard *ku* and then continue with the 7-5 meter.

Until the age of *Man'yōshū*, poetry followed the 5-7 meter and this had a nice rhythm, but from the time of *Kokinshū* this switched to 7-5, and the reason that we find that to be the best rhythm, which is a change from ancient times, is because of the natural change in rhythm. There are many people presently who compose poetry in a *Man'yō*-style and in all things they treat traditions from later eras as bad, but when you examine a *chōka* they have written you find that they are still composing in the 7-5 meter as they have not been able to comprehend the ancient meter. They cannot escape the natural rhythm of these later ages. Regarding the *chōka* in *Kokinshū*, the first two are a mixture of 5-7 and 7-5 meters, but the last three are generally written in a 7-5 meter.

[425] ON THE VAST AMOUNT OF MISTAKES IN MODERN POETRY

The poetry and prose composed lately by people appears on the surface to be well written, but there are many mistakes. However, there are few people in the present who can discover these mistakes, because most people composing poetry or writing prose do so using elegant phrases and putting on airs of elegance. They think this is proper, and they do it so they can be the center of talk and praise, and when this happens, they put on that self-satisfied look. I think this is quite absurd, even ignorant, but if these people came to a realization about how many mistakes are in their poetry and prose, they would certainly feel small. These people are able to spot a mistake in someone else's work, but they cannot notice the mistakes in their own, so they become self-conceited about their ability. Nevertheless, since there are myriad paths to understanding the true significance of the ancient lexicon, it is almost impossible to proclaim there is no other correct usage for a certain instance.

[426] IT IS DIFFICULT TO KEEP A TIGHT STRUCTURE IN YOUR POETRY AND PROSE

Having looked at a fair amount of poetry and prose composed by recent writers, I find that there are various places where interesting things have been said, catching the eye of the reader. Among these interesting passages are sections where I wonder about the propriety. I have seen very few works that were written without mistakes. In the present, it is very difficult to imitate the writers from the past. Even superior writers in the past had trouble producing an error-free text. Since this is true of them, how much so for the person in the present. Perhaps it is difficult to say anything about minor mistakes. Nonetheless, if you are going to the trouble to write something, then it is best not to include mistakes that will later cause criticism. I must say that writing in an affected, self-satisfied air is something chastised by the scholars of ancient China.[243]

[427] ON LECTURES, READING GROUPS, AND TAKING NOTES

No matter what field of study you are in, it is the normal practice to attend a lecture and listen to an exposition on the import of old works. In the Middle Ages this was called *dangi* (a sermon), but to use that word in the present conjures up images of a priest gathering together a group of unlearned people and teaching them about the doctrine. It is different from a lecture.

Modern Confucian scholars insist that at these lectures if you do nothing but listen to what is being said, avoiding any analysis on your own, then the lecture has no meaning as far as scholarship or research is concerned. They deny any value in simply listening. They turn a lecture into a meeting with the purpose of reviewing a

---

243. *The Analects* note, "Ran Qiu said, 'It is not that I do not delight in [the doctrine] of your Way. I do not have sufficient strength.' The Master replied, 'Those who do not have sufficient strength give up in the middle of things. You put limits on yourself'" ("Yong Ye" chapter).

8 ~ THE LOWER BRANCHES OF THE BUSH CLOVER

book. This is fundamentally different from a lecture, where in a book discussion group each participant must think on his own and announce the results of his analysis, probing aspects that do not satisfy the group, debating various points. This may appear to be good for scholarship, but it does not have that much value.

Having experienced a few book discussion groups in my time, I know that in the beginning it does appear that there is an active movement to question and answer, but as time goes on, people become slovenly, and they compete with each other, trying to see who can read the most material. What I do not care for is the affected air under which the meeting is conducted. There is thus no difference from reading on your own, and the whole purpose of gathering together loses its meaning.

Furthermore, beginners possess little ability to make their own thoughts clear, having no knowledge about this and that, so they are ashamed to asked questions in detail. Attending such a meeting for these people forces them to pass the time having done nothing fruitful, so a lecture is of much more value to beginners.

Even at a lecture, it is needless to say that the participants, who do nothing but listen, not attempting to use their own faculties of understanding, gain little. A student must work hard at a preliminary inspection of the topic, pondering what he can do by himself, paying attention to places he finds hard to believe, reading such passages repeatedly. Having done this, the student at a lecture gains much more insight and forgets much less.

Having attended a lecture, the student then should return home and review the principles learned, recalling things learned that day, reliving the experience. Taking notes refers to writing down what is being said while you listen. Normally, you should write down important points here and there that you feel you might forget later on, but the current practice is to write down everything said by the lecturer.

Lectures originally were places where you could relax, listen, and write down the essence of what was being said. However, later people took notes on everything being said, which made them tense, afraid they would miss something, and they paid little attention to important points, or missed important principles, or at worse, heard things different from what was actually said. A student who takes pride in being able to keep a minute record of everything being said means that the lecture has become an exercise in shorthand. This is surely a waste of time.

[430] *YŌSUTE*

In the vernacular is the usage of *yōsute* (用捨) used for *yurusu* (allow), which comes from a poem in the anthology of Bai Juyi: "If it is a change in my life and I take to being lost / then discard my consent as if it had never existed." This has the same meaning as that in the vernacular, but the graph should be the same (容). Writing the graph 用 (for this usage) comes from confusion with discarding (捨) something and using it (用).

[431] *TUBONE*

In the "Young Shoot" chapter of *Eiga monogatari* it says, "The [ladies-in-waiting] who came from the outside were jammed together in the Table Room inside flimsy enclosures of screens and curtain stands.[244] The meaning of *tubone* (a room for the ladies-in-waiting) comes from a place that is cramped and made narrow.[245]

[432] PILLOW WORDS

When one wishes to use the words "heaven," "moon," or "sun" in poetry, he places the modifier **fisakata no** before it. When he wants to use the word "mountain," he modifies it first with the words **asifiki no**. These kinds of set words are modifiers, and the designation of *makura kotoba* (pillow words), which is often used now, was never used anciently. This term appears to have originated

---

244. McCullough and McCullough (1980, vol. 2:646).
245. In an earlier essay Norinaga states, "*Tubone* is a cramped area that is appropriately decorated [for the ladies-in-waiting]" (Ōno and Ōkubo 1976, vol. 13:631).

from the end of the Middle Ages on.[246] It may appear that the reason for calling it "pillow" is because the modifying word is placed at the head [much like a pillow] of the poem, but this is not the case. *Makura* (pillow) is not something placed at the head. A pillow supports the head, but not only the head; it supports all things, whether they float or bridge two points. In each instance, we use the word *makura*. The reason there are pillow words in poetry is because one stanza is deficient in words, and the pillow word is placed in the space or opening to lend an allusion to the meaning of the word it proceeds, and that is apparently the reason that people began calling these *makura kotoba*. We find these in poems such as *ume no fana / sore tomo miezu / fisakata no* ... "The blossoms of the plum / and far off ... " (KKS 334). Or *sinoburedo / kofisiki toki fa / asifiki no* ... "Though I endure the longing / when I miss you / cramping my legs ... " (KKS 633). Now these describe a general phenomenon, but people in later eras took these as having a single function, and that is why they labeled them thus. Because these pillow words are usually placed at the head of the phrase, my teacher, Master Agatai, called his work on these *kanjikō* (crown-word-treatise), which makes sense. People now are accustomed to calling these *makura kotoba*, so regardless of the reason people cite why this usage is incorrect, I see nothing wrong with the label.

[433] CONCERNING *ZOKU FUDOKI* OF TIKUZEN PROVINCE

There is a work called *Tikuzen zoku fudoki*, compiled by Kaibara Atsunobu [Ekiken],[247] which includes minute details about this province. I have examined five volumes: 6, 7, 8, 15, and

---

246. From what we know, the word *makura kotoba* first appears in the early fifteenth century.
247. Kaibara Atsunobu (Ekiken) (1630–1714) was born in Chikuzen to a samurai family. In 1649 he was sent to Nagasaki to gain knowledge of things pertaining to Western science and technology. He incurred the wrath of the Daimyō Lord, Kuroda Tadayuki, and was a *ronin* for seven years. He spent over twenty years gathering data, which he put into *Chikuzen zoku fudoki*, completed in 30 volumes in 1710.

16. I have not yet seen the other volumes. Volumes 15 and 16 deal with things in Munakata District. Volume 15 consists of forty-four or forty-five leaves, and is generally concerned with events surrounding the Mimafe Shrine in Munakata. I made a copy of this one volume. The three volumes, 6, 7, and 8, concern Mikasa District. Now this elder gentleman, Kaibara, is a Confucian scholar of high reputation who has put together numerous works that have circulated through society, but this *Fudoki*, while it is a large compilation, is still relatively unknown, and even I myself only learned of it for the first time recently. He has written a very rare and splendid work.

[434] THE PRIEST CALLED GENSO

There is a Zen priest called Genso who appears in the records of Ming China,[248] having received an order to travel over to that country when Great Lord Toyotomi attacked Korea. He met with the king of that country, and exchanged diplomatic messages and other things. Genso came from Nisi Village in Munakata District in Tikuzen Province. He is the son of Kawazu Shinshirō, who is a descendant of Itō Yoshikiyo of Izu Province, who came to Tikuzen and homesteaded there. Genso was born in this village of Nisi in the sixth year of Tenbun (1537), and later moved to Tusima. He has a poetry and prose collection called *Sensōkō*. On the twenty-second day of the twelfth month of the sixteenth year of Keichō (1611) he passed away in Tusima at the age of seventy-five. This is recorded in *Tikuzen zoku fudoki*.

[435] *KANNA* AND *MANNA*, *FINGASI* AND *MINNAMI*

Kana (*hiragana*) should be pronounced *kanna*. It is a mistake to pronounce *mana* [Chinese writing] as *manna*. Since *kana* originally was *karina* (borrowed name), and the *ri* weakened and

---

248. Genso's full name is Keitetsu Genso. He is perhaps most well-known for his diplomatic work between Hideyoshi and the parties in Korea, the Tokugawa government, and Ming China.

8 ~ THE LOWER BRANCHES OF THE BUSH CLOVER   219

changed to *n* people say *kanna*, but there is no reason why *mana* should be pronounced as *manna*. People unexpectedly say this, adding *n* analogous to the pronunciation of *kanna*. It is also a mistake to pronounce "south" as *minnami*. This pronunciation also originates by analogy from *fingasi* (east), where people carelessly insert *n*. As "east" originally was *fimukasi*, the *mu* undergoes a similar sound change [as *karina*] to *n*, and this is an example where *n* causes the following *ka* to become voiced to *ga*.[249] Therefore, there is no reason to pronounce "south" as *minnami*. Now when there are these kinds of sound changes, we find many examples where an *n* gets inserted. However, the words *manna* and *minnami* are not examples of this, but these are definitely confused usages based on the example of *kanna* and *finagasi*.

[438] CONCERNING THE WORD WOTI IN *MAN'YŌSHŪ*

In the fifth volume of *Man'yōshū* there are two poems that use the word **woti**:

wa ga sakari	The height of my life
itaku kutatinu	has completely weakened.
kumo ni tobu	Even if I take the medicine
kusuri famu tomo	so I can fly above the clouds
mata wotime yamo	I wonder if I will return to my youth.
	(MYS 847)

kumo ni tobu	Rather than taking
kusuri famu yo fa	medicine to fly above the clouds,
miyako miba	if you see the capital
iyasiki a ga mi	then your helpless body
mata wotinu besi	will return to its youth. (MYS 848)

It cannot be **oti** (to fall) because the phonograms used to represent it are different, and the meaning of the poem would not make sense. I have pondered these poems, which have been be-

---

249. This later becomes known as prenasalization. It is very perceptive of Norinaga to notice these phonological changes.

yond comprehension since ancient times. First, these two were written by poets far off in Tukusi and were written because of a longing for the capital. The meaning of the first poem is that the zenith of the poet's life has passed and he has greatly weakened in health, but even if he were to take that medicine of the sage of King Huainan who lived in China, he cannot become young like he was in the past. The second poem means that rather than taking the medicine of the King of Huainan, if you were to look at the capital, you would return to your youth of the past.

The word **woti** has the general meaning of returning to the original state of something and refers to the body returning to its former state of youth. In a *chōka* in Volume 17 written on hawks by Master Yakamochi we find this word: **tabanare mo / woti mo kayasuki** (even when I release them / they return back quickly) (MYS 4011). These stanzas praise the hawk and this use of **woti** refers to the bird returning to the hand that had released it ... .

[439] CONCERNING THE WORDS TADAKA AND MASAKA IN *MAN'YŌSHŪ*

The words **tadaka** and **masaka** that occur in *Man'yōshū* appear to be easily confused, but the difference in the two words can be discerned with ease by looking at the context of the word in question and the meaning of the poem. While there is no confusion in meaning, there are mistakes in the present manuscript, which may cause people to believe that the two words are ambiguous as to their meaning.

First, the word **tadaka** appears in stanzas such as **kimi ga tadaka** (written 君之直香 or 公之正香 or 吉美賀多太可, your scent), or **imo ga tadaka** (written 妹之直香 or 妹之正香, my beloved's scent). There are no other usages than these. Regarding **masaka** it appears in stanzas such as **masaka fa kimi ni yorinisi mono wo** (in the present my heart lists to you); also **itu no makasa mo tune wasurayenu** (no matter when, [your words] will never be forgotten); also **masaka mo kanasi** [(my love) at this moment is poignant]; or **masaka si yokaba** (if the present time is agreeable with you); and **ima no masaka mo** (even now at the present time).

The usage of **tadaka** is vastly different from **masaka**. However, when the scribe copied down 正香, he attached the gloss of **masaka** and that is where the ambiguity originated. 正香 is not **masaka**, but clearly **tadaka**, as one can glean from the examples I have provided. Now the word **tadaka** points directly at "you" (*kimi*) or "your beloved" (*imo*) and is only used with these two pronouns and thus sounds the same. **Masaka** points to the destination in which one is headed and is a word that refers to the present time. One can discern this from looking at the poems in the anthology that use these words. Among these poems there is the word **yuri**, which is used in a poem that replies to a previous poem. **Yuri** also means "later" and is in opposition to "now." Even in the present vernacular we have the phrase *masaka no toki* (at the present time). The meaning of this word *masaka* is a holdover.

[441] CONCERNING A MAN FROM CHINA NAMED BING JI

When one reads the juvenile book *Meng qiu*,[250] you notice that during the Han era there was a man called Bing Ji who was a minister. During one spring, he was going somewhere when he met a man pulling an ox. The ox stuck out its tongue and sneered. Bing Ji said, "It is not even summer yet, but this ox is so hot that it sticks out its tongue and gasps. When cold and heat do not follow their appointed seasons, it means that some disaster is about to occur. Though a minister [like me] is supposed to use *yin* and *yang* to keep the natural elements in harmony and thus avoid disasters, this ox is proof that such is not so. This shows that I am not fit to be a minister."

People read this event and think that this is a reasonable turn of events, and everyone believes this to be a superior story. My own personal opinion is that this is a terribly stupid story. Even

---

250. A work in three volumes, *Meng qiu* was written by Li Huan during the Tang dynasty. The author took quotes from ancient works and arranged these by topic. The quotes were then set to a four-grapheme rhyme pattern to make it easy for young people to memorize.

though it is not the season of heat, why should an ox not behave thus? In addition, if one were truly that worried about the state of *yin* and *yang*, then he should have watched over them from the very beginning—what is the significance of merely meeting an ox on the way to some place and be inspired to realize that something is amiss? If he had failed to notice the behavior of the ox then he would not have known anything about the state of *yin* and *yang* and the story would not have been handed down. Because of these reasons, I think that this is not an actual story, but one that someone invented to make people think it is a remarkable event. If this man had actually said and done these things, then he is the greater fool. It is also foolish for the author to have included this story in his work.

Let me reiterate that there never was anything such as "preserving the order of *yin* and *yang*," for everything that occurs in this world, whether it is in the heavens or on the earth, all events originate from the actions of the deities. It is not the fate of man to know whether a certain element is in balance or in confusion. Recording all sorts of details like these is another example of a very bothersome and trifling affair of the Chinese people.

[442] THE STORY OF ZHOU GONG DAN EATING HIS RICE, VOMITING IT UP, AND MEETING A WISE MAN

In the same juvenile book, we find the words of Zhou Gong Dan,[251] who instructed his students by saying, "When I wash my hair, I wring it three times. When I eat my food, I spit it up three times, and then I go out and meet high-ranking officials. I often worry if this will not lead to the loss of the wise men in the kingdom."

If this man actually did what he said, then it would merely be

---

251. Zhou Dan was also known as the Duke of Zhou, dates unclear. Much about his story is wrapped in legend, but he appears to have helped his older brother, King Wu, during the Zhou dynasty, consolidate power. He is credited with writing *I ching* and the *Book of Songs*. He later was called the God of Dreams. Confucius claimed to have met the Duke of Zhou in his dreams a number of times.

8 ~ THE LOWER BRANCHES OF THE BUSH CLOVER   223

a strategy to become a man of fame in the country. No matter how much you may wish to meet a learned scholar, could one not just hurry up, swallow his food first, and go out? Someone would certainly not hurry so, but take his time. It would be easy to chew and swallow while going on your way, so why make a show of throwing up one's food? There are many examples of Chinese customs where they do things just for show, because they have a strong desire for fame. As I have said before, this is a typical tendency of the Chinese, a very disgusting habit they have.

[443] ABOUT A PERSON KNOWN AS FUJITANI NARIAKIRA

Lately, a person named Fujitani Senzaemon Nariakira[252] lived in the capital. I have read his books, *Kazashishō*, *Ayuhishō*, and *Rokuun zuryaku*, and was astounded.[253] I had heard about him earlier, and thought he was nothing more than the typical affected poetic scholar, so I paid no attention to his works. But I finally picked up some of his works and he really impressed me. I talked to people who knew him and was again surprised to learn that he passed away not long ago.

---

252. Fujitani Senzaemon Nariakira (1738–1779) was born in Kyōto. He originally studied Chinese and poetry, much as Norinaga did. He later became interested in linguistics, and the three works he penned, noted below, have had a profound influence on early Japanese linguistic study, as he was one of the first to attempt a systematic and scientific analysis of Japanese grammar.
253. *Kazashishō* (挿頭抄, An Abridgement of Hair Ornaments), finished in 1767. Nariakira categorized parts of speech into Names (nouns), Garments (verbs), Leg Straps (particles and suffixes), and Hair Ornaments (pronouns, adverbs, prefixes, and conjunctions). This work explains the grammatical function of these "hair ornaments." *Ayuhishō* (脚結抄, An Abridgement of Leg Straps) was written in 1778. Fujitani describes the grammatical usages of "leg straps" as particles and suffixes. Finally, in *Rokuun ryakuzu* (六運略図, A Rough Diagram of the Six Revolutions, date of completion unclear) he analyzed poetic language, and by systematically categorizing the changes in the language of poetry, he established six "periods" for the Japanese language: ancient age, early Middle Ages, late Middle Ages, recent past, yesteryear, and present. Overall his work is of monumental importance, as he did his grammatical analysis in complete isolation. It is amazing that he labeled the last two groups as he did, showing his syntactic sensitivity, as both "leg straps" and "hair ornaments" *bind* words together (see Miller 1967:323–26).

Recent poets are so competitive and work so hard to be recognized in society that they pretend to have comprehended the Way of poetry and go around boasting about their ability. Reading their prose, poetry, or hearing them speak reveals how numerous their mistakes are and most of what they have attempted is immature. There are few people in this class that can be called talented, and there is not a single person we could label as distinguished. Fujitani was different from this brand of people, and though society is full of proud scholars engaged in the study of ancient learning, Fujitani was not like those people, either.

I do not know if he had mastered the principles of ancient learning that could take his scholarship back before the era of *Man'yōshū*. His theories in *Rokuun no ben* dealing with the poetic style prior to *Kokinshū* places him above the poetic scholars of our day. Having read his own poetic work, *Hokuhenshū*,[254] I do not find his own poetry that outstanding, but he commits very few of the errors that others of our day do. How pitiful that such a worthy man has already passed away. I have heard that his son, Senzaemon, is engaged in furthering the work of his father, in spite of his youth. I pray that he can bring his father's work to completion. Many of Fujitani's works are available today, and I have been fortunate in reading a few.

[445] *MAGO*

In *Saigūki* we find [phrases like] "*mago* (馬子) six people" or "*mago* four people." These are people that attend to the horses. In the present these are called *mago*.[255]

---

254. *Hokuhenshū*: Nariakira's poetic collection. Noringa's own copy of this work states that it was called *hokuhen* (北辺) because Nariakira dwelt on the land where Kitanobe Dainagon (北辺大納言) had lived.

255. Interesting that Norinaga does not quote from *Shoku Nihongi*, third year of Tenpyō Hōji (759), ninth month, twenty-sixth day, "Those used in the construction were men from the district offices, military affairs, soldiers from the *Chinzeifu*, and horse attendants, in all 8,180 men." Here 馬子 is glossed as *mago*.

[448] GRAFTING

In the same record [*Meigetsuki*][256] we find, "On the seventh day of the third month of the second year of Kanki (1230), both branches of the double-flowering cherry tree [one branch is grafted into a tree at the Ichijō Palace] gradually blossomed, and then on one long spring day, suddenly the chrysanthemums seedlings I planted sprouted forth [The weeds did not fear the flowerbed dirt]." It turns out that the act of *tugiki* (grafting) existed as early as this time.

[451] THE USAGE OF "SIR"

In correspondence in the present people will sometimes put 貴下 (sir) alongside the name of the addressee. In places here and there in *Taiki* you find examples of this "sir" where it should have 足下 (esteemed colleague).

[452] AFFLICTED WITH A RUNNY NOSE

In the same record [*Naka Mikado Gondainagon Nobutane nikki*], we see here and there, "Lately I am afflicted with a runny nose. Suddenly my body gets warm." Also, "Because of my runny nose I cannot count the rosary during my chants. However, today I did not have any fever." And, "Since I have had a runny nose, I can finally count the rosary during my chants [I bathed last night]." It sounds as if he had caught a cold. There is also an example of "last night" being written 夜前.

---

256. *Meigetsuki* "Record of the Clear Moon" is the diary of Fujiwara no Teika (1162–1241). He kept this diary religiously over a fifty-six-year period, starting in 1180 and ending in 1235.

[453] *SESERAGI*

A small ditch in the vernacular is called a *seseragi*, a word that is also seen in a poem in the last half of *Kanke Man'yōshū*:[257]

momidiba no	As the autumn leaves
nagarete sekeba	block the flow of the water,
yama kafa no	the shallow ditch
asaki seragi mo	of the mountain river also
aki fa fukaki wo	shows how autumn is deepening.

[455] WRITING A *TAN* OF CLOTH AS 反

In *Taiki* there are examples of three yards of cloth (布三反) or two yards of cloth (布二反). Even during those days they wrote *tan* 端 (yard of fabric) as 反.[258]

[456] *FIKIFADA*

In the same record [*Taiki*] it says, "Those of the fourth and fifth rank wear "half shoes" [These have *fikifada* (tanned) leather and lack embroidery]. Those of the sixth rank wear "deep shoes." [These have no *fikifada* and lack any embroidery.] This makes it sound as if even regular shoes had tanned leather. The meaning of this word (*fikifada*) is "toad-skin" (蟾蜍膚).

---

257. More commonly known as *Shinsen Man'yōshū* (Newly compiled *Anthology of a Myriad Leaves*). The compilation of the first half was completed in 893. The compilation of the last half was finished in 913. The first half is thought to be the work of the Sugawara Michizane (845–903), hence the name of "Kanke" [household of Sugawara].

258. Kojima Seisai (1797–1862), a Confucian scholar of the late Edo era, wrote in *Kanchu seiwa* (date unclear), "Presently people use the graph 反 to count the amount of silk fabric. They should be using the graph 端, but have borrowed the graph 段, which is used to divide up parcels of rice paddy land. When written in the running script [cursive], this graph becomes 反, and people mistake it for 反. It's the same mistake as 仮 originating from the running script form of 假" (Section 46).

[459] A CONCURRENT POST

In the "Flock of Cranes in the Rice Fields" chapter of *Utsuho monogatari* the word "concurrent post" is written *kakedukasa*.[259]

[460] CONCERNING THE EAR OF A NEEDLE

People in the present call the eye of a needle *mimidu*. In *Dōmōshō* it is called *fari no mimi* (ear of a needle). Perhaps this is the [same] meaning as ear.[260]

[463] CARPENTERS FROM FIDA

Anciently because so many carpenters came from the province of Fida, later carpenters in general were called "Fida carpenters," even when they were not from that province. There is a similar example of this in China. In the "Biography of Kuan" in *Shiji* it says, "He commanded that two generals of the Lou-Fan and five company commanders [of archers] be beheaded,"[261] which has an annotational note, "Lou-fan is the name of a prefecture. People from there were skilled at the bow on horseback. Thus skilled archers were named Lou-fan. This became a designation of honor, but not all of these archers were necessarily from Lou-fan."

[464] CONCERNING THE WORD *FAYARU*

In *Ōkagami* it says, "When the Horikawa Chancellor [Kanemichi] was at the height of his prosperity [*fayaritamafisi*], the present Lord of Higashi Sanjō [Kaneie] was forced to give up

---
259. Norinaga likely noticed this because the earlier reading would have been *make wo kaneru*.
260. This usage appears as early as Chapter 1, "Toshikage," in *Utsuho monogatari* (*A Tale of a Hollow Tree*, ca. 980). Here the text has *fari no mimi*. It is unclear what the *-du* is.
261. My translation is a slightly altered version of Nienhauser (1994, vol. 8:189).

his [former] high offices and was living in a most saddened state ...."[262] The word *fayaru* is understood to mean "prosper." The word used in the present has a slightly different meaning.

[475] CONCERNING 咄 (STORY)

In the present people call tales *fanasi*, and write this with the character 咄. In the Chinese dictionary *Shuowen*, it says that 咄 means to speak to one another. Moreover, because [of the example] in the Zhang Jing Yang historical poem in *Wenxuan*, which says, "This cicada speaking to the guests / My lord, naturally this was written to the gentry," the graph fits the meaning. So what does [the Japanese word] *fanasi* actually mean? Perhaps it is from *fanasi* (to release).

[477] WILLOW BOX

A willow box appears in the ninth volume of *Shoku Nihongi*.[263]

[478] THE DAY AFTER TOMORROW

The "day after tomorrow" (明後日) is seen here and there in *Shōyūki* written 明々日 (tomorrow tomorrow day).

[482] THE TITLE OF WAKE FOUND IN *MAN'YŌSHŪ*

The appellation **wake** attached to the end of the names of princes, like Prince "so and so" Wake, or that found in some titles, like "so and so" Wake is not the same **wake** found after people's name as a title. In the poetry in *Man'yōshū* there is a certain type of

---

262. See Yamagiwa (1967:147).
263. Found in an imperial edict issued on the nineteenth day of the twelfth month of the sixth year of Yōrō (722).

wake used as a label. It is not fully clear why all people understand this as a dishonorable label. Generally people have always treated it as dishonorable, but it is different than *yatuko*, which is a noun used to refer to oneself and not other people, and when you use it in relation to other people, it is a label that places you especially lower in status. In spite of this, some have used it in a joking manner, so it is not really that improper. In Book 4 of *Man'yōshū* we find **wa ga kimi fa / wake woba sine to / omofe kamo** (Is it because you want little ol' me to die ... " (MYS 552)? This is said in relation to the poet. Now because this is said to debase oneself, when a person should say "my beloved," and when the person wants to show respect to the other person they would say "my lord," which can be taken as said in jest.

In the same book of the anthology there is another poem that demonstrates the same usage:

kuroki tori	I have tried to serve
kaya mo karitutu	by taking black trees
tukafemedo	and by cutting thatch,
isosiki wake to	but he is not to be praised
fomemu tomo arazu	as an industrious chap. (MYS 780)

Here the poet sets up the phrase **isosiki mono** (an industrious chap) to refer to himself. Now in Book 8 we find:

wake ga tame	For your humble servant
a ga te mo suma ni	I will not rest my hands,
faru no no ni	but the thistle blossoms
nukeru tubana so	I plucked from the spring field—
mesite koyemase	come eat and grow fat. (MYS 1460)

Since this phrase reads "For your humble servant, I will not rest my hands" **wake** refers to "you." The next poem has:

firu fa saki	The sleeping flower
yoru fa kofinuru	which blooms in the day
nebu no fana	and sleeps at night—
kimi nomi mimeya	is it only right that my lord should see it?
wake safe ni miyo	You must see it, too. (MYS 1461)

As this ends in **miyo wake** it must refer to "you." Pondering the phrase, "is it only right that my *lord* should see it," this does not fit the meaning of the poem, so a scribe must have miscopied 吾 (I) as 君 (lord).

Now these two poems use **wake** to refer to other people, but the poem in Book 4 refers to oneself so these two usages are opposites, which is very misleading. Having pondered this, since Lady Ki sent these two poems to Minister Yakamochi, there is no reason why she should refer to the minister as **wake** and debase him, but what we can say is that this **wake** is used in jest. That is why **wake** is written 戯奴 (playful slave) with a note that says, "This should be read **wake**." This note was originally inserted by the poet. So she playfully debases "her lord" by calling him "a slave," and the insertion of the note regarding **wake** is to alert him to the fact that she is making fun of him ....

[483] WHAT SOME PEOPLE HAVE SAID

A certain person's statement that the study of ancient things was influenced by the Ancient Rhetoric School (of Sorai) is mistaken. The priest Keichū opened our field of ancient study. The ancient studies of the Confucian schools started by people like Itō[264] are from the same general time period as that of Keichū, but Keichū was chronologically ahead of him. Mister Ogyū was also a latecomer. Why should this group influence Keichū?

[486] SANSKRIT

The word for "crow" in Sanskrit is *kakaaka* (迦迦去引迦),[265] which is a name according to the cry of the bird. "Rooster" is *kurakuta* (矩羅倶姹),[266] which functions [as a name based on the sound

---

264. Itō Jinsai (1627–1705) rejected the modern interpretations of Confucius and went back to the original texts. This is often viewed as the start of Japanese philological studies in the Edo era.
265. Actually the Sanskrit word for crow is *kaaka*.
266. "Rooster" in Sanskrit is *kurkuṭa*.

of the bird] naturally the same as *kuda* of *kudakake* (chicken). "Roof tile" is *kyafara*.[267]

[488] VISITORS

In Ise they call people who come from other provinces to worship at the Ise Shrine *dōsha* (道者). In the record in *Shōchō Kumasha Shinkyō satabun*, there is a quote from a document dated the second year of Tenpuku (1234), which says, "A visitor (道者) named Minami Mumyōbō, a resident of Usuwi District in Simofusa Province came to worship at Kumano."[268]

[490] CAULDRON OF TWENTY-FIVE-BUSHEL CAPACITY

In *Uji shūi monogatari* it says, "Five or six cauldrons with a capacity of twenty-five bushels were brought and set up in the garden on stakes driven into the ground."[269] In the present we say that a cooking cauldron that has an *ittō* (five-gallon) capacity is called an *ittō* cauldron. This is it.

[492] CONCERNING GOLD COMING FROM SADO

In *Uji shūi monogatari* there is the event where people were digging for iron in Noto Province and on Sado Island someone said there were flowers that bloomed golden blossoms. Eight thousand taels of gold were collected and presented to Governor Sanefusa.[270]

---

267. It is not clear what word Norinaga has written. I have not been able to find a word for "roof tile" in any Sanskrit dictionary.
268. The record is found in Volume 1 of *Gunsho ruijū* (*Shōchō Kumasha Shinkyō* 1906:385).
269. Slightly altered version of Mills (1970:160). I have interpreted the original *nafa* (Norinaga's *nawa*) as "capacity."
270. Ibid., 219–20.

[493] *KURAKAKE*

In the same tale it relates that there were twenty "official business" saddles that were hanging on wooden horses (*kurakake*). While this is true, this object known as *kurakake* originally is the name of a tool to saddle a horse.

[494] A *KANA* CALENDAR

In the same tale it mentions a *kana* calendar. Were there calendars in Chinese and *kana* anciently? Now there are also days that are good for the Gods and the Buddha. Our present calendars have designated days that are good for the Gods. [This story] also points out days that are evil, as well as days that are good or bad [for certain events].[271]

[496] PROVERBS

In the present vernacular there is something called *sirikurafe kannon*.[272] In the record of Emperor Kinmei in *Nihon shoki*, we find a person called Tsuki Kishi Ikina who said, "King of Silla, kiss my ass!"

[499] *CHŪGOKU*

The provinces in the San'indō and San'yōdō are called *chūgoku* (middle states), and this is seen in an official tally from the second year of Gengyō (878), second month, third day, where it says, "Bowing we request information on the state of things. Because

---

271. Ibid., 244.
272. These are mainly proverbs about those who forget a debt or obligation owed them. It originates from someone praying to the goddess of mercy, receiving help, and then forgetting (or lacking gratitude) for the result. Norinaga seems to interpret *sirikurafe* to mean "kiss my ass," according to the quote from *Nihon shoki*.

8 ~ THE LOWER BRANCHES OF THE BUSH CLOVER   233

Mutu and Defa are so far removed, [we request information] every five years, and those places in the middle provinces of Inaba and Idumo we will request information every six years ... ." This is recorded in *Ruiju sandaikaku*.

[506] CONCERNING THE WORD *IRU*

In the vernacular, people say *kane ga iru* (I need cash), or *zeni ga iru* (I need coins), or even *ikura bakari iru* (How much do you need?) This word *iru* is seen in *Shōyūki*, "Do they need a thousand *koku* of sacrificial rice?" Also in *Genji monogatari* in the words of the Akashi Novice, "Letters written in *kana* take me time to read."[273] In the present vernacular people say they need some time [to do something]. It would appear that this word came to mean this from an early period. In the vulgar language of recent China they use the graph 没 with the same meaning.[274]

[514] CALLING "SERPENT" IN THE TWELVE-BRANCH SYSTEM *MI*

Calling "rat" in the twelve-branch system *ne* is based on an abbreviated form of *nezumi* (rat). "Hare" is called *u*, a truncated form of *usagi* (rabbit). In the ancient dictionaries this can be written phonetically as 宇, or with the graph 菟 (hare). Now that clearly explains where these two examples came from, but "serpent" is *mi*, and in *Wamyōshō* (serpent) is **femi**.[275] Now all the names of animals that are two syllables long, like *usi* (ox) and *tora*

---

273. See Tyler (2001, vol. 2:610).
274. It is difficult to explain why Norinaga uses this example, as 没 has never had the meaning of "need" or "necessary." In the vernacular in modern Chinese this means "not," as in 他還沒有吃 (He has not eaten yet).
275. Norinaga is suggesting that while the first two examples use only the first syllable of the longer word, "serpent" is an example where the last syllable is used, but the reason for this is never specified. This is possible, but difficult to prove or refute, as we have good phonological evidence that the first syllable of "serpent" *pemi* sounded like *pe* (< *pe₂*?) "fart," and was thus avoided (Bentley 2000:430, n. 21).

(tiger) are not abbreviated, aside from "serpent," and other than *fituzi* (sheep), all the three-syllable names are abbreviated.

[516] *RAKUGAKI* AND *RAKUSHU*

When someone has something to say but is afraid to say it in public, they write it so that no one will know who did it; in effect, they drop it on the way, and that is why even now we call this *otosibumi*. This is something they did even in the past, and they would write these on gates or on the walls of buildings, putting up something with the writing on it, or writing directly on the wall. Thus people took the Chinese reading of this word *otosibumi* (落とし書) and called this *rakusho*, and after people had become accustomed to calling it that, people later began to read the same characters as *rakugaki*. Even later people started using this word *rakugaki* to mean something written on walls without any purpose as a joke or sport [like graffiti]. In addition, in the provinces there is a kind of playful song called *rakushu*, which is also a spinoff of *rakusho*, the pronunciation becoming corrupted to *rakushu*. The section "Children's *rakushu* songs" found in *Gumon kenchū*[276] refers to this.

[518] CALLING THE DEATH OF SOMEONE "A DEATH FROM ILLNESS"

In official documents and other records in the present the death of a person is recorded as "death from illness" (病死). Generally speaking, from among hundreds or thousands of examples there are rarely one or two examples of a person dying without having been ill. In normal cases everyone dies from an illness, so everyone already knows this, and so it is not necessary to make a special case of this. This custom comes from the past when society

---

276. *Gumon kenchū* is a work compiled by Ton'a (1289–1372) and Nijō Yoshimoto (1320–1388), where Yoshimoto takes the persona of an ignorant person who addressed a number of questions concerning poetry, and Ton'a provides answers.

was in upheaval, and there were many who died in battle, so a "death from illnesses" was kept separate from death in battle.

[523] *WETA*

The name of the class of people in the present, Weta, is a corruption of *etori* (takes bait). The spelling of 穢多 (defiled-many) is a pretentious, vulgar usage. In *Wamyōshō* it says, "'A man who slaughters livestock' is **wetori** in the vernacular, and means someone who strips off the flesh of cows and horses, or who takes the bait of hawks and chickens. It is a person who slaughters or butchers cows and horses and sells the meat."

In the work *Fanyi mingyiji* it says, "Candala, this is a butcher. In *Fang xian chuan* it says that these are called evil people. They live separately from people and when they enter a city they slap bamboo sticks together to let people know that they are uncommon and [allow] people to stay away from them." This refers to the custom in India and these people resemble the *weta* in our times.[277]

[524] *TABI*

What people today call *tabi* (*tabi* socks) is referred to as "simple cloth shoes" (単皮履, **tanbi kutu**) in *Wamyōshō*. It goes on to say, "Considering this in the present, people in the fields take deer hide and make half-shoes, and call these *tabi*. They get this word from the two graphs 単皮 (*tanbi*, simple hide)."

---

277. The class *eta* [earlier *weta*] has unclear origins, but the word appears as early as the fourteenth century. No clear etymology has been proposed, other than that which Norinaga has listed. It is unclear if Norinaga knew, but the Heian-era dictionary, *Meigoki*, has the same etymology, quoting from *Wamyōshō*.

[527] THE WORD FOR "GOODBYE"

When people take leave of one another, they say *saraba* (goodbye). This is seen in a poem in *Gosenshū*, in the section on the "names of things":

saraba yo to	Because you said
wakaresi toki ni	"I hope to see you again"
ifamaseba	when we parted,
ware mo namida ni	I felt the same emotion
oboforenamasi	and almost drowned in my tears.[278]

[530] ROLLING UP THE HEM OF ONE'S SKIRT

In the vernacular people say "roll up the hem of your robes" (*koromo no suso wo tumageru*), and this usage is a contraction of an earlier from of the verb *tumiage* as found in a *chōka* poem in Book 20 of *Man'yōshū*: **mimo no suso / tumiage kakinade** (she pinched together the hems of my robes and caressed me) (MYS 4408).

[532] *KŌJŌ*

In the thirteenth volume of *Sandai jitsuroku*, in an imperial edict, there is the word 口状 (*kōjō*, a verbal message).[279] The word *kōjō* (口上) in the present is the same thing. The reason that 口状 is written 口上 is based on the same kind of rewriting seen in tales where *kichō* (几帳, a veil) is written 几上, or where *honjō* (本性, one's true colors) is written 本上.

---

278. *Gosenshū*, 1341. There is some debate as to how much to read into the word *saraba* here.
279. This edict appears on the twenty-second day of the ninth month of the eighth year of Jōkan (866).

9 | SNOW OF BLOSSOMS

Around the month of Yayoi [the third month] I was at a certain place and saw a cherry tree with blossoms scattered around the base, and I suddenly recalled that a year earlier when I had traveled to Mount Yosino I had beheld the same kind of sight, so I composed a poem:

fumiwakasi	Walking across the mountain
mukasi kofisiki	I longed for the past—
miyosino no	how I would like to envision
yama tukuraba ya	that scene on Mount Miyosino—
fana no sirayuki	the blossoms were white like snow.

I gathered the poems [blossoms] together, and made this the title of this chapter. One sees a number of examples in various works where someone has gone to the mountain and thought they saw it covered in snow [when it was just the white cherry blossoms].

[545] ON THE WORD *MORAFU*

In *Shinsen jikyō* it says, "餬 means to supply with food, and is read **morafifamu**." In the modern vernacular, when we get something from someone we say *morafu*, and this is the same word. It originally only referred to getting food, but perhaps the meaning later expanded to include the reception of any object. Perhaps it originally was not just limited to food. I do not know.

[546] TEACUPS

In the regulations of the Ministry of Popular Affairs in *Engi shiki* in the section "Yearly Tribute of Food and Various Vessels" it mentions that among the tribute offered by the Nagato Province were twenty teacups of five *sun* in diameter. Teacups are a rare item.

[547] THE STONE IMAGE OF BUDDHA IN OFONO

On the road from Fatuse headed toward Nabari in Iga there is a temple called Ofonodera, where there is a tall, large boulder. On that boulder someone carved an image of Buddha. The inscription says, "Seventh day of the third month of the third year of Shōgen (1209), the emperor took an august excursion to Fatuse Temple and to the stone Buddha of Ofono in Uta District." This refers to this place; "the emperor" in question is Emperor Gotoba.

[549] USING THE CAUSATIVE 令 FOR RESPECT

In the classical language when someone demonstrated respect for something a person did, he would [conjugate words to show that respect], so words like *yuku* (go) would be *yukasu*, or *tatu* (stand) would be *tatasu*. In the Middle Ages people added *tamafu*, so you have *yukasetamafu* or *tatasetamafu*. In records and other documents they would write these with the graph 令: 令行給 and 令立給, respectively. The use of this causative [with 令] appears to be somewhat recent, but in the fourteenth book of *Man'yōshū* in a poem from Upper No Province we find something very rare:

asifumasimu na   Do not step on it. (MYS 3399)

In poetry from that anthology written around that time, the other examples all have *asifumasu na*.

[550] HOLDING A GRUDGE FOR UNFAIR TREATMENT

The word *katami urami* (holding a grudge for unfair treatment) is seen in *Hogen monogatari*.[280]

[551] CONCERNING *KAKIDASI*

In the ninth volume of *Gōke shidai*[281] you will find the word *kakidasi* (an announcement). *Kakidasi* found in front of the homes of merchants [announcing a coming of age ceremony] must have come from this word.

[554] THE DINING HALL

The dining hall [at court] is commonly called *aitandokoro*. In the diary of those serving in the interior ministry, the word *asitadokoro* appears here and there. The word *asita* undergoes a sound change to *aitan*, where *si* weakens to *i*, and *n* is attached. This kind of sound change is regular.

[557] ON THE RECORDS IN THE LIBRARY AT THE PEACH BLOSSOM ABODE

During the Ōnin Disturbance (1467–1477) the library at the Peach Blossom Abode in the great palace of Ichijō no Kaneyoshi[282] caught fire and became a wasteland. Thieves in the area came from

---

280. *Hogen Monogatari*: One of a number of military tales. *Hogen monogatari* is centered around the Hogen Revolt of 1156. The authorship and date of completion are unknown.
281. *Gōke shidai*: A book on Heian era ceremonies compiled in twenty-one volumes around the end of the eleventh or beginning of the twelfth century by Ōe Masafusa (1041–1111).
282. Ichijō no Kaneyoshi (1408–1481). While he was statesman and later a regent, he may be more famous because of his love of poetry and studying about the literary past of Japan.

here and there and scattered some seven hundred boxes of ancient works, and buried the great avenue in scraps of used paper. This event is recorded in the preface to this minister's [Sōgi] work, *Chikurinshō*.[283] The events in a world in turmoil are miserable. Now, if we calculate this, supposing that one box contained a work in fifty volumes, then we would have thirty-five thousand volumes or more that have been lost.

[558] CONCERNING THE DEITY OF TAMATU ISLAND

One year I was employed by someone in the province of Ki and had spent so much time at Wakayama that I was able to view a variety of works written about things related to various famous places in that province by a person from that area. Among the works I saw was a work written by a man named Iwahashi Jinemon Hidenaga[284] in which there was a section called "Thoughts on the Deity of Tamatu Island." It claimed that the deity of Tamatu Island was Princess Sotoori. It also quoted from *Fukuro zōshi* and a commentary to the preface of *Kokinshū* by Kitabatake Chikafusa, who quoted some abridged work, but none of these has any substance.

In recent times another theory that the deity of Tamatu Island is Waka Hirume has also surfaced, but this is a forced theory, based on the toponym Waka Bay [*wakaura*]. As I have quietly pondered the origin of this deity of Tamatu Island, I believe it should refer to Empress Jingū. The reason for this is that the fourth deity of the four deities enshrined at Sumiyosi Shrine in Settu Province is Empress Jingū, where one variant theory is that it is the deity of Tamatu Island.

Shūchūshō[285] also notes, "Thus, it was reported to the vice minister of the left capital that the foundation of the ruling deities of

---

283. *Chikurinshō*: A selective anthology of *renga*, compiled by Sōgi. It was completed in 1476 and was modeled after the Chinese idea of seven wise hermits in a bamboo grove (竹林七賢). Sōgi included *renga* from seven poets he greatly admired.

284. Little is known of Iwahashi Jinemon Hidenaga (dates unclear) who wrote *Kin'an meisekikō* in five volumes, which was published in 1805.

285. *Shūchūshō*: This is a poetic work written by Kenshō (d. 1209), outlining and defining three hundred poetic words. It was completed between 1185 and 1190. Kenshō cites a

Sumiyosi originally was the three shrines of Sumiyosi. The fourth shrine is the bright deity of Tamatu Island, also known as Sotoori Hime."

Thus in the theory of the foundation of the protector of the state who is the main deity of Sumiyosi, the fourth deity is the bright deity of Tamatu Island, so this then should be Empress Jingū of Tamatu Island; that is the tradition. However, blind adherence to a tradition is the reason that it claims that this is also Sotoori Hime, and it is in error.

Now the reason that people claim that the deity of Tamatu Island is the deity of *waka* poetry is based on the fact that this originally was the deity of Waka Bay (*waka*, "young" versus "Japanese song"). This toponym originally was *waka* (young). Furthermore, the reason that the deity of Sumiyosi is considered one of the deities of *waka* poetry is because Empress Jingū is worshipped by the fourth shrine within the Sumiyosi Shrine complex, from which the deity of Waka Bay also originated. Now the third syllable of the name "Tamatu Island" later underwent voicing, and became Tamadu Island. In ancient records and in song recorded in *Utsuho monogatari* this name is read Tamaizurusima. Thus, after some research it becomes clear that this refers to the area where Empress Jingū obtained the *nyōrai* pearl in the middle of the bay when she set out to attack Silla. Empress Jingū's enshrining of this deity appears in *Nihon shoki*, and this is the origin of it. Because this was the place where she was able to obtain the pearl, it is the place where she should be worshipped.

Another theory holds that there is a Tamade Island at the Sumiyosi Shrine in Tu Province, and when Empress Jingū left to attack Silla she obtained a pearl that would control the tide, and thus it has reference to that place. However, this theory is a corruption of the story handed down regarding Tamazu Island (*tamatu* > *tamadu* > *tamade*). As the deity of Tamazu Island was later also worshipped at Sumiyosi, it also came to be called Tamazu Island ... .

---

large number of lost works as proof of the usage of these words, making *Shūchūshō* a very important resource.

[569] ON SECRET TRADITIONS

In almost any field, there are many instances where one of the most important teachings is that the student should not divulge the teachings of his master to others. If that is truly an important aspect of a Way, then one naturally wants to tell many others. Something profound that is hard to convey to others becomes limited and dies out easily. However, when someone lightly or carelessly preaches his teachings, then others castigate him. This course of events may appear normal, but even if others scorn that person's teachings, it is still wise to spread their teachings. There are some points that naturally become valued simply because they were widely dispersed in society.

No matter how profound a teaching may be, it is not good to keep it locked up with a few people, which leads to extinction. What value is there in having taught something that eventually vanishes from society?

On the other hand, lately, there have been many secret traditions that appear to show how profound a certain tradition is, which turn out to be nothing more than a title. In reality no one is allowed to know anything about it other than one person. He has leaked out the information simply to lift himself in the eyes of others, while his actions only show how debased he actually is. I do not have much to say about those secret traditions related to various trivial artistic pursuits, but high-level scholarly and artistic groups should not engage in secret traditions.

[570] THE WAY

The Way was first given to the two deities Izanagi and Izanami through the birth of the parental deities Takami-musubi and Kami-musubi. Because it is the same Way bestowed upon Amaterasu Ōmikami, it is the Way that all countries between heaven and earth should wholeheartedly pursue. It ought not to be the private Way of a particular house.

9 ~ SNOW OF BLOSSOMS 243

[571] AS KEICHŪ EXPOUNDED UPON POETRY

Producing a commentary on poetry is difficult, and according to the way that one writes, the meaning and strength of the explanation often differs greatly. Keichū was gifted at interpreting poetry, and whether it was good or bad, the point of his explanations comes through clearly, being very easy to understand. So why is it that sometimes within his explanations there are bothersome commentaries? For example, we have the following in the commentary to the *amatu kaze* poem from Henjō Sōgi;[286] it says "Since the wind and clouds are originally floating objects, and because they are not objects that remain still for a long time, this word usage suits the meaning of 'for a while.'"

Nevertheless, the poets who wrote poetry during this period did not think that deeply upon these things. This type of commentary, which expounds upon minute points, however, is probably a habit Keichū picked up from reading commentaries on Buddhist scripture. All Buddhist scriptural commentaries expound upon bothersome points in ways that are difficult to explain to give the air of profundity. These are annoying works.

[572] FACTS IN THE REIGNS OF THE ANCIENT CHINESE PEOPLE THAT ARE INCONSISTENT

We see that even in China events that occurred in the eras before the Xia and Yin have not been transmitted to posterity in a clear manner, and there is no unity regarding these events as recorded in various histories. There are many places where things are varied and disjointed. If one wants an example or two, the record says that King Yu was a grandson of Zhuan Xu, and King Shun was a descendant in the seventh generation from Zhuan Xu, so how can one of these people be handing over the throne to the other in the same era? Also, considering that Yi Yin lived during the reign of King Tang, how can his son, Yi Zhi, be a minister to

286. Commentary to the *amatu kaze* poem from Henjō Sōgi, KKS 872.

King Tai Wu, who is a descendant of King Tang in the fifth generation? Since five generations is an incredibly long period of time, how could he have lived so long? Hou Ji, the ancestor of Zhou, is recorded as having been a person who lived during the eras of Yao and Shun, but King Wen is a descendant of Hou Ji in the fourteenth generation. It is recorded as being over a thousand years, so how could he go on living for fourteen or fifteen generations? We cannot accept that the ancient Chinese in those days were able to live such long lives. Even the ancient people found these facts strange.

[575] SINO-JAPANESE READINGS THAT DIFFER FROM THE COMMON ONES

There are many cases where different Sino-Japanese readings appear for graphs instead of the ones that we are accustomed to seeing. We have 周礼 (rites of the Zhou) read as *shurai*, while 檀弓 (a bow made from the sandalwood tree) is *dangū*, 淮南子 (*Huai nan zi*) is read *wenanzi*, and 玉編 (*Yu pian*) is read *gokufen*, 鄭玄 (Master Zheng Xuan) is *dzaugen*, while 孔穎達 (Master Kong Yingda) is *kueudatu*.[287] These kinds of readings are not problematic because they are based on *go'on*.[288] A different example where 越王句踐 (King Yue Wang Gou Jian) is read *wettōkōsen* is simply a shortening of something longer.[289] 子昂 [(Chen) Zi Ang] being read as *sugau* is originally based on *tō'on*,[290] just as 扇子 (a fan) is *sensu*, and 銀子 (silver coin) is *ginsu*, or 鑵子 (teakettle) is *kansu*. In modern Chinese 子 is pronounced *tuu*, but the pronunciation of *su* is likely from the Song or Yuan eras. Also when the emperor

---

287. As an example, the reading of 周礼 as *shūrai* is based on *go'on*, as the *kan'on* reading would have *rei* instead of *rai*.

288. *Go'on* (呉音) could be translated as the pronunciation of Wu China, but this is misleading. *Go'on* is actually the label for the earliest surviving pronunciations of Chinese characters, which Miyake (2003:100–109) has shown is an amalgamation of various strata of Chinese pronunciations.

289. This would have originally been read as *wetu-ou-kou-sen*, and when two vowels occur side by side, one elides and this is the shortening Norinaga mentions.

290. *Tō'on* (唐音) refers to pronunciations from Tang China.

9 ~ SNOW OF BLOSSOMS 245

went off on an imperial excursion and resided at various places along the way, the writer would record these as 行在所, which is pronounced *anzaishō*, but this does not mean that the graph 行 has a special reading just for this occasion [of *an*]. It is the same *an* found in examples like 行燈 (lantern, *andon*) and 行脚 (a walking tour taken by Buddhist priests, *angya*). This is likely an ancient Chinese reading.[291] In modern Chinese when the graph has the level tone or the departing tone, 行 should be pronounced *in*. Also the graph 明 as found in the name for the Ming dynasty is read *min*, which is also *tōon*. The present dynasty is called *sin* (清), which is a corruption of the Chinese pronunciation. The Chinese pronunciation of 清 is *tuin*.

At the end of the Ming dynasty there was a man named 鄭成功 (Zheng Cheng Gong) who is also called 国姓爺 (Guo Xing Ye, *Koku Sen Ya*), and the graph 姓 is read *sen*, because the Chinese pronunciation is *suin*, and this was changed to *sen*. The *koku sen* of this name, Koku Sen Ya, refers to the surname of the king, and it is said that he was given a Ming name. The *ya* is the same as Elder "so and so," or Mister "so and so"; it is an appellation of respect. In the recent past of China this graph was used especially often. I wrote this as an afterthought.

[580] CONCERNING THE WORDS *KUTI AKASANU*

In the language of the present, people say *kuti akasanu* (not say a word), which has the meaning 閉口 (keep one's mouth closed). In the "Hahagi" chapter of *Genji monogatari* there is the line: "Her erudition in Chinese studies was such that an inexperienced student would be put to shame and I could not say a word."[292] It is an ancient usage.

---

291. It should be noted that the graph 行 has four different readings in Chinese: *xing*² (walk, go), *xing*⁴ (behavior), *hang*² (line, row), and *hang*⁴ (ordered). According to Pulleyblank (1991:120), this graph underwent the following changes from about 600 CE on: ɣaŋ > xʱaŋ > xaŋ. The Japanese could not pronounce the h- initial, so they originally pronounced this as *au* or *an*, according to the era when the word was introduced.

292. The two modern translations both seem slightly off here. Tyler has, "Her daunting learning simply left nothing further to add" (2001, vol. 1:33). Seidensticker has, "Her erudi-

[582] CONCERNING THE MUSIC CALLED "NOH"

In the Sumo Section of *Saigūki* it says that Nōyū was the first thing performed after they finished Sumo wrestling. This "nōyū" sounds like *sarugaku*, and is the origin of what we presently call Noh. This graph 能 has the pronunciation of *tai*, and the reading of *nou* has been a mistakenly passed down from long ago.[293]

[583] A TESTIMONY OF AN ADMISSION OF GUILT

Currently in society there is an item called "a testimony of an admission of guilt." Anciently this was called "a report of negligence" (怠状). In the same work (*Saigūki*) it is seen as "an admission of guilt" (過状). In *Uji shūi monogatari* we see it as a "statement admitting his guilt" (おこたりぶみ).

[584] VARIANT COMMENTARIES WITHIN THE MAIN TEXT OF *NIHON SHOKI*

Within the various paragraphs of the "Age of the Gods" section of *Nihon shoki* where there is a variation to the orthodox text, the compilers have inserted the words "another work states." The reason that variants are given is that there were many old legends at the time of compilation. Needless to say that it is a good thing these variations were recorded because not everything variant could have been preserved. Since *Nihon shoki* was not compiled just from one ancient record, there are many old records quoted that are closely related to the Chinese Heart, as far as they were quoted. It appears that the compilers selected from among these

---

tion would have put any ordinary sage to shame. In a word, I was awed into silence" (1976:35).

293. Norinaga is considering the reading *tai* for 能 based on the graph 態. In actuality, 能 has always been n- initial, while 態 originated as *n-, or may have included a prefix of some sort that induced the shift to t-. In any case, Norinaga is wrong to conclude that reading 能 as *nou* is an error passed down from long ago.

variants as they deemed necessary, put them together, and interwove them into the text.

There are some quotes in which the beginning and end do not agree. In the beginning, the name for the sun goddess is only recorded as Ōhirume no Muchi without any explanation like, "She is also known as Amaterasu Ōmikami." Then, from the next line on she is recorded as Amaterasu Ōmikami. This is different from the beginning. The name of Amaterasu Ōmikami is a name seen in one of the variant quotes, and because it is first seen in the main text as, "Another record says, 'Amaterasu Ōmikami,'" it is certainly from a variant tradition. Nevertheless, how do we know that the record is talking about Ōhirume no Muchi in the next line when it mentions Amaterasu Ōmikami? It is just as if we did not know what kind of being the deity called Amaterasu Ōmikami is in the beginning. Also, the record says that the moon deity, Tsukiyomi, is next in brilliance to the sun, and in one of the variant quotes the highly honorific graph 尊 is always attached, making this deity highly honored. Why does the main record merely say, "And they gave birth to the moon deity," without even announcing the deity's name? Then the deity Takami-musubi appears in the beginning of the creation of the world, the most revered deity in the heavens with the honorific graph 尊 attached to his name. Emperor Jinmu worships this august deity, and sets up Michi no Omi to be the head priest in charge of worshipping Takami-musubi in that he is to be treated with special care; however, in the beginning of the record, his origins are only seen in one variant quote, and he is not seen at all in the first half of the main text of the "Age of the Gods," suddenly appearing in the second half, abruptly known as the imperial ancestor.

The sending down of the imperial grandson to rule over the central land of Asifara is all accomplished through the command of this deity. Thus, the beginning and the end do not match. Master Agatai said that he did not understand this either. Truly, like other deities, it is not fitting for an august deity to appear suddenly out of nowhere. How important it is that the beginning be clearly recorded when a deity comes into existence. Generally, it can be seen from this that the *Nihon shoki* text is not well organized due to the disposition of the compilers; they did not know what to include or discard.[294]

[585] CONCERNING THE EIGHT MILLION DEITIES BEING RECORDED AS EIGHT HUNDRED THOUSAND IN *NIHON SHOKI*

If we were to total the sum of the myriad deities, all the ancient records starting with *Kojiki* count them as eight million deities. Only *Nihon shoki* here and there labels them the eight hundred thousand deities, and we see no mention of the eight million deities within its pages. No matter how we slice it, we can see the intentions of the compilers. Even in the recording of the names of deities, Hitaka is changed completely in *Nihon shoki* with the addition of *fiko* to his name, perhaps to avoid the name of the ruler in that reign.[295] I cannot imagine what this number of eight hundred thousand is based on. This kind of rewriting, along with the spelling of the names of the deities, has been the sole source for later works, which have only had reference to *Nihon shoki*. However, in society today people still say that there are eight million deities, following the case of *Kojiki*, which is rare.

[586] THE CUSTOM OF PEOPLE'S NAMES FOLLOWING SINO-JAPANESE

We see that the custom of calling people according to the Sino-Japanese reading of the graphs of their name is quite prevalent, considering people like Minister Shihei (時平大臣), Tada no Manchū (多田満仲), Minamoto no Raikō (源頼光), and Abe no Seimei (安倍晴明). Later the custom was to pronounce most

---

294. No doubt to Norinaga's vexation, it must be said that the ancient Japanese myths were not of a pure strain. Many strains were intermixed by the era of *Nihon shoki*. The compilers did their best at trying to portray an air of organization and unity from a chaotic tradition, but Norinaga is correct that the compilation could have been done more smoothly.

295. *Nihon shoki* was presented to Empress Genshō, whose name was Hitaka (氷高), and this may have seemed too close to 日高, Norinaga argues.

names according to the Sino-Japanese reading of their graphs: Minister Shunzei, Minister Teika, Minister Karyū, Kamo no Chōmei, and so on. When we listen to mendicant priests recite *Heike monogatari*, this is usually not the case. It seems that anciently the practice of pronouncing people's names according to the Sino-Japanese reading of their graphs was quite popular.

[590] LIST OF CONTENTS

In the "First Flower" chapter of *Eiga monogatari* we find mention of a list of contents, where it says, "[He] came with a willow-wood box that contained a list of the Emperor's gifts."[296]

[591] JUG (BY) THE INKSTONE

In the "Iwakage" chapter of the same tale it says, "the jug beside her inkstone."[297] In the vernacular this is called a "pitcher."

[592] THE WORD *SAGASU*

People in the present say *sagasu* when they are searching for things. This word appears in the separate volume "Bays" in the same tale [*Eiga monogatari*].

[593] LOSING A HAWK

In the "Paper-Mulberry Strips" chapter of the same tale it says, "Someone who loses a hawk from the arm."[298]

---

296. McCullough and McCullough (1980:280).
297. Ibid., 314.
298. Ibid., 462.

[598] SORROW FOR THE CURRENT TREND OF NEGLECTING THE DEITIES

It causes me great sorrow to see people in society neglecting the deities. While one cannot say that they do not render worthy service to the deities, it is all a facade, as they do not render *sincere* service. Their thoughts are not upon the deities.

The deities are not visible to us in the present sphere, but there is nothing in this world that does not exist because of the blessings of the deities, be it the creation of all existence, great and small events in the past and present, or even every person's food, clothing, and lodging. People forget about this, and then they incur the disastrous consequences of that awful deity, Magatsubi.

The learned scholars in society have filled themselves with the heart of Chinese literature, and in the rare event that they hear about events from the "Age of the Gods," they act as if it is some old story from long ago. They treat it as if it is someone else's problem. They cannot comprehend the basic fact that everything that occurred in the "Age of the Gods" is still pertinent to everyone in the present.

One of the most lamentable affairs is the decline of shrines and their religious ceremonies, and it is equally regrettable that in such a prosperous reign as we now enjoy, we have so few people with the intention of helping the various old shrines that have fallen on hard times.

I have harped on this point before, and the listener will think I am nagging, but since the sad plight of the ruin of old shrines has yet to be addressed, I have taken up my brush again.

osamareru	In such an era
miyo no sirusi wo	where we enjoy prosperity,
tigi takaku	how I long to gaze at
kami no yasiro ni	the crossing beams that support
miru yosi mogana	the roof of the divine dwelling.

🌿 10 | MOUNTAIN SEDGE

fate mo nasi There is no end—
ifu beki koto fa Though I say the things
ifedo ifedo that I ought to say,
nafo yamasuge no the mountain sedge is even now
midareafitutu still a mass of confusion.

This work that I write to comfort myself:[299] And while I feel like a madman as I selfishly and exaggeratingly add a poem and thus name each chapter of this work where I write down these trifling things, with what kind of contempt will people later view this work? Near the end of the first paragraph of the beginning of the first chapter I had said, "Without any thought I composed one poem," and named the first chapter for it, and with this I have titled the next and then the next chapter, and now it has naturally become a habit. Now I feel that each chapter has to be titled this way, and no matter how much I think about changing this pattern at this point in time, I continue to name my chapters according to a poem.

In general I get despondent from time to time and let my thoughts wander, thinking about what poem can be used as a title, and I will just compose a poem, or I will use a poem I had composed on something different and I will bring these out. When I find one that I think is suitable, or even when I do not have one that is suitable, I do as I did now. Holding my brush I think about

---

299. This sentence has reference to the poem that he wrote and attached to the beginning of *Tamakatsuma*. In the first poem at the beginning of Chapter 1 he has *nobe no susabi*, which I translated as "in the field of life," but *susabi* has a dual meaning: (i) the passage of time in one's life, (ii) to be in a state of ruin. Thus Norinaga is saying that the mountain sedge is in a state of ruin, just like his writings in this book (*Tamakatsuma*).

various things, but when the words to a poem only come to me slowly, I put the end of the handle of my brush in my mouth, which seems like something a madman would do. At length I was finally able to compose the poem on mountain sedge, but it is such a poorly written poem!

[599] THE PROPER ATTITUDE TOWARD SCHOLARSHIP

There was no specialization in ancient times dealing with the study of our imperial country. Scholars only concentrated on Chinese studies, and with the passage of time, people became disaffected with anything related to their native country. On the other hand, they grew more attached to things Chinese, and even their feelings and attitudes have become Sinicized. Words related to antiquity, including the meaning, are unknown, and sound foreign to our people.

After this occurred, there were people who began specializing in the study of our imperial country. Nonetheless, as I stated above, they have been associated with the Chinese Heart for such a long time that it infects their thinking, and these "native studies" are performed in name only. What these scholars proclaim and believe has not changed at all, remaining tainted with Chinese thinking. It seems that these scholars do not even notice this condition.

Therefore, scholarship has lately become popular and people have become more intelligent. A side effect of this is that [the influence of] the Chinese Heart has also increased, so the spirit of the ancient Japanese has only grown dimmer. Very recently there have been a few people who have noticed this phenomenon, coming to the realization that everything in society is somehow connected to China. These people now desire to elucidate those things that are purely Japanese with origins in the ancient past. Their work has begun to illuminate the ancient way of our land. So bright our future is, since the awe-inspiring deities Kamu Naobi and Ōnaobi[300] dwell in this world.

---

300. Ancient traditions state that these two deities rectify and remedy faults and mistakes; thus Norinaga is announcing that these two deities have begun to rectify the errors of the past.

[600] LAMENTING THE DISAPPEARANCE OF TRADITIONS FROM THE PAST

There are also examples of many traditions from the past falling into ruin, or disappearing altogether. During this time of prosperity, I desire to strive toward reviving all things, looking into the relics of things that have already vanished, and bringing them back. Taking no thought about whether it is too early or too late to start such a work, I still have the desire to repair mistakes, a desire inspired by the divine influence of the deity Naobi no Mitama. There is no means or evidence, however, to use in reviving something that has already vanished. Needless to say, this is regrettable.

There are many families from the ancient periods, or from the "Age of the Gods"—even families that were not that honorable—that have vanished with their posterity. No matter what kind of plan you come up with, there is no way to reconstruct their lineage. Using this fact as a guide, anything from the ancient period that still exists, even fragmentarily, must be located without missing anything, dealt with, and firmly established so that it will never face extinction again.

[601] ABOUT DEMONS

The thing we call "demons" in the present refers to what women, children, and others call *oni*. There are many appearances of these in old tales and works from the Middle Ages, and generally, these describe the same phenomena. Now in the record of Emperor Saimei in *Nihon shoki* we find "A demon appeared in the palace,"[301] and "A demon appeared on Mount Asakura," and these are what we still call **oni**, which reading we also can glean from graphs such as "evil demon," "demon spirit," and "lecherous demons" as these appear in the same record. As these are more than just evil demons, they should not be read as *oni*. *Oni* may also be labeled deities, but we should be careful not to call deities *oni*. In the section on spirits

---

301. Perhaps Norinaga's text is corrupt, because the text actually has 亦見宮中鬼火 (The demon of fire was spotted in the palace). The text Norinaga has relied on has dropped the character 火 "fire."

of the dead in *Wamyōshō* we find, "The spirit of man is called a 'ghost.' The work *Si sheng zi yuan* says, 'Ghost' refers to the spirit of men when they die. The Japanese reading is **oni**. Another record states that **oni** is derived from a corruption of the sound of *yin* (hidden, from 隠). **Oni** are entities that are hidden and do not wish to show their form. That is why they are called such." In the section of *Wamyōshō* dealing with apparitions, it says, "The Japanese name for these are **oni**. Another theory is that this word is derived from *yin* 'hidden' and the pronunciation has been corrupted. Apparitions are hidden (*kakurete*) and do not wish to show their form. Thus in the vernacular they are referred to as *in*." All these theories are incorrect. The reason that the word *oni* is attached to the character 鬼 is derived from 魅. The character 魅 refers to monsters.

In addition, the categorization of *tenjin* (heavenly deities), *tigi* (earthly deities), and *ninki* (spirits of men) notes that the spirit of the dead is also called *oni*.[302] But the spirit of dead men does not equal *oni*. However, there is no distinction mentioned between the two, so that the spirits of men and demons are both called *oni*, which is an error caused by the graphic representation of the word. As both words use the same character, people get confused and err regarding the meaning. This is a common occurrence from ancient times with the learned. Also, the theory that the word *oni* is derived from a corruption of *yin* (hidden) is a dreadful blunder. If the thing were named after the fact that it hides its form, then it should be called **kakure**. Using the Chinese sound of the character 隠 to give it a label is far off the mark and is not how to establish the etymology. Furthermore, the theory where something that is hidden is labeled *in* based on the character 陰 (shade) is the same kind of error. The word *oni* is of an ancient origin, and if that is what they called it back then and we still call it that now, then we should understand that these are one and the same thing. There are many examples in the world where those who pretend to be learned will propose mistaken theories regarding the origin of objects and explain this according to the characters that are used to represent their names. Now the words *oni* and *kami* were originally written with the Chinese graphs 鬼 and 神 (and read *kijin*

---

302. This three-part categorization first appears in *Xinshu* (ca. 169 BCE), an early Confucian text from by Jia Yi.

in Japanese), and these two graphs, while dealing with things in the realm of the deities, were not demonic, and in texts like the preface to *Kokinshū*, we see where *oni* and *kami* are written in Chinese and this is how both came to be used in relation to each other. So two entities were grouped into one, and they are neither demons nor deities, but refer to things that are violent and frightening, as *oni* and *kami* can be.

What people in the present called *kijin* does not have the meaning of spirits as in Chinese, nor are these demons in the Japanese sense, but are *oni* with a slight change in meaning. In a common proverb, "a wicked man gets a demonic wife" or "one becomes an *oni*," clearly a wife is being compared with *kijin*. The phrases people in the world create are indeed strange and written using a variety of graphs, causing the meaning to change far and wide.

[602] HOW I WISH THERE WERE WORKS WRITTEN ON EVERY TOPIC

I wish there was a work that informed us in detail about everything from the ancient past in relation to plants, trees, birds, and beasts. There have been many such works dealing with herbs, animals, and minerals from ancient times in China. In our country, there is only the work of Minamoto Shitagau,[303] *Wamyōshō*. This work is full of errors, and makes the mistake of quoting from Chinese works. It is barely related to ancient things, and everything between its covers is incomplete. Since there are no other ancient works of this type, people including myself have relied on it when pondering all the various things in the world.

Recently, someone discovered a work called *Shinsen jikyō*.[304] Though it has been around since ancient times, it has not spread

---

303. Minamoto Shitagau (911-983) also helped in the compilation of the imperial anthology, *Gosen Wakashū*.

304. *Shinsen jikyō*: An early Heian dictionary of Chinese characters used in Japan at the time. It is important because it attaches Japanese readings to each character. It was compiled around 798, so it is contemporary with *Wamyōshō*. The interesting thing, however, is that *Shinsen jikyō* still preserves the spelling distinction between ko_1 and ko_2, while *Wamyōshō* does not.

throughout society very much, and moreover many suspicious characters are used within the text; it is indeed a strange work; however, there are many places that supplement *Wamyōshō*. There are many other works created in later eras, but all are mere imitations of Chinese works. When studying about things anciently in our land, *Wamyōshō* is rarely of any use, so I wish someone would first study all the ancient works like *Kojiki, Nihon shoki,* and *Man'yōshū,* and then add the works from the Heian era down to the present, and compile a work to be used in place of *Wamyōshō*.

From an early time on, I have had this great desire to compile such a work, but because it is not an easy task, I have not been able to do it while engaged in other projects. There is very little time remaining to my life, and since my desire to compile such a work has vanished, I wish that some new student armed with great knowledge would be engaged in the work.

Six or seven years ago, there was a young man named Itō Tōshirō Tara from Etizen Province.[305] He paid me a visit and related to me, "My father is fond of studying natural history and is engaged in that sort of work. I also have had interest in such things since my childhood. Nevertheless, everyone engaged in this work has a penchant for Chinese ideas, and there are many books in this area. I have not been able to locate a single book solely about things in our land. I have thus decided to do something about this, and work in that direction."

He then showed me one or two volumes he had written. I read some of the passages and found that they agreed with what I had desired. His ideas were very gratifying. "Please continue and finish this work," I said. I sent him away with these words of encouragement, but have not heard a word from him since.

Lately, I met a person from Etizen who lived not far from Tara, and I inquired into the matter. The man did not know very much, and said, "I believe I heard that he passed away." If this is true, then it is painful to have lost such an important person.

---

305. Itō Tōshirō Tara (1766–1822). He compiled a work called *Man'yō dōshoku kō* (A Treatise on the Animals and Plants in *Man'yōshū*).

[603] CONCERNING THE NAME *WAMYŌSHŌ*

Since the work *Wamyōshō* (Excerpts of Japanese Words) is a compilation of quotes from many Chinese works, recording the names of things in Chinese, I now feel that the title of this work should have been *Kanmyōshō* (Excerpts of Chinese Words).[306] The reason it is titled *Wamyōshō* is that it takes Chinese as the root and the main thing, and treats Japanese words as the branches and as something secondary, which is an unsatisfactory arrangement, but if you read [Minamoto] Shitagau's own preface to the work, the original intention of the work was to show which Japanese words corresponded to particular Chinese words, and that is the intent behind his compiling the work, and naming it thus, so the title is logical.

Be that as it may, it is the work of Chinese, both Han and Tang, to divide everything globally. Regarding things related to the imperial state, they should not be labeled Wa (倭 or 和), Nihon (日本), the original land (本邦), or "our state" (吾国). These phrases are meant to flatter China and are extremely useless. Therefore from now on when someone wants to put together a work that deals with the myriad objects in the world as *Wamyōshō* did, needless to say, the title of such a work should reflect the makeup of the work, where the core is Japanese, such as "**ame** (firmament), the Chinese name is *ten*," or "**tuti** (earth), the Chinese name is *chi*." Thus the name of the object should first be given in *kana* and then the Chinese name given. If we speak about it logically, the Chinese name is a foreign thing and need not be mentioned, but as all the graphs originate from China, and the custom is to write the names of objects in Chinese script, then without a knowledge of the characters everything else becomes confusing, so after the Chinese graphs, the argument for each entry should be listed.

---

306. This is a rather unfair criticism of *Wamyōshō*. The work is named thus because it gives Japanese readings (Japanese names, if you will) to a variety of Chinese words. This was the reality in Heian Japan, and the work is a valuable resource.

[604] KAGURA

Kagura is what anciently was known as "deity entertainment." These songs are still known as "deity entertainment" in *Kokinshū*. Even the current spelling of 神楽 (deity music) was originally glossed as *kami asobi* (deity entertainment). We do not know the origin of the word, or when it began to be used, but it appears as the topic of a song in *Kokin waka rokujō*.

[605] ON THE WORD *TATOFE*

There are many cases where the meaning of something cannot be expressed directly, so it is easier to make the meaning clear by using examples. Thus, these examples were employed even in the "Age of the Gods" and appear in poetry and even those in the present employ this technique. This is not only true of our country, but in foreign lands they have employed this usage from ancient times. The Chinese were very adept at using metaphorical phrases, and there are many cases where they could make difficult concepts clear with only a few words. However, the many parables seen in the Buddhist sutras are pitifully written, unduly circumspect, expressing ideas with muddled expressions. Were the [original] words of Sakyamuni like this also?

[606] EXPOUNDING AND COMPREHENDING THINGS

It is difficult to comprehend the color, shape, or purpose of many things in the world, no matter how detailed an explanation we have. If you give an example within the same parameters, like "It is the same color as this, or has the same shape as that," or if you give one or two examples to explain what you are trying to describe, then it is easier to understand.

[610] AN EXAMPLE OF HOW TO READ *GENJI MONOGATARI*

[Someone said,] "*Genji monogatari*, a work the world finds interesting, comprised fifty-four chapters and I tried reading it one day to see what was so interesting, and when I opened its pages, I found that it was like string that is all tangled up, and you can't find the end of the string. What in the world caused someone to create a work that when you read you can't make heads or tails of it?"
I replied, "That is true. You should read and become accustomed to the text. If you read it repeatedly, you will not get lost in the text. If I were to give an example of this, it is like during the sixth month when you have endured the heat of a blistering sun and have been walking outside, and then you suddenly enter your house. Everything is dark and you cannot make out the shapes of things or their color. But if you stay in the house long enough, you find that things naturally come into focus and become visible and you can make out the fine details. It is the same with the text of this work." This example is from a collection of the poetry and essays by Kinoshita Chōshōshi.[307]

[615] CONCERNING *SIWORI*

In a poem in *Kokin waka rokujō* written on the topic of "mountains," we find:

siwori site	I should have traveled
yukamasi mono wo	along Mount Aizu
afidu yama	with broken branches as a guide—
iru yori madofu	From the start I am lost,
miti to siriseba	if I had known the way.

---

307. Kinoshita Chōshōshi (1569–1649) was also known as Kinoshita Katsutoshi. He was a *daimyō* in the beginning years of the Edo era but is perhaps better known as a poet and a poetic commentator.

Is the object *siwori* mentioned here and in other places the first instance of this?[308] Or is it older than this? How unexpected.

[618] THINGS FOUND IN *SARASHINA NIKKI*

Among the things recorded in *Sarashina nikki* we find, "In the Futamura Mountains we stayed the night. At the base of a persimmon tree we put up a simple hut, and all night long persimmons would fall from the tree and hit the roof of our hut, so people would go and pick these up." This event was recorded by the wife of Sugawara Takasue, and even though this event did not happen in the distant past, we see that lodging during a trip like this was primitive. When I think on this and how people are writing poems like *kusa no makura* (grass for a pillow), I realize that in the distant past things were really primitive.

[619] A POEM COMPOSED ON THE TOPIC OF "RETURNING GEESE"

On the topic of "returning geese" I composed the following:

faru kureba　　　　When spring comes
kasumi wo mite ya　and I see the mists on the mountains,
kaferu kari　　　　the geese returning home
ware mo to sora ni　will likely take flight to the sky
omofitaturamu　　thinking, "I am next."

I also composed another:

kaferu kari　　　　The geese returning home—
kore mo kosidi no　will the scent of the plums
ume ga ka ya　　　on the road to Kosi

---

308. Perhaps Norninaga did not make the connection with the infinitive of *siwori* here and the verb *siworete* in *Man'yōshū* poem 4282: 梅花・雪爾之平礼氏 (**UME NO FANA / YUKI ni siworete,** the blossoms of the plum / drooping under the weight of the snow).

kaze no tayori ni beckon to these,
sasofisomekemu borne on the wings of the wind?

Later I thought about the second poem lacking a connection to the geese in the final two stanzas, and I wondered what I had intended, so after focusing on this and that, I rewrote the poem as:

ume ga ka ya	Beckoned and encouraged by
sasofisomekemu	the scent of the plum
kaferu kari	these geese returning home
kore mo kosidi no	will follow the news borne on
kaze no tayori ni	the wings of the wind from the road to Kosi.

Here I have switched *kosidi* (Kosi road) to the final two stanzas and now the connection with geese is clear, but now I think the sophistication of the poem has been compromised a bit. Please give me your criticism, you readers who understand poetics well.

[620] CONCERNING TEXT OUTLINING THE ORIGIN OF THE NAME OF OU DISTRICT IN *IZUMO FUDOKI*

The reason it is called **Ou** is because Yatuka Midu Omitunu no Mikoto who pulled the land together decreed, "The land of Idumo where the eightfold clouds rise is because it is a young land like fine-woven cloth. I have created small pieces of land in the beginning. Now let us sew these together." He looked over at Misaki in Silla, a land white like mulberry trousers, to see if there was any leftover land and said, "There is leftover land." He took in his hand a large spade, broad like the breast of a maiden, and cut away the land, as if he were prying open the gills of a large fish and sliced the land as if he were waving a banner of bundled ears of pampas grass. He threw a great rope woven of three strong strands and tied the pieces together, and as one would haul in the black stalks of frost-bitten grass, he hauled in the rope back and forth. And like the slow movement of a ship on the river little by little, "Come here, land! Come here, land!" he said.

The land that he hauled in and sewed together is now land from the tip of Kodu to the cape of Yafonikiduki. Thus, the strongly driven wooden stake is the border of the land of Ifami and Idumo; it is this, called Mount **Safime**. The rope that he held in his hand and used to pull in the land is Nagafama of Sono.

He then looked around to see if there was extra land in the northern entrance of the land of Saki, and decreed, "There is extra land!" He took in his hand a large spade, broad like the breast of a maiden, and cut away the land, as if he were prying open the gills of a large fish and sliced the land as if he were waving a banner of bundled ears of pampas grass. He threw a great rope woven of three strong strands and tied it together, and as one would haul in the black stalks of frostbitten grass, he hauled in the rope back and forth. And like the slow movement of a ship on the river little by little, "Come here, land! Come here, land!" he said.

The land that he hauled in and sewed together is now land from the tip of **Taku** to the land of Sada. He then looked around to see if there was additional land in the northern expanse of Nonami, and decreed, "There is additional land!" So he took the large spade, broad like the breast of a maiden, and like prying open the gills of a large fish, he sliced the land as if he were waving a banner of bundled ears of pampas grass. He threw a great rope woven of three strong strands and tied it together, and as one would haul in the black stalks of frostbitten grass, he hauled in the rope back and forth. And like the slow movement of a ship on the river little by little, "Come here, land! Come here, land!" he said.

The land that he hauled in and sewed together is now land from the tip of **Ufa** to the land of Kurami. He then looked around to see if there was more land by **Tutu** Cape in Kosi, and decreed, "There is more land!" So he took the large spade, broad like the breast of a maiden, and like prying open the gills of a large fish, he sliced the land as if

10 ~ MOUNTAIN SEDGE 263

he were waving a banner of bundled ears of pampas grass. He threw a great rope woven of three strong strands and tied it together, and as one would haul in the black stalks of frostbitten grass, he hauled in the rope back and forth. And like the slow movement of a ship on the river little by little, "Come here, land! Come here, land!" he said.

The land that he hauled in and sewed together is now the cape of Mifo. The rope that he used to haul in the land is the island of Yomi. Thus the strongly driven wooden stake is the peak of Finokami in the land of Fafagi. He decreed, "I have finished pulling the land together." He stuck his staff in the ground at the sacred forest in Ou and said, "**Owe**." Thus this area was called Ou.[309]

The text above includes very ancient words here and there with many places that are difficult to understand. The present text also has many miscopied characters that make it even harder to comprehend the text, but if I am forced to interpret it, this is what I have.

"Pulling the land together" [some texts have 坐 miscopied as 座] as it is used in the text means that land from other areas was stripped away and added to the deficient parts of Idumo and means to finish creating the province. This is how they use this meritorious work to praise this deity. As we called Ōkuninushi the great deity who created everything under heaven, Yatuka Midu Omitunu is seen in *Kojiki* as Omitunu and he is a great grandson of the great deity Susanoo in the fourth generation, the son of the deity Fukafuti no Midu Yarefana. He is thus the grandfather of Ōkuninushi. Even in this *fudoki* this deity appears here and there in the land of Sanuwaka. The character 堆 is a miscopied graph. Uchiyama Matatsu,[310] a person from Tofotuafumi Province, created an annotational note for this *fudoki* and claims that the

---

309. Noringa is correct about the text he has relied on being somewhat corrupt. My translated version has relied on the modern text in *Nihon koten bungaku taikei*.
310. Uchiyama Matatsu (1740–1821) was born in Tofotuafumi Province, the son of a village mayor. His father read Shintō and Buddhist texts, and his maternal grandfather learned poetry from Kamo no Mabuchi. In 1762 he joined Mabuchi's school, and in 1775 he visited Norinaga in Matsuzaka, and they began corresponding. He wrote *Izumo fudoki-kai* in 1787.

proper character is 稚. The continuation from Sanu is very quick, and this land should be known as Waka Province.

In both *Kojiki* and *Nihon shoki* it records the name as Kuni Waka [or Kuni Wakasi] which will remind you that this is the origin. The meaning of "I have created small pieces of land in the beginning" refers to the beginning when the two great deities Izanagi and Izanami first gave birth to the islands and they also created the smaller pieces. The deities created this land of Idumo, and the northern reaches were insufficient, like a slender cloth, making it narrow and thin. Thus it is called **waka kuni** (young land), because the creation of this area was not yet completed. The phrase "let us sew these together" refers to piecing together the places that were insufficient, and creating a broader area. "Misaki in Silla" [the character 埼 is erroneously copied as 椅 in one manuscript] is a cape that juts out into the sea on the southeastern coast of Silla.

The phrase "if there was any leftover land" refers to whether this cape contained excessive land that could be used to expand the land in Idumo, whereupon he looked and searched and found that there was extra land. The wording "a large spade, broad like the breast of a maiden" refers to the shape of the spade resembling the shape of a beautiful girl's breast, and is said in reference to its being broad, straight, and flat. In *Man'yōshū*, Book 9, there is a poem that praises the beautiful form of a woman: **muna wake no / firoki wagimo** (a young maiden with a broad breast valley). This makes it sound as if her breasts were straight and flat. "Great fish" refers to fish like the tuna. **Kida** refers to the gills (*agito*), and it is said that this form is from the dropping of the *a* and the *to* changing. However, *agito* is always pronounced with the *ki* voiced [as *gi*] and with the *to* voiceless, but there is the claim that originally the *ki* was voiceless and the *to* was voiced. In the ancient records *da* is written with a voiced graph.

Regarding "prying open," I asked a fisherman, and he said when they catch a large fish they aim for the gullet and catch it by piercing it there. In ancient song we find **sibi tuku** (pierce a tuna), and this is the same usage. But as a preface to the verb **tuki**, it talks about the gills of the great fish. As the gills are to the side of the mouth it is slightly different from the gullet, but as the gullet is inside the mouth, when one pierces from the outside, it ends up being the same thing. Now "prying open" refers to breaking off the leftover land from that other area and means to split off and take.

The word **fatasusuki** (banner of pampas grass) is a preface for "ears of grass." **Fofuriwake** (wave and separate the ears) is to slice and separate something. "Slice" means to cut off the meat and other parts of beasts. This same word appears in *Kojiki* in the section regarding Emperor Sujin, where it says, "They cut down the men of the army." This is the same meaning. Thus, this leftover land was sliced away with the spade.

The phrase "rope woven of three strong strands" is miscopied. The character 身 (body) is miscopied, and Matatsu claims that this is an error for the character 舟 (ship), and he has altered all examples to this, but I wonder if this is correct. In a poem in the fourth book of *Man'yōshū* we find **mitu afi ni yoreru** (woven with three threads), and this refers to a cord woven with two threads and a third thread added, and this phrase refers to a strong cord. Also in the record of Kōtoku in *Nihon shoki* we find **mise no tuna** (a rope of three strands) which again means the same thing. Perhaps the error comes from this word **yori** (weave) being written with the graph 自 (from). That seems clear from the example of **mitu afi**.

The words (throw [a rope] around) refer to the throwing of a rope around the leftover land that had been sliced away and pulling it across the sea. The phrase "black stalks of frostbitten grass" is perhaps the name of a type of black vine. Or does it refer to a vine upon which frost has descended? It is not clear. The graphs 聞々耶々爾 contain miscopied graphs. There are no examples in *Fudoki* where the graphs 聞耶 are used as phonograms. This section is very difficult to decipher, but if I am forced to try to explain, perhaps this phrase is an error for 閇々那々爾?[311] In the present we say *fe nara fe nara* or *funara funara* (rocking back and forth). *Fe* and *fu* are related sounds and refer to the same thing. Here this

---

311. Norinaga is correct that this section is difficult, but most scholars agree that the archetype had 闇々耶々, where the blackness of the stalks introduces the blackness of night 闇, which is a rebus graph for **kuru** (wind, spin). Thus the apparent winding of a rope as it pulls something ashore.

refers to being tossed to and fro by the waves as the ship is pulled across the sea. When others write about the great ship tossing back and forth (**yukura yukura**) or rocking back and forth (**yuta no tayuta ni**) it refers to the same thing. As I think further about this, maybe the name **fune** is alluded to in the phrase *funara funara yuku*. Also "black stalks of frostbitten grass" is a preface and the attending meaning seems to be that the black vine that meets the frost is broken [under the weight of the frost] and waves back and forth. If this refers to a variant name of a plant, then maybe it is clubmoss that perhaps is rocking back and forth. More thought needs to be put into this.

The phrase **mosoro mosoro ni** is the same thing as the modern word *soro soro* (gradually). The word *soro soro* is a form with the *mo* abbreviated. "Of a ship on the river" is a preface; it means that if compared with a ship on the sea, a ship on the river travels quietly. This demonstrates the interlude of the ship tossed on the waves as it is pulled across the sea. The phrase "Come here, land! Come here, land!" [in one manuscript there is only one set of this doublet of three graphs with the comment that this is dittography; another manuscript has included *yura yura*, but that is a mistake] is corrupted. It is very difficult to comprehend, but if forced to again given an explanation, I believe that perhaps the graph "come" is a mistake for "approach" and it should be "land approaches." As the example above has a doublet, perhaps "land approaches" was doubled accidentally and then corrupted by the following line, which has "come," and so "approach" was altered to "come."[312] Thus "land approaches" refers to the leftover land from the august cape in Silla being pulled closer and approaching. The phrase "the land sewed together" refers to the land being pulled over and attached to the land of Idumo.

The phrase "from the tip of Kodu" includes Kodu, which is a place name. In the district of Tatenufi you will find Kodu Shrine, Kodu Island, Kodu Beach, and other such names. It says these are on the border of the two districts of Idumo and Tatenufi. The

---

312. Norinaga has been led astray by several poorly copied manuscripts, as most witnesses in the present have 国々来々, which I have translated directly as "come here, land!"

character 乃 (of) is a mistake. I have not been able to figure it out.[313] The phrase "strike till it is gone" [the graph 打 has been miscopied as 折[314]] forms the border and is used to refer to a limit. The phrase "Yafome" is a corruption, as *me* (米) is a mistake for *ni* (尔). **Yahoni** is a pillow word for Kiduki. The cape of Kiduki is a place that we call in the present Finomisaki, but this refers broadly to the area up to the border of Tatenufi District. Even the area up to the mountains east of Kiduki is called "cape." **Kasi** (pier stake) is found in *Wamyōshō* as a small implement for boats. *Tang rhymes* notes, "A boat stake is used to tie down boats. *Kangoshō* records that this is a thing called **kasi**." The geographical section of *Qian Hanshu* writes this as 样舸 and has an attached note, "A stake to tie up boats." It also appears in a poem in *Man'yōshū*. Thus, we can state here that this is a wooden stake to tie off the land that has been stitched together to prevent it from coming apart. Mount **Safime** is found in Ifisi District. "The rope that he used to haul in" is the rope to pull in the land. "Nagafama of Sono" appears in *Fudoki* as, "There is a mountain between this sea and the ocean. The length is 22 *li* and 234 steps, with a width of 3 *li*. This is the rope used when Omitunu no Mikoto pulled the land together. People of that area called it Mount Matu of Sono." In another part of the same record it says, "Sono, length of 3 *li* ... . This is boundary of the two districts of Idumo and Kamuto." This should say Nagafama, but there is an error after 長 (length) as *nagafama* has been dropped. It is the same place as Mount Matu in Sono. The mountain includes Kamuto District and the beach [*nagafama* means "long beach"] attaches to the Idumo District.

"The northern entrance" refers to the sea north of Idumo. "Land of Saki" is a mistake, as *sa* has been miscopied and should be *o*, and surely points to Oki Island, as this is what is in the sea north of Idumo. Nonetheless, this is still doubtful. I will give my reasons below ... .

---

313. It is unclear to me why 乃 is problematic for Norinaga. It is simply the phonogram *no* (of).
314. Current research believes that 折 is the correct form and 打 is actually the corruption.

"From the tip of **Taku**" is the border of Simane and Aika Districts, as there is a Taku Shrine in Simane as well as the Taku River. Perhaps the character 乃 (of) is a mistake for 川 (river). However, as the phrase above "from the tip of Kodu" and now this, there is no river seen in Kodu, so one also wonders why this character is here ... .

"Land of Sada" is what we see as the Sada River in Aika District and the Sada Sea. However, this has reference to both districts of Aika and Tatenufi. "Northern expanse of Nonami"[315] is beyond me. Considering that there are no words that start with *ra, ri, ru, re,* or *ro*, perhaps *ra* is a mistake. However, as there are no islands or lands in the great sea north of Idumo aside from Oki Island, if we consider the cape that came from Silla mentioned above, perhaps both Saki and Ranami are names of a foreign land up north. More work should be done on this.

"From the tip of **Ufa**" [one text has 縫 added after this, but this is a stray mistake; the phrases above "from Kodu" and "from Taku" had the character 乃 after each, and it is only here that this character is not seen], this land is not seen anywhere. Considering that one manuscript has 宇 (*u*) as 手 (hand) perhaps this should be 手染 (Tesimi). There is a Tesimi Village in Simane District, and following precedent, this should definitely be located east of Taku, and west of Mifo Cape, which appears below. Tesimi fits the geography nicely ... .

"Land of Kurami" appears as Kurami Shrine (久良彌社) and Kurami Shrine (椋見社), both found in Simane District. Here this refers broadly to the area between Taku River and Tesimi. "Kosi" refers to the province of Kosi. "**Tutu** Cape" [one manuscript has this as 都乃三埼], it is not certain, but in *Wamyōshō* in the Fagufi District of Noto Province there is a **Tuti** Village, and in Kubiki District of Etigo Province there is **Tuu** Village. *Jinmyōchō* records that in Turuga District and Sakawi District of Etizen Province there is a Misaki Shrine. It must be one of these. More research should be done. "Cape of Mifo" is found in Simane District, on the far eastern side.

---

315. The text Norinaga has relied on has 良波, but this should be 農波 (*Nonami*). There are no native words in Old Japanese that are r- initial.

Considering the examples above, this last paragraph should include "the strong driven wooden stake," but as it does not, which means that as for this cape of Mifo, its eastern boundary is the sea. Below it should also have the two characters, "This is it." The reason it does not is that it was abbreviated and is included at the end ... .

The sentences "I have finished pulling [one manuscript has 訖 miscopied as 記] the land together. He stuck his staff in the ground at the sacred forest of Ou and said, 'Owe.' Thus this area was called Ou" demonstrates the sigh he let out as he rested from his backbreaking and agonizing work. Now **we** is a contraction of **ue** [**uye**], and follows the initial *u* and naturally later becomes **ou**. All the lands that this Omidunu no Mikoto pulled and stitched together became the four districts of Simane, Aita, Tatenufi, and Idumo, which continued from east to west. These were connected from the west in a continuous fashion. Of these four districts the three aside from Idumo are located south of Ou and are in the midsection, in a long, slender line to the sea. Only Idumo District connects directly with the two districts of Ou and Kamuto. Uchiyama Matatsu has pondered this and said that in the "Age of the Gods" from this inlet to the great sea even Idumo District came from the northern half of the area like the other three districts, and was pulled through the inlet. Ou and Kamuto Districts were separated. Pondering the text of this "land pulling" account I believe that this is actually how things happened. Now appreciating the events in this account as nothing more than fantasy is an attitude infected by the Chinese Heart I have mentioned before. In the "Age of the Gods" unexpected events occurred, strange and wondrous events, and as the creation of our land came to an end one should not doubt the ancient traditions. These are all facts. One should understand the texts as they are.

[621] CONCERNING THE CAVE OF YOMI IN IDUMO

My student Ozasa no Minu around the third month of last year, the sixth year of Kansei (1794), visited and worshipped at the great shrine of Idumo and found a place called "the cave of Yomi" on a mountain in an area not far from Mount Wanibuti. I quickly inquired of someone about what it was and found that there are few people who have traveled there to see it. When I heard a person from Kituki talk about it, I earnestly wanted to go and see it, but I am now old and my legs are weak, so I cannot do some things myself. My student Saitō Hidemaro, however, was here and available, and as he is often asked to do, I asked him to go and see it and off he went. This Hidemaro is a person from the same Misumi of Ifami Province as Mr. Minu. As he is someone who has often traversed back and forth through the mountain paths, he did not think it a burden to go up there, and joyfully went to take a look and returned to report. He wrote a detailed account of what happened there and has shown it to me.[316]

First, from Kituki to the east you cross over Mount Wanibuti, and toward the northeast, at a place close to the ocean, you pass through a place called Kafasimo Village and reach Okuwoka Village. The so-called cave of Yomi is in the mountain within this village. It is 18 *chō* [1.2 miles] up from the coast. And while the mountain is not very high, the path up the mountain is very steep, with a mixture of rocks and grass that has grown high. There are many thorns and the path is difficult to climb. The "cave" is in the midsection of the mountain deep in the thick grass and is barely visible. The entrance is a bit narrow. The lower part is about two *shaku* and four or five *sun* across [about thirty inches]. Some places are as large as three *shaku* [three feet] across. It is round like a well and one cannot see the bottom. The inner walls from the entrance down are made from stones placed one upon another. All the stones have corners, and the surface of the stones is white with many cracks. There are also some yellowish stones mixed in.

Now to the south side there is one large boulder that has a surface area of about two *shaku* [two feet] and a length of one *jō* and five or six *shaku* [roughly sixteen feet] where one could put a wooden plank. The bottom of this boulder can be seen a little way to the north of the entrance if one bends a bit. All the stones by the

---

316. According to a record in Uga Village in Shimane a doctor from Iwami named Saitō Hidemaro visited the cave in the third month of 1798.

entrance are covered in moss, and they are crumbling on the bottom and seem to lack moisture. The villagers call this cave "the path of darkness." Most of the people in the area do not know about the cave. When Hidemaro enquired of the people of Okuwoka Village, he found an old man in his seventies who told him that there are very few people who come to see the cave. Even the youth of the village have said that they knew nothing of the cave.

The old man talked about how there originally was a Wanibuti Temple until he was about sixty years old. When he was younger he came to see the cave, but as the years passed, he no longer remembered the path to it well. Thus, the old people of Okuwoka Village have continued to talk about the place. The old man also said that there is a story handed down that at times a poisonous vapor would come up out of the cave and if a person encountered it they would immediately expire. Hearing this Hidemaro felt great fear about even just peeking inside, but he had come all the way out there and could not return without having a look. Therefore, he kept the fear tightly gripped in his breast and took a good look inside.

The old man also said that many years ago if you dropped a rock down inside, the sound of the rock striking the other rocks as it descended could be heard deep inside. However, about forty some years ago someone dropped a large rock inside, and after that, even if you dropped a rock inside the sound of it dropping does not last very long, probably because that large rock created a blockage and made it much more narrow inside.

Also, the old man said that he had heard that the record that recorded the origins of Wanibuti Temple also mentioned that anciently a person called Chishō Jōnin, who established the temple, would enter the cave to perform meditation. Now the name of this mountain is called Mount Okuwoka, and close to the cave is the valley of Zōga. He also writes that Mount Wanibuti continues behind this mountain for a short distance. There are things written about the goings and comings along this path that he has recorded that I have read and that do not seem certain, and I would like to ask whether they are correct or not, but for now I will accept what he has written ... .

[622] DECIDING UPON A TEACHER

In the "Red Plum Blossom" chapter of *Genji monogatari* we find, "When selecting a teacher for dance [or something else], select one who is not common, but who is exceptional, and then each of you make sure you practice in private." We find the words in the present "take a teacher" or "take a student," and we find that these are originally ancient ideas.

[623] CONCERNING WORDS THAT START WITH A VOICED CONSONANT

There are rare cases where a word starts with a voiced consonant, such as *gama* (bulrush), *zakuro* (pomegranate), *zuwae* (staff), *buti* (dapple), and *beni* (rouge). These words are also seen in old works. In later eras these were pronounced with a voiced initial, but anciently these were all pronounced with a voiceless initial.[317] There are other kinds of examples but they all follow the same pattern. Regarding *gama*, when we say *kamafu* (bulrushes growing) it is said even now with a voiceless initial. *Zakuro* is simply taken from the pronunciation of the characters 石榴. It is also the poetic topic in *Kokin waka rokujō*, and words like *bashō* (banana) are seen in the "Names of Things" section of *Kokinshū*, where we have *fase wo ba*, but the characters 芭蕉 anciently were pronounced with a voiceless initial. The character 楚 (*zuwae*) means "tip of a stick." The pronunciation of "end, tip" (末) as *suwa* undergoes the same kind of change as *kowe* (voice), changing to *kowadukuri* (making one's voice strong).[318] *Buti* (dapple) also appears in the "Age of the Gods" in *Nihon shoki* as *futigoma* (a dappled horse). It can also be read as *mutigoma*, but that is because anciently they

---

317. In principle Norinaga is correct, as Old Japanese did not allow voiced initial words. However, unless we have phonetic spellings in ancient records, it is difficult to know if all five of these words were originally voiceless (or more accurately lacked prenasalization). For example, *zakuro* is a loan from Chinese, and likely was introduced with a voiced initial.
318. Very astutely, Norinaga notices the phonological change within words compared to their free form versus their bound form: *suwe* (tip, end) versus *suwa-* or *kowe* (voice) versus *kowa-*.

did not realize that this was *fu-* and since *muti* (whip) was also called *buti*, they read it *mutigoma* based on this. This is conjecture, however.

Beni (rouge) is found in *Wamyōshō* as **feni**. Other examples include *geni* (actually), which is based on the pronunciation of the character 現 (visual, actual), which is a later phenomenon. The character *ba* 場 (place) is anciently seen in words like *ofoba* (大庭, great garden) and *umaba* (馬場, stables), but you never see *ba* as an independent [free] form. Originally it was *fa*, so "great garden" originally was *ofonifa*, and "ranch" was originally *umanifa*, and with the elision of the syllable *ni* the last syllable became voiced. Furthermore, words like *besi* (can, should) and *gotosi* (similar to) are formed according to the preceding words, and these are classified differently.

[624] *TANZAKU*

In the twenty-seventh volume of *Sandai jitsuroku*, we find the word 短籍 (*tanzaku*, small slips of paper), and in the thirty-fifth volume we also see 短冊 (small squares of paper). Yet these are not for writing poetry.

[631] CONCERNING *NOSAKI*

The reading of *no* in Nosaki (荷前), where *ni* (burden) is read *no*, is the same phenomenon as *ki* (tree) being read *ko* in examples like *kozuwe* (treetops) or *konofa* (leaves of trees). *Fi* (fire) is read *fo* in compound words like *fokage* (a light), and *fonofo* (flames). This phenomenon is where the second vowel [in the sequence of a-i-u-e-o] transforms into the fifth [in the sequence]. In the record of Jingū in *Nihon shoki* the word *notori* is written phonetically in a note as 能登利 (**notori**). In *Wamyōshō* in Simodi District of Bitchū Province is a village name written as 近似 and glossed as 知加乃里 **tikanori**. Even in texts written in Chinese the character 似 (*niru*) is glossed as *noreri*. This is an example of the same phenomenon.

[632] CHANGING THE REGNAL YEAR

In *Saigūki* it says, "The minister received the imperial edict to change the regnal year, and he commanded the professors of literature to consider what to designate [the new] regnal year. They reported to the emperor after they had considered [the graphs] and designated what the new regnal year should be, and then commanded the secretary from the Central Affairs Ministry to produce a written edict. The command was to write out a draft, and then rewrite it in clean script. They received the final copy and passed it to the Central Affairs Ministry. The Central Affairs Ministry looked over the plan with an official of the Council of State, and this official then put his seal on it. The major councilor read through it again, and having done that, he gave the official tally to the officiator ... ."[319]

[633] MINTING NEW COINAGE

In the same work it says, "Minting new coinage. The minister received the imperial edict to mint new coinage, and commanded the professors of literature to consider what [auspicious] graphs to put on the coins. Having done this, they selected an auspicious day. They summoned a skilled calligrapher, and had him write out the inscription in front of the palace guard's office. They presented to the emperor a mold of the coin together with an official tally given to the director of the imperial mint. The director of the imperial mint submitted a new coin, and after he had reported on the inscription for the coins, the first batch of new coins was offered to the shrines of the deities and Buddhist temples ... ."

---

319. The very next sentence, which Norinaga has abbreviated, states that the regnal year was changed to Kōhō (康保), which is the year 964.

[643] RETURN MARKS AND JUDGMENT MARKS

Regarding marks [added to judge] poems, there are "return marks" and "judgment marks," something seen in a document written by Minister Ietaka.[320]

[646] *FIWINA*

The object that children play with, which is a miniature version of a person, is called *fiwina* in tales. This label is based on the word *fina* (chick), because a chick is a small version of its parental bird. People also write this with the graph 雛 (chick), and people in the present even call these dolls *fina*, which anciently was pronounced as *fiwina* [with a lengthening of the vowel], written examples of this vowel lengthening we see in words like 詩歌 (*siika*, poetry), or 四時 (*siisi*, the fourth hour), or 女房 (*nyoubau*, ladies-in-waiting). Because the vowel in *fi* is lengthened, one should write *fiina*, so the spelling of *wi* here is an error. Calling the shape of small objects *fina* originates from these being miniature versions of the original.

[647] *TEDUTU*

In books that argue about poetics, you will see the words, "it is clumsy (*tedutu*)." Anciently even in *Murasaki Shikibu nikki* you find, "Ever since then I have avoided writing even the simplest character. My handwriting is appalling."[321]

---

320. As the editors of *Nihon shisō taikei* point out, there is a document sent by Minister Ietaka to Minister Teika in which he writes, "Even a few 'return marks' and 'judgment marks' here are very important" (Yoshikawa et al., 1978:338, headnote).
321. See Bowring (1982:139).

11 | KADSURA JAPONICA

konu mono wo
omofitaenade
sanekadura
matu mo kurusi ya
kururu ya goto ni

I cannot have pity
for the person who did not come.
Like the long vines of *kadura*
how painful to wait for you
night after night.

This poem was composed on the topic of waiting every night, and I made it the name of the chapter following the example of the previous chapters.

[662] CONCERNING THE FESTIVAL FOR THE THIRTY-SIX THOUSAND DEITIES

In the same record (*Nakahara Yasutomiki*)[322] it says, "Twelfth day of the seventh month of the first year of Bun'an (1444). This evening there was a festival for the thirty-six thousand deities held at the private estate of Minister Abe Arishige of the Junior Third Rank. It was held because of the appearance of a comet on the twenty-third day of the previous month." These kinds of festivals were held at homes where the traditions of *yin* and *yang* were perpetuated.

---

322. This is usually called *Yasutomiki*, the diary of Nakahara Yasutomi (ca. 1400–1457). While it contains much about the affairs of government in the fifteenth century, it also includes entries about poetry and other forms of entertainment.

[672] CONCERNING LIFE BEFORE AND AFTER THIS ONE

It is the common concern of man to want to know about life before and after he is born into this world, and looking at the doctrine as contained in the Buddhist sutras we find that there is much detailed discussion about the meaning of life and death and the nature of man; however, since these all originate from ideas invented by mortals, one look will tell you that this will be of no value for people wanting an answer. In addition, the Confucian idea that when the body dies, the spirit and soul vanish into nothingness may appear on the surface to be the most reasonable answer, but this doctrine is difficult to accept. The logic of all things is as deep as to be beyond human comprehension—fire is red, but things burned by fire turn black, while ash, the remains of this blackness, turns white. There are many unexpected events like this one in the world and many results are quite different from the results thought up by men. Therefore, it is beyond the comprehension of man to know what happens after death, and cannot be envisioned by the limited nature of man. This is another example of such unexpected events. Pondering this, in the traditions handed down from the "Age of the Gods" in our imperial land it says that [the dead] go to the land of Yomi, a tradition that is very noble. The pretentious, clever doctrines of logic from China all sound quite shallow.

[673] CONCERNING THE THEORIES IN THE CHINESE WORK *HUANGJI JINGSHI SHU*

During the period called Song in China, a man named Shao Kangjie[323] appeared on the scene, and in a work called *Huangji*

---

323. Shao Kangjie, also known as Shao Yong (1011–1077), was a Confucian scholar from the Northern Song dynasty. He is well-known for using Daoist-based numerology in expounding about the universe and the changes it goes through. His ideas later influence the Zhu Xi School.

Jingshi shu[324] he claims that the duration of heaven and earth begins and ends in the cycle of one day and night. He claims that there are eight layers—heaven, time, cycle, world, year, month, day, hour— and this forms one revolution. The time of one revolution equals 129,600 years. Regarding what this was based on, he claims that it is the formation from the number of hour-blocks in a day multiplied by the number of months in a year, twelve, multiplied by the number of days in a month, multiplied by the number of years in a generation, thirty [12 x 12 x 30 x 30 = 129,600]. These connected together are the numbers of the measure of time and form a natural equation.

Pondering this, I find the entire theory difficult to believe. First the number of hour-blocks in a day is twelve, and the number of days in a month, and a generation just happen to be thirty. There is no reason to pile these numbers one upon another as an explanation of how the universe was created. Especially since the division of a day into twelve time periods is the work of man. In reality there is no template saying that there must be twelve time periods, no matter how you slice it, it is still one day. Also, claiming that one generation is thirty years is also the doing of men, and there is no sign that such *must* be the case. The basis for using the number twelve lies simply in the number of months in a year. The basis for using the number thirty [for a generation] lies simply in the number of days in a month; is it not extremely reckless for one man to force this equation on us? Why should anyone label these "natural numbers"? There also is no evidence for the number eight in the eight layers from heaven to hours, but it could be twelve layers, as you can layer as many as you like and get the same effect, as the four pieces of hours, days, months, and years is the first pattern, and then the person imitates that for the next four, and creates the theory of the creation of the universe, which you now see is only a man-made theory.

---

324. *Huangji jingshi shu*: written around 1070 CE. Shao argued that sentient beings originated from the "great extreme" (太極), and therefore to preserve order, a proper numerical relationship is crucial. Based on the Eight Hexagrams as found in the *I Ching* (where one is divided into two, two into four, four into eight) society and man will either experience peace or upheaval. It is this numerology that Norinaga castigates.

In reality there is no such law. Also the number twelve is based on the twelve trunks of the Chinese calendar, which is said to start with the rat and end with the boar, but if this is the case then the number thirty should be based on something also. So it is strange that there is no basis for the number thirty. How can you obtain the beginning and end of the creation of heaven and earth when everything is based on the shallowness of things? There is absolutely no sign that this is worthy; it is a trivial and stupid theory. The so-called theories of the Zhu Xi School are generally these kinds of insipid things. No matter how much thinkers in later eras lavish praise on these theories, they discuss the creation of heaven and earth from inside a cave as if they could discern these things. How silly this is. Like all the theories in the texts of Buddhism, it is easy to give labels to all the things that cannot be seen by the eyes of people. It is the tendency of people to believe the things that the thinkers suppose based on the logic of their theories, but reasoning based on the wisdom of men often turns out to be wrong in unexpected ways, so it is difficult to place your belief in these. This theory about the creation of heaven and earth is the same as that in Buddhist texts, and as these deal with things no one has ever seen, they speak of things based on a false logic, it being a completely fabricated thing—these are born at the same time as the theory. Why do people fail to understand that the reason the theory seems to fit is that it deals with things unseen?

[674] POETRY PRODUCED BY BEGINNERS

When a master corrects difficult-to-comprehend parts of poetry composed now in society by beginning poets, we find that the poetry usually resembles the poetry of the ancients. This is how it should be. The reason for this is that when one is a beginner, and his master gives him a general topic to compose his poem, he is more likely to go back to the ancient anthologies and look at other poetry composed on that topic.

With that, the beginning poet usually selects one poem, constructing his own verse by changing the words a little here and there. For the most part, the good poems of the ancient poets are such that the words are exactly as they should be, and it is very difficult to change even one character. Immature poets do not understand this. When the student changes the original poem a little here and there, it becomes impossible to arrange the newly created poem properly. If some discerning person reads the newly created poem, he is able to tighten the structure, edit it, and it becomes a poem equal to the original.

There may seem to be little value in composing new poetry that is basically old poetry, but it is an important step for the beginner; later on, the poet should not include these imitated poems in his private collections. For a beginner to comprehend poetry, it is good to leave the beginner as he is as was discussed above. One would be embarrassed to enter upon the evil and abnormal practice of putting on airs from the beginning and composing a poem on a rare topic that appears to be rustic.

[676] CONCERNING THE SAYING THAT TEIKA HAD POOR HANDWRITING

In the work, *Ama no mo kuzu*,[325] it mentions the handwriting of that famous person, Minister Teika, as being exceptionally poor. However, in the famous diary *Meigetsuki*, Part 6, we have examples of his actual handwriting. A person who may seem good and with ample care, whether they are a priest or a layman, will write in their own hand, no matter how poor their handwriting, but will write content that is fine. It is said that having someone else write things for you is very regrettable.

The saying that Teika's handwriting was poor is very refreshing and unexpected. People in present society are self-righteous, and they are always dropping that kind of criticism, but I do not judge this as that kind of thing. The standard of people at that time is that he truly had poor handwriting.

---

325. Written by the monk Senshu at the Keimei'in Temple in 1420, *Ama no mo kuzu* deals with ceremonies, and ceremonial robes, especially those of the nobility at court.

[679] THE USUAL FOOD FOR THE IMPERIAL FAMILY

In the same work [*Ama no mo kuzu*] it notes that the standard three meals a day included seven types of side dishes and two types of soup. As for their rice, it says that they ate portioned servings of sticky rice steamed with red beans.

[693] ON LATER ERAS BEING AWKWARD

In *Sennen sanshū*, Andō no Tameakira[326] praised Keichū's commentary on *Man'yōshū*, saying that if we compared his work to the great works of Kenshō[327] and Sengaku,[328] their works would be worthy of being called "old gray mares." Tameakira has spoken the truth. When comparing Keichū's commentary with that of Kenshō, we find that there is nothing in Keichū's commentary requiring correction, but he has expounded upon the matter accurately. Everyone must have appreciated this feat, but when we compare the work of Keichū and those before him to our master, Master Agatai, we find that the former are now the old, gray mares. In all things, those in later eras make wonderful advances, making one feel embarrassed.

---

326. Andō no Tameakira (d. 1716). He was born in Sen'nensan in Tanba Province. In 1685 he moved to Edo and served Tokugawa Mitsukuni. He worked on various philological projects, and in 1698 was put in charge of the annotation of *Man'yōshū*. Two years later, Mitsukuni ordered him to spend several months studying with Keichū.

327. Kenshō: A late Heian era monk who excelled in poetry. His dates are unclear, though scholars believe he was born around 1130 and died sometime before 1210. He wrote a number of poetic treatises and served as a judge at poetic contests. He greatly prized *Man'yōshū* and its poetic style, and wrote one work on the poetry in *Man'yōshū*, and another work on Hitomaro.

328. Sengaku (b. 1203). Little is known of Sengaku (仙覚), aside from his Buddhist name. What information we do have is gleaned primarily from his writings. He appears to have been born in Hitachi Province. From youth he studied *Man'yōshū*, and in his mid-forties he was able to view a number of manuscripts and collated these. Through a number of stages of copying and collating texts, he eventually felt confident enough to put together *Man'yōshū chūshaku* (1269). In many respects, this is the beginning of serious work on *Man'yōshū*.

[694] WHAT OCCURS WHEN YOU PONDER COMPOSING A POEM

When a person wants to compose a poem and thinks of various ways he could construct the verse, he gets an interesting idea, but usually finds that there is no appropriate way to express the image. He ponders long, sometimes for days, obsessed with the same connections, varying a word here or there, but an unsuccessful poem is all he creates. At times like this, the poet should purge his thoughts on that one image and look at the poem from a different angle. People, however, often find it difficult to let go of the first thought they entertained, falling into a maze of dismay because a sense of dissatisfaction swells inside them from not being able to compose the poem. It is despicable to force words into the structure of poetry, but this is the common tendency of people.

At times, when the poet is consumed with trying to arrange his poem, a fresh and new idea will appear in his mind and the poet finds that he can compose this new poem with ease. Nevertheless, this second, new poem owes its existence to the fact that the poet was consumed with different thoughts, and all the trouble the poet went through has not been in vain. This was just a bunch of meaningless nonsense that popped into my mind, and I wrote it down here.

[695] CONCERNING THE SHRINE ON MOUNT ASO IN FIGO PROVINCE

Mount Aso in Figo Province is about three *li* from the base to the top of the mountain, where on top there is a large pond with hot water always bubbling up and beautiful rocks strewn here and there. When the fearsome fire that burns there is at its height it spews molten rocks, making it difficult to approach the pond. Established in Miyati Village, the shrine is located down from the mountain. I provide the layout of the shrine in the picture below:

```
                    ┌──────┐
                    │      │
                    └──────┘
                  Various Shrines

  ┌─┐ ┌─┐ ┌─┐ ┌─┐  ┌──────┐        ┌──────┐  ┌─┐ ┌─┐ ┌─┐ ┌─┐
  └─┘ └─┘ └─┘ └─┘  │      │        │      │  └─┘ └─┘ └─┘ └─┘
   9   7   5   3  └──────┘        └──────┘   4   6   8   10
                  Ichi no Miya     Ni no Miya

  ┌──────┐                                    ┌──────┐
  │      │ Front                        Front │      │
  └──────┘                                    └──────┘
  Kunitukuri                                  Kanagori
  Shrine          ┌──────┐                    Shrine
                  │      │
                  └──────┘
                    East
```

The "Ichi no Miya" Shrine worships Take Iwatatsu no Mikoto. The "Ni no Miya" Shrine worships Aso Hime. The Kunitukuri Shrine worships Haya Kametama no Mikoto. The Kanagori Shrine worships Emperor Suizei. The surname of the head shrine officiator is Uji Ason. His residence is not far removed from the aforementioned Miyati Village, located in a place called Ofomiyasi Yasiki. A person from Figo relayed this information. As I have pondered things, referring to the character 瓶 [in the name of the deity worshipped at Kunitukuri Shrine] as *kame* is a mistake. His august name should be Haya Mikatama. Furthermore, the report that Kanagori Shrine worships Emperor Suizei is an error for Kamu Yawi Mimi. I also wonder what the origins of the surname of the head shrine officiator as Uji Ason are, as well as when this family originated. *Kojiki* only mentions Aso Kimi so I wonder if they understood that family to be from this.

[697] CONCERNING THE FRAUDULENCE OF *SANBU SHINKYŌ*

There is a collection of works called *Sanbu shinkyō*, which includes *Tengen shinpen shinmyō kyō* [the sutra of the heavenly origin-changing-deity-of-mystic power], *Chigen shintsū shinmyō kyō* [the sutra of the earthly origin-of-supernatural-mystic power], and *Jingen shinryoku shinmyō kyō* [the sutra of mortal origin-divine-strength-of-mystic power]. One person has claimed that these are the divine decrees of Ama no Koyane no Mikoto, whose descendant, Sukuma Kimi of the Great Dipper, came to earth, copied these decrees into Chinese writing, and put them together as sutras. Though one should say that anciently they had such trivial things, people in the present have been deceived. I have yet actually to see these works, but just from the titles, I can say that these are bizarre works infected with the envy of Chinese and Buddhist texts and pay lip service to them. There are many such strange works in the houses of people who claim to be scholars of Shintō.

[698] ON THE FRAUDULENCE OF *KUJI TAISEIKYŌ*

There is a fraudulent book in seventy-two chapters called *Sendai kuji hongi*,[329] also known as *Sendai kuji taiseikyō*. A priest named Chōin conspired with some person in charge of the Izaha Shrine in the province of Siga and put the work together. The fraudulence of the work became known, and in the first year of Tenwa (1681), the government banished both people, and burned both the work and its printing blocks. Chōin was a Zen priest after the tradition of Ōbaku.[330]

[700] CONCERNING THE EXISTENCE OF ONE TYPE OF WRITING IN THE ANCIENT PAST

A recent work[331] claims, "Using logic, and thinking upon this, we find that Japan probably had some kind of writing in the ancient past. Why would this not be passed on through time? Perhaps the

---
329. *Sendai kuji hongi*. Not to be confused with *Sendai kuji hongi* (abbreviated to *Kujiki*) in ten chapters. The work Norinaga is refuting here is radically different than the original *Kujiki*. See Bentley 2006b.
330. Chōin (1592–1673). His real name was Yin Yuan (J. Ingen). He came to Japan from China around 1654.
331. Norinaga records in a separate essay much the same content as here, but claims it

beginning of written history occurred during the reign of Emperor Richū. From the time of Jinmu to Richū hundreds of entries have been recorded, with a reformation in government to lineages of the upper and lower classes, with many linguistic and poetic things recorded already. Surely from the creation down to the present there is nothing that was not preserved orally." On the surface, anybody would believe this to be reasonable, but this is because we use a priori reasoning based on the idea that we have always had writing, and judge all things based on this. In the period when there was no writing they made do with things at their disposal; things like this are unexpected. Nevertheless, if you were to relate these theories to a person from the ancient periods they would turn and laugh at you.[332]

[701] CARICATURE PICTURES

In *Konjaku monogatari*[333] it says, "It was a long time ago, but at the Mudōin Temple on Mount Fie there was a priest called Gisei Ajari who enjoyed drawing, and was skilled at drawing caricature pictures. He drew incoherently, his brush like a stick, but when he drew with one stroke, his drawings appeared to dance, and his talent was absolutely marvelous."[334]

---

comes from a work titled *Shintō shiyō*, written by a Shintō scholar from the province of Kai named Minamoto Mitsuakira, completed sometime during the Meiwa era (1764–1772).

332. In Book 1 of *Kojiki-den*, Norinaga stated, "Since we did not originally have a writing system in our august country (needless to say, the syllabary in existence now which is called '*zindai mozi*' ('god-age script') is the forgery of a person in a later era), ancient things were transmitted merely by speech in human mouths, which was heard by human ears" (Wehmeyer 1997:75).

333. *Konjaku monogatari*: The largest collection of tales in Japan. The date of its compilation and its authorship are unknown, though it seems clear the work was finished before the move of the capital to Kamakura. It contains tales from India, China, and Japan.

334. For whatever reason Norinaga has edited this entry. It is possible that he wrote this down from memory, or he had a corrupt text at his disposal. This is the only quote from *Konjaku monogatari* in *Tamakatsuma*.

[703] TAMAYA

In the "Toribeno" chapter in *Eiga monogatari* when it talks about the death of the empress of Emperor Ichijō and the preparations for her burial, it says, "As a shelter for the body, he built a resting place [*tamaya*] by an earthen wall at a spot two hundred yards south of Toribeno Plain."[335] In the present the label *o-tamaya* is the same as *tamaya*. However, I do not believe that the earlier *tamaya* is precisely the same as the modern *o-tamaya*. We can judge that things change slightly over time.

[704] NECROMANCERS

In the present when someone has died, there is a practice where a necromancer speaks words of the dead [*kuti wo yoseru*]. This is also seen in the same tale [*Eiga monogatari*] in the "Major Captain's Regrets" chapter, "The weeping nurse Sakon decided to visit a necromancer."[336] Now these necromancers are also seen as mediums [in the tale], and in the present are called *miko*.

[705] A FISH CALLED *UGUFI*

There is a river fish called *ugufi*. Presently this is the name of a type of fish, but originally it was the name of any fish that cormorants (*u*) ate (*kufi*). In a poem from Akinaka Ason,[337] director of the native religion, we have:

kagaribi no	In the gem weed
fikari ni magafu	where the light from the fishing fire
tamamo nifa	intermixes
ugufi no iwo mo	even the *ugufi* fish
kakurezarikeri	could not remain hidden.

---

335. See McCullough and McCullough (1980, vol. 1:232).
336. A slightly altered version of McCullough and McCullough (1980, vol. 2:613).
337. Fujiwara Akinaka (1059–1129), a descendant of the powerful Fujiwara Saneyori (900–970), was a poet and compiled *Horikawa hyakushu*.

People have interpreted this to mean fish eaten by the cormorant.

[706] THE STATE OF *KANA*

In the "Plum Branch" chapter of *Genji monogatari* it says, "Compared to the ancient past all things are in decline. During our time, the end of the world, things are becoming shallower, but it is only *kanna*[338] where things have really progressed magnificently. Ancient writing was set to one standard, but it lacked a broad characteristic depth and everyone conformed to one type of writing. Beautiful and elegant writing is something of recent times, and there are people who excel at this."

Kanna mentioned in this passage refers to the writing we call *iroha* characters. It is said that Priest Kūkai invented this script, but when we consider that in the beginning of anything the object is simple and immature, when *kana*[339] was first invented, people generally used it in convenient ways, and people did not judge between those who were good at it or not. As time passed and this type of writing spread throughout society, people began to judge whether a person was skillful at writing or not. When *Genji monogatari* was written, it had not been that many years since the advent of *kana*, so it should have been a period when people with great talent for writing were appearing on the scene.

[707] CONCERNING WHAT SHOULD HAVE BEEN INCLUDED IN BOOK 6 OF *KOJIKI-DEN*

In *Kojiki*, from the birth of the deity Yaso Magatubi, in the section where Izanagi purifies himself, to the line about Susanoo, fourteen deities are created, but the text says only ten, and no

---

338. I have followed Norinaga's spelling, which writes *kana* (as opposed to *kanji*), while most manuscripts of *Genji monogatari* have 仮名, written in Chinese.

339. It is difficult to know why Norinaga vacillates between the spelling *kanna* (かんな) and *kana* (かな). I have kept the spellings according to Norinaga's own text.

matter which manuscript you look at it is the same. On the surface it appears that the number four has been dropped, but this is not so. The Nobuyoshi edition is the only one with "fourteen deities," and Nobuyoshi has brazenly added the number four here. The reason the book has only "ten" is that the three Watatsumi deities are counted as one deity, and the three Tutunoo deities are also counted as one. Other examples of this kind of counting were found previously, noted in Volume 5 of *Kojiki-den*, on leaf 62 of the work. This should be considered together. It was poor judgment on my part to have blindly believed the Nobuyoshi edition and written "fourteen deities." We should follow the other editions in accepting the archetype as having "ten deities." I should have included this in *Kojiki-den*, and because I could not put it there, I include it here.

[708] THE STRANGE HABIT OF SCHOLARS IN OUR IMPERIAL LAND

In all things, people should follow the customs of their own country first. They should not abandon native practices for those of foreign countries. In spite of this, it is the bizarre habit of scholars in our country to think it wise to follow foreign customs while they denigrate the practice of adhering to native traditions.

A very simple example of this regards our practice of calling China *morokosi* or *kara*. When we compose in Chinese, we write 漢 (Han) or 唐 (Tang), but these scholars think this is trivial, so they use the characters 中華 (middle flower) or 中国 (middle country) thinking it shows how intelligent the writer is, a practice I have already criticized in my work, *Gyojū gaigen*,[340] so I say nothing further here.

Also, scholars who recognize the mistake of calling China 中華 or 中国 apparently still think it silly to refer to China as Han or

---

340. Matsumoto translated the title as "Complaint on the Failure to Bridle the Chinese" (1970:71). The essay was written in 1778 and published in 1796. The title as presented here is the Chinese reading of the graphs, but purists have argued that Norinaga wanted the title to be read in native Japanese, as *Kara osame no ureta migoto*. This essay outlines the political history of Japan from ancient times until the invasion of the Korean peninsula by Hideyoshi and includes a marvelous outline of Yamataikoku and its problems.

Tang. Some of these scholars write the name of China as 震旦 (*Shintan*) or 支那 (*Shina*). These two are better than the other two above, but these last two examples are appellations applied from Western countries, so this is another example of scholars who have discarded their own country and are blindly following some other. If one feels that it is not strange to refer to China as Han or Tang, then is it ridiculous to refer to China in rebus script such as 諸越 (*moro-kosi*), or phonetically as 毛虜胡鴟 **morokosi**?[341]

Thus, if writing in a masculine style is what makes those things of our country prominent, then writing out of flattery regarding a foreign country is feminine and foolish. This does not have to do just with the usage of the name of China, but deals with a broad range of topics. To give one or two examples of what I mean, the far-off Western countries divide the many countries of the world into five major divisions, and among the names of each division, our imperial land is located in the division known as Asia, which also includes China and India.

This division into five regions and the names of each region are all inventions of foreign countries often heard recently. These scholars adopt such foreign ideas and abandon the knowledge we have had since the "Age of the Gods." This is the suspicious habit I mentioned above of revering and believing things from foreign countries, following them at will.

Also, it is terribly inconvenient to use Chinese sounds to translate a foreign language. Anciently, there were many errors committed when the sutras from Indian Buddhism were translated into Chinese. During the recent Ming era, when the Chinese began translating the names and numbers of the distant countries of the West, out of ten pronunciations of Chinese characters, seven or eight do not match the sounds of Western words. Since there are so many strange areas, no one can know the reading without an intermediary script, like *kana*, and continuing the Chinese practice of representing words with rebus script is meaningless.[342]

---

341. In this final example Norinaga does to China what Chinese histories had done to other countries throughout history: write foreign toponyms in phonetic script, but by selecting graphs that tend to be pejorative in nature. Norinaga's example of 毛虜胡鴟 means "hairy-prisoner-why-kite."

342. Naturally, this is difficult, because Chinese has such a limited vocalism in the present (as well as during the Ming dynasty). What should further be pointed out is that Japa-

When I say this I do not mean the ancient Japanese tradition of following the phonology of *kan'on* or *go'on*, but I am particularly pointing to modern *tō'on* phonology. Trying to understand the phonology of the Western world through the eyes of Chinese rebus script creates too many mistakes, but *kana* of our imperial land is quite accurate in representing the foreign phonology, and there are few examples of mistakes. Therefore, scholars in this imperial land should completely abandon the practice of writing in Chinese rebus script, and adopt the native practice of *kana* script. However, since *katakana* is unseemly, and difficult to write Chinese with, these scholars should use "true script" (*mana*). "True script" is really just *man'yōgana*, a form of phonetic writing where a Chinese graph represents one sound in Japanese.

By renewing the use of this script, it would be quite convenient to write the names of these five areas, like 阿自夜 (*aziya*, Asia) or 要呂波 (*yōrofa*, Europe). It is an unparalleled example of desultoriness and foolishness that our native scholars refuse to use this convenient native method, but opt to continue to use Chinese script, which is strange, awkward, and inaccurate. Yes, this is just another example of the bizarre habit of our native scholars who follow foreign countries, and their sophism.

[709] CONCERNING THE WORD ARETUKU IN *MAN'YŌSHŪ*

In Book 1 of *Man'yōshū* there is the poem:

fudifara no	How enviable
ofomiya tukafe	are those young maidens
aretuku ya	who were able to be born
wotome ga tomo fa	as servants of the throne
tomosikiro gamo	of the Fujiwara Palace. (MYS 53)

---

nese also has a limited vocalism, so writing foreign words in *kana* is not much of a solution, either. Consider that the English word "cola" is written in Japanese as コーラ, with an -r-, while in Chinese the same word is written 可樂 (可乐): *kělè*, where the vowels are simply approximations of those in English.

First, the last graph of the third stanza 哉 is really a mistake for 武 **mu**.[343] Examples of this kind of error are found here and there. Now regarding the final stanza, Tanaka Michimaro argues that 之 (**tomosi**) is really a mistake for 乏 (**tomosi**, rebus for **tomosi**, poor), which is a fine emendation.

Also, in Book 6 there is a *chōka* that in part reads:

yati tose ni	For eight thousand years
aretuka situtu	being born a prince and
ame no sita	going forth to rule all
sirosimesamu to	under the heavens. (MYS 1053)

Concerning these two examples of **aretuku**, in *Ruiju kokushi* in the twelfth month of the eighth year of Tenchō (831) it says, "The Imperial Prince Kamo no Iwahi proclaimed those words, 'to the maiden given birth by the great imperial deity, and even the age of the imperial princess' and in their place at the time we determined through divination the child of this princess we come forward and announce the result of this divination … '." Also in *Sandai jitsuroku* on the twenty-fourth day of the second month of the nineteenth year of Jōkan (877) in the proclamation establishing the ritual representative of the imperial household it says, "Divination determined that Princess Atsukiko should be the representative, and she was advanced as the princess born for this position." Thus we see that these princesses who serve in the rituals at the Kamo Shrine are called *are wotome* (maidens born). This *are* used here is the same as that seen above and means to serve in a position.[344] The reason that the Kamo Festival is also called *miare* should be interpreted as meaning "service." The word *tuku* is the same as *tuki* seen in the record of Jingū in the name of the deity Tsuki Sakaki Itsuno Mitama, and simply lacks the *i* (as in *ituki*, purified, holy).

Now, the stanza **aretukamu wotome** refers to women who served the throne in the Fudifara Palace and who served Empress

---

343. Norinaga interprets 哉 *ya* to be *mu*, and corrects the graph accordingly to 武.

344. Later scholarship has determined that this line of argument is incorrect, and *are* is simply another word meaning "be born," based on *ar-* (to exist).

Jitō. This evidence should be considered along with the word **are wotome**. **Tomo** means "companion." **Tomosiki** means "envious." However, Keichū's interpretation that this is "born to inherit" is an unbelievable mistake, and such a meaning is not fitting for this poem. The final *ku* of "inherit" and "attach" are different in voicing, so how could the former be borrowed to represent the latter?

Now Book 6 has the poem continue with the verb "rule all under heaven," so it refers to the emperor, but when we compare that with the poem in Book 1 it is not something said to or in place of the emperor, but surely refers to someone who serves someone in the palace. Because we can interpret this with the modifying words of "even for eight thousand years" or "served by the myriad officers and will rule all under heaven," we realize that *tukamu* is a modified form of *tuki*. I also think that the graph 之 is a mistake for either 兄 (older brother) or 衣 (robe), both of which would be read *e*. Thus the stanza would be read *aretukae*.[345] Here *tukae* is really *tukare*. If this line of reasoning is correct, then it means the multitude of officials who rendered service to the august person of the emperor.

[710] THE PROPER ATTITUDE WHEN READING *MAN'YŌSHŪ*

There are many places in the current edition of *Man'yōshū* where graphs have been incorrectly copied. This is not a mistake of recent eras, but it appears that there has been a long tradition of scribal error. Recently, however, the study of ancient things has been established, and since there are many colleagues who have directed their attention mainly to the text of *Man'yōshū*, things have taken a turn for the better. These scholars have finally brought many of the mistaken graphs to light. Having said that, there are still many areas that are unknown. Scholars should be careful when they read the text. Places that do not sound proper generally contain incorrectly copied graphs.

---

345. Recent textual work on this poem shows that it should likely be read *aretukasitutu* [being born as (an imperial prince) and going forth].

Now, there are also many incorrect readings.[346] In the beginning, when the compilers committed the poems to paper, there were no readings. Later scribes added these readings. It is these later readings that are terribly foolish and unspeakably incorrect. The tradition of these foolish readings lasted until the Middle Ages, when a priest named Sengaku worked diligently, correcting many of the errors. The present edition of *Man'yōshū* is the one in which Sengaku corrected many of the errors, comparing his text with the original condition of [a variety of other] texts. It is a major improvement. There are, needless to say, still many places that are not satisfactory.

In recent times, the priest Keichū made corrections, and he improved the text immensely. However, there were many times when Keichū did not realize that some graphs were mistaken, and forced readings upon them. In addition, there are still many unsatisfactory places in the overall readings. After Keichū's era, some scholars have done minute research upon this text, and every time research is conducted, the condition of the reading improves, but it is hard to say that the archetypal readings have been restored.

First, if one does not know about all the erroneous graphs, then it is very difficult to correct completely the interlinear reading. Miscopied graphs are still hard to grasp, and if one tries to read the poetry with the mistaken graphs, then many times he is forcing a reading on the poetry. This issue should be well researched. In addition, one should think deeply about the condition of the reading and the way that the graphs represent that reading, using precedence to read the poems. In general, these are the principles for reading this text.

[711] ON BEING SATISFIED WITH HOW YOU ARE

The Chinese believe that being satisfied with how you are is a splendid state of mind, and I agree with them.[347] If you can come

---

346. The *Man'yōshū* text is a complex mixture of phonograms and ideograms. Because of this, the exact reading of many poems is unclear. Thus, from early on, interlinear readings were added next to the characters.

347. Laozi writes, "He who knows contentment is wealthy."

to this understanding, then everyone, regardless of who they are, would feel peace of mind. Nevertheless, it is the basic feelings of humans, whether they are noble or base, to feel that one has not done enough to insure his place in society. Though we may not feel that we are truly satisfied with what we have accomplished, those who follow Chinese learning put on airs of satisfaction and wander around society deceiving others. Indeed very few people actually feel satisfied with their present state. It is not something easily found.

[716] CALLING FALSEHOODS "LIES"

In a poem in Book 4 of *Man'yōshū* we find,

afi mite fa	Though it has been
tuki mo fenaku ni	less than a month
kofu to ifaba	since we met,
wosoro to are wo	if I said I yearn for you
omofosamu kamo	would you think me impetuous?
	(MYS 654)

In Book 14 we see:

karasu to fu	The crow known
ofo wosodori no	as the reckless bird—
masade nimo	even though it is accurate
kimasanu kimi wo	that it is not you who is coming,
koroku to so naku	it cried out *"cawm cawm."* (MYS 3521)

The meaning of this last poem is, "Even though you surely are not coming, the crow who tells great lies is crying out, 'Coming now, coming now.'"[348] The *ro* in the word *koroku* is a weakened variation of *ko*, so it is *koko fe ku* (I'm coming here). It does not

348. Several points need to be made here. The cry of the crow in Old Japanese was *ko-roku*, which is nearly homophonous with 此来 (*kono ku*, at this moment I come). That is the pun in the poem. The major problem is the interpretation of *wosoro* and *woso*, which Norinaga interprets as related to *sora* (sky, emptiness), the supposed etymology of *soragoto* (falsehood). The traditional explanation is that *woso* is related to *uso* (lie). In reality,

mean "children are coming." All examples of 子 **ko** (child) are written with the same set of characters like 古故, but here it is written with 許. Because the stanza *kimasanu kimi* (it is not you who is coming) is a phrase a woman uses on a man, it cannot refer to children.

Now [Fujiwara] Kiyosuke's *Ōgishō*[349] records, "A certain person said that people in the eastern provinces say *wosogoto* when they refer to *soragoto* 'falsehood.'" The poem above from the fourth book of the anthology is not written by someone from the eastern provinces, but anciently people in the capital also called "lies" *woso*. The word in the present, *uso* (lie) is the word that was used anciently. The initial *wo* and *u* have a special affinity for change.

[719] BIRTH FATHER AND MOTHER

In the present people make a distinction between the father and mother who gave them birth and their father- and mother-in-law by calling their parents "real father and mother." In the same work, *Hokuzanshō*, it calls these "birth father and mother," which is a splendid way to say this. As "real" is used in contrast to "fake," it does not have a very good connotation when you call your own parents "real father and mother," and your in-laws "pretend parents."

[720] CONCERNING "WORD" WRITTEN *KOTOBA* OR *KOTONOFA*

"Word" is seen in the preface to *Kokinshū* as *kotoba* and as *kotonofa*, but in *Man'yōshū* it only appears as **koto**, and there is only one occurrence of **kotoba** in Book 20 of the anthology, in an

---

woso(ro) appears to be related to *wasa* (quickly, hurriedly), which from a phonological standpoint is easier to explain. This leads to the interpretation of reckless or hurried.

349. Fujiwara no Kiyosuke (1104–1177) was a late Heian poet who appeared to have devoted much of his early life to the study of early Japanese poetry. He assisted his father, Akisuke, in the compilation of *Shika wakashū*. His poor relationship with his powerful father meant that he had no post or rank for much of his life. It is unclear when, but around 1140 Kiyosuke had completed his manuscript of *Ōgishō*. This poetic treatise lays out a variety of ideals about poetic style, poetic ills, and other advice. It is an important work in that it deals with *Man'yōshū*.

eastern province poem **ifisi kotoba zo / wasurekaneturu** (I cannot forget those words).[350] However, 婆 (**ba**) is a mistake for 波 (**fa**), and it is difficult to know if this **fa** functions as a case marker. There are various examples in this anthology where **fa** and **zo** are used together.

[721] WRITING ⁄ WHEN YOU SHOULD WRITE 封

This is also seen in *Hokuzanshō*, but instead of writing the graph 封 (letter sealed), in recent years people "just suddenly drag ink across."[351]

[723] YUKATABIRA AND KATABIRA

What is known in the present as *yukata* (unlined cotton garment), a light robe one puts on after bathing, is seen in the "Jeweled Decorations" chapter of the same tale [*Eiga monogatari*] as "august *yukatabira*." Let me just add that *katabira* (a hemp summer garment) is only used in the present to refer to cloth robes, but that was not always the case. All clothing that was unlined, no matter the variety, was called *katabira*.

[726] FATAZINE/ZARU/MORAFU

People in the present call left over thread from weaving at a loom *fadazine*. In *Shinsen jikyō* it says, "纑 'Left-over thread' refers to thread left over after an article has been woven. [In the vernacular] called **sine-ito**." This is the same thing. In addition, a bamboo basket is called *zaru*, and in the same work it says, "筲

---

350. This is from MYS 4346. Modern textual work reconstructs this stanza as 伊比之気等婆是 (**ifisi ketoba ze**), which is a dialectal version of what Norinaga is talking about. It does not necessarily change his theory, however.
351. Typical of Norinaga, he laments the sloppiness of people. When a letter was written and then sealed, it was the custom to write the graph 封 (sealed) across the envelope. In recent years, people had begun to just write ⁄ across, which looked like people were just dragging ink over the back of the envelope.

'Bamboo basket' called **sitami** or **azika** or even **izaru**." Also, "笆 'Bamboo bowl' is a bamboo vessel in which you pile up grain, called **izaru**." These are the same thing. And the word *morafu*, which means to receive something, appears in the same work as "餬 means to supply with food, and is read **morafifamu**."

[728] *KUTIAMI* AND *MOROMOTI*

In *Tosa nikki* it says, "The party from the residence ... helping one another along like fisherman dragging a net."[352] Kanehara Kiyokata, a person from Tofotuafumi Province, told me, "Fishermen in the present use something called *fikiami* [dragnet], along with *kutiami* [drawnet], and *okuami* [seine]. *Kutiami* is six or seven feet wide and fifty or sixty feet long. They spread this out over the ocean and catch fish. When they drag in the net many fishermen stand in a line, heft it over their shoulders, and pull it in. This is called *naramu*. It is exactly as the diary states. The author was making light of the people, finding it difficult to compose a poem by using the weight of the net as an example, where many people pulling in the net make the job easier to accomplish.

---

352. McCullough (1990:76).

12 | JAPANESE YELLOW ROSE

There are people who have said, "There is no one who knows my feelings,"[353] but at any rate I do not care what people say:

omofu koto	I will not cease
ifade fa yamazi	to give voice to what I think.
yamabuki mo	Even the yellow rose
sareba zo fana no	does not care but blossoms;
tuyukekaruramu	I have become all misty.[354]

[732] CONCERNING THE WORDS *TUTUMINAKU* AND *TUTUGANAKU*

In *Man'yōshū* there is the phrase *tutuminaku* (without hindrance), but people in later ages say this as *tutuganaku*. In works composed in Chinese this is written as 無恙 (without hindrance), and we understand these to be the same; thus, we see that the ancients used the same kind of graphs, as in Book 13, where they appear as 無恙 (**tutuminaku**) (MYS 3253), but in present manuscripts this is glossed as *tutuganaku*, which is a later word. In this poetic anthology, every example of these graphs should be read *tutuminaku*.[355] Now in Chinese records the graphs 無恙 are annotated in reference to "being distressed" or "being ill."

---

353. Based on a famous line in *Ise monogatari*, dan 124.
354. This poem alludes to KKS 19.
355. Norinaga is thinking of examples where the word is written phonetically, such as in MYS 894, where it is spelled out: 都々美無久 (**tutumiNaku**).

In *Fengsutong*[356] it says, "恙 [malady] is a biting insect, and is able to consume the heart of a person. People in the ancient past lived in the grasses and many were afflicted with this poison. Thus they searched and worked together, and that is why we say 'without hindrance.'" Based on this we also have the name of an insect called *tutuga*. However, it is an abominable mistake to argue that the meaning of the word in *Man'yōshū* is based on this kind of reasoning.

Even the graph 恙 in Chinese works, which is defined as "having distress, or having an illness," sounds like it is a safe bet, but the theory that claims that the name of the insect was based on this is difficult to accept. In our imperial land, the word *tutuganaku* is simply a corruption of *tutuminaku* and *tutuga* is *not* the name of an insect. Even if 恙 became the name of an insect it is unrelated to the word in *Man'yōshū*. Using the graphs 無恙 simply helps the reader understand the meaning, because the meaning is similar, nothing more. One may know that this is not the name of an insect by examining examples of *tutumu koto naku* and *tutumafazu* in *Man'yōshū*. In Book 6 of the same anthology, we have the stanza 草管見 / 身疾不有, which some read as **kusa tutumi / mi yamafi arazu** (MYS 1021). There are likely people who think that perhaps the graph in question is 草 because of the story above about people living among the grasses, but this is not the case. The graph 草 (grass) is actually a mistake for 莫 (not) and that again makes it *tutuminaku*. The meaning of *tutumi* is found in my treatise on the interpretation of the liturgy of the great purification, so I have left it out here.

[735] THE EIGHT YOUNG MAIDENS

In the vernacular people say "the eight young maidens." In the record, *Itsukushima gokōki*, written by the internal minister of Tsuchimikado, Minamoto no Michichika,[357] we see the phrase "the eight young maidens of the august *kagura*."

---

356. The full title is *Fengsu tongyi* (風俗通義), written in the Later Han dynasty by Ying Shao (ca. 204). He is best known for his annotation of *Hanshu*. *Fengsutong* was printed in Japan in 1660.

357. Minamoto no Michichika (1149–1202). The official title of this record is *Takakura-in Itsukishima gokōki*, because it deals with a trip taken by Emperor Takakura in 1180.

[736] TOKINAKA

Half a period of time is called *tokinaka*.[358] In the same record it says, "He fell on the ground and for half a time period was unconscious."

[737] READING "EIGHTEENTH DAY" AS *TOWOKAYAUKA*

In "An Imperial Visit to the Horse Races" chapter of *Eiga monogatari* in the section where it mentions Yoshishige no Tamemasa, the date "eighteenth day of the ninth month" is glossed as *nagaduki no towokayauka*. It should be *tawoka amari yauka*, and while one wonders why they shortened it, at least they kept the first *ka*, which is archaic. People in the present do not use the first *ka*, but write the date as *towo amari yauka*, which differs from the ancient precedent.

[738] CONCERNING CALLING "NIGHT" *YOSARI* OR *YŌSARI*

The usage of people in the present who call "night" *yosari* or *yōsari* is based on an old word.[359] In the "Sticking in the Comb" song in *Saibara*, we have the words **asina tori / usari tori**, which means "take tomorrow, take tonight."

[739] CONCERNING "DEFECATION" BEING CALLED CHAMBER POT

Some people from the mountain villages in this province of Ise call defecating *hako*. That is because anciently these people would take out their defecation in a chamber pot (*hako*) and dispose of it

---

358. The Japanese divided a twenty-four-hour day into twelve periods of two hours each. Thus "half a time period" equals an hour in our time.

359. One of the earliest usages of this is found in *Taketori monogatari*, where it means "the night comes," based on *yo* (night) and *saru* ([time] comes).

outside. It is found in old phrases. In a certain tale, we find the story of Heichū, who deeply longed for a attendant lady named Hon'in no Jijū: "Worrying about things, this person [speaking of Jijū] thus thought that even if she was superior, her going in the chamber pot would yield the same results as anyone else. He searched for this, looking and sniffing inside, and thought that he should give up on this idea."[360] What it means by "her going in the chamber pot" refers to defecation.

[741] CONCERNING THE SONGS OF RYŪKYŪ

Regarding the songs of Ryūkyū, there are two songs recorded in a certain collection.[361] One is *yamanto te fu fe / kiyaru naru / wan mo turerete / kiyare / wan fa nokorite / sode no namida* (To the land of Yamato / if you go / take me with you / if you go / and I stay / my sleeves will be wet with tears). The other is *okinan te fu to / yamanto te fu to / riku turuki nara / koma ni norite / itaritui / kitaritui* (Regarding Okinan, if it was connected / to the land of Yamato / we could ride horses / and reach it. / We could come back from it). "Okinan" refers to a place name in that country.[362]

[742] USING *KUTI* TO REFER TO BEING ON THE VERGE OF BEGINNING SOMETHING

In the vernacular when someone is on the verge of beginning something, we say *nani kuti*, which is an old usage. In the "Name of Things" section of *Shūishū* on the topic of "The Square Tray the Color of Autumn Leaves About to Fall" we find:

---

360. This episode is mentioned in Videen (1989:132–35).
361. The logical choice would be *Omoro sōshi*, but neither song appears in that collection.
362. "Okinan" is an archaic form of Okinawa. In the vernacular, this word is pronounced as *uchinaa*.

asifiki no If the leaves
yama no konofa no on the trees of the mountains
otikuti fa that pull at one's feet
iro no wosiki zo are about to fall, I will have profound
afare narikeru regret at the loss of their color.
(SS 417)[363]

[743] REGARDING *NO*

In *Horikawa-in hyakushu* there is: *nugikakesi / nusi fa tare tomo / siranedomo / fito no ni tateru / fuzibakama kana* (Though we do not know who the owner is who took off and hung them, there they are—that one pair of wisteria trousers).[364] This is a pun with "one field" (一野) and "one pair of trousers" (一幅).

[746] CONCERNING WORSHIPPING THE DEITIES WHILE HOLDING A FAN

When people in the present worship the deities, they take a fan and worship as if they were holding a ritual baton, but this is not an ancient ritual. In the regulations of the twenty-eighth day of the sixth month of the tenth year of Jōkan (868) it says, "Sumiyosi, Hiraoka, Kasima, Katori, and others: the ritual officiator and the Shintō priests will wear [at their waists] the ritual baton. Many shrines do not yet adhere to this precedent. On the day of a festival or ritual, the officiator will fold his arms and follow through with things." Considering what it says here, anciently if an officiator was not wearing a ritual baton, then they worshipped by folding their arms.

---

363. Norinaga has interpreted the original おちくちは as "when the leaves are about to fall," but most modern scholars now interpret this as *otikutiba* [if (the leaves) fall and rot].

364. This poem alludes to KKS 241: A scent diffuses / from an unknown source. / Who has taken off his / wisteria-trousers / and hung them in the autumn field? (McCullough 1985:60). A different issue concerns the interpretation of *fito no*, which Norinaga believes is actually 一幅 (one length of cloth).

[747] CALLING THE FIFTEENTH DAY OF THE SEVENTH MONTH *CHŪGEN*

In *Tang liudian*[365] it says, "There will be seven specified [times] for fasting for observers of the Way .... The fourth one is called the Sanyuan, "the three basic day" fasts. On the fifteenth day of the first month, the officers of the heavenly institution fast. This is "upper basic day." The fifteenth day of the seventh month the officers of the earthly institution fast. This is "middle basic day." The fifteenth day of the tenth month the officers of the water institution fast. This is "lower basic day."

[751] A THING CALLED *NAGAMOTI*

In the "Young Shoot" chapter of *Eiga monogatari* it says, "Pairs of bearers carried stacks of trunk and chest lids, packed with unbelievable quantities of clothing."[366] This has been understood as *nagamoti* (trunk) in the present. This noun is also seen in *Utsuho monogatari*, but I have forgotten which chapter it is in.[367]

[752] THE WORD *SAKAYAKASU*

In *Shōyūki* it says, "The name of the great councilor was 隆家, and is read **ife wo sakayakasu**. Accordingly there were prosperous events." The word *sakayakasu* resembles a vulgar word, and even back then as it was pronounced, it reminds me of other words, like the examples *tayasu* (to die out) and *moyasu* (to burn).

---

365. "The Six Statutes of Tang." This is a work outlining the procedures and regulations of posts at the Tang court. It was completed in 738, but it took fifty years for the regulations to be implemented.
366. See McCullough and McCullough (1980:647).
367. It appears in the eighth chapter, "Matsuri no tsukai."

[754] CONCERNING *SIKIGAMI WO TUKAFU*

In *Uji shūi monogatari* there is the usage *sikigami wo tukafu*.[368] It has been interpreted to mean "powers that are like that of the Izuna."[369] With this power one has the ability to suddenly kill someone.

[756] HANAKURA

In the same tale (*Uji shūi monogatari*) we find, "There was ... an Archivist-and Sometime-Respondent Ein. Having a long red nose, he was called 'the big-nosed Archivist-and-Sometime-Respondent,' and later, since that was too long, 'Hanakura [the Nose Archivist].' In the end, he came to be referred to always as Hanakura [the Nosed Arch.]."[370] That [famous poet] So vice governor of Tango Province had his name shortened and abbreviated down to just Sotan.[371] This is also seen in the same tale.

[757] *KIGAFE*

In the same tale it says, "to fetch a change of robes. Having changed."[372] This usage comes from having robes available for a person to change into. In the present changing of robes or clothing is *kigafe*, which is an extension of the original meaning.

---

368. *Sikigami* 式神 (a deity whose power is controlled by diviners of the Bureau of Divination) appears three times in *Uji shūi monogatari*, but the phrase *sikigami wo tukafu* only appears in episode 126.
369. This is a belief in the magical power of the foxes of Mount Izuna in Sinano Province.
370. Slightly modified version of Mills (1970:344).
371. This refers to Sone no Yoshitada (dates unclear). He was a poet during the Heian Period (active between 960 and 985). He was later known as So, the vice governor of Tango Province.
372. A slightly altered version of Mills (1970:347).

[759] CONCERNING THE DROPPING OF *NO* IN THE VERNACULAR

In the modern vernacular, there are many instances where people are dropping *no* (of) when it should be included. When we say the names of districts and villages in provinces, we would say such and such *of* district, or such and such *of* village, but now people generally say X district or Y village; there is a lack of the connecting *no*. Also, in the names of people the rule was to say Fujiwara *no* X, or Minamoto *no* Y, and though people still say it this way in the present, they do not add the *no* with so-called titles and personal names. This *no* is rarely used in unreserved conversation, but this should be viewed as incorrect. In elegant speech one should always insert the *no* between the title and personal name. In general people who are learning to speak should take heed regarding these subtle issues, and make a distinction between vulgar and elegant speech.

[760] CONCERNING THOSE WHO DISPARAGE THE POETRY OF MINISTERS SHUNZEI AND TEIKA

Recently among students who are studying the poetic style of *Man'yōshū* some say recklessly arrogant things, disparaging the poetry written by Minister Shunzei, Minister Teika, and others, spouting off with such ease that their poetry is horrible. This is because in the present poets have worshipped these two people as if they were divine, which has led to aggravation, so these students who are critical use violent words of censure, which censure is forced. Now, granted I am not saying that the poetry of these two poets is devoid of any weaknesses, but in general their poetic form is traditional, following the form of the successive reigns and has great beauty. No matter how much poetry these critical students compose they will never be able to approach the feet of these great poets.

[761] SHRINES SHOULD BE ESTEEMED

In the codes dealing with public documents,[373] the title of Great Shrine is seen under the "Omitted Name" section. This title of Great Shrine is seen in the *Jinmyōchō* as shrines of importance. Through this usage in official documents, and the use of omitted names,[374] we know that anciently people esteemed these shrines. Presently, though a certain shrine may be known as a Great Shrine, the usage of Omitted Name is no longer employed. Moreover, is it not cruel when people make mention of these shrines in official documents and fail to use the honorific prefix 御?

[762] THE DEBATE OF THE LEARNED ON LOGIC

Scholars in the present debate in a proud manner, as if they are wise, about what happens to man or about the various forms of logic, but they are simply reiterating ideas found in Chinese works. Why in the world can they not even set one foot outside the box [of Chinese learning]?

[763] THERE ARE SIX PRINCIPLES IN POETICS

People respect the theory that there are six principles in poetics, but this is insipid. "Six principles" is something established anciently in China, and *waka* has absolutely nothing to do with it. Regarding the six principles and their relation to *waka*, it started with the idea found in the preface to *Kokinshū*, where it states that there are six types of poems, and Ki no Tsurayuki divides poetry into six groups. However, this was done in imitation of poetry in China, which divides poetry into six types; this is wholly unsuitable for *waka*. There are classifications such as poetry, metaphorical poetry, allegorical poetry, and so on, but these three are really the

---

373. Pointing to the Taihō and Yōrō codes promulgated between 701 and 718.

374. Article 38 of the Code on Official Documents allows for the omission of certain names or titles out of respect.

same. At the time of Tsurayuki, poets tried to force *waka* into this classification, and called it "the six principles." It is also unsatisfactory to put poems of celebration in this classification. If one is to include celebratory poetry in this classification then it is not right that they exclude love and lamentation poetry.

Generally this preface in *Kokinshū* does not classify poetry very well, and in many points merely copies verbatim discussions that originally applied to ancient poetry in China. Among all these ideas that are not suitable to *waka*, this idea of six principles really does not work, and while Tsurayuki employs his emotions deeply and argues for these principles in various ways, it is useless and of no value. Even the six principles applied to Chinese poetry have a number of differing versions and scholars have found it difficult to decide on just one, so why should we imagine that it would be easy to stuff *waka* into these six categories? In the old annotations of the (*Kokinshū*) preface it says, "It is impossible to classify *waka* according to the six types." This indeed is a reasonable argument. With this one phrase the arguments about the six principles should be considered finished.

[769] A DISH CALLED FISH *SASIMI*

In the same record [*Nakahara Yasutomiki*] in the fifth year of Bun'an (1448), eighth month, fifteenth day, it says "Two courses of cold noodles and sea bream *sasimi* were prepared."

[774] HALL FOR VISITORS

In *Shōyūki* it says, "They came to the Hall of Abstinence. In the Hall for Visitors ... ."[375]

---

375. Norinaga seems to have made mention of this, because 客殿 appears here for the first time. It refers to a building set up in temple precincts and other areas to host guests.

[775] CHILDREN'S NAMES CONTAINING -*MARU*

In the same record, it says, "On the sixteenth day of the second month of the third year of Kan'nin (1019), Senjumaru underwent his coming of age ceremony in the guard's house of the family residence" [He was given the name of Tametoki]. So people back then gave their children names that included *maru*.

[776] REFERRING TO SOMEONE AS "HONORABLE RESIDENCE," AND RESIDENCES OF OTHER PROVINCES

In the same record [*Shōyūki*], in an entry from the same year, we find the record referring to other people as "your honorable residence" (貴殿). In addition, there are examples of "Funya Tadamitsu, a resident of Sima District in Tikuzen Province," or "Taji Hisaakira, a resident of Ito District, same province." It turns out that calling people "residents" (住人) is somewhat archaic.

[777] *SHINKYŌ* AND *KŌKYŌ*

In the same record, entry of the same year, we find the usage of *shinkyō* (神郷, shrine villages) and *kōkyō* (公郷, imperial villages). *Shinkyō* are villages within *shinryō* (land controlled by a shrine), while *kōkyō* are villages within imperially controlled land.

[780] CONCERNING A BANQUET WITH SOUP

In Governor Kanroji Motonaga's record it says, "At the mansion of the elder sister of Koji of the Third Rank we had soup." Also, "I was invited for something by the chief of the imperial storehouse, and soup was laid out for us." These and other examples are in there. Even in the present if you go into the provinces they have "soup." The various guests bring rice from their own houses and go to the house [where they have been invited] and are provided with vegetables and soup and given a banquet. In some provinces it is called *siru kau*.

[784] ANCIENTLY THE RITUALS OF THE DEITIES WERE VALUED

In the record of Emperor Tenchi in *Nihon shoki*, in the third month of the ninth year we find, "Close to Mii of the mountain various places of enshrinement were laid out, and paper offerings were presented. Nakatomi Kane Murazi read the liturgy." At that time the ranks of the Nakatomi were large, and one may know how important the rituals of Shintō were at the time because Kane Muraji is the one who read the liturgy. This great Muraji held the rank of superior messenger upper greater brocade, which corresponds to the later rank of superior forth rank upper, but at that time he was the second highest-ranking minister, and in the first month of the next year the court promotes him to minister of the right, so he was a very important official.

Now this emperor [Tenchi] had a special affinity for things Chinese and during his reign the court studied all things regarding China; however, it is important to note that even with this trend events relating to the rituals of Shintō did not cease.

[785] SCHOLARSHIP IS TO WISELY SELECT ONE'S WAY

When one has the intention to enter scholarship, first he should carefully select his teacher. Then he should ponder his teacher's beliefs and teachings. Then he should follow him. A wise person—and of course, even an ignorant person—is usually drawn to his master's theories in the beginning, but if the master's theory is incorrect, the student generally does not notice. Though the student may notice later on that the theory is incorrect, it is very difficult to rid yourself of old habits; add to that the evil spirit of egoism, and the student stretches truth here and there to defend his master's theory. In the end, there are many people who cannot leave to posterity anything of value, having spent their entire lives in pursuit of mistaken ideas. People like this work hard and learn profound things, and as they proceed down the path to learning, only bad habits flourish, and not only do they lead themselves astray, they lead other people astray as well.

As I have said repeatedly, it is critical to select your master well in the beginning. I should have said this in *Uiyamabumi*, and since I did not include it there, I have put it here.

[786] ON THE EIGHT BEAUTIFUL SCENIC VIEWS

There are many places in the country where there are eight revered spots, and this is in imitation of the Chinese habit of setting up a list of eight scenic places. In Japan, the first one established appears to have been the eight beautiful spots of Afumi. There are many other examples of "eight beautiful spots" around the country, all done in imitation of Afumi. Some of these places even include spots that have no inherent beauty, so why label them one of "the eight beautiful spots"? If one truly reveres natural beauty, then he would only select excellent places, not worrying about fitting them into some predetermined number. Fine if many, and fine if few. It is the insipid practice of the day to be obsessed with fitting things into a preconceived mold.

[787] ON COLLECTING POETRY FROM OLD-AGE CELEBRATIONS AND ESTABLISHING MONUMENTS FOR THE DECEASED

When celebrating old age, it is the current custom in Japan and China to request that people compose various forms of poetry for the occasion. This is a popular practice, and though it is refined, there are people who pretend to have an interest in this, even when they actually have none. Their true interest is in seeing how many poems they can collect, so in the end I think they are caught up in the custom of the day.

In addition, it is a widening practice in society to erect monuments to people, though the deceased person was not that important a figure in society. There are many examples of this, decreasing the value of the custom, and in the end I think it is bothersome and unbecoming.

[788] PRETENDING YOU DO NOT WANT RICHES

Another example of the deception of China is when people say that they do not want riches. Though scholars or other writers want to get their hands on a good book, they put on airs and pretend that they actually do not seek after riches. This is a clear example of deception. In this era of prosperity, if you pay enough, you can get your hands on almost anything. If these scholars actually want a good book, then why would they not desire money? Nonetheless, in this era of coveting anything at the expense of your neighbor, putting on the air of not wanting riches is clearly the lesser of the two evils.

[789] THE DIFFERENCE BETWEEN MAFE AND SAKI, AND USING SAKI TO MEAN *NOTI*

Mafe (before) is the opposite of "behind" and means "the direction from the eyes" (目方). So the word is modeled after the human form, but even when talking about the shape of things you use the character 前 [to illustrate in front of something]. Nevertheless, when you use **saki** (before) in opposition to *noti* (later) you can never use **mafe** in its place. In the present vernacular there are people who say things like *mafekata* for "before I go," or "Bon, which is before *Sekku*." Alternatively, there are written examples where people use *mafe* as in "before a certain time." These examples are all errors. I myself did not notice this distinction early enough and I have written **mafe** when I should have used **saki**, and I now realize that I made a mistake. Regarding these, the Chinese graphs are the same for both words, but the Japanese underlying word is different. One should never make a mistake because of the graph .... .

[794] "HAVE A WIFE" AND "POUR *SAKE*"

In poetry composed in the present, it seems to be the custom now as found in poetic works to celebrate someone who is to be betrothed (*tuma wo mukafe*) and they send congratulatory poems written on "getting married" (*tuma wo mukafu*). This is not an elegant usage, and these words were never used in ancient times. They would have written "prepare to have a wife" (*tuma wo mauke*). In all things in the ancient past people would say "prepare a young man" (*wotoko wo mauke*) or "prepare to have a child" (*ko wo mauke*).

Furthermore it is the tradition in present poetry to talk about "pouring *sake*" (*sake wo kumu*), but this is not an elegant usage, either. Pouring *sake* and drinking it is a vulgar custom from that foreign land. There has been no such custom in the imperial land, in the past or the present. Thus in poetry and prose there are no examples of the verb *kumu* (pour). In the past they only said "drink."

Therefore, poets in the present do not ponder the precedents of the ancient past, but simply guess at words, and since words like "have a wife" (*tuma wo mauku*) and "drink *sake*" (*sake wo nomu*) still exist in our present speech, they feel that these have no elegance, and try to sound elegant by using *mukafu* and *kumu* [in place of *mauku* and *nomu*]. These people should understand that these usages are much like *ka wo kiku* (test incense). These provincialisms differ from the ancient usages.

[796] CONCERNING CLOTH OFFERINGS MADE OF MULBERRY BARK

Anciently the object called *yufu* was something woven of fibers from the bark of the paper mulberry tree, and was used in all kinds of general things anciently, but from the Middle Ages people have only made paper objects and I believe that the weaving of this kind of cloth has died out. Even in the present in the province of Afa they have something called *tafu*, which is woven from the fibers of the bark of the paper mulberry tree. It is white in color and the fibers are strong, and even if you wash it you do not need to use glue. The more you wash it the whiter it becomes.

These things were recently made known in a work written by Senge Kiyonushi[376] of the province of Idumo. He said that he had obtained a specimen from that province [Afa], and mentioned that he had some minute scraps that he brought for me to see. In actuality the fabric was of very solid fibers, and of a brilliant whiteness. How I would like to ask and ascertain about this from someone in Afa Province. As I have pondered these things, surely there are other specimens in other provinces. How I wish someone would research far and wide for these things.

[797] ABOUT TEA

Ruiju kokushi says, "On the twenty-second day of the fourth month, summer, of the sixth year of Kōnin (815), the emperor journeyed to Karasaki of Siga in Afumi Province, and passed in front of Sōfukuji. Senior Prelate Zuyōchū, Priest Gomyō, and others came outside the gate at the head of a great many monks, and greeted the emperor. He descended from his palanquin, entered the Golden Pavilion, and paid his respects to the Buddha. At last when he passed in front of Bonshakuji he had his palanquin stopped and he composed a poem. His younger brother, the crown prince, and many in the crowd composed poems in reply. Senior Prelate Zuyōchū himself boiled water and presented tea to the emperor, and in return received the emperor's blanket. From there the emperor got on a boat and headed out across the lake. The governor had people perform a local dance, and the emperor presented robes and bedding to those above the fifth rank, and those holding the post of judge and lower. Those holding the post of provincial scribe down to those serving in district offices

---

376. Senge Kiyonushi, more commonly known as Senge Toshizane (1764–1831), was born a descendant of the Izumo Kokuzō Senge family. He went to Kyōto and studied the Chinese classics. In 1792 he became a disciple of Norinaga, and had a steady correspondence with him till his master's death. He published *Teisei Izumo fudoki* ("Corrected" *Izumo fudoki*) in 1806.

received wool fabric according to their status." Again, "On the third day of the sixth month of the same year, the court ordered the capital provinces and the provinces of Afumi, Tanba, Harima, and others to plant tea and present it to the court." This is the beginning of records about tea.

[798] THE CHIEF PRIEST AT THE GREAT SHRINE OF ISE PERFORMS BUDDHIST RITES, AND IS RELIEVED OF HIS CURRENT POST

In the same work [*Ruiju kokushi*] we find, "On the twenty-second day of the sixth month of the seventh year of Kōnin (816), Chief Priest at the Great Shrine of Ise, Ōnakatomi Ason Kiyomochi, Junior Seventh Rank Lower, did not observe the ritual taboo, but performed Buddhist rites. Divination was performed in the Office of the Native Religion, and it was judged that a curse would ensue. A fine consisting of the value of 'great purification' was ordered, and he was relieved of his current post."

[801] VERBS THAT USE FIVE BASES AND THE CONJUGATION OF *U* (GET)

Regarding the class of inflected words [verbs], we have verbs that conjugate from one base up to four, but there are no cases of verbs with five bases.[377] Regarding *ku* (come), we only have one other base, *ko*.[378] It is extremely rare to find a word that has five bases. And among all the words in the language, no verbs have a

---

377. Kamo no Mabuchi and Norinaga described verbal declension according to a *kana*-based description, where a verb is analyzed as consisting of a base and an attending suffix. Thus a verb like *saku* (bloom) in classical Japanese had four bases: *saka-*, *saki-*, *saku*, and *sake*. There are four different vowels, which equal four different bases. In classical Japanese there were no verbs with five bases.

378. It is not completely clear what Norinaga means here, as *ku* (come) has at least three bases (depending on the analysis): *ko-*, *ki-*, and *ku*. It is possible that Norinaga had trouble finding an example of *ki-* in his *Kojiki* or *Man'yōshū* texts. MYS 3571 contains this stanza: 見都々曾伎奴流 (**Mitutu so kinuru**, while watching I have come).

base with a vowel from the *a-i-u-e-o* group, other than *u* (get), which conjugates from *u* to *e*. This verb is also rare.[379]

[802] THE OLD CHINESE TRADITION OF READING BOOKS BY THE LIGHT OF SNOW OR FIREFLIES

In ancient China, there was a man named Sun Kang who thoroughly enjoyed learning, but his family was poor and had no money to buy oil for their lamp, so at night he would read by the natural light reflected from the snow. And in the same country, there was another man named Che Yin who also was fond of studying, and like Sun Kang, his family was too poor to afford oil for their lamp, so in the summer, he would gather fireflies together and read by the light they emitted. These two stories are quite famous, and there is not a person who has not heard of them. There are even many poems written about these two stories.

However, when you think about these two stories, you realize these are examples of the Chinese trying to gain popularity, and both are pure fiction. The reason for this is that if one's family were too poor to buy oil, then the person would go to a neighbor's house and beg to be allowed to use their lamp. And even if that light were not as good as one had hoped, being faint, surely it would be brighter than reading by light reflected from the snow, or the light from fireflies. Also, there is only a limited time during the year when snow or fireflies are available for use, so does that mean that these people did not read in the evenings when there was no snow or fireflies? These stories are extremely bizarre.

---

379. Norinaga does not appear to realize that he has hit upon an important discovery, likely because he has not accurately described the verb. Here Norinaga writes that *u* (get) conjugates into 宇延, which he is interpreting as *ue*, but historically this is really **uye**. He is correct, however, that there are no verbs with a simple vowel as a base; all bases have a consonant (or glide) plus a vowel.

❧ 13 | BROOMRAPE

suwe firoku	How broad the tips are
sigerikeru kana	of the broom rape
omofigusa	that grows thickly.
wobana ga moto fa	The base of the miscanthus
fitomoto ni site	is a single rod.

The reason for composing this poem is that there are always love poems that include "the herb that makes me think of the miscanthus." If we look into the beginning of this reading, we find a poem in *Man'yōshū*:

miti no fe no	Like the broomrape that lies
wobana ga sita no	in the shadow of the miscanthus
omofigusa	on the side of the road,
ima sara sara ni	what would lead you
nani ka omofamu	to have doubts now? (MYS 2270)

This is the only poem of this kind in *Man'yōshū* and there are no others, but this one poem spawned a large number of love poems later, including the one that I composed and added above.

Now it is not clear what kind of plant this *omofigusa* is. One year I got a letter from Tanaka Michimaro, who lived in Nagoya in Ofari Province, in which he wrote,

> Even now we have a plant that we call *omofigusa*, a small plant that grows among the pampas grass. It is three or four inches in height, but some can grow to five or six inches, and the flowers bloom late in autumn. The color of the blossoms is purple with a hint of black, and if you see

one it looks like a violet, but the color does not have the luster of the violet. When the blossoms bloom, the leaves have already fallen. This plant is only found growing among pampas grass, nowhere else. At the tip of the flower you will see a seed about the size of a black soybean. If you pick this seed and plant it you can grow this plant very easily. But if you plant the seed, you must plant it among pampas grass or it will not grow. Perhaps this is the same *omofigusa* from ancient times. Or was it called *omofigusa* in the recent past by someone who knows things from the ancient past, calling it such only because it grows among pampas grass?

He also drew me a picture of this plant and sent it to me to look at. The picture looks like this [see right]. Then at a later date after this letter he brought me one plant he had dug up along with some pampas grass, transplanted in a bamboo box, and showed me what it looked like. I transplanted this here and looked after it. For a while it looked like it would take, but in the end it died in the winter. The next spring I waited to see if anything would spring forth from the dead base, but it remained lifeless. The pampas grass also did not sprout again. When I asked about this later, I was told that it is the same plant that you find growing among pampas grass in the mountains and fields in this area. It is very doubtful that this is the same *omofigusa* that grew in the ancient past.

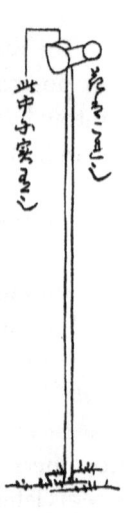

[814] EXAMPLES WHERE THE GRAPH 不 (NOT) IS LEFT OUT IN *MAN'YŌSHŪ*

In Book 7 of *Man'yōshū* there is the poem

awo midura	On the plain of Yosami
yosami no fara ni	of green dangling hair

13 ~ BROOMRAPE

fito mo afanu kamo	will we not meet anyone?
ifabasiru	Let us read
afumi agata no	the tale of Afumi District
monogatari semu	where the boulders dash. (MYS 1287)

The second and third stanza 依網原 / 人相鴨 should be read as yosami no fara ni / fito mo afanu kamo. Afanu kamo is an example of a word meaning that the person desires to meet someone else. In Book 9, we have

kumogakuri	Hidden in the clouds
kari naku toki fa	when the wild geese cry
akiyama no	we wait for the autumn leaves
momidi kata matu	to appear on the fall mountains,
toki fa suginedo	the time has not yet passed.
	(MYS 1703)[380]

If we do not read the concluding stanza 時者雖過 as **toki fa suginedo**, then the poem does not make sense. In Book 10, we also have:

kasumi tatu	Spending the long spring day
faru no nagafi wo	when mists have appeared
kofikurasi	longing for you—
yo mo fukeyuku wo	the night also deepens;
imo ni afanu kamo	will my beloved not meet me?
	(MYS 1894)

If we do not read the concluding stanza 妹相鴨 as **imo ni afanu kamo**, then the poem does not make sense. In the same book we also find:

satuki yama	On a night when
unofana tukuyo	the deutzia flowers bloom
fototogisu	on the mountain in May—

---

380. This poem is open to various interpretations. Most scholars in the present interpret the final stanza 時者雖過 as **toki fa suguredo** (Has the season already passed?).

kikedo akanu wo	I tire not of hearing the cuckoo's cry;
mata nakanu kamo	will he cry again, I wonder.
	(MYS 1953)

This also should be **nakanu kamo**, and means "cry out!" In Book 11, we have:

wa ga seko fa	That my beloved
sakiku imasu to	is safe and sound—
kaferikite	won't someone return
ware ni tugekomu	and come to me and
fito mo konu kamo	tell me it is so? (MYS 2384)

This must be read **konu kamo**, and means "come!" as she is waiting. In the same book we also find:

fi narabeba	Lining up the days
fito sirinu besi	surely people will find out.
kefu no fi no	The day of today
titose no goto mo	I wish could last a thousand years—
ari kosenu kamo	won't you come to see me? (MYS 2387)

In the same book there is also:

kakusitutu	Is there no sign
wa ga matu sirusi	that it was worth waiting
aranu kamo	for you like this?
yo no fito mina no	Even though no one in society
tune naranaku ni	lives their lives out in the same place.
	(MYS 2585)

The third stanza is 有鴨 (**aranu kamo**), and means "so be there." Again in the same eleventh book we have:

sikitafe no	Spread out on the floor
makura ugokite	the pillow moves
ineraezu	and I cannot sleep.

13 ~ BROOMRAPE 321

monomofu koyofi   Tonight as I am filled with thoughts
faya mo akenu kamo won't the dawn hurry and break?
(MYS 2593)

This is the same as above. All of these poems were composed without the negative graph 不. I likely have left out more examples than these. In all of these cases the reading in the manuscript is mistaken. However, thinking that there are cases where the reading must be *nu* (not) or it will not make sense, there are likely people who wonder if the character 不 (not) has been dropped from the text, but there have yet to be people who have realized that the graph has been dropped. And it is not just one or two cases. Among a large number of examples, we should understand that there would be a few rare cases where the character has been purposely abbreviated.

Again, in Book 7, there is:

ikenobe no   Please do not cut the slender bamboo
wotukigamoto ni at the base of the small zelvoka tree
sasa na kari so ne ... growing by the side of the pond ....
(MYS 1276)

Also,

kono woka ni   Child cutting grass
kusa karu wara fa on this hill—
sika na kari so ne you should not cut it so much!
(MYS 1291)

Perhaps both of these have left out the character 莫 (do not). However, I cannot find any others apart from these two, so perhaps these simply were miscopied. It is difficult to decide which is correct. Now regarding whether the character 不 should be included or not, it depends on the context; why would a person abbreviate a graph when it is a grammatical marker that must be there, as the meaning is implicit from the graph? When you verbally say things like *narinu* (had become) or *tirinu* (had scattered) it is homophonous with the negative *nu* when articulated. This is especially the case as *na-ni-nu-ne-no* are soft and light sounds [nasals], so they should be clearly articulated.

To say a bit more about this, *sirazu* (I don't know) in Old Japanese can be *sirani*, and you find places here and there where it is written 不知爾, and this is a case where the graph 不 is superfluous, and is this also not clear from context?

[817] AN EXAMPLE OF *YAMA* MISTAKENLY WRITTEN AS *TAMA* IN *MAN'YŌSHŪ*

There are many examples in *Man'yōshū* of the graph 山 (*yama*, mountain) written 玉 (*tama*, jewel), and this is because the two graphs look alike when written in cursive form. In Book 2 of *Man'yōshū*, the poem **miyosinu no tamamatu ga e ni** (MYS 113) and in the poem **yama matu kage ni** (MYS 3655) in Book 15, the character *tama* is a mistake for *yama*. Nevertheless, in later poems, all the readings of *tama matu* are mistakes. There is no such thing as a jeweled pine tree (*tama matu*).[381] In Book 2 of the same anthology we have:

fito pa yosi	Other people
omofi yamu tomo	even if they stop longing for someone,
tamakadura	will continue to see that face
kage ni miyetutu	that stunning face.(MYS 149)

Here this is **yamakage** (mountain shadow) and points to a vine that grows in sunlight and is used as a pillow word. It is intended to continue as **yamakage fikage**, and is the same as that found in a poem in Book 14, **asifiki no yamakadurakage** (the vine of the mountain shade which pulls at the feet) (MYS 3573). In Book 18, we also have **yamakage**. In every case *kage* points to the vine that grows in the sunlight. However, in later periods people

---

381. Scholars today generally accept *tama* as the correct reading, stating that *tama* is an honorific embellishment.

read this as *tamakadura* without realizing it was a mistake for **yamakadura**, so it is a mistake to interpret this through the association of *kake* (to hang), because *kage* follows.

Also in Book 13 there is **igusi tate** (Standing the divine skewers) ... **uzu no tamakage / mireba tomosi mo** (when I look at the jeweled vine in her hair / I am drawn to her) (MYS 3229). This is a vine that drapes down the girl's hair. In Book 16 we have **asifiki no / tamakadura no ko** (the maiden of the jeweled vine that pulls at one's feet) (MYS 3789), and it goes without argument that *tama* is a mistake for *yama* because of the pillow word **asifiki no,** which only attaches to mountains, not jewels. So in this poem it should be **yamakage no ko**. Considering the evidence from these quotes, even the poem in Book 11 **tamakuse no / kiyoki kafara ni** (at the pure stream of the beautiful Kuse River) ... (MYS 2403) points to the Kuse River in Yamasiro Province, so *yama* has been miscopied as *tama*, and 能 'able' has been miscopied as 清 'pure,'" and because the graph 代 (reign) has been dropped I do not think that it should be read as *tamakuse*.[382]

[819] ADDING GRAPHS WHEN ONE WRITES

In the same anthology we find examples where graphs have been added that are not necessary, such as 雖干跡 **fosedo** (though they hang them to dry) (MYS 1186); 将有裳 **aramu mo** (whose name is it)? (MYS 3105); 不知爾 **sirani** (do not know) (MYS 167). In these cases the graphs 跡・裳・爾 are extraneous. Examples of this also appear in the edicts in *Shoku Nihongi*, and the Sugawara family *Man'yōshū*; there are likely other examples of this in other works.

---

382. Norinaga is often right in emending corrupted readings, but he is off the mark here. There are no textual witnesses that support the amount of changes he insists on here. There simply is no evidence that 玉 at the beginning of this poem is a mistake for 山.

[821] CONCERNING THE WORD *AYENUGANI* IN *MAN'YŌSHŪ*

In Book 8 of *Man'yōshū* we find:

ofuru tatibana	The orange tree with many branches
tama ni nuku	will be strung with fruit
satuki wo tikami	because the fifth month is close,
ayenugani	and the tree is in full bloom
fana sakinikeri	and the blossoms spill forth.

(MYS 1507)

In Book 10 we have:

aki tukeba	When autumn comes
mikusa no fana no	though I think about how
ayenugani	the blossoms of the water grass
omofedo sirazi	drop off quickly,
tada ni afazareba	I have not met you, so you don't know.

(MYS 2272)

It is a mistake to interpret this **ayenu** as "We do not associate with each other." "Associate" is **afe**, so the spelling is different. One should not be deceived into thinking that **tatibana no tama ni afenuki** (stringing together the jewels of the orange) (MYS 4189) is the same usage. **Aye** refers to trees and vegetation bearing fruit and the **nu** shows the completion of that action. **Gani** is a contraction of **ganeni**, and is the same word as **mukogane** (future groom) and **kisakigane** (future queen). This usage also appears in *Kokinshū* in *oi kakurugani*.[383] In *Man'yōshū* this usage is especially prevalent, and we find both examples of **gane** and **gani**. The meaning originates from preparing something beforehand. Thus, the poem in Book 8 has reference to the blossoms blooming first in preparation for the appearance of the fruit. The poem in Book 10 is an allusion

---

383. There is no such poem in *Kokinshū*. Perhaps Norinaga had KKS 349 in mind, but the wording is different.

to love bearing fruit while the poet mentions the flower blooming in preparation for the production of the fruit. The meaning of the poem is, "I think my love will bear fruit, but as we have yet to meet, how will it happen? I have no way of knowing." Considering the line in the *chōka* in Book 18 written about the orange, **ayuru mi fa / tama ni nukitutu** (threading a string through the fruit which has dropped), one may know that **ayu** refers to "bearing fruit." It is a verb that conjugates as **aye** and **ayu**.[384]

[822] ON PLUM BLOSSOM POETRY DEALING WITH FRAGRANCE

Among poetry composed on plum blossoms, there are many poems about plum blossoms in *Man'yōshū*, but there is only one with the fragrance as its core element, which is the following poem from Book 20:

ume no fana	The wondrous fragrance
ka wo kagufasimi	of the plum blossoms!
tofokedomo	Though you are far off,
kokoro mosi no ni	my heart gently thinks of you,
kimi wo si zo omofu	and how you are. (MYS 4500)

There are no other examples. Anciently there was no general appreciation for the fragrance of the blossoms. There are also many poems written about the orange blossoms, but there are only two poems (in Books 17 and 18[385]) that praise the fragrance. In Book 10 there is a poem about mushrooms:

---

384. This is not completely accurate. *Ayu* is "fruit falling as it is ripe." This verb undergoes a slight semantic change in the Heian era, where it is used for blood or sweat dripping. The verb *ayu* (or *aeru*) still is used in some dialects such as Ōita and Miyazaki, meaning fruit dropping from trees.
385. MYS 3916 and 4111.

takamato no[386]	On Mount Takamato,
kono mine mo seni	on this narrow peak
kasa tatete	I stand my parasol.
miti sakaritaru	How wonderful is the fragrance
aki no ka no yosa	at its peak during autumn. (MYS 2233)

Other than these poems, there are no other poems composed in appreciation of fragrance. All the other many poems using the word **nifofi** (color, fragrance) have reference to the beauty of reflecting color and do not refer to the sense of smell. As a minor detour, the above poem was composed about mushrooms, but the text has "Composed about the sensation of smell." The character 芳 (sensation of smell) is a copyist's error for 茸 (mushroom).

[824] THE NAME OF EMPEROR NARA

The real name of Emperor Nara [Heizei] was Wotono in the beginning, but later was altered to Ade. At that time, the precedent for naming the imperial princes and various other princes was to take the *kabane* of their nursing maids as their name, and even in the case of this name *wotono*, we see in the thirty-ninth volume of *Shoku Nihongi* that there is a nursing maid named Abe Wotono Ason Sakafi, and her *kabane* was *wotono*. Even the name *ade* is a fusion of the *a* of Abe and the *de* of *tono* [the Chinese reading being *den*], and it is read with its Chinese reading of *ade*. The district of Arita in the province of Kii originally was called Ade District, written 阿提郡 in *Nihon shoki* and *Shoku Nihongi*. Looking through the changes of the name of this emperor, you see that in the first year of Daidō (806) the district name was altered to Arita.

---

386. Norinaga's text has 高円, which is also seen in MYS 230 and read as **takamato**. However, in the poem quoted here, MYS 2233, the critical text has 高松 (**takamatu no**).

[825] CONCERNING POETRY WRITTEN IN A "GRASS" STYLE

In the "Beneath the Oak" chapter of *Genji monogatari*, it says regarding a poem by the eighth prince of Uji, "'Winds from off the hills sweep away lingering mists with strains of music, yet there still stretch between us distances of tossing waves,' the gentleman had written. It was beautifully done in the running [grass] style."[387] "Written in a grass style" refers to a script where *man'yōgaki* is written in a cursive style. It seems that they wrote that way even back then.

[827] A STABLE OF THE IMPERIAL GUARDS OF THE RIGHT

Because we find mention of "a stable of the imperial guards of the right," it should be remembered that not just the guards of the right, but all branches of the six offices of guards had their own stables for horses.

[829] CONCERNING *KIN'YŌSHŪ* CALLING PRINCE SUKEHITO THE THIRD PRINCE

In the same work [*Ima kagami*],[388] it notes that *Kin'yōshū* records that Imperial Prince Sukehito wrote his name, and Retired Emperor Shirakawa replied, "Why did you write it so that I could see it?" So the prince signed it as "the third prince." Since this prince was the child of Retired Emperor Shirakawa, I believe it was prudent of him not to write his name down. Thus he presented the poem as he did.

---

387. See Tyler (2001.2:850).
388. Norinaga uses the more common title of *Shoku Yotsugi*. The narrator of *Ōkagami* calls himself Yotsugi. As *Ima kagami* is a continuation of *Ōkagami*, it received the name of "Yotsugi, continued." *Ima kagami* is of unknown authorship, though tradition records Fujiwara no Tametsune as the compiler.

[830] THE READING OF 式乾門院

The usual reading of 式乾門院 is *sikiken*, but in *Izayoi no nikki* kept by Abutsu-ni,[389] the name is written phonetically as *sikikamumonwin no mikusigedono*.[390] Is not this the correct reading? I wonder.

[836] *OFOTETE*

In the "Jewel in the Robe" chapter of *Eiga monogatari* in the words spoken by a child, the child refers to his grandfather as *ofotete*.

[837] A BIOGRAPHY OF SŌGI

A certain record contains this:[391] Priest Sōgi, his *kabane* was Nakatomi and his surname was Inoo. He is the son of Sōjū. In the past he lived in Ki Province. His mother was a Fujiwara, and being grieved, as she had no heir, she prayed to the deity of Tamazu Island for one hundred days. On the night when the one hundred days were fulfilled, she saw in a dream an egg enter her mouth and thus she became pregnant. Thirteen months later she gave birth to Sōgi. The time was the twenty-eighth year of Ōei (1421). From the time he was a child he enjoyed *waka*. He studied at the feet of his uncle, Sōzei. Because of the miraculous event of his mother getting pregnant by swallowing an egg, he called himself Shugyokuan (Egg Hermitage). He traveled to the capital and made Shinkei his teacher. He built a grass hermitage in Nagatani of Ifakura, and enjoyed studying Laozi and Zhuang Zi. He styled himself Shizensai. In the third year of Bunmei (1471) he visited Tō Tsuneyori, became

---

389. A diary and travelogue kept by a nun named Abutsu (hence, Abutsu-ni). She was the wife of Fujiwara no Tameie. This work basically marks the end of Heian literature.

390. This name refers to the female poet, Shikiken-Mon In no Mikushige (dates unclear), who lived during the Kamakura period. She was the daughter of Koga Michiteru.

391. It is unfortunate that Norinaga did not actually name his source, as this "certain record" is unknown in the present.

close friends with him, and Sōgi asked him to increase his learning of the Way of poetry. Tsuneyori taught him the secret teachings of the Way of poetry and there was nothing forgotten. After this Sōgi thanked him and Tsuneyori sent him back to the capital. Furthermore, he worked at poetry and sent some of his work with a Zen priest. Afterward his residence was not permanent and he became a wanderer and journeyed to various provinces. Those who received Sōgi's teachings were Shōhaku, Sojun, Sōchō, and Sōseki. On the last day of the seventh month of the second year of Bunki (1502) he passed away at an inn at a hot spring in Sagami Province. He was eighty-two years of age. He is buried at Teirinji Temple in Momosono in Suruga Province. There is a pine tree planted on top of his grave.

[844] THE WORD *FUKUSA*

Tanaka Michimaro claims that in Afumi, Mino, and Ofari the word *fukusa* refers to something that is soft. Also, when one has washed a robe and has yet to starch it, this is called *fukusame mono*. To wash cloths and leave them unstarched is known as *fukusamete oku*. They also say *fukusa naru* in reference to many objects.

[845] A PLANT KNOWN AS *MARUSUGE*

The plant known in society as *kayaturigusa* (*Cyperus microiria*) is a small plant, growing in agricultural fields, and is extremely vexing to farmers. In Mino Province, this plant is known as *maruko*, but in Mikafa Province they call it *marusuge*. This same person [Michimaro] wondered if this is not the same plant, *marokosuge*, mentioned in poetry.[392]

---

392. Seen in SS 829.

[846] THE ASH TREE

The tree known as the ash tree is white, the leaves much like the hackberry, and this tree can grow to become very large. The fruit of this tree is shaped like this:
The top is flat like a leaf. Many types of this tree can be found in Fannoki Village in Mino Province. People in that area say these trees do not grow in any other village. Tanaka Michimaro is from Fannoki Village, which is in Tagi District.

[847] A NUMBER OF NAMES FOR A VARIETY OF WILD GEESE

This same person has told me that wild geese can generally be divided into four large groups. The largest group is called *magamo*, the next one is called *fidori*, the next is called *adi*, and the variety that is the smallest is called *takabe*. These are all wild geese, but the name of the bird changes according to its size. Both the *adi* and *takabe* appear in poetry in *Man'yōshū* (cf. MYS 258 and 2751). There is also another variety called *aisa*, and while this is also a variety of wild goose, it is slightly different. It is called *akisa* in a poem in Book 7 of *Man'yōshū* (MYS 1122).

[850] LIVING DEEP IN THE QUIET OF THE MOUNTAINS

Scholars from various ages as well as those in the present tend to live far from town in the quiet of the mountains. I do not see the point with being obsessed with living in the mountains. I am attracted to places full of people and a lively atmosphere. Places far removed from the city are lonely and gloomy. On the other hand, going to such a place on a rare occasion and spending one night is quite interesting, but I would not want to settle down in such a lonely spot and live my life there.

There are many kinds of people, and their desires are varied, so it is only proper that some want to live in such a secluded place. There are probably many people in society with this desire, but there are also others mixed in with this group who are putting on a facade and following in the Chinese practice of deception, which differs from the average person in society, only saying that it would be ideal to live in the mountains. Perhaps I have this kind of suspicion because of my own vulgar habits.

[851] WHEN I SPENT TIME IN THE CAPITAL

When I, Norinaga, went up to the capital in the first year of Kyōwa (1801), I stayed at a place east of Karasumaru, located on the southern side of Fourth Avenue. The place is situated somewhat away from the road, so the bustle of the city is not as loud. I went out to the gate morning and evening. The avenue is wide and gave me a feeling of freedom. The street was filled with people coming and going and the atmosphere was full of activity. Above all else, as someone who has spent most of his time in the provinces, this scene amazed me. The scene left me with my eyes wide open.

The capital is not always like this, but Fourth Avenue is especially crowded with people. Among the three great cities of our country, Edo and Ofosaka are so full of people and the confusion so great that I feel that the capital is perfect. There are many shrines and temples and there are many things with long histories. Perhaps this image of mine makes everything that much more respectable, beautiful, and elegant. There is nowhere else I would rather live than in Kyōto, the capital.

[859] CONCERNING A GREAT MUGWORT TREE

A certain work records that in an area around Miyagino in the province of Mitinoku many mugwort plants grow to about two *jō* (twenty feet) in height. In the same province, about two *li* this side of Firusaki in Tugaru there is a place called Ofowani where there is a building called Dainichidō. In front of this building out in the forest is a large tree, some ten or twenty *jō* in height, and a circumference of four *wi* (two feet). When a certain person saw this tree, he saw that the leaves and flowers were all like mugwort. Also in the province of Satuma there is a large mugwort tree. I wonder if this is true.

[864] CONCERNING MEN SENDING STRAW BOUND TOGETHER TO ASK FOR THE HAND OF A WOMAN IN SANUKI PROVINCE

When a man in Sanuki Province wants to seek the hand of a woman in marriage, they have a custom of binding up straw and sending it to the woman. This custom is relatively unknown even in this province among the people who live nearby in castle towns, but generally the villagers all do this. When the man has bound up the straw thus and sent it to the woman, if her reply is "no," then the straw is unbundled and part of it is sent back. If the woman agrees to the proposal, then she moves the tied rope to the middle of the bundle like this [see picture].

Perhaps the *tamadura* spoken of in *Man'yōshū* was the same as this. In present society when people call the seed of the fruit of vegetation *tamadusa*, it is much like this custom of binding up straw. This information was provided by a person named Yamada Rokurō from the village of Taka.

[865] CONCERNING THE SONG SUNG DURING A SHINTŌ RITUAL IN VARIOUS VILLAGES IN SINANO PROVINCE

A certain person told me that in Sinano Province, upstream of the Tenryū River in various villages such as Kafamura, Wada, Kisafa, and others, during Shintō rituals they boil water in a cauldron and place paper offerings around the cauldron, and through the night villagers, men and women, old and young, mingle together by the cauldron. They take a paper offering, and sing the following: *oyu mesu toki no na / omikage kogu omikage kogu / yaku mo da nobore yaku mo da nobore* (When you partake of the hot water / let your august spirit, let your august spirit sway back and forth / climb, up to the multilayered clouds, climb)!

[866] A CELEBRATION OF EMPEROR SAGA'S FORTIETH BIRTHDAY

Ruiju kokushi records, "On the twenty-eighth day of the eleventh month of the second year of Tenchō (825) the court held a celebration for the fortieth birthday of the previous ruler, Emperor Saga. At the banquet the sun started to set in the west, and lanterns were lit and the banquet continued. The Bureau of Music provided music. Middle Counselor Yoshimine Ason Yasuyo who held the senior third rank descended from the staircase to the south of the palace and danced. The audience joined in and danced, also."

[868] MOUNT ARATI IN ETIZEN PROVINCE

In *Ruiju kokushi* we find, "On the twenty-eighth day of sixth month of the ninth year of Tenchō (832), the court presented three hundred bundles of tribute rice from Etizen to Hata no Otomaro, who cut through and opened the Arati Pass into Etizen Province." In an old document there is an example of 愛発関, which is located in the Arati Pass, and both of these should be read *arati*. This place name still exists.

[872] SIDURI

In a poem in *Kigoshō*[393] it says,

oku yama no   Are these my sleeves
siduri no sita no   under the falling snow
sode naru ya   in the deep mountains?

omofi no foka ni   I wondered if they had become wet
nurenu to omofeba   from something other than my thoughts.

(It includes a quote from) *Shijō Dainagon Utamakura*,[394] which says that *siduri* is snow that has fallen on branches of trees, and then drops off those branches.

[874] THE THEORY ABOUT *SINONOME*

In the same work (*Kigoshō*) there is an annotational note after the word *sinonome* by Nōin,[395] which says, "It resembled *sinonome*, with the clouds of the sky when dawn is fully breaking." What does that mean, that *sinonome* resembled *sinonome*?[396]

[877] CONCERNING TEN (*TOWO*) READ AS *TUTU*

The question arose: "In some of the old readings added to the manuscript of *Wenxuan*, the character 十 (ten) is glossed as *tutu*, where the second *tu* is the same as the *tu* in *fitotu* (one), *futatu*

---

393. *Kigoshō*: A poetic treatise written by Fujiwara no Nakazane (1064–1122) sometime between 1107 and 1116. This three-volume work categorizes poetic vocabulary under fourteen topics.

394. *Shijō Dainagon Utamakura*: This work no longer survives, other than in a few quotes in *Kigoshō*. It was written by Fujiwara Kintō.

395. Nōin is the Buddhist name of Tachibana no Nagayasu (988–1051?). He is one of the thirty-six medieval poets.

396. It seems unlikely that Norinaga did not know that *sinonome* means "sunrise"; it is more likely that he was being critical of Nōin for defining a word by using the word itself.

13 ~ BROOMRAPE 335

(two). The first *tu*, being in the same series of sounds as *to*, would therefore be the word for (ten). In certain dialects people say *tutu ya fatati* "nineteen or twenty years," where *tutu* is the number nineteen. Is this assumption correct?"

My guess is that originally people said *tutu* (ten)[397] and *fatati* (twenty) [as a set phrase], and later this was mistaken as "nineteen and twenty."

[878] THE THING CALLED *WOYAMI*

The word *woyami* does not refer to just rain [stopping for a little while]. In the first part of the "Spring Shoots" chapter in *Genji monogatari*, where His Highness Emperor Suzaku is ill, it says, "He was not in fact continuously unwell."[398] This word is also used on illness.

[880] CALLING SOMETHING IN ORDER *ITIBAN, NIBAN*

In the present people call everything *itiban* (first) or *niban* (second). The reason that the order of numbers is called *ban* is because originally *ban* referred to a progression, but the meaning changed and is now used in relation to anything. This word appears in *Uji shūi monogatari* where it says, "said a demon three places from the chief" [literally "in the third seat"],[399] and so this has been used as far back as five hundred years in the past.

---

397. Martin (1987:550) wonders if the etymology for *towo* (ten) comes from an earlier *tu-bo. Leaving the question of *-bo aside for now, it is possible that *tu later lowered to *to* in Central Japanese, but remained *tu* in Eastern Japanese, and with the addition of the suffix –*tu* for counters, became *tutu*. The difficulty with this theory is that the languages of the Ryūkyūs preserve the form *tu*, which must go back to an earlier *to.
398. See Tyler (2001.2:578).
399. See Yamagiwa (1967:138).

[884] BANQUET OF BLOSSOMS

In *Ruiju kokushi* it says, "On the twelfth day of the second month of the third year of Kōnin (812), the emperor journeyed to Shinsen'en to survey the flowers and trees. He commanded the literary people to compose poems, and presented wool fabric to those attending according to their rank. This is the beginning of holding the Banquet of Blossoms at this season." Also, "On the twenty-eighth day of the second month of the sixth year of the same period (815), the emperor journeyed to Shinsen'en, and held the Banquet of the Blossoms. He commanded the literary people to compose poems, and presented wool cloth to his attendants and the literary people according to their rank."

[896] GRANTING THE VARIOUS SHRINES IN THE COUNTRY ALL THE RANK OF SENIOR SIXTH RANK UPPER

In *Montoku jitsuroku*[400] it says, "On the twenty-seventh day of the first month of the first year of Ninju (851), the emperor issued an edict stating that all the various shrines under heaven, regardless of whether they have a rank or not, will be granted the senior sixth rank upper."

[898] THE CHINESE-COLORED FESTIVAL OF THE HEAVENLY DEITY AND CALLING THE EMPEROR "ONE GIVEN AUTHORITY FROM HEAVEN"

In *Shoku Nihongi*, on the fifth day of the eleventh month of the sixth year of Enryaku (787) it says, "The deity of heaven was worshipped with a festival at Katano. The text of the festival reads as follows, 'On this the first day of *kanoe inu* of the eleventh month

---

400. This is the fifth of the *Rikkokushi* (Six Imperial Histories). The full title is *Nihon Montoku tennō jitsuryoku* (The Veritable Record of Emperor Montoku of Japan). It records only the era of Montoku (r. 850–858).

of the year *finoto u*, which is the sixth year of Enryaku, I who am the son of heaven, the inheritor, have dispatched [Fujiwara Ason Tsugunawa] ... and dare to proclaim to the Upper Emperor, the God of Heaven. I have finally received the benevolent, brilliant command .... I pray that Emperor Takatsugu will be given authority from the heavenly deity, and please accept this.' The text also said, 'On the sixth year of Enryaku ... I, the emperor who is a filial son, dispatched [Fujiwara Ason Tsugunawa] ... and dare clearly proclaim to Emperor Takatsugu. I ... please accept this' ... ." These are festivals that are stained with Chinese traditions and this was not the intention [of the festival originally] of the imperial land.

[899] BANQUET ON THE DAY OF THE RAT

In the same record (*Montoku jitsuroku*) it says, "First year of Ten'an (857), spring, first month, day of the ox ... a casual banquet was held in the forbidden precincts, and those who received this did not exceed the twenty or so ministers and their attendants. Anciently this event was always held in the middle of the previous month, and sometimes was called the event of the day of the rat. Today's banquet was carried out at the old site."
This event was always held on the day of the rat, so it is suspicious that it is recorded on the day of the ox. Pondering this, we see that previous to this account on the day of the monkey a document was submitted from Minister of the Right Yoshifusa, and then another document was submitted on the day of the ox in conjunction with the banquet, so this banquet is recorded after this official document; perhaps the compiler wrote down both of these official documents in succession and perhaps the banquet was to have been recorded as the intervening day of the rat. Is it not confusing?

[901] CONCERNING THE VOICING OF *SI, TI, SU, TU*

In the language of people from Tosa there is still a natural distinction between the voiced and voiceless counterparts of *si, ti, tu*, and *su*, and there is no confusion. The people in Tosa say that even a small child who can just barely write *irofa* will not make any mistakes when he writes these *kana*.

[905] WHITE PEOPLE

In the same record [*Sandai jitsuroku*], it records, "In the seventh month of the eighth year of Jōkan (866), the province of Kii made a report, 'In Ito District is a man, Mutōbe Yukitsugu, who gave birth to two children, a boy and a girl. The boy is two years of age, and is two feet and four inches in height. The girl is five years old, and is three feet and one inch in height. When both children were born, their skin, their hair, and their eyes, all over their bodies, is white like the snow. Because of this, they are visible on a dark night. They cannot face the white sun. Their father and mother raised them in secret, and because of that they are now providing this information.'" The recording of this event lacks a quote from the Later Interpretation of the Great Purification Liturgy.[401]

[906] PRIVATE OWNERS

In the thirteenth volume of the same record [*Sandai jitsuroku*] it says, "Tsuneyama and others reported, 'We followed the instructions of the private owner, Satomo Sukune Nakatsune of the Right Palace Gate Guard.'" "Private owner" (私主) is now just called "owner" in the present, also called "master." In tales this is called *siu*.

[907] CALLING SHRINES BY THE SPECIAL LABEL OF "PALACES"

In the same record it says, "On the second day of the eighth month of the ninth year of Jōkan (867), the emperor issued an

---

401. The birth of white children was considered a "national sin."

edict that altered the label of 'shrine' for the deities Izanagi and Izanami in Ise, and changed it to 'palace.' In relation to the monthly festival at the Grand Shrine of Ise the court appointed one person to be in charge." As this record notes, the label of "palace" or "shrine" was determined according to the honor that each shrine holds, or would it not be generally determined? Even regarding great shrines there are some still labeled "shrine." I wonder why so many shrines are still not labeled "palace."

[908] AN OBJECT CALLED *FORO*

In the seventeenth volume of the same record, in the words of a petition filed by Ono Ason Harukaze, the governor of Tusima, we find, "The supplies of our troops consist of only armor. Even though our armor is thin we are aided by having **foro**. We would like to petition that we sew together tribute cloth and make a thousand cloth **foro** with which to prepare for the unexpected." In the present woodblock print of this record, the first instance of **ro** has been dropped from the text, which makes it difficult to figure out the meaning.[402]

[910] THE SEVEN HIGH MOUNTAINS

In the same record, in the second year of Gangyō (878), it says, "The emperor issued an edict to the Protective Temple of Ibuki Yama in Sakata District of Afumi Province. The temple is to be included in those temples with a specified amount of tribute, and as Samon Sanshū[403] has petitioned ... . During the time of the regnal year Ninju [851-854] he (Sanshū) climbed to the top of this mountain. It is one of the seven high mountains ... ."

---

402. *Foro* is a cloth capelike object a warrior wears on his back over his armor to protect him from being hit with an arrow.
403. Samon Sanshū (829-900). Tradition states that he founded the four protective temples on Mount Ibuki. It is said that he died on the peak of the mountain.

[912] COCK FIGHTS

In the same record [*Sandai jitsuroku*], it says, "On the twenty-eighth day of the second month of the sixth year of the same regnal period (882), the emperor went to the area in front of the Kōkiden building to observe a cock fight." This event of causing cocks to fight is also seen in the record of Emperor Yūryaku in *Nihon shoki*.

[913] THE FAMANA BRIDGE

In the same record, it says, "On the first day of the ninth month of the eighth year of the same regnal period (884), [it was reported about] the Famana Bridge in the province of Tofotuafumi. It is 560 feet in length, 13 feet wide, and 16 feet high. It was repaired during the fourth year of Jōkan (862). Over twenty years had passed and it had already fallen into disrepair. The emperor issued an edict that from the tribute rice of that province, 12,630 bundles of rice be taken to build the bridge."

14 | COUNTLESS CAMELLIAS

In Book 1 of *Man'yōshū* there is a poem that begins:

koseyama no	The countless camellias
turatura tubaki	lined up on Mount Kose—
turatura ni	I continuously gaze at ... (MYS 54)

I remembered this poem and so I produced the following:

yo no naka wo	The countless camellias
turatura tubaki	lined up in this world—
turatura ni	I continually think
omofeba omofu	about the many things
koto zo ofokaru	lined up in my own life.

I did not write this poem regarding the sadness in my own life. I wrote it about the general circumstances of the world, and people in society, considering the good and the bad, things that are hard to keep to oneself, things that cannot be kept in one's heart. There are many times that I have given vent to these feelings in this book, but no matter how much I write about it, I cannot get rid of them all.

[915] THE PERVERSION OF THINGS LIKE KILLING ONE'S LORD OR KILLING ONE'S FATHER

In *Nihon shoki*, in the record of Richū, there is a person called Sashihire, who stabs Prince Suminoe Naka, a person who is Sashihire's ruler. In the record of Emperor Sushun, Soga no Umako has someone murder the emperor. The person who murdered the emperor is none other than a servant of this Soga individual. The story of Prince Mayowa murdering Emperor Ankō is also an example of someone murdering his lord. Now since he was avenging the murder of his father, it is difficult to say if we should group this with the other examples above.

In the record of Keikō, we have a woman called Ichifukaya from the province of Hyūga who kills her father. In the record of Yūryaku, Princess Kusu kills her husband. These two cases were committed for the sake of the court and since they show their loyalty to the ruler it is difficult to call these excessive. In the same record, Ihokibe Muraji Kikoyu kills his son, Take Hiko. In the record of Suiko, one Buddhist priest takes an ax and strikes his grandfather. There are many examples of this kind of thing in *Nihon shoki*, and I have only mentioned these few examples.

In the barbaric country of China from the era known as Zhou, through the ages there have been examples of people murdering their ruler and sons killing their fathers. Pondering the many examples of these in the various Chinese records and comparing them, one can comprehend the good and evil of a country, and the superiority or inferiority of their teachings. Now Gong Dan of the Zhou era established and ordered his Way; although he did not teach people to kill their lord or father, naturally such things came about.

[916] PRAYING TO THE DEITIES AND SEARCHING FOR A PRINCE

In the same record [*Nihon shoki*], in the account of Emperor Keitai, it says, "Ohotomo Kanamura Ohomuraji addressed the Emperor, 'I beg of you to set up Tashiraka Hime as empress, send the patriarch of the office of the deities of heaven and earth to worship the gods, and pray for a son.' The Emperor replied, 'It will be done.'" The ancient Way was like this. When someone wants to have an heir, he ought to go out of his way to petition the deities.

[917] CONCERNING PRAYING TO THE DEITIES WHO DESCENDED FROM HEAVEN TO PAEKCHE AND ESTABLISHED A COUNTRY

In the same record, in the account of Emperor Kinmei, we find,

"Second month, sixteenth year. Prince Yosiau of Paekche dispatched Prince Kuwei to report, 'King Mei has been killed by the enemy.' ... Soga Omi appeared, and with his condolences, asked ... Kuwei responded ... Minister Soga said, 'Anciently, during the reign of Divine Ruler Ohohatsuse [Yūryaku], your country was invaded by Koguryŏ, and the situation of your country was precarious, like eggs stacked one upon another.' At that time, the Divine Ruler commanded the patriarch of the office of the deities of heaven and earth and inquired of the deities as to what policy to follow. The deities possessed a medium, instructing us, 'If you entreat the deity who founded the country, and go to the assistance of the ruler about to be destroyed, you will surely bring peace to that land, and the people we be subdued.'

'With these words, the divine ruler entreated the deities, sent military help, and your country obtained peace. If we analyze the origins of this, we find that this is the deity who descended from heaven and founded the country when heaven and earth were divided, and plants still had the power of speech. We have heard reports that your country no longer worships this deity. If you repent of your carelessness, repair the shrines, and worship the spirit of the deities, your country will prosper. Take care not to forget.'"

Regardless of which country or which period this concerns, these words are very noble. Regarding "the deity who descended from heaven and founded the country," it should be Susanoo. In the record of the "Age of the Gods" we see that this deity descends from heaven to the land of Kara.

[918] REGARDING THE DECREE WHERE THE KOGURYŎ KING IS CALLED THE SON OF A DEITY

In the same record, in the account of Emperor Kōtoku, in the great command given to the ambassador from Koguryŏ we find, "The Divine Ruler, a visible deity who rules over Yamato, declares— The servant dispatched by the divine ruler, and the servant dispatched by the son of Koguryŏ's deity ... ." Here the king of Koguryŏ is called the son of a deity.[404] Perhaps this is in reference to the deity that first established the land, and being a descendant of that deity, he is a son. Or perhaps he said this in response to the decree as a visible deity that he was being familiar with him? Either way it is a rare decree written in Chinese with an appellation that is rare and profound.

[919] GIVING CEREMONIAL *SAKE* TO AN ENVOY FROM A FOREIGN COUNTRY

In the same record in the account of Emperor Jomei, we find, "Fourth year, Tang sent Gao Biao Zhen ... and his party docked in Nanifa ... . On this day ceremonial *sake* was presented to the guests." In the "Foreign Guests Lodging" section of *Engi shiki* we also find, "When the guests of the envoy of Silla enter court, present them with ceremonial *sake*." Regarding this ceremonial *sake*, the regulations state,

> The rice to be used when brewing this *sake* will be taken from the four shrines of Kamo, Ofo, Makimuku, and Sidori in Yamato Province. Along with one shrine from Omuti in Kafati Province, one shrine from Anasi in Izumi Province, and two shrines from Isagu in Sumudi in Tu Province. Each shrine will provide thirty bundles of rice for a total of 240 bundles, which will be sent to Sumudi. One shrine in Katawoka in Yamato Province,

---

404. Norinaga's interpretation here seems forced. The decree makes more sense if addressed to the ambassador who is standing in their midst, not the king who is across the sea.

three shrines of Firota, Iketa, and Nagata in Tu Province will contribute fifty bundles of rice each for a total of two hundred bundles that will be sent to Iketa Shrine. The ceremonial *sake* in all cases will be produced by the Kamube, overseen by one member of the Nakatomi. It will be made and presented in full. The *sake* brewed at the Iketa Shrine will be presented to the deities at Minume Cape. The *sake* brewed at Sumudi will be presented at the Nanifa Lodge.

The presentation of ceremonial *sake* to foreign envoys appears to have first begun in the reign of Empress Jingū.

[920] CONCERNING THE STATUS OF SHRINES

In the same record, in the account of Emperor Tenmu, we find, "After the disturbance was over, the generals related the words of the deities to the emperor, who issued an edict and raised these three shrines in status." Perhaps 品 (grade) refers to status. If this is the case, then this is the first time that we see shrines being given a rank. On the other hand, this does not necessarily mean that shrines were ranked as a group, but may refer to a certain shrine being given a distinction. The instructions of the three deities [worshipped by the three shrines] appear in the text of the disturbance.

[922] SOUTHERN PALACE

In *Shoku Nihongi*, it says, "Eighth year of Tenpyō (736), spring, first year, seventeenth day. The emperor held a banquet for the various officials in the Southern Palace." Also in the twentieth year of the same regnal period (748), spring, first month, seventh day it says, "The emperor went out to the Southern Palace and held a banquet for those of the fifth rank and higher." This Southern Palace is either a different name for the Main Palace of the complex as we see later [in the Heian era], or perhaps the original name was Southern Palace and later this was renamed the Main Palace.

Generally, the names of the palace gates like the Suzaku Gate of the Throne Hall have Chinese-style names, but none of these is seen until the palace built in Nara. We find many examples but only of the type like Ofoyasumi Palace, Woyasumi Palace, Inner Yasumi Palace, Outer Yasumi Palace; so the Chinese names of the various gates were first given when the palace in the present capital [Kyōto] was established.

[923] CONCERNING THE RECORD OF EMPEROR KINMEI IN *SHOKI*

In the record of Emperor Kinmei in *Nihon shoki*, the entire record dealing with events from the fifth page of the second year of the record, which reads, "Summer, fourth month, ambassadors from Ara," down to page 19 of the fifth year of the record where it says, "should we not give the plans deep and careful study?" is information solely focused on the king of Paekche trying to reestablish the land of Mimana. The record is wholly about this event dealing with foreign procedures and the total sum of these fifteen pages is nothing but a waste of time. What reason is there for recording the completely bothersome, drawn-out event? Of the fifteen pages, from page 9 with "Autumn, seventh month, the king of Paekche" to page 10, "It goes without saying," everything here can be discarded aside from the middle section, which deals with the court. Every time I read this volume, I find this section very bothersome and I feel how annoying it all is. I would like to know what other people think.

[924] CONCERNING THE ORIGIN OF *FUDOKI*

In *Shoku Nihongi* we find, "On the second day of the fifth month of the sixth year of Wadō (713), the royal region and the various provinces in the seven circuits will record in pleasing characters the names of the districts and villages. You will record each instance of items produced with each district, including silver, copper, dyes, vegetation, fowl, beasts, fish, insects, and other things. Also record in this history whether the earth is fertile or not, the origins of the names of mountains, rivers, plains, and moors. Also record old stories passed down by the elderly and other strange occurrences."

This is the origin of the *Fudoki* of the various provinces. Perhaps the graph "decree" (詔) has been dropped before "royal region."

[925] REGULATIONS REGARDING THE HAIR OF WOMEN

In *Nihon shoki*, in the account of Emperor Tenmu we find, "Fourth month of the eleventh year (682), the court decreed, "From now on all men and women will tie up their hair." "On the sixth day of the sixth month, the men and women tied up their hair for the first time, and wore varnished thin silk caps." Also, "On the intercalary fourth month ... another decree was issued, 'For women over forty years of age we leave it to your discretion whether you tie your hair up, or ride your horse sidesaddle or not. Also we leave it to the discretion of female shrine attendants and functionaries at shrines whether to tie your hair up or not.'" "In the seventh month of the first year of Shuchō (686), the court issued an edict, 'Henceforth men may wear waist skirts, and the women may let their hair down to their backs as before.'"

This decree in the first year of Shuchō was issued because the emperor was very sick and as many different rituals were performed, perhaps the court was afraid to alter an ancient custom regarding women's hair that had continued since the "Age of the Gods." Thus, in *Shoku Nihongi* in the twelfth month of the second year of Keiun (705) we find, "Regarding women throughout the realm, both married and single, all will tie their hair on top of their heads, while female officials who serve the deities and officiate at the Ise Shrine will be exempted." [The details of this are in the previous record, and the regulation was simply reestablished here.]

Thus, I believe that this standard for hair had not been adhered to, and by later eras, all women just let their hair hang down. However, since the recent past, all women again tie up their hair, and this custom is common again.

[926] THE IMPORTATION OF SWEET CITRUS

In *Shoku Nihongi*, in the eleventh month of the second year of Jingi (725) we see, "The court granted both Sami Ason Mushimaro of the junior sixth upper rank, a judge in the Central Affairs Ministry, and Harima Atae Otoe of the senior sixth upper rank, a clerk in the Casting Office, the rank of junior fifth lower rank. Otoe was the first to bring sweet citrus back from Tang China. Mushimaro was the first to plant some seeds and the [resulting] trees bore fruit. Because of this, the court granted these two men a promotion in rank." "Sweet citrus" is known as a mandarin orange.

[927] *TANZAKU*

In the record of Emperor Saimei in *Nihon shoki* it records, "Another manuscript says that Prince Arima and Soga Omi Akae [and others] ... divined the chances for their plan of rebellion [to succeed] by drawing small slips of twisted paper." This is the first time that this object, *tanzaku* (短籍), appears. It is glossed as *fineribumi* (twisted strips of paper). It also appears in the tenth volume of *Shoku Nihongi*, and appears later in other works here and there. In *Shoku Nihongi* it is still correct to refer to this as *fineribumi*. However this object includes more than just twisted strips of paper. In all kinds of instances you can also write down simple things on it. Yet the idea of writing poetry on these [strips of paper] is something from much later.

[928] CONCERNING SMALLPOX

In *Shoku Nihongi* in the seventh year of Tenpyō (735) it says, "From summer to winter everything under heaven was afflicted with smallpox [note: in the vernacular this is called *mogasa*] and there were many who died young." Perhaps this is the first occurrence of smallpox in the imperial land. However, the way it is recorded makes it sound as if this is not the first occurrence. And even in the ninth year of Enryaku (790) it says, "This year, in the autumn and winter, almost all of the men and women under the age of thirty living in the capital and the surrounding districts contracted smallpox and many of them became bedridden. Those with severe symptoms died. This disease appeared from time to time in the various provinces under heaven."

The graph 垸 (earthen wall) is a mistake for 豌 (type of small bean). The name of this pox is called 皰瘡 *hōsō*, skin eruption pox" in later records, and this is the same thing as smallpox. Even in the present we call it *fausau* (> *hōsō*). It is also called *imo*. Perhaps the ancient name *mogasa* is an abbreviated form of *imogasa*.

[929] CHARTS OF THE VARIOUS PROVINCES AND DISTRICTS

In the same record we find in the eighth month of the tenth year of the same regnal period (738), "An edict was given to the various provinces to create charts of the [individual] provinces and districts."

[930] SWEETFLAG HAIR ORNAMENTS FOR THE FIFTH DAY

In the same record, in the nineteenth year of the same regnal period (747), in the fifth month on the fifth day, "The dowager empress decreed, 'Long ago on the fifth day [of the fifth month] during the royal banquet people always adorned their hair with sweetflag hair ornaments, but this custom is no longer observed. Henceforth, those who do not have their hair adorned with sweetflag hair ornaments will not be allowed to enter the palace.'"

[931] *MISO*

In the forty-ninth volume of *Sandai jitsuroku*, we see "two *gō* of *miso* [roughly two cups]." This is the first time that this word [*miso*] appears. In *Wamyōshō* it says, "**Miso** (未醬): In Mr. Yang's *Kangoshō* it says, 'Koryŏ *jiang* (醬, something pickled) is called **miso**. Now considering the evidence, *Benshiki* came up with the same theory; however, the etymology of this word is unclear. In the vernacular people use the two graphs 味醬, but it would be better to write the graph 味 'taste' as 末. At any rate these seem to be interchangeable in vernacular texts, as we have 末楡莱醬. The graph 末 has the meaning of the end of pounding. The graph 末 was later corrupted to 未.'" In another version of *Wamyōshō* the entry word 未醬 is written as 末醬. Recently we have the theory of Mr. Arai [Hakuseki] where he says that **miso** is a word from a dialect on the Korean peninsula. In *Kyelim yusa* it says, "Syrup is called *miso* (蜜祖)."[405] Considering that it said "Koryŏ *jiang*" this theory is right on. I doubt the theory in *Wamyōshō* that 末 changed to 味.

[932] DEW AND FROST IN *MAN'YŌSHŪ*

There are many poems with examples of dew and frost in the various books of *Man'yōshū*. In poetry of later eras there is a distinction made between dew and frost, but in the era of *Man'yōshū* both were simply called **tuyu** (dew). Therefore in Book 7 (MYS 1116), and Book 10 (MYS 2170) we have poems that were composed on the topic of **tuyu** "dew," and among many of these poems the text has 露霜 (dew and frost) so it sounds as if the poet is writing about two different phenomena, but such is not the case. It simply points to dew. There are a number of theories about this,

---

405. *Kyelim yusa* (雞林類事) was compiled in 1103 by a Chinese government official named Sun Mu, and records a number of Korean words in Chinese characters to represent their sounds. For example, "moon," Middle Korean *tol*, is recorded as 月羅理, interpreted to be something like TO-lali (Vovin 2000:147). Thus, "syrup" written as 蜜祖 represents *myit-tsuə*, which is close to the Sino-Japanese reading of *mitsu* "honey."

but none of them hit the mark. I have thought about why one would write "dew and frost" when writing only about dew, and as I have thought about this noun, *simo* (frost), it anciently also referred to dew, and when it referred to frostlike particles, it was called *tuyu simo*, and the poet could abbreviate the word and only say *tuyu*. This word originates from *tubuyu* (grain-pure), where *yu* (忌) is what we call things that are clean and pure. It is the same *yu* as in *yuki* (snow). Therefore, *tuyusimo* refers to frost that is pure and grainlike.

[934] CONCERNING THE USE OF THE GRAPH 和 IN PEOPLE'S NAMES

It is a mistake for people to read the graph 和 found in names as *kazu*. It should be *katu*, with the final syllable voiceless. This is based on the conjugation of the verb, *kate, katu, katuru*, which means to harmonize. In a *Man'yōshū* poem we find:

fisifosu ni   Adding leeks to
firu tuki katete   soy sauce and vinegar. (MYS 3829)

This is read *katete*.

[935] ON JUDGING THE GOOD OR BAD OF PEOPLE BASED ON ONE WORD OR ACTION

It is common sense in Chinese books to judge whether a person is good or bad according to one thing the person said or one thing the person did, but this is not very applicable. Even if a man is a good person, he cannot help but do unreasonable things sometimes. Though a man may be evil, he sometimes does good deeds, because very few people spend their entire lives doing only good deeds or only bad deeds. Because of this, how can it be proper to judge a person's entire existence according to one word or one action?

[936] CONCERNING THE NAMES OF PEOPLE IN THE PRESENT

Recently we have found that many people's names have Chinese graphs that are not suitable for their name. Moreover, among the many names whose readings are not normal, we find that recently people are using strange graphs or insisting on rare and strange readings, and we find many names that are hard to read. Generally, names should be written using uncomplicated graphs, and the reading should be transparent to everyone. When I say "name," I am referring to the actual [legal] name of the individual. I am not talking about names like "so and so" Uemon or Zaemon. It is also foolish when people argue that a person's name should also match the person's personality. There is no such thing as a person with a "fire" personality, or a "water" personality. It is also terribly stupid to select graphs for a person's name based on *fanqie*.[406] *Fanqie* is used simply to supply a hint to the pronunciation of a graph, so why would a person's name have anything to do with that?

[938] CALLING A DEER *KASEGI*

People believe that calling a deer *kasegi* is something from the ancient past, but this word is not found in any of the ancient records, so it is unclear where the word came from.[407] Perhaps it has

---

406. In China *fanqie* (反切) developed as an aid in the pronunciation of difficult or obscure graphs. A person selects two common graphs; the first graph provides the initial, while the second graph provides the rhyme. In *Nihon shoki* in Book 1 the complex graph 夒 has this note: 夒音力丁反, informing the reader that this is *leng* (l- from 力 and the rhyme -eng from 丁). However, Norinaga here is addressing a related issue in Japan, where not only the pronunciation, but also the semantics are involved. Yoshikawa et al. (1978:451, headnote) provide a helpful example: people considered the name 忠経 to be a good name, because its *fanqie* is *zhēng*, which is the same reading as 貞 (virtuous, chaste), and this reflects back on the original name 忠経 which means (go through [life] loyal).

407. This is a strange statement, as a number of manuscripts of *Nihon shoki* gloss "white deer" in the story of Yamato Takeru as *siroki kaseki*. It is possible that the manuscripts Norinaga had available did not contain this gloss.

something to do with the word *kaseduwe*, (deer staff) as recorded in the section on "Tools of Priests" found in *Wamyōshō*.

[939] SACRIFICING AN OX IN WORSHIP TO A CHINESE DEITY

In *Shoku Nihongi* in the ninth month of the tenth year of Enryaku (791), we find, "The court prohibited the people of the provinces of Ise, Ofari, Afumi, Mino, Wakasa, Etizen, Kii, and others from killing an ox and worshipping a Chinese deity." I wonder what kind of deity the record means by "Chinese deity." Also in the first year of Empress Kōgyoku, we see an account where people sacrifice oxen and horses to the deities of various shrines and pray for rain according to the teachings of the Hafuribe. Tanigawa Kotosuga[408] also said that it is a Chinese custom to worship the deities by sacrificing horses and oxen.

[940] LINEAGE CALLED *FARA*

In the record of Emperor Seinei in *Nihon shoki* it says, "Prince Hoshikawa, the son that Princess Waka Hime had given birth to. ... " *Fara* (given birth [from inside her belly)] points to lineage.[409] It should be read **udi** or **ugara**. Also in the record of Emperor Kenmei we find "peninsular by birth [Korean-belly]," and in the Emperor Suiko record "the eight royally sanctioned lineages." All of these have the same meaning. In the thirty-second volume of *Shoku Nihongi* it says, "The three royally sanctioned lineages were appointed in rotation," and in the thirty-eighth volume "the eight royally sanctioned lineages" and in *Shinsen shōjiroku* under the section of Hata Imiki, "The descendants of the Hata lineage all have the same ancestor, and are divided up into

---

408. Tanigawa Kotosuga (1709–1776) was a physician who lived in Tu in Ise Province. He is perhaps most renowned for his work, *Nihon shoki tsūshō* (1762). While he established a nativist school much like Noringa, and they corresponded frequently, Norinaga criticized him for holding to the beliefs of Suika Shintō, a form of Shintō greatly influenced by Confucian thought.
409. Norinaga writes this as 氏族. For a detailed explanation, see footnote 79.

different lineages." These are all the same usage. This label originally came from Korea, and it is of the same type as "district" (郡) being called *kofori* (評) in that country.

[941] CALLING CONFUCIUS PRINCE WENXUAN

We see the following in the seventh month of the second year of Jingo Keiun (768) in *Shoku Nihongi*, "Professor at the Imperial University, Kashiwade Omi Ōwoka of the senior sixth rank upper reported, "I accompanied the envoy to Tang China in the fourth year of Tenpyō Shōhō (752) and entered Tang China. There I inquired into the doctrine left by the ancient sages, and examined the afterglow of the ancient school. There are two gates to *Guozijian*,[410] above which it reads, 'Ancestral Temple of Prince Wenxuan.' At this time there was a student of the Guozi University named Cheng Xian, who told me, 'Our current emperor greatly reveres the teachings of Confucianism and changed [Confucius's] name to Prince Wenxuan.' The influence of the virtue of the ancient sages still resonates there. However, [in our land] we follow an old system and still refer [to Confucius] by his old appellation. Perhaps this is an attitude that goes against our revering the virtue [of the sages], and we may lose the way of revering the sages. We should apply the things that I have heard in China. In any event, this is simply my narrow opinion, and I look to you for guidance. The emperor issued an imperial decree and changed the [usage of Confucius's] name to Prince Wenxuan." Calling Confucius "Prince Wenxuan" at our imperial court started from this period.

[942] CONCERNING WRITING 尸 (CORPSE) FOR THE *KABANE* OF LINEAGE NAMES

I have wondered why in later eras the *kabane* of lineage names was written with the graph 尸 (corpse), but in the eighteenth volume

---

410. Known as "the institution [to educate] the sons of the state." This university for the sons of the nobility was established in the Sui era, and expanded under the Tang.

of *Shoku Nihongi* we find within the words of a declaration by Sasakibe Ason Mabito the following: "The source of the 'bone name' of our family had been lost, and for a long time my family became a lineage without an origin." Since they could also write *kabane* with the graph 骨 (bone), I suppose the graph 尸 has some deeper meaning.

[943] THE DAIJINGŪ TEMPLE OF ISE

In *Shoku Nihongi* in the eighth month of the third year of Hōki (772) it says, "The court moved the Jingū Temple of Watarai to the area by Mount Watase in Ifidaka." Also in the second month of the eleventh year of the same regnal period (780) it says, "The head of the Native Cult reported, 'Because there was a curse on the Daijingū Temple of Ise previously we moved the temple and built it in another location, but as it is still close to the divine district the curse does not cease. We would like to move it to a district other than the Ifino District.' The emperor gave his permission."

[945] HUNTING AT KATANO

In the same record, in the tenth month of the second year of Enrayku (783), fourteenth day, we find, "The Emperor went to Katano, released his hawks, and enjoyed himself with hunting." Apparently this is the beginning of the custom of hunting at Katano.

[946] *SHINSEN JIKYŌ*

Shinsen jikyō is a work that was not widely known at one time, but that recently has made an exceptional appearance, and now is a work that scholars of the study of ancient things use universally. The text of the preface to the work is obviously written very clumsily by the person who compiled it, and the dictionary is very difficult to comprehend as it records everything. First, it lists the Chinese characters, many we are not accustomed to seeing, including strange graphs, and many that, to say nothing of Chinese works, do not even appear in Japanese works of the past or present. In the preface it claims that the characters have been taken from the various works and private compilations of the imperial land as well as mathematical works, commentaries, and character dictionaries from China, but it is not clear at all what works have been used as sources. Also, the entry character, the note, and the reading vary here and there, and there is little consistency. In all aspects it is substandard work.

Nevertheless, it is not a fabrication of a later era, but is a product of the Kanpyō (889–897) or Shōtai (898–900) eras, as it claims in the preface.[411] Thus, while it is a substandard work, the attending readings are all ancient, including many rare words, as it was written at a point far back in time, making it superior to *Wamyōshō*. It is thus a work that should complement *Wamyōshō*. People wishing to learn should always check its entries. But as I mentioned above, there are many characters or annotational notes that are difficult to trust, so the student should only rely on the readings. The spellings are also correct and match with older works. The one case where it does not match is the reading of 美麗 [Old Japanese **urufasi**] written 宇流和志 (*uruwasi*), and I wonder why that is. Furthermore, there are not a few cases of characters unknown to the world that are not preserved in other records, but are found in *Shinsen jikyō*. In that case this is especially fortunate.

[952] FIVE POINTS ON PAINTINGS

When drawing a portrait of a person, it is important to create the likeness as close as possible. Of course, the face must be an accurate representation, but care also must be applied to the atmo-

---

411. The preface notes that the compilation process occurred in several stages. The second leaf of the preface notes that during the summer of the fourth year of Kanpyō (892) a rough draft was completed, and titled *Shinsen jikyō*. Then during the Shōtai era the compiler was able to obtain a copy of two Chinese dictionaries, *Yupian* (543) and *Qieyun* (601). Having obtained these two other sources, the compiler added characters and other information.

sphere and the clothing. That is why the painter must put precision and detail into the portrait of a person.

However, the practice in the present is to let the brush move itself, even when painting a portrait, and put great emphasis on elegance, so that many portraits do not resemble the subject. And when the painter tries to capture freedom and elegance, he ends up creating a simplistic and vague portrait. With swift strokes the face ceases to belong to the subject, but it becomes a feature of a grotesque common person, like a woodcutter. It is not the face of a gentleman who possesses virtue. We should despise such paintings.

[953] POINT TWO

When a painter creates a portrait of an ancient person, there is no way to know what the face looked like, so the painter should create a portrait accurately reflecting the person's social status and virtue. With people of high status, not only the face, but also the entire atmosphere of the painting must be elevated, so that the subject appears truly exalted. Unfortunately, current painters do not feel this way, only having interest in showing off their own ability, and they portray even lofty and virtuous people like rustics and buffoons.

[954] POINT THREE

Even when someone wants to paint a portrait of a beautiful woman, because their main purpose is just to let their skill show through, the face of the individual turns out ugly. People say that if the painter adds too much refinement and beauty to a face it ends up lowering the value of the picture, but that is only because the person is not skilled at painting. If the face of the individual is good, then the painter should try not to paint a bad picture. Because one's pictures always turn out poorly is not an excuse to paint a beautiful person poorly. A painter should apply himself to painting a beautiful woman as skillfully as he can. A picture with an ugly portrait does not leave anyone with a good feeling. However, in the present we have a portrait style called Edo painting, and because this style tries too hard to make everything appear beautiful, the value of the picture decreases, and of course, the individual looks ugly. Many portraits are so poorly drawn.

[955] POINT FOUR

Presently there is a style called "warrior prints" (*musha-e*), where men are portrayed as being warriorlike and strong. The face of the subject does not look human, with eyes that are round and large, flared nostrils, and a large mouth. These look just like demons. Should they paint the individual like a nonhuman demon, no matter how much they want to portray the individual as intrepid? They should paint the individual in a peaceful atmosphere, but showing a fearless intensity.

In a certain Chinese work it talks about paintings from our country, and makes the comment, "The person looked like a violent demon or a malignant spirit."[412] Likely the Chinese said this when they say a picture painted in this Musha style. However, because the Chinese are ignorant of how the Japanese look, then surely they would look at such pictures and believe that we all resemble demons. In all things, because Japanese people read about things in Chinese works, they know a lot about China, but because Chinese do not read Japanese works, they know little about our imperial land. In the rare event that something is recorded in Chinese works about our imperial land, they take that as a standard to judge our country. As foreigners will look at a Japanese portrait and decide that this is what Japanese people look like, if the painter portrays a person of nobility like a commoner, or if he portrays a beautiful woman like a hag, then they think that the men look base and the women look ugly. This

---

412. It seems highly likely that Norinaga has reference to the Ming Chinese work, *Wu za zu* (ca. 1592), written by Xie Zhaozhe (1567–1624). There it mentions that Xie received some paintings from Wa [Japan] that contained many depictions of people. He said, "The forms are ugly and strange, and they look just like *yakṣa* [demons who are violent and eat human flesh]."

does not apply just to foreigners. Even among Japanese, if a person sees the portrait of an ancient person, then he will think that this is how they looked.

[956] POINT FIVE

I know next to nothing about paintings so it would seem that I should not criticize this or that, but even without being able to comprehend the superior or inferior points about the details, as an outsider looking in I can offer my own critique. This is true of all kinds of esthetic pursuits, where a person in that path cannot easily comprehend the faults, but on the other hand, an outsider can see the good and the bad very clearly. Because paintings fall within this realm, I will elaborate on what I feel. First, I have not looked at many ancient paintings from either Japan or China, and do not feel I know much about these, so I will confine my comments to modern paintings.

First, among the various types of drawings, be these charcoal drawings, light-colored drawings, or brilliant-colored drawings, charcoal drawings are only smudges of charcoal with a few details added by brush, where everything is simplified and drawn very quickly to represent the object being drawn. Because these simply demonstrate the power of the brush and its energy, when the painter is very skilled, it leaves the observer impressed that things can be represented in such a manner, with such high quality. However, if something is drawn by an average painter, then there is no such quality and it does not leave the viewer with a good feeling. It is the trait of our society to praise such charcoal drawings as wonderful works of art, but in reality there is nothing of quality there. Recently there are people who enjoy the Japanese tea ceremony who lavish high praise on these paintings, and completely ignore the light-colored drawings. But these people do not actually feel this way. They are simply preserving a doctrine taught by the founder of the tea ceremony [Sen no Rikyu], and that is why they praise charcoal drawings. It is completely beyond my comprehension why those affiliated with the tea ceremony faithfully preserve this tradition where they lavish praise on everything, be it paintings or works of calligraphy, which have few praiseworthy qualities or any elegance.

Now regarding light-colored drawings, these are attractive and interesting. Many types of these paintings are splendid, up to the brilliant-colored drawings. There are rare examples where some drawings are overembellished and bothersome; those that represent water with a dark blue color are especially annoying. Now among the various schools there are houses that have established this as their occupation since ancient times. In their painting, these houses generally have their particularly transmitted styles and strictly uphold their own methods, but that does not mean that they think about accurately representing the object. There are good characteristics to the paintings from these houses, as well as poor ones. First there are terrible ones, where people of noble stature are depicted with grotesque faces, and the faces of beautiful women appear plump and ugly. It is also defective to portray the edges and creases of their robes with fat lines. This is an ancient act of trying to show off the power of one's brush. When people paint Chinese pine trees they call it one type, Tang Pine, and the reason they always portray a strangely shaped pine tree probably comes from a tradition handed down by someone who anciently had seen this kind of tree portrayed in a Chinese painting. It does not mean that this kind of tree exists in China! They are only incompetent at drawing a regular pine tree. And this school has made this kind of painting a good tradition worthy of preserving, which is truly odd.

Among the various kinds of paintings, I find annoying and bothersome the ones that disgust you with one look, and leave you with no intention of viewing it a second time. Examples of these are the poorly drawn charcoal drawings, this Chinese pine tree, the ones where the creases in a person's robes are drawn with thick lines, or paintings of Daruma, Hotei, or Fukurokujū.[413]

In general it is a wonderful thing to preserve an ancient tradition, but it depends on what is being preserved, and what the purpose is. This does not necessarily apply to paintings. It is

---

413. Hotei and Fukurokujū both belong to the seven gods of good fortune.

terribly arrogant to see a better method of painting and not be able to incorporate those traits into one's own school. Now that is not to say that no wonderful methods of painting have been handed down from the past by various schools. Paintings where a building is portrayed with no roof so the interior can be seen, or where clouds are represented so the distance between near and far is clear are indeed good, while there are many examples of poor paintings that drift from these traditions. Many paintings in the present are lacking, where the painter draws whatever his heart feels at the moment.

There are also a number of modern methods labeled Chinese that imitate Chinese paintings. In almost all respects this school tries to paint an accurate image of whatever object they choose. This is called *shō utusi* (copying live). I believe this is a very good method of drawing; however, there are times when the painting and the object do not look alike. So sometimes you get bad results when an artist will attempt to accurately portray an object, but the result does not resemble the object in question. And that is why various artists in a number of schools do not give much thought to trying accurately to represent the object they are painting. This is an excellent method, and one that is hard to dismiss.

All schools of art excel at the *sansui* (mountain and water) style, but most Chinese pictures painted in the style of *sansui* are dreadful and difficult to enjoy. Likely because the artists do not follow the rules and just draw any way they feel. On the other hand, there are those artists who paint a path into a scene where there ought not to be a path. Or they paint a bridge where there should not be a bridge. Or they insert boulders, trees, and shrubbery in bad places in a scene. There are very few paintings where this is done well. Most are of the type where these objects are often placed in inferior places in a scene, and most of their depictions are poorly done; you will notice that the shapes of the boulders, trees, and shrubbery as well as the steepness of the peaks are amateurish and ugly. Even in paintings done by skilled artists we see this weakness. This flaw is due to all the painters of these schools painting according to a traditional methodology, not because they are unskilled.

In Chinese paintings, when they portray a boat, it is very unfortunate that most of these portray the boat at an angle. Granted in general, we observe a boat sailing away at an angle, but it is dreadful to portray this scene that way. When the boat is painted at an angle, it does not appear to be gliding cleanly on the surface of the water. It appears as if the stern of the boat will lift up and capsize. This is not according to some style of drawing, but simply a weakness in trying to portray the object exactly as one sees it. Also, when an artist draws birds or insects these are drawn in clear detail, but many of these do not portray the energy of flight. In addition, when trees or shrubbery are drawn, the artists do not portray the distance from the leaves or stalk to the ground with a line, which is unseemly. Because there actually is no line showing distance the portrait is accurate in this respect, but when drawing the artist must put in a line, or the viewer cannot tell the dimension.

In all things when the actual object has no outstanding characteristics, it becomes just a plain object, and when it has no color, there is no shade. In a picture white is the background, and when there is nothing there, it is white. Because the artist draws in the white area, it is different from drawing in emptiness, so one cannot draw without having a line. Chinese paintings do not have this line, because they do not understand this distinction. When drawing the face of a person, even in a Chinese portrait, one cannot draw without having a line on the canvas to distinguish the face from the canvas. It appears to me that in Chinese paintings there is no method for drawing the spread of the branches of a tree, or the outline of roots of grass and flowers, or the shape of leaves. They draw these as they feel, which leads to a complete lack of coherence in the picture. Every school of painting has a traditional way they paint, so their paintings have coherence and are well done. In general, these are the common failings of Tang paintings.

However, compared to our paintings, Tang paintings, when portraying birds or beasts, insects or fish, trees or shrubbery, if they are skillfully done, accurately portray the object, because they are drawn with fine detail and care by a skilled artist. In paintings by Japanese artists of the various schools, because they all simplify the details when drawing the fur of beasts, or the feathers of birds, or the stamen and pistil of flowers, or the veins on leaves, in most cases, when compared with Tang paintings, the Chinese overpower the Japanese. This is because the paintings that Japanese produce for such things as the sliding screens of a large house are something viewed from afar, making the artist feel that it is useless to give such detail to tiny objects—and they feel it is bad to do that, because it is better to just draw quickly and smoothly—so the Tang paintings appear superior with their detail and delicate features.

In general, both paintings from the various schools of Japan and paintings from China have their strengths and weaknesses. As I noted earlier I cannot declare who wins or who loses. Recently there are many artists who do not feel obligated to follow one school's tradition or even imitate Chinese paintings. They paint any way they feel, taking what they believe are the good characteristics of Japanese and Chinese paintings. Their paintings take the good and eliminate the bad in earlier paintings, so I have found very few weaknesses in their paintings.

[957] DO NOT BE RECKLESS AND BELIEVE EVERYTHING IN CHINESE WORKS

It is very foolish for the scholars in our time to read about suspicious events in Chinese works, and yet they believe the whole thing. Most stories in Chinese works are unfounded, mistaken, or simply fabricated. One should not recklessly believe these things, being deceived by the skillful wording in the text.

[958] SOLAR AND LUNAR ECLIPSES

It is funny how the sages of China did not comprehend why we have solar and lunar eclipses, but treated these as a calamity.

[959] EVERYTHING IN THE WORLD COMES FROM THE DOINGS OF THE DEITIES

People do not comprehend that the myriad events that occur in the world are remarkable, and these are a result of the mysterious doings of the deities. It is very dimwitted for people to say things based on their own conjecture and logic. It is the convention of the Chinese to judge things based on their own logic, when they themselves rely on logic that is terribly lacking. The reason that they declare conclusions like this is surely apparent. There are many times when the error in their logic that has been transmitted from ancient times by the Chinese becomes clear in later eras. Moreover, when they eventually meet something difficult to explain according to their logic, then they dodge the subject by claiming it has to do with heaven, but this is because they do not realize everything originates from the actions of the deities.

[960] RESPECTING THE SAGES

Among the sages that successive generations of Chinese have revered, there are some who are truly worthy of respect; however, there are many people society reveres as sages, even though some people do not believe this in their hearts, but they are afraid of being censured by others. This makes them appear to agree with others in society. Among the various sages, Confucius was not a king, but was simply someone who propagated the Way of the kings, and the reason it seems that numerous people revere him among all the other sages is because he praised the kings and made their Way prosper.

[961] ABOUT DIVINATION

It becomes clear when one looks at the art of divination that in ancient China people did not originally engage in so much speculation on their own about the logic of things. Divination cannot be established by the will of a person, but is the form used to petition the deities and receive their instruction. The resulting information from divination is divine instruction. In spite of this, people in later eras have used their own intellect to ponder the logic of existence and establish doctrine. This was made popular by Minister Zhou and his self-wise scholars.

[962] CHINA AND BARBARIANS

When one looks at later records from China, within the country generally, the southern regions prospered in all things, but the northern regions were terribly impoverished. However, the origin of Chinese culture is based in the northern regions, and the Chinese ridiculed the southern regions as the land of barbarians. With this we can prove that the idea of "China and the barbarians" is a baseless lie.[414]

[963] THE WORDS OF THE CHINESE SOUND WISE

When we examine the various wise sayings of Chinese scholars from the successive eras, we find that they were skilled in telling parables, and even when they employed everyday words, they used interesting expressions. The imagery of their words tends to have originally been understood even by average people who were not educated, and these sayings are not that rare. Nevertheless, since the expressions are so skillfully uttered, people are moved to say, "I see your point."

[964] FIVE POINTS ON *THE ANALECTS* OF CONFUCIUS, POINT ONE

In an annotational note by Zhu Xi in the "Yong Ye" Section of *The Analects* he says, "Zhong Gong perhaps still did not understand the master's use of the character 可." This person known as Zhu Xi always taught the investigation of things and the extension of knowledge, but this Zhong Gong, who was one of Confucius's best students, could not even understand the use of the graph 可 by his master, so how could he obtain an extension of knowledge? Even the brightest student of Confucius was like this, so how could

---

414. Written 華夷 (China and barbarians). This term was coined to show the limits of Chinese civilization, and debase those ethnic groups that lived outside the "Chinese sphere."

a regular person comprehend such contrived thinking? There are so many forced and unreasonable things in the doctrine of Zhu Xi, and they are just like this example of Zhong Gong.

[965] POINT TWO

It also says that Ran Bo Niu was afflicted with a disease. Confucius said, "Such is the destiny of life. But why him? Why did he get sick?" If the will of heaven always blesses the good, then why this event? That is why the idea about the will of heaven is erroneous.

[966] POINT THREE

Also in *The Analects*, unparalleled praise is lavished on kings Yao, Shun, Yu, Tai, Bo, and Wen, but not one word of praise for kings Shang or Wu. Is there not a reason for this? At the end of *The Analects*, it quotes the words of King Shang. These are not the words of Confucius.[415]

[967] POINT FOUR

In the same work it says, "Confucius says, 'Who says that Wei Shang Gao is upright? One person begged some vinegar from him, so Wei begged vinegar from his neighbor, and gave it to this man.'" You can see from this example that the teachings of men are cruel. People should not label this as something so dishonest when this incident with the vinegar is trivial. So criticizing a person for being dishonest when they have only done such a small thing is a terrible way to teach. And even if this had been a very dishonest occurrence, it is not right to label the man a liar based on this single transgression. Even a fine, upstanding person has weaknesses and

---

415. Norinaga's intent here is to show that these two kings were guilty of atrocities and should not be interpreted to have been sagacious rulers.

bad habits. On the other hand, an evil person also does some good things. It is thus the pernicious habit of the Way of Confucianism to decide the good or evil of people on one incident. It is wrong.

[968] POINT FIVE

In the same work we find, "The stable having burned to the ground, Confucius having been at court and on his way back asked, 'Has anyone been injured?' He did not inquire regarding the horses." This is a very humorous incident. Even if a person's house catches fire, in most cases people are not burned. However, in the case of a stable catching fire, many times the horses are burned alive. When a stable catches fire, people are not usually in any danger, but the horses are in great danger. That is why Confucius should have asked about the welfare of the horses. That is the true feelings of a person. Even if we are to doubt the intent of someone who inquires primarily into the welfare of people, the phrase, "He did not inquire regarding the horses," shows that Confucius lacks discernment. Because he asked regarding people, it is only proper that this event be recorded, but what good is there in recording that he did not ask about the horses? However, because the students of Confucius wanted to show that their master was different from normal people they ended up showing that he actually was a person of little mercy. It would have been better to leave out those three graphs (不問馬, He did not inquire regarding the horses).

[969] *FAYARU*

People in the modern vernacular call times of prosperity when things are going well *fayaru*. They say that a disease is spreading (*byōki no fayaru*) or that doctors are doing good business (*isha no fayaru*) and so forth; it is used to describe a myriad things. This word appears in works from the Middle Ages so I wrote down some examples. The original meaning of this word is somewhat different from how it is used now. One example is *sono fito no fayari tamafisi toki*. This only refers to when you meet someone, and you find that he is prospering. When we say *isha no fayaru* we mean that the doctor's business is doing well. In the past it only meant that a person was doing well.

[970] ON THE GRAPH 御

Regarding the use of the graph 御 (imperial), in China it was only used in relation to events surrounding the ruler, and not for anything else. It was not used for events related to ministers or people below them. It seems that the graph 御 refers directly to the ruler. In our imperial land, we use the graph 御 when we use the prefix *mi-*, but this prefix is not limited to events surrounding the emperor, but naturally is widely used by others when they show respect. We generally limit our use of 大御 (great-imperial) to things surrounding the emperor. When we deal with things surrounding the deities, as deities are treated in the same manner as the emperor in all things, we then employ usages of the following type: the imperial wife is called "empress," and taking a journey is called "an imperial procession." Thus, our use of 大御 is close to the Chinese use of 御.

Later the reading of 大御 (*ofomi*) became *ofon* through a sound change and this has become widely applied to things other than the emperor. Later the medial *fo* elided and people now say just *on*, and even later the final *-n* has been dropped so people just say *o*. When common people write something and use the graph 御, they read it as *on*, but in speech they only say *o*. It is very rare to hear instances where someone will say something like *omi-obi* (great august belt), *omi-afase* (great august lined *kimono*), or *omi-tabi* (great august *tabi*), and this is a rare case where the old word *ofo-mi* has survived. In general this word is not used.

[971] THE CIRCUMSTANCES THAT PEOPLE ARE BORN INTO

The nature of man is different from person to person. Even when a person understands the logic of existence, there are people in the world who cannot describe these things verbally. And while there are things people can express verbally, there are people who cannot put these things into practice. Though there are people who cannot express these things verbally, they perform the principles in their lives. Also, there are people who are able to express the principles, but cannot put them into writing. Of course, there are people who cannot verbally express the principles, but can put them down on paper.

[972] THE USE OF PAPER

There are many uses for paper other than just for writing things down. First you can wrap things in it, wipe things, or use it for labels on boxes and baskets. You can also make a twisted paper string that lets you tie up things. There are likely a number of other uses for paper than what I have just mentioned. Chinese paper, however, is only good for writing on. It is not convenient for doing the other things I just noted. In our imperial land there are a number of kinds of paper made in the various provinces, some are thick and others are thin, some are strong and others are soft. There are so many kinds it is difficult to number them all, but none of these is better than Tang paper for writing. I do not know what others think, but this is how I feel.

[973] THE PRESENT IS BETTER THAN THE PAST

There are many instances where objects and affairs are better in later eras than they were in ancient times. Just to give one example, anciently the orange (*citrus tachibana*) was an unparalleled fruit highly valued, but in more recent times, there is a fruit called the mandarin orange (*mikan*), which is by far more popular than the orange when the two are compared. Among the varieties of the mandarin, however, like *kōji mikan*, citron (*yuzu*), bergamot orange (*kunebo*), and bigarade (*daidai*), the mandarin itself is especially delicious, the one most like the *tachibana* orange, a matchless fruit. From this one example, one can guess what I mean about later items being better than the ones in the past. Also, there are many things that did not exist in the past which exist in the present. Or there are many objects that were inferior in the past but are superior now. When we consider this aspect of life, what will happen in the future? Certainly many things superior to those in the present will appear. When we look at the minds of the people in the present, probably many things were very unsatisfactory and dissatisfying. The people in those past eras, however, did not feel this dissatisfaction. In the future, surely better things will appear, and the people in those eras will think that our era was unsatisfactory and that we were dissatisfied with life, but the people in the present are happy with the current state of things, feeling no dissatisfaction.

[975] FAMOUS PLACES

When one argues about famous places in the provinces that appear in poetry, the person needs to think well about the old poem in which the place appears and then determine which province this is in. Later poetry simply uses a place name based on the feeling of the earlier poem, and because the poet has not actually been to the place, that newer poem has no real effect. It is not just poetry composed on a certain topic, there are times when you cannot trust the poet who claims to have gone to the place and composed a poem. The reason this is so is that there are many errors in later works that attempt to point out where these ancient place names were located. Later poets then compose poetry based on this erroneous information about where a place was located. Others claim that this is the same mountain that is found in a poem composed in *Man'yōshū*. As time has passed, the place name has migrated to other places, so poets from other provinces come to this new location and compose a poem having heard the place name, and that is why you cannot trust them.

[976] MIXED POEMS

In the "Mana" preface to *Kokinshū* there is mention of a style of poem called "mixed style" (混本), and as I have thought about this it seems to refer to a kind of poem where the basis is a mixture of styles, so it seems to be another name for *sedōka* (repeating head style). Surely there is no other style than this. However, perhaps the [writer of the] preface to *Kokinshū* understands there to be another style, or in order to create tension between the four graphs 長歌短歌 (long poems, short poems) maybe he intended to place "repeating head" (旋頭) with "mixed style" as 旋頭混本. Either way, there should not be any other styles of mention. In later works we find one or two poems recorded that claim to be of this style, but these were purposely created according to the preface of *Kokinshū* and are poems unworthy of mention. Other than this, there are no other instances of poetry from the ancient times written in this "mixed style."

[977] ALLEGORICAL POETRY

Metaphorical poetry, figurative poetry, and indirect poetry[416] all refer to the same thing, but in the preface to *Kokinshū* there are these three divisions, a distinction that is forced based on the six types of poetry in China. In all respects there are not six types of Japanese poetry. This distinction is a terrible mistake.

[979] *SAKIFAFI*

Regarding the word 幸 (*sakifafi*, good fortune) in ancient records of our land, many times this word is employed with the meaning of 福 (prosperity) and people make no distinction in meaning. However, the meaning is different from the semantics of the graph; 幸 refers to receiving blessings for no overt reason; one

---

416. I have used McCullough's translations of these three terms (1985:4).

obtains it by chance. The usages in the works from China all use it in this context.

[980] TEACHINGS AND MANDATES

It is truly disagreeable that ancient Chinese works generally do little more than teach and declare mandates. People do not become good simply because they follow teachings. Naturally if one forces teachings on someone who is not waiting to be taught you will actually create someone who will do evil and commit many acts of deception. Gong Dan of Zhou was so strident in his various teachings that it caused a revolt at the end of the Zhou era. In the Warring States period the evil acts and wily wisdom of the times all came from the teachings of Gong Dan. In the ancient works of our imperial land, there is not even a shred of such moral teachings. Ponder on this distinction [between China and Japan]. It is silly to put so much weight on teachings and mandates.

[981] MENCIUS

Mencius said, "There are three kinds of unfilial deeds. The worst of these is having no posterity." By this we may know that *having* posterity is considered filial. If having posterity is considered something filial, then seeking riches and honors for yourself should be the greatest kind of filial piety. I understand that Confucian scholars do not desire wealth or status, but only try to keep themselves pure and take no thought for their parents. This should also be called a great unfilial act.

[983] I HAVE HEARD IT THUS

The various Buddhist sutras start with the words, "I have heard it thus." The various authors use this phrase as if it had some great import or meaning, but it is not suitable here, as it should come at the end. At any rate, it is a mistake to introduce something this way; it is silly. It would be better if they started with the words, "I have heard the following." The order of the words is also very laborious. Now this all ultimately comes from the learning of India, but the translators [from Sanskrit to Chinese] were also not very good. When someone studies Chinese texts, whether it be learning the graphs, or writing text, the person is always being criticized as "too Japanese, too Japanese," thus we see that in Buddhist texts there is a great tendency of being "too Indian."

[985] THE BUDDHIST WAY

The Way of Buddhism is simply to be able to make a distinction between enlightenment and confusion, and only being able to obtain said enlightenment. Everything else is simply branches and leaves;[417] therefore, enlightenment is an empty, vain doctrine; dew does not provide any benefit to the world. It just goes to show what dimwitted minds these people have because they are blinded by the teachings of the branches and the leaves.

[986] THE HEARTS OF PEOPLE ARE NOT DRAWN TO THE TRUE WAY

In China, Taoism has been widely practiced for many eras, reaching a point of popularity equal to Buddhism. Taoism was founded by Laozi, but the doctrine as it now stands varies quite differently from what Laozi preached, and now is little more than a strange form of amusement. Having looked into the doctrine, I find it has no value. We are lucky that this doctrine never came over to Japan.

Nonetheless, it is truly unfortunate that the people of our imperial land have had their hearts stolen by Buddhism and Confucianism. There is not a person in our land who does not embrace the doctrine of Buddhism, be he upper, middle, or lower

---

417. In other words, it is not the actual tree.

class, wise or foolish, even the woodcutter in the depths of the mountains. Among people who have a little learning, they mix half the teachings of Confucianism with Buddhism and take this as their standard by which they judge everything in life.

In spite of this, among all these believers, there are perhaps one or two from among ten million who believe in the Way of the gods. While there are also others who serve at shrines, rarely are there people at these shrines who think it is their duty to their family to know the Way of the deities. Thus, there are people who revere the true Way, but most of these people do it from the point of view of Buddhist or Confucian philosophy. And the common interpretation of Shintō so far has followed the twisted thought of Buddhism or Confucianism, and this has pushed the true Way to the brink of extinction.

That is a fair description of the current state of affairs, and in all provinces, temples continue to prosper while shrines fall into decay and ruin, and there is no one to lament the decline of the shrines. The people view the deities as entities to pray to in sickness or disease, and they treat the true Way as if it were some kind of useless thing. And like other ancient traditions, the true Way has come to the verge of extinction, and hangs on in an extremely emaciated state. The true Way should be used to rule the empire and the state. I have not seen in my dreams nor in the world anyone who believes that the Way is important. Is this not a truly lamentable fate?

[987] THE SONG ERA, THE MING ERA

In China during the Song era everything the government did was filled with logic, and in government, in all things, the people engaged in meaningless debate. People in the Ming era had their minds opened to the fact that the logic of the Song era was problematic, and there were many people who discovered the weaknesses of the theories of the ancient thinkers as well as other problems people had not noticed, and this is praiseworthy. However, in the end no one found the true Way, and the reason that the Ming era ended is that it was not part of the divine country of the deities.

[990] HEAVEN

The Chinese are fond of saying, "This is related to heaven, or that is something from heaven." This erroneous idea has its origins in the people's ignorance of the deities. Heaven is simply a place where the deities dwell, and it has no independent mind, behavior, or Way. What people call "the mandate of heaven," or "the Way of heaven" is in reality the doings of the deities. It is also an erroneous conclusion to say that heaven and earth are the procreators of all existence. Heaven and earth are merely the stage upon which the deities procreated everything. Heaven and earth do not create things.

The Chinese say, "Heaven gives commands to the sages, subjugates the barbarians, and protects the people." If this were true, the actions of heaven would be correct. This signifies that heaven would not do anything that goes against logic, but how can you ignore all the illogical events that have taken place in the world? When something goes against logic, they say, "It is the command of heaven, and there is nothing we can do about it." It is strange that no one chastises heaven for these illogical events. If heaven does things that go against logic, then we must say that heaven is barbaric when it commands a sage to put the emperor to death and seize the realm.

[991] RULERS OF COUNTRIES SHOULD ENGAGE IN SHOLARSHIP

If people who rule over countries were to engage in scholarship, in a well-governed age there would be no harm at all in Song Confucianism, even though it was of little relevance. The scholarship of the school of Ancient Rhetoric of recent years is liable to bring about terrible mistakes. Now, in a world full of confusion, all the various books should be put aside, and leaders should carefully read the military works of recent and past eras. They should scrutinize the good and the bad, the wise and foolish in the people of those eras, their hearts, and their battles.

[995] A METAPHOR FOR THE STORIES IN CHINESE TEXTS AND THE ANCIENT TRADITIONS OF THE IMPERIAL COUNTRY

The stories in Chinese works are a lot like looking at the nearby mountains that are right in front of our eyes, while the ancient tales of the imperial land are like gazing at far-off mountains that are ten or twenty *ri* in the distance. The stories in Chinese works agree with the emotions of people, and people find these to be reasonable. The events of the "Age of the Gods" in the ancient past of the imperial land are thought to be insipid and lacking in substance, but this is because the import of the events are so profound that they exceed the common wisdom of the average person, so they do not see the logic, but treat it as something worthless. Back to the metaphor of the distant mountain, the person can only see the mountain dimly in the distance, and cannot see the scenery associated with it, and the viewer then treats it as if it has nothing worthy of praise; however, this mountain is not without scenery worthy of praise. It is simply that the worthiness exceeds that of the power of the person's vision. Regarding the stories in Chinese works as containing deep logic and sounding wonderful, these are human stories, and as such touch the human heart superficially, and so like the mountain that is nearby, one can observe the scenery clearly, and it is like finding an interesting place there.

[996] FOOD, PART ONE

When one prepares food, this is called *ryōri* 料理 (arranging things in a proper order)[418] in the vernacular, and by association with this, the food that has been prepared is also called *ryōri*. "I have prepared the august *ryōri*" or "This is fine *ryōri*." These all refer to food.

---

418. In modern Japanese 料理 means "cooking," but to an educated person like Norinaga, back in his day it still had the original meaning of taking care of business.

[997] FOOD, PART TWO

An average meal should consist only of a thick soup and a vegetable. If the meal has many different dishes, then one is distracted by this and that, then in general it is not a pleasant experience, and no one thinks it is felicitous. On the other hand, when the event is a banquet, then having only a few dishes leaves one feeling dissatisfied. But if there are too many dishes then one just does not feel very joyous. When too many dishes are prepared, one finds this bothersome, and later the guests become weary. One could simply vary the different kinds of soup and that would be fine. Anciently these were all called "soup," but in the recent past one of the appetizers was called *siru* (broth), and the next dish brought out was called "the second broth." The rest after that was not labeled *siru*, but was called *suimono* (sipping thing). Thus *siru* and *suimono* are different objects.

Also, regarding what we call "vegetables," anciently this was called *afase* (side dish). This word appears in works like *Makura no sōshi* from Sei Shōnagon. In the records of the Ise Shrine there is the word *mafari*, which is perhaps a dialectal form in Ise. In this province people in the mountain villages and others still say *mafari*.

[998] THE PROVINCE OF ISE

The province of Ise was also called *kata kuni no umasi kuni* (a wondrous land located on the edge [by the sea]) in the ancient records. From the northern limit to the southern, along its western edge there is a continuous line of mountains, truly forming an azure barrier. To the east is a sea called the Sea of Ise. The province is a flat basin sandwiched between sea and mountains. From Kufana in the north to Yamada in the south is a distance of twenty *ri*, and there is not a single mountain in the way. It is one large basin. Among the many towns and villages in the basin, there is Yamada, Anotu, Matuzaka, and Kufana, among others—these are especially busy places. Traveling from the capital to Kyōto, one must pass through seven or eight provinces, and there are no other large cities like in Ise, other than perhaps Ofotu and Kokufu in Suruga. I think the same is true in other provinces.

After the towns I mentioned above, other good towns are Yokkaiti and Sirako. Thus, the province of Ise lacks nothing, be it sea or mountain products. The heat and cold of the seasons are not as severe as in other provinces. Concerning the cold, the farther north you go, the colder it becomes. Ise is a land of wind.

One reason the province is so busy is due to the Ise Shrine, to which travelers come to worship. At these times, there is no end to the travelers. During spring and summer, this area is so merry as to rival all other places in Japan. The land is very good for agriculture and rice production thrives. Most of the rice and other agricultural products are good.

Of special mention is the town of Matuzaka. This town is larger than any other, except perhaps Yamada. There are many wealthy families, many of these also have shops in Edo, and they send people up there to help. After doing business, the owners come back to Matuzaka for entertainment. The place does not seem that prosperous on the outside, but it is quite blessed. Overall, the streets are not straight but winding. The houses jut in or out toward the street every one or two feet and nothing is well balanced, the whole outlay loosely organized. The residential areas are not that magnificent, but the interiors of many of these houses are quite fine.

The quality of its water resources is irregular, with some water of good quality and other poor. There are few rivers and the ocean does not reach this far, so there are no ports. The mountains are about one *ri* away, while the ocean is half a *ri* distant. This place is very convenient for going to other provinces, especially if you want to go to the capital, Edo, or Ofosaka. Since this is where people from other provinces come, you can depart for anywhere from here.

The hearts of the people here are not that good. Many are proud and few are sincere. The outward appearance of the people is quite modern. Most women are well supported and their appearance is fine. Few places here would lose to the capital in a contest.

There are many strange phrases in the language of the area

when compared with the standard language of the people east of Ofari. There is almost no slur in the language of the people in Ise. However, if you compare Ise's language with Yamato or Yamasiro, the pronunciation sounds vulgar and there are many slang words.

When it comes to *kimono* fabrics and everyday items, Matuzaka has many good shops, and the quality is better than that in Yamada or Tu. Because of the high quality of goods in Matuzaka, middlemen from the capital come here frequently to buy goods. Matuzaka even keeps up with the popular items that come and go so fast.

When we talk about various arts and their places, there is none worth recommending in the area [in spite of the wealthy and their influence]. There are many skilled artisans here, though. All merchants enjoy prosperity, and the theaters, sightseeing places, shrines, and temples are all quite busy. Since this place is a magnet for people from other provinces, there are many no-good people and theft is a problem. Matuzaka is blessed with a large quantity of fish and vegetables, but there is a shortage of carp and crucian carp. There is also a shortage of arrowhead and lotus root. My biggest complaint about Matuzaka is the chaos in the layout of the roads, the looseness in the organization of the city, and the fact that there is no port.

[999] USING A GRAIN OF RICE AS A METAPHOR BY THE BUDDHIST LAW OR A BODHISATTVA

When one wants to talk about not being careless with grain [food], a grain of rice is called the law of Buddha, while in the eastern provinces it is called a Bodhisattva. Because it means to treat food with care, and refrain from wasting it, the core meaning of this saying is most welcome; however, if one means to imply that there is nothing worthier than Buddhism and the Bodhisattva, then this saying is a great error. One should use the deities as an example. As grain is most precious above all, one should label it a deity among deities.

[1000] ON PEOPLE THINKING SOPHISM IS GOOD

The proud scholars in society compose didactic poetry and talk as if they were enlightened. Others talk about being secure and compose poetry about the peace of mind they have obtained. This all comes from the hypocritical teachings of Confucianism and Buddhism. In reality, people who are secure with a concrete peace of mind do not exist. Since there are few people who live to be seventy, a person should feel satisfied if he has lived to be seventy, but all do not feel that way, merely lamenting the shortness of life. Everyone wants to live to be ninety or one hundred years old. This is the true state of the human heart.

[1001] *KANA*

The language of the imperial land was written in Chinese in the ancient records, because there was no *kana*, so there was no other method available to record the language. We now have *kana*, and we can write freely, so what kind of crooked heart does a person have who throws this writing system aside and writes in the restricted system of Chinese?

[1002] THE LANGUAGE OF CHINA

Compared to the language of the imperial land, the language of Tang China is very brusque. For example, they have the word *hăn yán* (罕言, rarely said), but in the imperial land we would just say *mare ni ifu* (rarely said), while "to rarely say something" has a different meaning. "Rarely said" puts the emphasis on what is said, meaning that while it is rare (罕), there are times when it might be spoken. "To rarely say something" places the emphasis on the rarity. There are many other examples like this related to this language. They all have the same problem.

[1003] THE TEXT OF BUDDHIST SUTRAS

All Buddhist sutras have obtuse texts. When dealing with a subject that is short, the sutra goes on and on, and while this can be said of things from India, it is all very bothersome and unenlightening.

[1004] THE BLESSINGS OF THE DEITIES

A person of high birth rules over a province or over a district, possessing many retainers, and is the object of reverence from the populace. These people lack nothing and live their lives in pleasure. A person of humble birth eats so he can escape hunger, wears clothes to avoid the cold, and resides in a house. We owe everything to our ruler, our ancestors, and our parents, and needless to say, if we searched into the origins of all things, we would find that everything in the world owes its existence to the deities. Because of this, a person should not be able to survive in the world without venerating the deities, but this has become commonplace; this has become the norm, and the people do not spend much time or energy thinking about it. It is the tendency of people to forget things, and then they lack gratitude for the things we have because of the ruler or our ancestors. Naturally, they think nothing of the blessings we get from the deities, and this is extremely improper.

If a person spent a day without food, what would he do? What would he do without clothing? We must never forget that we owe these things to the ruler, our ancestors, and parents. People in society do not even try to understand or ponder this, and they think the deities have nothing to do with them. However, when something they have prayed for does not come to pass, they despise the deities. How terrifying. Is it permissible to despise the deities simply because the slightest thing does not match one's desires, even though you continue to enjoy the blessings of the deities from birth to death? And how can people say that they do not revere the deities unless they give ear to their prayers?

If one always remembers that everything in this world exists because of the blessings of the deities, then you will come to realize that you cannot keep from revering the deities. For example, you will notice that the prayer you offered and that did not come to pass was likely the time you prayed to get one hundred *ryō* and in the end you only received ninety-nine. Should we not be pleased to have even received ninety-nine? Or should we hold a grudge because of the one *ryō* we did not get? Should the giver be pleased or angry? Despising the deities because your prayer remained unfulfilled is like the fellow holding a grudge because he got only ninety-nine *ryō*. How can a person have such feelings, having received the ninety-nine and forgetting the blessings of the deities?

[1005] THE WAY

The Way of the gods is the superior and true way of the world, and a person in our imperial land cannot survive without knowing about it. Only a small fragment of the Way remains in the world now. Why have other various ways from foreign countries that are not the true Way grown so thickly in our country? There is nothing that can be done about the will of the evil deity, Magatsubi.[419]

---

419. In essence: this is all the doing of the deity Magatsubi who has brought about this terrible state of affairs, and since we cannot control him, we are doomed to vexation.

❧ | ALPHABETICAL LIST OF ENTRIES

*The articles *a*, *an*, and *the* have been omitted from the titles. Numbers in brackets [ ] refer to the entry numbers in the main text.

About a Person Called Uemura Nobukoto [129], 106
About a Person Known as Fujitani Nariakira [443], 223
About Demons [601], 253
About Divination [961], 364
About Tea [797], 314
About the Chinese Ascetic Practice of Mourning the Death of a Parent [122], 104
About the Upper and Lower Designations in the Ranks of Courtiers [43], 52
Adding Graphs When One Writes [819], 323
Afflicted with a Runny Nose [452], 225
Allegorical Poetry [977], 371
Ancient Records and Their Impostors [422], 210
Anciently the Rituals of the Deities Were Valued [784], 310
Appealing Directly to the Face of the Emperor [309], 170
Argument of Priest Kenkō [231], 133
Arikinu [326], 177
Around the Fire [341], 180
As Keichū Expounded on Poetry [571], 243
Ash Tree [846], 330

Auspicious Signs of the Sages of China [76], 71
Awikuti [334], 179

Banquet of Blossoms [884], 336
Banquet on the Day of the Rat [899], 337
Biography of Master Agatai [303], 166
Biography of Sōgi [837], 328
Birth Father and Mother [719], 296
Blessings of the Deities [1004], 381
Bridge of Famana [401], 202
Buddhist Way [985], 373

Calling a Deer *Kasegi* [938], 352
Calling a New Year Illness "Pleasure" [56], 57
Calling Confucius Prince Wenxuan [941], 354
Calling Falsehoods "Lies" [716], 295
Calling People "Miya" [186], 120
Calling "Serpent" in the Twelve-Branch System *Mi* [514] 233
Calling Shrines by the Special Label of "Palaces" [907], 338
Calling Something in Order *Itiban*, *Niban* [880], 335
Calling the Fifteenth Day of the Seventh Month *Chūgen* [747], 304
Calling the Death of Someone "A Disease from Illness" [518], 234

Caricature Pictures [701], 286
Carpenters from Fida [463], 227
Cauldron of Twenty-Five-Bushel Capacity [490], 231
Celebration of Emperor Saga's Fortieth Birthday [866], 333
Changing the Regnal Year [632], 274
Charts of the Various Provinces and Districts [929], 349
Chief Priest at the Great Shrine of Ise Performs Buddhist Rites, and Is Relieved of His Current Post [798], 315
Children's Names Containing –*Maru* [775], 309
China and Barbarians [962], 365
Chinese-Colored Festival of the Heavenly Deity and Calling the Emperor "One Given Authority from Heaven" [898], 336
Chinese Heart [25], 39
Chinese Know Nothing about Other Countries [372], 194
Chūgoku [499], 232
Circumstances That People Are Born into [971], 368
Cock Fights [912], 340
Concerning 者 as "Accordingly" [158], 115
Concerning a Banquet with Soup [780], 309
Concerning a Fish Called *Isibusi* [399], 201
Concerning a Great Mugwort Tree [859], 331
Concerning a Man from China Named Bing Ji [441], 221
Concerning Adopted Sons [233], 136
Concerning an Inner Buddha Hall [308], 170
Concerning Calling Cherry Blossoms Just "Blossoms" [190], 123
Concerning Calling "Night" *Yosari* or *Yōsari* [738], 301
Concerning Cloth Offerings Made of Mulberry Bark [796], 313

Concerning Confucian Scholars Who Feign Ignorance When Asked about Japan [9], 28
Concerning "Defecation" Being Called Chamber Pot [739], 301
Concerning Events of Ifawi, Tukusi no Kimi [322], 174
Concerning Gold Coming from Sado [492], 231
Concerning How the Posthumous Name of Emperor Shijō Was Selected [30], 42
Concerning How the Posthumous Name of Emperor Shijō Was Selected [29], 42
Concerning *Kakidasi* [551], 239
Concerning *Kin'yōshū* Calling Prince Sukehito the Third Prince [829], 327
Concerning *Kuni no Miyatuko* [321], 173
Concerning Life Before and After This One [672], 278
Concerning Long Verse in *Kokinshū* [46], 54
Concerning *Man'yōshū* Using the Graphs 義之 to Transcribe *Tesi*, and the Writing of 大王 for the Same [325], 175
Concerning *Matsushima no nikki* [97], 85
Concerning Men Sending Straw Bound Together to Ask for the Hand of a Woman in Sanuki Province [864], 332
Concerning Minister Yoshida Kanetomo's Lecture on *Nihon shoki* [17], 34
Concerning Mizukuki no Woka [6], 24
Concerning *Nosaki* [631], 273
Concerning Poetry in *Kokinshū* that Deals with the Moon [87], 79
Concerning Poetry Written in a "Grass" Style [825], 327
Concerning Poets and Private Poetic Compilations [192], 123

LIST OF ENTRIES 385

Concerning Praying to the Deities Who Descended from Heaven to Paekche and Established a Country [917], 343
Concerning Prince Munetaka's Principal Wife Being Labeled "Miyasudokoro" [60], 59
Concerning Privately Compiled Historical Works [7], 27
Concerning *Ryōbu* and *Yuiitsu* [72], 69
Concerning *Shinpai Kuden* [18], 36
Concerning *Sikigami Wo Tukafu* [754], 305
Concerning *Siwori* [615], 259
Concerning Smallpox [928], 348
Concerning Soga no Umako [298], 165
Concerning Stanzas Repeating 5 and 7 or 7 and 5 in Chōka [424], 212
Concerning 咄 (Story) [475], 228
Concerning Surnames [79], 75
Concerning Syncope [41], 49
Concerning Ten (*Towo*) Read as *Tutu* [877], 334
Concerning Text Outlining the Origin of the Name of Ou District in *Izumo fudoki* [620], 261
Concerning the Cave of Yomi in Idumo [621], 269
Concerning the Criticism of Flowers [304], 168
Concerning the Debate about It Being Good to Not Seek Riches and Fame [123], 105
Concerning the Deity of Tamatu Island [558], 240
Concerning the Demon of the Mind [145], 110
Concerning the Difference Between *Okasi* and *Wokasi* [26], 40
Concerning the Divine Will of the Three Shrines [18], 36
Concerning the Dropping of *No* in the Vernacular [759], 306
Concerning the Ear of a Needle [460], 227

Concerning the Eight Million Deities Being Recorded as Eight Hundred Thousand in *Nihon shoki* [585], 248
Concerning the Existence of One Type of Writing in the Ancient Past [700], 285
Concerning the Festival for the Thirty-Six Thousand Deities [662], 277
Concerning the Festivals of the Four Borders and Four Corners [118], 99
Concerning the Fraudulence of *Sanbu Shinkyō* [697], 284
Concerning the Graph 妖 [148], 111
Concerning the Graphs 朝臣 [144], 110
Concerning the Last Words of Hōjō Tokiyori [59], 58
Concerning the Limited Amount of Money in the Past [54], 56
Concerning the Music Called "Noh" [582], 246
Concerning the Name *Wamyōshō* [603], 257
Concerning the Names of People in the Present [936], 352
Concerning the Object Called *Fata no Kazari* [267], 147
Concerning the Origin of *Fudoki* [924], 346
Concerning the Passing of Shōhaku [114], 99
Concerning the People of the Yin Dynasty Revering Demons and Deities [37], 45
Concerning the Poetry Composed by Minister Tamekane [209], 125
Concerning the Presentation of the Ceremonial Articles and the Recitation of the Liturgy after an Imperial Ascension [61], 61
Concerning the Raising of the Bow [115], 99
Concerning the Reading of *Fase* for *Fatuse* [196], 124

Concerning the Record of Emperor
  Kinmei in *Shoki* [923], 346
Concerning the Saying that Teika Had
  Poor Handwriting [676], 281
Concerning the Shrine on Mount Aso
  in Figo Province [695], 283
Concerning the Song Sung During a
  Shintō Ritual in Various Villages in
  Sinano Province [865], 332
Concerning the Songs of Ryūkyū
  [741], 302
Concerning the Status of Shrines
  [920], 345
Concerning the Theories in the
  Chinese Work *Huangji jingshi shu*
  [673], 278
Concerning the Theory about the
  Thatch on Ise Shrine [47], 55
Concerning the Titles of Officials
  [42], 50
Concerning the *Tuki Ya Aranu* Poem
  by Narihira Ason [289], 163
Concerning the Use of the Graph 和
  in People's Names [934], 351
Concerning the Voicing of *Si, Ti, Su,
  Tu* [901], 337
Concerning the Word **Aretuku** in
  Man'yōshū [709], 291
Concerning the Word *Ayenugani* in
  Man'yōshū [821], 324
Concerning the Word *Faberu* [176],
  119
Concerning the Word *Fayaru* [464],
  227
Concerning the Word *Iru* [506], 233
Concerning the Word **Woti** in
  Man'yōshū [438], 219
Concerning the Words *Kuti Akasanu*
  [580], 245
Concerning the Words **Tadaka** and
  Masaka in *Man'yōshū* [439], 220
Concerning the Words *Tutuminaku*
  and *Tutuganaku* [732], 299
Concerning Those Who Call Shrines
  the Ancestral Temple and the Altars
  of Soil and Grain [311], 171
Concerning Those Who Disparage
  the Poetry of Ministers Shunzei and
  Teika [760], 306
Concerning What Should Have Been
  Included in Book 6 of *Kojiki-den*
  [707], 288
Concerning "Word" Written *Kotoba*
  or *Kotonofa* [720], 296
Concerning Words that Start with a
  Voiced Consonant [623], 272
Concerning Worshipping the Deities
  While Holding a Fan [746], 303
Concerning Writing 尸 (Corpse) for
  the *Kabane* of Lineage Names [942],
  354
Concerning Writing "Cuckoo" as 時
  鳥 [197], 124
Concerning Yuki / Suki [5], 23
Concerning *Zoku fudoki* of Tikuzen
  Province [433], 217
Concurrent Post [459], 227
Confusion in Confucian Names [93],
  84
Council Hall of the Imperial Palace
  [2], 19
Custom of People's Names Following
  Sino-Japanese [586], 248

Daijingū Temple of Ise [943], 355
Daimyō [319], 173
Day After Tomorrow [478], 228
Debate of the Learned on Logic [762],
  307
Debating from One Point of View
  [167], 117
Deciding upon a Teacher [622], 272
Dew and Frost in *Man'yōshū* [932], 350
Difference Between Chinese Works
  and Shintō Works [242], 143
Difference Between **Mafe** and **Saki**,
  and Using **Saki** to Mean *Noti* [789],
  312
Dining Hall [554], 239

LIST OF ENTRIES 387

Dish Called Fish *Sasimi* [769], 308
Dismantling and Rebuilding the Various Shrines [136], 108
Do Not Be Reckless and Believe Everything in Chinese Works [957], 363
Do Not Stick to your Master's Theories [106], 92

Eastern Quarter and Western Quarter of the Capital [313], 172
Eight Young Maidens [735], 300
Events after a Person Has Died [188], 121
Everything in the World Comes from the Doings of the Deities [959], 363
Example for Reading Works [89], 80
Example of How to Read *Genji monogatari* [610], 259
Example of People in Society Being Deceived by False Appearances [165], 117
Example of *Yama* Mistakenly Written as *Tama* in *Man'yōshū* [817], 322
Examples Where the Graph 不 (not) Is Left Out in *Man'yōshū* [814], 318
Explaining the Fifty Linking Sounds to the Dutch [108], 94
Expounding and Comprehending Things [606], 258
Expounding Upon the Way, Whether or Not It Resembles Other Ways, Is Not Conditioned on Whether People Accept It [411], 204

Facts in the Reigns of the Ancient Chinese People That Are Inconsistent [572], 243
Famana Bridge [913], 340
Famous Places [975], 370
Fatazine / Zaru / Morafu [726], 297
Fayaru [969], 367
Festival at Sirayama Shrine in Kaga [34], 43
Fikifada [456], 226

Finding the Way Through Study [23], 38
Fish Called *Ugufi* [705], 287
Five Points on Paintings [952–56], 356–63
Five Points on *The Analects* of Confucius [964–68], 365–67
Fiwina [646], 275
Food [996–97], 376–77
Foya no Izusi [397], 201
Frozen Ice [338], 179
Fugusi and *Kugutu* [398], 201
Futon [271], 148

Giving Ceremonial *Sake* to an Envoy from a Foreign Country [919], 344
Grafting [448], 225
Granting the Various Shrines in the Country All the Rank of Senior Sixth Rank Upper [896], 336

Hall for Visitors [774], 308
Hanakura [756], 305
"Have a Wife" and "Pour *Sake*" [794], 313
Hearts of People Are Not Drawn to the True Way [986], 373
Heaven [990], 375
Holding a Grudge for Unfair Treatment [550], 239
How I Wish There Were Works Written on Every Topic [602], 255
How to Read Chinese Poetry [45], 54
Hunting at Katano [945], 355
Hut Where the Priest Keichū Lived [157], 114

I Have Heard It Thus [983], 372
I Have Nothing Special to Tell People [409], 202
Imperial Edict When the Imperial Procession Went to Kamo [66], 65
Importation of Sweet Citrus [926], 348
Inner Attendant [164], 115

Instructions I Leave to My Students [107], 94
Interpreting Shintō Works [85], 76
It Is Difficult to Keep a Tight Structure in Your Poetry and Prose [426], 214

Jug (by) the Inkstone [591], 249

Kagura [604], 258
Kana [1001], 380
Kana Calendar [494], 232
Kanna and *Manna, Fingasi* and *Minnami* [435], 218
Karazae [244], 144
Key Being Drawn in *Takaradukusi* [307], 169
Kigafe [757], 305
Kōjō [532], 236
Korean Language [392], 199
Kudoku [342], 181
Kurakake [493], 232
Kutiami and *Moromoti* [728], 298
Kyōka [265], 146

Lamenting the Decline of Shintō Festivals [369], 193
Lamenting the Disappearance of Traditions from the Past [600], 253
Language of China [1002], 380
Last Words of Narihira Ason [282], 157
Learning of Holland [373], 195
Lineage Called *Fara* [940], 353
List of Contents [590], 249
Liturgy of the Nakatomi [1], 14
Living Deep in the Quiet of the Mountains [850], 330
Losing a Hawk [593], 249

Mago [445], 224
Mana Edition of *Ise monogatari* [274-75], 149-52
Master Agatai Is the Father of the Study of Ancient Things [4], 23
Mekakau [333], 178
Mencius [981], 372

Metaphor for the Stories in Chinese Texts and the Ancient Traditions of the Imperial Country [995], 376
Minase River [71], 68
Minting New Coinage [633], 274
Miso [931], 350
Miti no Kuni Mutu [283], 158
Mixed Poems [976], 371
Most People in Society Admire Shrines That Look Desolate [370], 193
Mount Arati in Etizen Province [868], 333
Mountain Passes [340], 180

Name of Emperor Nara [824], 326
Necromancers [704], 287
Number of Names for a Variety of Wild Geese [847], 330
Number of *Sake* Jars During the Kamakura Era [58], 58

Object Called *Foro* [908], 339
Ofotete [836], 328
Ofotori Shrine in Izumi Province [371], 193
Old Chinese Tradition of Reading Books by the Light of Snow or Fireflies [802], 316
On a Person's Theory Changing from Time to Time [168], 118
On Aliases [80], 75
On Ancient Elegant Words That Still Exist in the Provinces [415], 206
On Being Satisfied with How You Are [711], 294
On Calling People *Jin* [312], 172
On Chinese Theories Being Profuse and Verbose [212], 127
On Collecting Poetry from Old-Age Celebrations and Establishing Monuments for the Deceased [787], 311
On Judging the Good or Bad of People Based on One Word or Action [935], 351
On *Kana* Usage [347], 182

On Kande Kōji [250], 144
On Later Eras Being Awkward [693], 282
On Lectures, Reading Groups, and Taking Notes [427], 215
On *Manyōshū* Poem 9 [354], 187
On My Learning from Master Agatai [105], 91
On Penmanship [288], 163
On People Thinking Sophism Is Good [1000], 380
On Plum Blossom Poetry Dealing with Fragrance [822], 325
On Rearing a Child Safely [257], 145
On Secret Traditions [569], 242
On Students Asking Difficult Questions First [234], 137
On the Chinese Officials Who Had both Authority to Worship the Imperial Deities and Perform Funerals Together [48], 56
On the Color Called Light Yellow [329], 178
On the Color of the Document Paper for Edicts [137], 108
On the Damage Done to the Divine Mirror When the Palace Caught Fire [64], 64
On the Deity Homusubi [237], 137
On the Discussion by Mr. Kumazawa on Shintō Texts [239], 139
On the Diversity of Commentaries on the Confucian Classics [211], 126
On the Eight Beautiful Scenic Views [786], 311
On the Emperor Giving a Name to the Kamakura Minister of the Right [21], 37
On the Fraudulence of *Kuji Taiseikyō* [698], 285
On the Graph 乙 [178], 120
On the Graph 和 in the Name Izumi (和泉) [284], 158
On the Graph 俵 [350], 186
On the Graph 御 [970], 368

On the Kosizuka Tomb [127], 105
On the Poem of Priest Keigetsu at Kiyomizu Temple [57], 57
On the Practice in Society of Building Facades [232], 135
On the Records in the Library at the Peach Blossom Abode [557], 239
On the Remnants of Ancient Practices Surviving in the Provinces [419], 209
On the Shrine of Saho Hime [208], 125
On the Vast Amount of Mistakes in Modern Poetry [425], 213
On the *Waza Uta* in the Saimei Record of *Nihon shoki* [121], 100
On the Word *Morafu* [545], 237
On the Word *Tatofe* [605], 258
On the Words *Fosaku* and *Fiki* [260], 145
On the Work *A Treatise on Voiceless and Voiced Words in the Ancient Lexicon* [230], 131
On Trying to Give the Position of Crown Prince to Each Other [27], 41
On Wanting to Know the Etymology of Words [423], 211
On Wanting to Know Which Deity Is Worshipped at Which Shrine [355], 189
One Point about the Use of the Honorific Prefix *Mi* [175], 119
One's Native Area [155], 113

Perversion of Things Like Killing One's Lord or Killing One's Father [915], 341
Pillow Word *Arakane* that Modifies the Word "Earth" [110], 97
Pillow Words [432], 216
Place Where Priest Sōgi Was Born [75], 71
Plant Known as *Marusuge* [845], 329
Poem about *Kotatu* [111], 98

Poem Composed by the Go Kyōgoku
　Regent [49], 56
Poem Composed on the Topic of
　"Returning Geese" [619], 260
Poem in *Ise monogatari* [273], 149
Poem of the Jingi [86], 77
Poetry in *Fūgashū* [88], 80
Poetry Produced by Beginners [674],
　280
Poetry Written about *Samisen* [390],
　198
Praying to the Deities and Searching
　for a Prince [916], 342
Present Is Better Than the Past [973],
　369
Pretending You Do Not Want Riches
　[788], 312
Priest Called Genso [434], 218
Principles to Adhere to When Following the Way [74], 71
Private Owners [906], 338
Proper Attitude Toward Scholarship
　[599], 252
Proper Attitude When Reading
　Man'yōshū [710], 293
Proverbs [496], 232
Province of Ise [998], 377
Putting Forth a New Theory [39], 47

Rakugaki and *Rakushu* [516], 234
Reading "Eighteenth Day" as *Towokayauka* [737], 301
Reading of 式乾門院 [830], 328
Reading of the Ten Trunks [177],
　120
Reading the Chinese Graph 言 as
　Mozi [38], 46
Referring to Someone as "Honorable
　Residence," and Residences of
　Other Provinces [776], 309
Regarding *No* [743], 303
Regarding the Decree Where the
　Koguryŏ King Is Called the Son of
　a Deity [918], 344
Regarding the Governing of Things

Under the Heavens and Putting
　Shintō Affairs First [353], 186
Regulations Regarding the Hair of
　Women [925], 347
Reputable Scholars in China Also
　Believed in Buddhism [413], 205
Researching Old Names [348], 183
Respecting the Sages [960], 364
Return Marks and Judgment Marks
　[643], 275
Rihōōki [199], 124
Rolling Up the Hem of One's Skirt
　[530], 236
Roosters Announcing the Dawn
　[339], 179
Rulers of Countries Should Engage in
　Scholarship [991], 375
Ryōbu Shintō [213–15], 127–30

Saburō [259], 145
Sacred Stone [343], 181
Sacrificing an Ox in Worship to a
　Chinese Deity [939], 353
Safabokuri [394], 200
Sakifafi [979], 371
Sanskrit [486], 230
Scholars Do Not Accept New Theories
　Readily [90–91], 81–82
Scholarship [24], 38
Scholarship Is to Wisely Select One's
　Way [785], 310
Seseragi [453], 226
Seti at the Beginning of the Year, and
　Calling One's Wife *Utikata* [416],
　207
Seven High Mountains [910], 339
Shinkyō and *Kōkyō* [777], 309
Shinsen jikyō [946], 355
Shōya [266], 147
Shrines Should Be Esteemed [761],
　307
Shunki [96], 85
Siduri [872], 334
Sino-Japanese Readings That Differ
　from the Common Ones [575], 244

Six Points on Ancient Records [10–15], 28–34
Solar and Lunar Eclipses [958], 356
Song Era, Ming Era [987], 374
Songs That Have no Voiced Syllables [44], 53
Sorrow for the Current Trend of Neglecting the Deities [598], 250
Southern Palace [922], 345
Spoken Title of Gokyōgoku [302], 166
Stable of the Imperial Guards of the Right [827], 327
State of Commentaries on Shintō Works [133], 107
State of *Kana* [706], 288
Stone Image of Buddha in Ofono [547], 238
Story of Zhou Gong Dan Eating His Rice, Vomiting It Up, and Meeting a Wise Man [442], 222
Strange Habit of Scholars in Our Imperial Land [708], 289
Sweetflag Hair Ornaments for the Fifth Day [930], 349

Tabi [524], 235
Tama arare [346], 182
Tamaya [703], 287
Tanzaku [624], 273; [927], 348
Tatuta River [3], 21
Tatuta River, Part Two [70], 67
Teachings and Mandates [980], 372
Teacups [546], 238
Tedutu [647], 275
Testimony of an Admission of Guilt [583], 246
Text of Buddhist Sutras [1003], 381
The Words of Minister Ietaka [8], 27
The Words of the Chinese Sound Wise [963], 365
Theory about *Sinonome* [874], 334
Theory about Strange Phenomena [240–241], 141–43

Theory That Beginning Students Should Compose Poetry [217], 130
There Are Six Principles in Poetics [763], 307
There Are Some Points in the Doctrine of the Chinese Thinker, Laozi, That Resemble Parts of Our Way [410], 203
Thing Called *Nagamoti* [751], 304
Thing Called *Woyami* [878], 335
Things Found in *Sarashina nikki* [618], 260
Things I Want to Say about Reading *Ise monogatari* [280–81], 153–56
Things in the World That Do Not Suit the Way [73], 70
Things Not Found in China [374], 196
Things to Keep in Mind When You Write [389], 196
Thinking It Rude to Call a Person by His Given Name [55], 57
Tikusiyau [270], 148
Title of **Wake** Found in *Man'yōshū* [482], 228
Titles of Kōson and Tenson [357], 191
Tokinaka [736], 301
Tosa Province Does Not Cremate People [395], 200
Tubone [431], 216
Two Points about the Chinese Heart [35–36], 43–45
Two Points Concerning *Udi* Titles [77–78], 72–75

Ukiyo [156], 114
Usage of "Sir" [451], 225
Use of Paper [972], 369
Use of *Sama* to Show Respect to People [367], 192
Using a Grain of Rice as a Metaphor by the Buddhist Law or Bodhisattva [999], 379
Using *Kuti* to Refer to Being on the Verge of Beginning Something [742], 302

Using the Causative 令 for Respect [549], 238
Usual Food for the Imperial Family [679], 282

Variant Commentaries within the Main Text of *Nihon shoki* [584], 246
Various Palaces in Asuka [128], 106
Various Place Names in Edo [268], 147
Verbs That Use Five Bases and the Conjugation of *U* (Get) [801], 315
Visitors [488], 231
Vulgar Usage of *Kō Wo Kiku* [412], 205

Way [570], 242; [1005], 382
Way I Came to Scholarship [103], 87
Way of Poetry and Cherry Blossoms [261], 146
Weta [523], 235
What a Person Once Said [393], 200
What Occurs When You Ponder Composing a Poem [694], 283
What Some People Have Said [483], 230
When I Spent Time in the Capital [851], 331
When One Copies Down a Manuscript [287], 162
White People [905], 338
Why Buddhism Is Easy to Believe [414], 206
Why Commentaries on Poetic Works Are Called *Shō* [81], 76
Why It Has Become Easier to Locate Various Works [102], 86

Why *Mori* Is Written 杜 [99], 86
Why Provinces Are Called "States" [92], 82
Why the Chinese Avoid the Given Name of Confucius [112], 98
Why We Call China *Kara* [143], 109
Why You Want to Revere the Deity You Worship [356], 191
Willow Box [477], 228
Wise Admonition of My Master [104], 90
Word about Reading Chinese Works [40], 47
Word for "Goodbye" [527], 236
Word *Fukusa* [844], 329
Word *Sagasu* [592], 249
Word *Sakayakasu* [752], 304
Words of the Child Seen in the Sujin Record, Who Was Divinely Possessed [164], 116
Writing 〆 When You Should Write 封 [721], 297
Writing a *Tan* of Cloth as 反 [455], 226
Writing the Word *Tomi ni* with the Graph 早 [245], 144

Yagi [315], 173
Yōsute [430], 216
You Compose Poetry by Carefully Selecting the Words [218], 131
You Should Read Chinese Works Also [22], 37
Yukatabira and *Katabira* [723], 297

BIBLIOGRAPHY

Aoki, Kazuo, Sasayama Haruo, Yoshimura Takehiko, eds. 2000. *Shoku Nihongi.* Five volumes. Tokyo: Iwanami Shoten.
Aoki, Shūhei. 2005. *Kojiki ga wakaru jiten.* Tokyo: Nihon Jitsugyō Shuppansha.
Asada, Tōru. 2000. "*Gekanshū no shohon.*" *Kokubungaku kenkyū shiryōkan kiyō* 26:81–136
Bentley, John R. 2000. "A New Look at Paekche and Korean: Data from *Nihon shoki.*" *Language Research*, 36.2:417–443.
—. 2006a. "Gengogaku-teki na takara o himeru *Nihon shoki.*" *Kokubungaku* 51.1: 132–40.
—. 2006b. *The Authenticity of Sendai Kuji hongi: A New Examination of Texts, with a translation and commentary.* Leiden: Brill Academic Publishers.
Bowring, Richard. 1982. *Murasaki Shikibu: Her Diary and Poetic Memoirs.* Princeton: Princeton University Press.
Brown, Delmer M. and Ichirō Ishida. 1979. *The Future and the Past: A Translation and Study of the* Gukanshō, *An Interpretive History of Japan Written in 1219.* Berkeley: University of California Press.
Hérail, Francine. 2004. *Notes journalières de Fujiwara no Sukefusa—traduction du* Shunki. Geneve: Droz.
Inoue, Nobutaka, Okada Shōji, Sakamoto Koremaru, Sugiyama Shigetsugu, Takashio Hiroshi, eds. 1999. *Shintō jiten.* Tokyo: Kōbundō. A translation of this encyclopedia is available on-line: http://eos.kokugakuin.ac.jp/modules/xwords/
Katagiri, Yōichi. 1968. *Ise monogatari no kenkyū, kenkyū-hen.* Tokyo: Meiji Shoin.
Katagiri, Yōichi, Teisuke Fukui, Yoshiko Shimizu, Shōji Takahashi, eds. 1994. *Taketori monogatari, Ise monogatari, Yamato monogatari, Heichū monogatari.* Vol.12 of Shinpen Nihon koten bungaku zenshū. Tokyo: Shōgakkan.
Kojima, Seisai. Date unclear. *Kanchu seiwa.* Manuscript from Waseda University e-brary: http://archive.wul.waseda.ac.jp/kosho/i05/i05_01832/
Kurano Keishi. 1976. *Kojiki / Norito.* Vol. 1 of Nihon koten bungaku taikei. Tokyo: Iwanami Shoten.
Martin, Samuel Elmo. 1987. *The Japanese Language through Time.* New Haven: Princeton University Press.
Matsumoto, Shigeru. 1970. *Motoori Norinaga: 1730–1801.* Cambridge: Harvard University Press.

McCullough, Helen Craig. 1985. *Kokin wakashū: The First Anthology of Japanese Poetry*. Stanford: Stanford University Press.
—. 1990. *Classical Japanese Prose: An Anthology*. Stanford: Stanford University Press.
McCullough, William H. and Helen Craig. 1980. *A Tale of Flowering Fortunes: Annals of Japanese Aristocratic Life in the Heian Period*. Stanford: Stanford University Press.
Miller, Roy Andrew. 1967. *The Japanese Language*. Chicago: University of Chicago Press.
Mills, D.E. 1970. *A Collection of Tales from Uji: A Study and Translation of Uji shūi monogatari*. Cambridge: Cambridge University Press.
Miner, Earl Roy. 1985. *The Princeton Companion to Classical Japanese Literature*. Princeton: Princeton University Press.
Miyake, Marc Hideo. 2003. *Old Japanese: A Phonetic Reconstruction*. New York: Routledge Curzon.
Muller, Charles. 2012. "Digital Dictionary of Buddhism". www.buddhism-dict.ne.
Nakada Norio. 1982. *Kogo daijiten*. Tokyo: Shōgakkan.
Nienhauser, William H., Jr., ed. 1994. *The Grand Scribe's Records*. Bloomington: Indiana University Press.
Nihon Zuihitsutaisei Henshūbu. 1974. *Nihon zuihitsu taisei—dai niki*, vol. 7. Tokyo: Yoshikawa Kōbunkan.
Nishimura, Sey. 1987. "First Steps Into the Mountains. Motoori Norinaga's *Uiyamabumi*." *Monumenta Nipponica* 42.4:. 449–55.
—. 1991. "The Way of the Gods: Motoori Norinaga's *Naobi no mitama*." *Monumenta Nipponica* 46.1:21–41.
Nosco, Peter. 1990. *Remembering Paradise: Nativism and Nostalgia in Eighteenth-Century Japan*. Cambridge: Council on East Asian Studies, Harvard University.
Philippi, Donald. 1959. *Norito: A New Translation of the Ancient Japanese Ritual Prayers*. Tokyo: Institute for Japanese Culture and Classics, Kokugakuin University.
Omodaka Hisataka et al. 1967. *Jidai betsu kokugo daijiten: jōdai-hen*. Tokyo: Sanseidō.
Omodaka Hisataka. 1977. *Man'yōshū chūshaku*. 22 volumes. Tokyo: Chūō Kōronsha.
Ōno Susumu. 1993. Supplement three of *Motoori Norinaga zenshū*. Tokyo: Chikuma Shobō.
Ōno Susumu and Ōkubo Tadashi. 1976. *Motoori Norinaga zenshū*. Tokyo: Chikuma Shobō.
Seno, Yoshinobu. 2010. "*Kanke suma no ki* no seiritsu to ryūfu nit suite no shiron." *Hiroshima Daigaku daigakuin bungaku kenkyūka ronshū* 70:15–29.
Seidensticker, Edward. 1976. *The tale of Genji*. New York: Knopf.
Shōchō Kumasha Shinkyō. 1906. Contained in Volume one of *Gunsho ruijū*. Tokyo: Keizai Zasshi-sha.
Sugito, Kiyoaki. 1984. "*Tamakatsuma* no shoban-bon to sono kankō." In *Gotō*

Shigeo Kyōju teinen taikan kinen kokugo kokubungaku ronshū. Nagoya: Nagoya Daigaku Shuppankai, 477-89.
Tahara, Tsuguo. 1973. "The Kokugaku Thought." *Acta Asiatica*, 25:54-67.
Tyler, Royall. 2001. *The Tale of Genji*. Two volumes. New York: Viking.
Videen, Susan Downing. 1989. *Tales of Heichū*. Cambridge: Council on East Asian Studies, Harvard University.
Vovin, Alexander. 2000. "Pre-Hankul Materials, Koreo-Japonic, and Altaic." *Korean Studies* 24:142-55.
Wehmeyer, Ann. 1997. *Book 1 Kojiki-den*. Ithaca: Cornell East Asia Series.
Yamagiwa, Joseph K. 1967. Ōkagami: A Japanese Historical Tale. London: George Allen and Unwin Ltd.
Yanagisawa, Eizo and Wilfrid Whitehouse, trans. 1965. *Ochikubo monogatari; or, The tale of the Lady Ochikubo, A Tenth Century Japanese Novel*. Tokyo: Hokuseido Press.
Yosano, Hiroshi and Masamune Atsuo, eds. 1930. *Wamyō ruijushō*. Three volumes of Nihon koten zenshū. Tokyo: Nihon koten zenshū kankōkai. Quotes from this work are cited by book, and page (verso or recto).
Yoshikawa, Kōjirō, Satake Akihiro, and Hino Tatsuo, eds. 1978. *Motoori Norinaga*. Vol. 40 of Nihon shisō taikei. Tokyo: Iwanami Shoten.

INDEX

Age of the Gods, 27, 30, 35–36, 82, 107, 121, 128, 140–44, 181, 190, 205, 246–47, 250, 253, 258, 269, 272, 278, 290, 343, 347, 376
Ama no Koyane no Mikoto, 14, 285
Ama no mo kuzu, 281–82
Amaterasu Ōmikami, 9, 27, 44, 108, 191, 242, 247
Ame no Osikumone no Mikoto, 14–16, 19
Andō no Tameakira, 282
Ayuhishō, 223
Azuma kagami, 56–59

Bai Juyi, 216
Bentley, John R., 100, 233, 285
Buddha, 43, 70, 78, 119, 126, 129, 185, 232, 314, 379
Buddha, image of, 170, 238
Buddhism, 27, 69, 79, 107, 126, 128–29, 135, 139, 165–66, 194, 204–06, 280, 290, 373–74, 379–80
Bungo fudoki, 29

calendar, 100, 120, 232, 280
Chikuma Shobō, 1, 10
Chikurinshō, 240
China, 9, 27–29, 38–39, 43–45, 52, 66, 71, 74, 76, 83, 98, 104, 109, 117, 121–22, 126, 126–27, 136, 148, 161, 172, 174, 194–96, 203, 205, 214, 218, 220, 227, 233, 243–45, 252, 255, 257, 278, 289–90, 307–08, 310–12, 316, 342, 348, 352, 354, 356, 358–60, 363–65, 368, 371–74, 380

Chinese customs, 38–39, 223, 353,
Chinese Heart, 5, 7, 23, 38–40, 43–45, 55, 77, 90–92, 107–08, 140, 157, 210, 246, 252, 269
Chinese learning, 1, 38–39, 77, 86, 144, 196, 203, 295, 307
Chinese loans, 272
Chinese painting, 360–63
Chinese thinking, 40, 44, 76, 90, 107, 252
Chinese traditions, 172, 337
Chiteiki, 173
Chu hsi (see Zhu xi)
chōka, 54, 102, 109, 212–13, 220, 236, 292, 325
Chunqiu (Annals of Spring and Autumn), 84
Confucianism, 8, 88, 108, 126, 128–29, 139, 204, 354, 367, 373–75, 380
Confucian classics, 126–27
Confucian scholars, 8, 28, 44, 83–84, 94, 105, 107, 109, 122, 127, 130, 136, 140–42, 205, 214, 218, 372,
Confucius, 8, 11, 45, 84, 98, 136, 222, 354, 364–67
Council Hall, 19–20

Dōmōshō, 54, 227
Dutch, see Holland

Eiga monogatari, 145, 216, 249, 287, 297, 301, 304, 328
Engi shiki, 14, 67, 158, 183, 186, 238, 344

397

etymology, 41, 75, 97, 180, 211–12, 254, 295, 335, 350

Fanqie, 352
Fanyi mingyiji, 235
Fengsu tongyi, 299
First Fruits Ceremony, 14–15, 18–19, 23, 67, 179
Fudoki, 22, 255, 289, n39
Fugashū, 77, 80
Fujitani Nariakira, 95, 223–24
Fujiwara Akihira, 146
Fujiwara Akinaka, 287
Fujiwara Ietaka, 27, 203
Fujiwara Kintō, 32, 334
Fujiwara Kiyokawa, 109
Fujiwara Kiyosuke, 296
Fujiwara Michinaga, 179
Fujiwara Morotsugu, 80
Fujiwara Nakazane, 334
Fujiwara Norikane, 54
Fujiwara Sanesuke, 51
Fujiwara Saneyori, 287
Fujiwara Shunzei, 182, 225
Fujiwara Sukefusa, 85, 171
Fujiwara Taikō, 109
Fujiwara Tameie, 328
Fujiwara Tametsune, 327
Fujiwara Teika, 4, 225
Fujiwara Tsugunawa, 337
Fujiwara Yorinaga, 14
Fukuro zōshi, 240
Futo Norito, 17

Gengenshū, 111
Genji monogatari, 3, 7, 25, 46, 119, 123, 205, 233, 245, 259, 272, 288, 327, 335
Goi Ranshū, 114
Gōke shidai, 239
Gong Dan, 222, 342, 372
Goʾon, 244, 291
Gosenshū, 236
Gukanshō, 37, 144, 165–66
Gumon kenchū, 234

Gyokuzui, 178

Harima fudoki, 26
heaven, 14–17, 25, 43–44, 45, 70–72, 108, 128, 136, 169, 177, 194, 211, 216, 222, 242, 279–80, 336, 343, 364, 366, 375
Heike monogatari, 249
Heikoki, 42–43
High Plain of Heaven, 14, 61, 108, 190
Hikima gusa, 167
Hogen monogatari, 239
Hōjō Tokiyori, 58
Hokuzanshō, 32, 51–52, 125, 296–97
Holland, 195–96,
Homusubi, 137–38
Honchō monzui, 146–47, 172
Hori Keizan, 2
Horikawa-in hyakushu, 179, 303
Huangji jingshi shu, 278–79

Ichijō Kaneyoshi, 239,
Idumo, 116–17, 233, 261–64, 266–69, 314
Ifawi, 174–75
Ima kagami, 327, 337n391
Imibe, 63
Ise, 1, 55, 64, 78, 89, 231, 301, 339, 353, 377–79
Ise monogatari, 3, 88, 119, 149–56, 164, 299
Ise Shrine, 79, 108, 115, 190, 231, 339, 347, 377–78
Ishō Nihon-den, 74
Isonokami sasamegoto, 3, 46
Itō Jinsai, 159, 230
Itō Tōshirō Tara, 256
Itsukushima gokōki, 300
Iwahashi Hidenaga, 240
Izumo fudoki, 22, 138, 192
Izanagi, 111, 137, 242, 264, 288, 339
Izanami, 111, 137, 242, 264, 339
Izayoi no nikki, 328
Izumi, 115, 158–59, 171, 344

Izumi-shi, 159, 193
Izumi Shikibu, 77-78

Jinmyōchō, 17, 67, 172, 188-89, 194, 268, 307
Jōgūki, 29
Jōkan gishiki, 32, 179

Kada Azumamaro, 103, 167
Kaibara Ekiken, 217-18
Kaikoku zakki, 147
Kakinomoto no Hitomaro, 53, 146, 282
Kami-musubi, 166, 242
Kamo no Mabuchi, 4, 5-7, 22, 23, 34, 82, 88-92, 150, 154, 155, 166-67, 176, 183, 202, 217, 247, 263, 282, 315
kana usage, 4, 10, 95, 124, 131-33, 151, 182-83, 288, 291
Kanjikō, 4, 88-89
karagokoro, see "Chinese heart"
Kazashishō, 223
Keichū, 3, 21, 22, 82, 86-89, 95, 100, 114-15, 123, 155-57, 180, 182, 183, 230, 243, 282, 293-94
Kenshō, 181, 240, 241, 282
Kichibu hikunshō, 178
Kigoshō, 334
Kitabatake, Chikafusa, 111, 186, 240
Kitamura Kigin, 3
Kitamura Nobuyo, 169
KKS 287, 153
KKS 300, 21
KKS 334, 217
KKS 343, 205
KKS 388, 21
KKS 473, 53
KKS 520, 53
KKS 633, 217
KKS 668, 162
KKS 747, 163
KKS 861, 157
KKS 955, 53
KKS 1001, 54

KKS 1072, 25
KKS 1450, 164
Kōdai wana shōshi, 106
Kogo shūi, 97
Kogontei, 183
Kojiki, 3, 5-7, 23, 29-30, 34, 44, 77, 90-93, 100, 106, 128, 131-32, 188, 190, 248, 256, 263-65, 284, 288, 315
Kojiki-den, 6, 7, 26, 92, 121, 133, 172, 181, 286, 289
Kojima Seisai, 226
Kokinshū (individual poems are listed under KKS), 21-23, 25, 27, 42, 46, 53-54, 68-69, 79, 88, 113, 123, 140, 146, 153, 156, 157, 162, 164, 205, 212-13, 224, 240, 255, 258, 272, 296, 307, 308, 324, 371
Kokinshū tookagami, 156
Kokin waka rokujō, 124, 258-59, 272
Kokin yozaishō, 22, 88
Konjaku monogatari, 286
Korean language, 145, 350
Koyane no Mikoto, 14, 285
Kumazawa Banzan, 139
Kunitokotachi, 128, 191
Kurano Keishi, 17-18
Kuzimati, 17
Kyelim yusa, 350

Laozi, 78, 140, 203-04, 294, 328, 373
Li ji, 45, 72, 121, 172
liturgy, 14-17, 19, 35, 61-62, 111, 300, 310, 338

Magatsubi, 74, 194, 250, 382
make-up of *Tamakatsuma*, 8-9
Makura no sōshi, 3, 168, 377
Man'yō Daishōki, 87
Man'yō no shō, 29
Man'yōshū (individual poems are listed under MYS), 3-6, 22-23, 25, 30, 41, 48, 53, 68, 69, 76, 86, 89, 90-92, 98, 101, 102, 109, 113-14,

120, 131–32, 135, 137, 149–50, 161,
175–76, 177, 187–88, 201, 212–13,
Man'yōshū (continued)
219–20, 224, 226, 228–29, 236, 238,
256, 260, 264, 267, 282, 291, 293–
96, 299, 300, 306, 317–18, 322–25,
330, 332, 341, 350, 351, 370
Martin, Samuel E., 110, 150, 335
Master Agatai, see Kamo no Mabuchi
Matsumoto Shigeru, 2, 3
Matsushima no nikki, 85
Meigetsuki, 225, 281
Mencius, 72, 84, 140, 372
Meng qiu, 221
Mibu no Tadami, 207
Mikawaki, 167
Miller, Roy A., 223
Mills, D. E., 322n272,
Minamoto no Kenshō, 181
Minamoto no Toshiyori, 181
Miwa monogatari, 139
Miyake, Marc H., 244
mono no aware, 7
Mononobe, 15, 115
Montoku jitsuroku, see *Nihon Montoku Tennō jitsuroku*
Mount Arati, 333
Mount Aso, 283
Mount Kaminabi, 21–22, 67–68
Mount Yosino, 237
Murasaki Shikibu nikki, 275
MYS 9, 187–89
MYS 53, 291
MYS 54, 341
MYS 113, 322
MYS 149, 322
MYS 524, 98
MYS 552, 229
MYS 598, 68
MYS 654, 295
MYS 780, 229
MYS 847, 219
MYS 848, 219
MYS 1021, 300

MYS 1053, 292
MYS 1276, 321
MYS 1287, 319
MYS 1291, 321
MYS 1362, 161
MYS 1460, 229
MYS 1461, 229
MYS 1507, 324
MYS 1703, 319
MYS 1894, 319
MYS 1953, 320
MYS 2233, 326
MYS 2270, 317
MYS 2272, 324
MYS 2384, 320
MYS 2387, 320
MYS 2403, 323
MYS 2585, 320
MYS 2593, 321
MYS 2712, 68
MYS 2817, 69
MYS 3229, 323
MYS 3399, 238
MYS 3481, 177
MYS 3521, 295
MYS 3741, 177
MYS 3791, 177
MYS 3829, 351
MYS 4011, 220
MYS 4153, 109
MYS 4240, 109
MYS 4262, 109
MYS 4331, 102
MYS 4408, 48, 236
MYS 4500, 325

Nakahara Yasutomiki, 277, 308
Naka Mikado Gondainagon Nobutane nikki, 34, 225
Nakatomi, 14, 16, 19, 35, 63, 328, 345
Nakatomi Kamatari, 115
Nakatomi Kane Murazi, 310
Nakatomi no Takakuni, 62
Namikawa Seisho, 159
Naobi no Mitama, 252–253

Nihon Montoku Tennō jitsuroku, 336-37
Nihon shoki, 3, 19-20, 23-25, 29, 30-31, 34, 35-36, 41, 44, 51, 52, 74, 77, 92, 100-02, 115-16, 120, 121, 124, 128, 131-32, 137, 169, 170-71, 174, 176-77, 188-91, 232, 241, 246-47, 248, 253, 256, 264-65, 272-73, 310, 326, 340-42, 346-48, 352, 353
Nishimura, Sey, 9, 126
Nisuiki, 99
Nomori no kagami, 125
Norito, see liturgy
Nosco, Peter, 90

Ochikubo monogatari, 145
Ōgishō, 296
Ogyū Sorai, 2, 114, 230
Ōkagami, 144, 178, 227
Ōkuninushi, 263
Old Japanese, 11, 268, 272, 295, 322, 356
Ono Ason Harukaze, 339
Ono Miya Sanesuke, 63
Ōno Susumu, 4, 6-7, 95
Ozasa Daiki Minu, 94-95, 199, 269
Ozu Sadaharu, 2
Ozu Sadatoshi, 2
Ozu, Okatsu, 2

painting, 356-63
pillow word, 24-25, 97, 132, 178, 216-17, 267, 322-23
pronunciation, 1, 46, 48-49, 54, 69, 120, 132, 219, 234, 244-45, 246, 254, 272-73, 352, 379,

Qian Hanshu, 267

Rikkokushi, 31, 67, 336
Rinji saishiki, 67
Rokuun ryakuzu, 223
Romanization scheme, 10
Ruiju kokushi, 69, 123, 292, 314-15, 333, 336

Ruiju sandaikaku, 147, 186, 233
Ryūkyū, 302, 335

Saigūki, 32, 51, 99, 108, 124, 224, 246, 274
Sakaki Kenshō, 181
Samisen, 198
Sandai jitsuroku, 31, 144, 236, 273, 292, 338, 340, 350
Sanskrit, 230-31, 373
Sarashina nikki, 202, 260
Seigo okudan, 88, 155
Sendai kuji hongi, 106, 285
Sendai kuji taiseikyō, 285
Sengaku, 29, 282, 294
Senge Toshizane, 314
Senjūshō, 20
Sennen sanshū, 282
Shaku Nihongi, 29, 107, 111
Shangshu, 110
Shibun yōryō, 3
Shiji, 83, 86, 122, 227
Shiki, 23, 107
Shin Kokinshū, 27, 109, 164
Shinsen jikyō, 10, 41, 237, 255, 297, 355-56
Shinsen Man'yōshū, 226
Shinsen shōjiroku, 166, 353
Shintō, 1, 8, 36-37, 55, 69-70, 76, 79, 86, 89, 107-08, 127-30, 139-40, 143, 157, 172, 186, 193, 285, 303, 310, 332, 353, 374
Shōchō Kumasha Shinkyō satabun, 231
Shōkanshō, 182
Shokugenshō, 186
Shoku Nihongi, 19-20, 29, 31, 41, 51, 92, 115 191, 228, 323, 326, 336, 345-48, 353-55
Shōyūki, 51, 61, 64, 65, 173, 228, 233, 304, 308, 309
Shūchūshō, 240
Shūishū, 22, 123, 302
Shunki, 85, 170-71
Si sheng zi yuan, 254

Silla, 109, 121, 232, 241, 261, 264, 266, 268, 344
Sino-Japanese readings, 54, 244, 248–49, 350
Sino-Korean readings, 199
Soga no Umako, 165, 341
Sōgi, 71, 147, 240, 328–29
Suga Naomi, 41, 80
Sugawara no Michizane, 54, 69, 75, 86, 226
Suma no ki, 85
Sun Goddess, see Amaterasu Ōmikami
Sun Kang, 316
Susanoo, 263, 288, 343,

Taiki, 14, 125, 225, 226
Takano sankei no ki, 125
Takami-musubi, 242, 247
Tama arare, 182
Tamakatsuma, reading, 13
Tanaka Michimaro, 40, 41, 292, 317, 329–30
Tang liudian, 304
Tang rhymes, 267
Tatuta River, 21–22, 67, 69
Tenmu, emperor, 19–20, 24, 52, 110, 170, 345, 347
The Analects, 45, 84, 104, 214, 365–67
Tikuzen zoku fudoki, 217–18
Tosa nikki, 3, 201, 298
Toyotomi no Hideyoshi, 289
Tsurezure gusa, 133,

udi, 53–54, 295n79
Uemura Nobukoto, 77
Uiyamabumi, 1, 228, 306n141
Uji shūi monogatari, 169, 170, 180, 224, 246, 334n371
Utsuho monogatari, 166, 177, 223, 322n263

Verbs, 223, 315–16,
Vovin, Alexander, 350

waka, 3, 125–26, 131, 146, 151, 241, 307–08, 328
Wamyōshō, 10, 25, 50–52, 111, 124, 147, 158, 233, 235, 254, 255–56, 257, 267–68, 273, 350, 353, 356
warrior prints (*musha-e*), 358–59
Way, the, 38, 43–44, 58, 70, 71, 76, 78, 79, 80, 86, 87, 89, 92, 93, 94, 98, 108, 119, 126, 128, 129, 146, 202–03, 224, 242, 304, 329, 364, 367, 374–75, 382
waza uta, 100–02, 137
Wenxuan, 124, 146, 228, 334
weta, 235
woodblock prints, 31–32, 339

Yamato Takeru, 210, 352,
Yin dynasty, 45–46

Zhou, 46, 222, 244, 342, 372
Zhou Gong, 8, 222
Zhou li, 56
Zhuang Zhou, 140
Zhuang Zi, 328
Zhu Xi, 114, 127, 139, 278, 280, 365–66

CORNELL EAST ASIA SERIES

4 Fredrick Teiwes, *Provincial Leadership in China: The Cultural Revolution and Its Aftermath*
8 Cornelius C. Kubler, *Vocabulary and Notes to Ba Jin's Jia: An Aid for Reading the Novel*
16 Monica Bethe & Karen Brazell, *Nō as Performance: An Analysis of the Kuse Scene of Yamamba.* Available for purchase: DVD by Monica Bethe & Karen Brazell, "Yamanba: The Old Woman of the Mountains"
18 Royall Tyler, tr., *Granny Mountains: A Second Cycle of Nō Plays*
23 Knight Biggerstaff, *Nanking Letters, 1949*
28 Diane E. Perushek, ed., *The Griffis Collection of Japanese Books: An Annotated Bibliography*
37 J. Victor Koschmann, Ōiwa Keibō & Yamashita Shinji, eds., *International Perspectives on Yanagita Kunio and Japanese Folklore Studies*
38 James O'Brien, tr., *Murō Saisei: Three Works*
40 Kubo Sakae, *Land of Volcanic Ash: A Play in Two Parts*, revised edition, tr. David G. Goodman
44 Susan Orpett Long, *Family Change and the Life Course in Japan*
48 Helen Craig McCullough, *Bungo Manual: Selected Reference Materials for Students of Classical Japanese*
49 Susan Blakeley Klein, *Ankoku Butō: The Premodern and Postmodern Influences on the Dance of Utter Darkness*
50 Karen Brazell, ed., *Twelve Plays of the Noh and Kyōgen Theaters*
51 David G. Goodman, ed., *Five Plays by Kishida Kunio*
52 Shirō Hara, *Ode to Stone*, tr. James Morita
53 Peter J. Katzenstein & Yutaka Tsujinaka, *Defending the Japanese State: Structures, Norms and the Political Responses to Terrorism and Violent Social Protest in the 1970s and 1980s*
54 Su Xiaokang & Wang Luxiang, *Deathsong of the River: A Reader's Guide to the Chinese TV Series Heshang*, trs. Richard Bodman & Pin P. Wan
55 Jingyuan Zhang, *Psychoanalysis in China: Literary Transformations, 1919–1949*

56 Jane Kate Leonard & John R. Watt, eds., *To Achieve Security and Wealth: The Qing Imperial State and the Economy, 1644–1911*

57 Andrew F. Jones, *Like a Knife: Ideology and Genre in Contemporary Chinese Popular Music*

58 Peter J. Katzenstein & Nobuo Okawara, *Japan's National Security: Structures, Norms and Policy Responses in a Changing World*

59 Carsten Holz, *The Role of Central Banking in China's Economic Reforms*

60 Chifumi Shimazaki, *Warrior Ghost Plays from the Japanese Noh Theater: Parallel Translations with Running Commentary*

61 Emily Groszos Ooms, *Women and Millenarian Protest in Meiji Japan: Deguchi Nao and Ōmotokyō*

62 Carolyn Anne Morley, *Transformation, Miracles, and Mischief: The Mountain Priest Plays of Kyōgen*

63 David R. McCann & Hyunjae Yee Sallee, tr., *Selected Poems of Kim Namjo*, afterword by Kim Yunsik

64 Hua Qingzhao, *From Yalta to Panmunjom: Truman's Diplomacy and the Four Powers, 1945–1953*

65 Margaret Benton Fukasawa, *Kitahara Hakushū: His Life and Poetry*

66 Kam Louie, ed., *Strange Tales from Strange Lands: Stories by Zheng Wanlong*, with introduction

67 Wang Wen-hsing, *Backed Against the Sea*, tr. Edward Gunn

69 Brian Myers, *Han Sōrya and North Korean Literature: The Failure of Socialist Realism in the DPRK*

70 Thomas P. Lyons & Victor Nee, eds., *The Economic Transformation of South China: Reform and Development in the Post-Mao Era*

71 David G. Goodman, tr., *After Apocalypse: Four Japanese Plays of Hiroshima and Nagasaki*, with introduction

72 Thomas Lyons, *Poverty and Growth in a South China County: Anxi, Fujian, 1949–1992*

74 Martyn Atkins, *Informal Empire in Crisis: British Diplomacy and the Chinese Customs Succession, 1927-1929*

76 Chifumi Shimazaki, *Restless Spirits from Japanese Noh Plays of the Fourth Group: Parallel Translations with Running Commentary*

77 Brother Anthony of Taizé & Young-Moo Kim, trs., *Back to Heaven: Selected Poems of Ch'ŏn Sang Pyŏng*

78 Kevin O'Rourke, tr., *Singing Like a Cricket, Hooting Like an Owl: Selected Poems by Yi Kyu-bo*
79 Irit Averbuch, *The Gods Come Dancing: A Study of the Japanese Ritual Dance of Yamabushi Kagura*
80 Mark Peterson, *Korean Adoption and Inheritance: Case Studies in the Creation of a Classic Confucian Society*
81 Yenna Wu, tr., *The Lioness Roars: Shrew Stories from Late Imperial China*
82 Thomas Lyons, *The Economic Geography of Fujian: A Sourcebook*, Vol. 1
83 Pak Wan-so, *The Naked Tree*, tr. Yu Young-nan
84 C.T. Hsia, *The Classic Chinese Novel: A Critical Introduction*
85 Cho Chong-Rae, *Playing With Fire*, tr. Chun Kyung-Ja
86 Hayashi Fumiko, *I Saw a Pale Horse and Selections from Diary of a Vagabond*, tr. Janice Brown
87 Motoori Norinaga, *Kojiki-den, Book 1*, tr. Ann Wehmeyer
88 Chang Soo Ko, tr., *Sending the Ship Out to the Stars: Poems of Park Je-chun*
89 Thomas Lyons, *The Economic Geography of Fujian: A Sourcebook*, Vol. 2
90 Brother Anthony of Taizé, tr., *Midang: Early Lyrics of So Chong-Ju*
92 Janice Matsumura, *More Than a Momentary Nightmare: The Yokohama Incident and Wartime Japan*
93 Kim Jong-Gil tr., *The Snow Falling on Chagall's Village: Selected Poems of Kim Ch'un-Su*
94 Wolhee Choe & Peter Fusco, trs., *Day-Shine: Poetry by Hyon-jong Chong*
95 Chifumi Shimazaki, *Troubled Souls from Japanese Noh Plays of the Fourth Group*
96 Hagiwara Sakutarō, *Principles of Poetry (Shi no Genri)*, tr. Chester Wang
97 Mae J. Smethurst, *Dramatic Representations of Filial Piety: Five Noh in Translation*
98 Ross King, ed., *Description and Explanation in Korean Linguistics*
99 William Wilson, *Hōgen Monogatari: Tale of the Disorder in Hōgen*
100 Yasushi Yamanouchi, J. Victor Koschmann and Ryūichi Narita, eds., *Total War and 'Modernization'*
101 Yi Chŏng-jun, *The Prophet and Other Stories*, tr. Julie Pickering
102 S.A. Thornton, *Charisma and Community Formation in Medieval Japan: The Case of the Yugyō-ha (1300-1700)*

103 Sherman Cochran, ed., *Inventing Nanjing Road: Commercial Culture in Shanghai, 1900–1945*
104 Harold M. Tanner, *Strike Hard! Anti-Crime Campaigns and Chinese Criminal Justice, 1979–1985*
105 Brother Anthony of Taizé & Young-Moo Kim, trs., *Farmers' Dance: Poems by Shin Kyŏng-nim*
106 Susan Orpett Long, ed., *Lives in Motion: Composing Circles of Self and Community in Japan*
107 Peter J. Katzenstein, Natasha Hamilton-Hart, Kozo Kato, & Ming Yue, *Asian Regionalism*
108 Kenneth Alan Grossberg, *Japan's Renaissance: The Politics of the Muromachi Bakufu*
109 John W. Hall & Toyoda Takeshi, eds., *Japan in the Muromachi Age*
110 Kim Su-Young, Shin Kyong-Nim, Lee Si-Young; *Variations: Three Korean Poets*; trs. Brother Anthony of Taizé & Young-Moo Kim
111 Samuel Leiter, *Frozen Moments: Writings on* Kabuki, *1966–2001*
112 Pilwun Shih Wang & Sarah Wang, *Early One Spring: A Learning Guide to Accompany the Film Video* February
113 Thomas Conlan, *In Little Need of Divine Intervention: Scrolls of the Mongol Invasions of Japan*
114 Jane Kate Leonard & Robert Antony, eds., *Dragons, Tigers, and Dogs: Qing Crisis Management and the Boundaries of State Power in Late Imperial China*
115 Shu-ning Sciban & Fred Edwards, eds., *Dragonflies: Fiction by Chinese Women in the Twentieth Century*
116 David G. Goodman, ed., *The Return of the Gods: Japanese Drama and Culture in the 1960s*
117 Yang Hi Choe-Wall, *Vision of a Phoenix: The Poems of Hŏ Nansŏrhŏn*
118 Mae J. Smethurst and Christina Laffin, eds., *The Noh* Ominameshi: *A Flower Viewed from Many Directions*
119 Joseph A. Murphy, *Metaphorical Circuit: Negotiations Between Literature and Science in Twentieth-Century Japan*
120 Richard F. Calichman, *Takeuchi Yoshimi: Displacing the West*
121 Fan Pen Li Chen, *Visions for the Masses: Chinese Shadow Plays from Shaanxi and Shanxi*
122 S. Yumiko Hulvey, *Sacred Rites in Moonlight: Ben no Naishi Nikki*

123 Tetsuo Najita and J. Victor Koschmann, *Conflict in Modern Japanese History: The Neglected Tradition*
124 Naoki Sakai, Brett de Bary, & Iyotani Toshio, eds., *Deconstructing Nationality*
125 Judith N. Rabinovitch & Timothy R. Bradstock, *Dance of the Butterflies: Chinese Poetry from the Japanese Court Tradition*
126 Yang Gui-ja, *Contradictions*, trs. Stephen Epstein and Kim Mi-Young
127 Ann Sung-hi Lee, *Yi Kwang-su and Modern Korean Literature*: Mujŏng
128 Pang Kie-chung & Michael D. Shin, eds., *Landlords, Peasants, & Intellectuals in Modern Korea*
129 Joan R. Piggott, ed., *Capital and Countryside in Japan, 300–1180: Japanese Historians Interpreted in English*
130 Kyoko Selden & Jolisa Gracewood, eds., *Annotated Japanese Literary Gems: Stories by Tawada Yōko, Nakagami Kenji, and Hayashi Kyōko* (Vol. 1)
131 Michael G. Murdock, *Disarming the Allies of Imperialism: The State, Agitation, and Manipulation during China's Nationalist Revolution, 1922–1929*
132 Noel J. Pinnington, *Traces in the Way: Michi and the Writings of Komparu Zenchiku*
133 Charlotte von Verschuer, *Across the Perilous Sea: Japanese Trade with China and Korea from the Seventh to the Sixteenth Centuries*, Kristen Lee Hunter, tr.
134 John Timothy Wixted, *A Handbook to Classical Japanese*
135 Kyoko Selden & Jolisa Gracewoord, with Lili Selden, eds., *Annotated Japanese Literary Gems: Stories by Natsume Sōseki, Tomioka Taeko, and Inoue Yasushi* (Vol. 2)
136 Yi Tae-Jin, *The Dynamics of Confucianism and Modernization in Korean History*
137 Jennifer Rudolph, *Negotiated Power in Late Imperial China: The Zongli Yamen and the Politics of Reform*
138 Thomas D. Loooser, *Visioning Eternity: Aesthetics, Politics, and History in the Early Modern Noh Theater*
139 Gustav Heldt, *The Pursuit of Harmony: Poetry and Power in Late Heian Japan*
140 Joan R. Piggott & Yoshida Sanae, *Teishinkōki: The Year 939 in the Journal of Regent Fujiwara no Tadahira*

141 Robert Bagley, *Max Loehr and the Study of Chinese Bronzes: Style and Classification in the History of Art*
142 Edwin A. Cranston, *The Secret Island and the Enticing Flame: Worlds of Memory, Discovery, and Loss in Japanese Poetry*
143 Hugh de Ferranti, *The Last Biwa Singer: A Blind Musician in History, Imagination and Performance*
144 Roger des Forges, Minglu Gao, Liu Chiao-mei, Haun Saussy, with Thomas Burkman, eds., *Chinese Walls in Time and Space: A Multidisciplinary Perspective*
145 Hye-jin Juhn Sidney & George Sidney, trs., *I Heard Life Calling Me: Poems of Yi Sŏng-bok*
146 Sherman Cochran & Paul G. Pickowicz, eds., *China on the Margins*
147 Wang Lingzhen & Mary Ann O' Donnell, trs., *Years of Sadness: Autobiographical Writings of Wang Anyi*
148 John Holstein, tr., *A Moment's Grace: Stories from Korea in Transition*
149 Sunyoung Park in collaboration with Jefferson J.A. Gatrall, trs., *On the Eve of the Uprising and Other Stories from Colonial Korea*
150 Brother Anthony of Taizé & Lee Hyung-jin, trs., *Walking on a Washing Line: Poems of Kim Seung-Hee*
151 Matthew Fraleigh, trs., with introduction, *New Chronicles of Yanagibashi and Diary of a Journey to the West: Narushima Ryūhoku Reports from Home and Abroad*
152 Pei Huang, *Reorienting the Manchus: A Study of Sinicization, 1583–1795*
153 Karen Gernant & Chen Zeping, *White Poppies and Other Stories by Zhang Kangkang*
154 Mattias Burell & Marina Svensson, eds., *Making Law Work: Chinese Laws in Context*
155 Tomoko Aoyama & Barbara Hartley, trs., *Indian Summer by Kanai Mieko*
156 Lynne Kutsukake, tr., *Single Sickness and Other Stories by Masuda Mizuko*
157 Takako U. Lento, tr. with introduction, *Tanikawa Shuntarō: The Art of Being Alone, Poems 1952–2009*
158 Shu-ning Sciban & Fred Edwards, eds., *Endless War: Fiction & Essays by Wang Wen-hsing*
159 Elizabeth Oyler & Michael Watson, eds., *Like Clouds and Mists: Studies and Translations of Nō Plays of the Genpei War*

160 Michiko N. Wilson & Michael K. Wilson, trs., *Of Birds Crying by Minako Ōba*
161 Chifumi Shimazaki & Stephen Comee *Supernatural Beings from Japanese Noh Plays of the Fifth Group: Parallel Translations with Running Commentary*
162 Petrus Liu, *Stateless Subjects: Chinese Martial Arts Literature and Postcolonial History*
163 Lim Beng Choo, *Another Stage: Kanze Nobumitsu and the Late Muromachi Noh Theater*
164 Scott Cook, *The Bamboo Texts of Guodian: A Study and Complete Translation, Volume 1*
165 Scott Cook, *The Bamboo Texts of Guodian: A Study and Complete Translation, Volume 2*
166 Stephen D. Miller, translations with Patrick Donnelly, *The Wind from Vulture Peak: The Buddhification of Japanese Waka in the Heian Period*
167 Theodore Hughes, Jae-yong Kim, Jin-kyung Lee & Sang-kyung Lee, eds., *Rat Fire: Korean Stories from the Japanese Empire*
168 Ken C. Kawashima, Fabian Schäfer, Robert Stolz, eds., *Tosaka Jun: A Critical Reader*
169 John R. Bentley, *Tamakatsuma—A Window into the Scholarship of Motoori Norinaga*
170 Dandan Zhu, *Mao's China and the Hungarian Crisis*

eap.einaudi.cornell.edu/publications

www.ingramcontent.com/pod-product-compliance
Lightning Source LLC
Chambersburg PA
CBHW022007300426
44117CB00005B/68